D1482761

EPIC AND ROMANCE

ESSAYS ON MEDIEVAL LITERATURE

BY

W. P. KER

DOVER PUBLICATIONS, INC.
NEW YORK

Published in Canada by General Publishing Company, Ltd., 30 Lesmill Road, Don Mills, Toronto, Ontario.

Published in the United Kingdom by Constable and Company, Ltd., 10 Orange Street, London WC 2.

This Dover edition, first published in 1957, is an unabridged and unaltered republication of the second revised edition originally published by Macmillan and Company, Ltd., in 1908.

This edition is published by special arrangement with Macmillan and Company, Ltd.

Standard Book Number: 486-20355-7

Library of Congress Catalog Card Number: 57-3853

Manufactured in the United States of America
Dover Publications, Inc.
180 Varick Street
New York, N. Y. 10014

PREFACE

THESE essays are intended as a general description of some of the principal forms of narrative literature in the Middle Ages, and as a review of some of the more interesting works in each period. It is hardly necessary to say that the conclusion is one "in which nothing is concluded," and that whole tracts of literature have been barely touched on—the English metrical romances, the Middle High German poems, the ballads, Northern and Southern—which would require to be considered in any systematic treatment of this part of history.

Many serious difficulties have been evaded (in *Finnesburh*, more particularly), and many things have been taken for granted, too easily. My apology must be that there seemed to be certain results available for criticism, apart from the more strict and scientific procedure which is required to solve the more difficult problems of *Beowulf*, or of the old Northern or the old French poetry. It is hoped that something may be gained by a less minute and exacting consideration of the whole field, and by an attempt to bring the more distant and dissociated

76241

parts of the subject into relation with one another, in one view.

Some of these notes have been already used, in a course of three lectures at the Royal Institution, in March 1892, on "the Progress of Romance in the Middle Ages," and in lectures given at University College and elsewhere. The plot of the Dutch romance of *Walewein* was discussed in a paper submitted to the Folk-Lore Society two years ago, and published in the journal of the Society (*Folk-Lore*, vol. v. p. 121).

I am greatly indebted to my friend Mr. Paget Toynbee for his help in reading the proofs.

I cannot put out on this venture without acknowledgment of my obligation to two scholars, who have had nothing to do with my employment of all that I have borrowed from them, the Oxford editors of the Old Northern Poetry, Dr. Gudbrand Vigfusson and Mr. York Powell. I have still to learn what Mr. York Powell thinks of these discourses. What Gudbrand Vigfusson would have thought I cannot guess, but I am glad to remember the wise good-will which he was always ready to give, with so much else from the resources of his learning and his judgment, to those who applied to him for advice.

W. P. KER.

LONDON, *4th November* 1896.

POSTSCRIPT

THIS book is now reprinted without addition or change, except in a few small details. If it had to be written over again, many things, no doubt, would be expressed in a different way. For example, after some time happily spent in reading the Danish and other ballads, I am inclined to make rather less of the interval between the ballads and the earlier heroic poems, and I have learned (especially from Dr. Axel Olrik) that the Danish ballads do not belong originally to simple rustic people, but to the Danish gentry in the Middle Ages. Also the comparison of Sturla's Icelandic and Norwegian histories, though it still seems to me right in the main, is driven a little too far; it hardly does enough justice to the beauty of the *Life of Hacon* (*Hákonar Saga*), especially in the part dealing with the rivalry of the King and his father-in-law Duke Skule. The critical problems with regard to the writings of Sturla are more difficult than I imagined, and I am glad to have this opportunity of referring, with admiration, to the work of my friend Dr. Björn Magnússon Olsen on the *Sturlunga Saga* (in *Safn til Sögu Islands*, iii. pp. 193-510, Copenhagen, 1897). Though I am unable to go further into that debatable ground, I must not pass over Dr. Olsen's argument showing that the life of the original Sturla of Hvamm (*v. inf.* pp. 253-256) was written by Snorri himself; the story of the alarm and pursuit (p. 255) came from the recollections of Gudny, Snorri's mother.

In the *Chansons de Geste* a great discovery has been made since my essay was written; the *Chançun de Willame*, an earlier and ruder version of the epic of *Aliscans*, has been printed by the unknown possessor of the manuscript, and generously given to a number of students who have good reason to be grateful to him for his liberality. There are some notes on the poem in *Romania* (vols. xxxii. and xxxiv.) by M. Paul Meyer and Mr. Raymond Weeks, and it has been used by Mr. Andrew Lang in illustration of Homer and his age. It is the sort of thing that the Greeks willingly let die; a rough draught of an epic poem, in many ways more barbarous than the other extant *chansons de geste*, but full of vigour, and notable (like *le Roi Gormond*, another of the older epics) for its refrain and other lyrical passages, very like the manner of the ballads. The *Chançun de Willame*, it may be observed, is not very different from *Aliscans* with regard to Rainouart, the humorous gigantic helper of William of Orange. One would not have been surprised if it had been otherwise, if Rainouart had been first introduced by the later composer, with a view to "comic relief" or some such additional variety for his tale. But it is not so; Rainouart, it appears, has a good right to his place by the side of William. The grotesque element in French epic is found very early, *e.g.* in the *Pilgrimage of Charlemagne*, and is not to be reckoned among the signs of decadence.

There ought to be a reference, on p. 298 below, to M. Joseph Bédier's papers in the *Revue Historique* (xcv. and xcvii.) on *Raoul de Cambrai*. M. Bédier's *Légendes épiques*, not yet published at this time of writing, will soon be in the hands of his expectant readers.

I am deeply indebted to many friends—first of all to York Powell—for innumerable good things spoken and written about these studies. My reviewers, in spite of all differences of opinion, have put me under strong obligations to them for their fairness and consideration. Particularly, I have to offer my most sincere acknowledgments to Dr. Andreas Heusler of Berlin for the honour he has done my book in his *Lied und Epos* (1905), and not less for the help that he has given, in this and other of his writings, towards the better understanding of the old poems and their history.

W. P. K.

OXFORD, 25*th Jan.* 1908.

CONTENTS

CHAPTER I

INTRODUCTION

I

The Heroic Age

II

Epic and Romance

III

Romantic Mythology

IV

THE THREE SCHOOLS—TEUTONIC EPIC—FRENCH EPIC—THE ICELANDIC HISTORIES

CHAPTER II

THE TEUTONIC EPIC

I

The Tragic Conception

II

Scale of the Poems

III

Epic and Ballad Poetry

IV

The Style of the Poems

V

The Progress of Epic

VI

Beowulf

CHAPTER III

THE ICELANDIC SAGAS

I

ICELAND AND THE HEROIC AGE

II

Matter and Form

III

The Heroic Ideal

IV

Tragic Imagination

V

Comedy

VI

The Art of Narrative

VII

Epic and History

VIII

The Northern Prose Romances

CHAPTER IV

THE OLD FRENCH EPIC

(*Chansons de Geste*)

CHAPTER V

ROMANCE AND THE OLD FRENCH ROMANTIC SCHOOLS

APPENDIX

EPIC AND ROMANCE

CHAPTER I

INTRODUCTION

I

THE HEROIC AGE

THE title of Epic, or of "heroic poem," is claimed by historians for a number of works belonging to the earlier Middle Ages, and to the medieval origins of modern literature. "Epic" is a term freely applied to the old school of Germanic narrative poetry, which in different dialects is represented by the poems of Hildebrand, of Beowulf, of Sigurd and Brynhild. "Epic" is the name for the body of old French poems which is headed by the *Chanson de Roland.* The rank of Epic is assigned by many to the *Nibelungenlied*, not to speak of other Middle High German poems on themes of German tradition. The title of prose Epic has been claimed for the Sagas of Iceland.

By an equally common consent the name Romance is given to a number of kinds of medieval narrative by which the Epic is succeeded and displaced; most notably in France, but also in other countries which were led, mainly by the example and influence of France, to give up their own "epic" forms and subjects in favour of new manners.

This literary classification corresponds in general history to the difference between the earlier "heroic" age and the age of chivalry. The "epics" of Hildebrand and Beowulf belong, if not wholly to German heathendom, at any rate to the earlier and prefeudal stage of German civilisation. The French epics, in their extant form, belong for the most part in spirit, if not always in date, to an order of things unmodified by the great changes of the twelfth century. While among the products of the twelfth century one of the most remarkable is the new school of French romance, the brilliant and frequently vainglorious exponent of the modern ideas of that age, and of all its chivalrous and courtly fashions of thought and sentiment. The difference of the two orders of literature is as plain as the difference in the art of war between the two sides of the battle of Hastings, which indeed is another form of the same thing; for the victory of the Norman knights over the English axemen has more than a fanciful or superficial analogy to the victory of the new literature of chivalry over the older forms of heroic narrative. The history of those two orders of literature, of the earlier Epic kinds, followed by the various types of medieval Romance, is parallel to the general political history of the earlier and the later Middle Ages, and may do something to illustrate the general progress of the nations. The passage from the earlier "heroic" civilisation to the age of chivalry was not made without some contemporary record of the "form and pressure" of the times in the changing fashions of literature, and in successive experiments of the imagination.

Whatever Epic may mean, it implies some weight and solidity; Romance means nothing, if it does not convey some notion of mystery and fantasy. A general distinction of this kind, whatever names may be used to render it, can be shown, in medieval literature, to hold good of the two large groups of narrative belonging to the earlier and the later Middle Ages respectively. Beowulf might stand for the one side, Lancelot or Gawain for the other. It is a difference not confined to literature. The two groups are distinguished from one another, as the respectable piratical gentleman of the North Sea coast in the ninth or tenth century differs from one of the companions of St. Louis. The latter has something fantastic in his ideas which the other has not. The Crusader may indeed be natural and brutal enough in most of his ways, but he has lost the sobriety and simplicity of the earlier type of rover. If nothing else, his way of fighting—the undisciplined cavalry charge—would convict him of extravagance as compared with men of business, like the settlers of Iceland for example.

The two great kinds of narrative literature in the Middle Ages might be distinguished by their favourite incidents and commonplaces of adventure. No kind of adventure is so common or better told in the earlier heroic manner than the defence of a narrow place against odds. Such are the stories of Hamther and Sorli in the hall of Ermanaric, of the Niblung kings in the hall of Attila, of the Fight of Finnesburh, of Walter at the Wasgenstein, of Byrhtnoth at Maldon, of Roland in the Pyrenees. Such are some of the finest passages in the Icelandic Sagas: the death of Gunnar, the burning of Njal's house, the burning of Flugumyri (an authentic record), the last fight of Kjartan in Svinadal, and of Grettir at Drangey. The story of Cynewulf and Cyneheard in the English Chronicle may well have come from a poem in which an attack and defence of this sort were narrated.

The favourite adventure of medieval romance is something different,—a knight riding alone through a forest; another knight; a shock of lances; a fight on foot with swords, "racing, tracing, and foining like two wild boars"; then, perhaps, recognition—the two knights belong to the same household and are engaged in the same quest.

> Et Guivrez vers lui esperone,
> De rien nule ne l'areisone,
> Ne Erec ne li sona mot.
>
> *Erec*, l. 5007.

This collision of blind forces, this tournament at random, takes the place, in the French romances, of the older kind of combat. In the older kind the parties have always good reasons of their own for fighting; they do not go into it with the same sort of readiness as the wandering champions of romance.

The change of temper and fashion represented by the appearance and the vogue of the medieval French romances is a change involving the whole world, and going far beyond the compass of literature and literary history. It meant the final surrender of the old ideas, independent of Christendom, which had been enough for the Germanic nations in their earlier days; it was the close of their heroic age. What the "heroic age" of the modern nations really was, may be learned from what is left of their heroic literature, especially from three groups or classes,—the old Teutonic alliterative poems on native subjects; the French *Chansons de Geste*; and the Icelandic Sagas.

All these three orders, whatever their faults may be, do something to represent a society which is "heroic" as the Greeks in Homer are heroic. There can be no mistake about the likeness. To compare the imaginations and the phrases of any of these barbarous works with the poetry of Homer may be futile, but their contents may be compared without reference to their poetical qualities; and there is no question that the life depicted has many things in common with Homeric life, and agrees with Homer in ignorance of the peculiar ideas of medieval chivalry.

The form of society in an heroic age is aristocratic and magnificent. At the same time, this aristocracy differs from that of later and more specialised forms of civilisation. It does not make an insuperable difference between gentle and simple. There is not the extreme division of labour that produces the contempt of the lord for the villain. The nobles have not yet discovered for themselves any form of occupation or mode of thought in virtue of which they are widely severed from the commons, nor have they invented any such ideal of life or conventional system of conduct as involves an ignorance or depreciation of the common pursuits of those below them. They have no such elaborate theory of conduct as is found in the chivalrous society of the Middle Ages. The great man is the man who is best at the things with which every one is familiar. The epic hero may despise the churlish man, may, like Odysseus in the *Iliad* (ii. 198), show little sympathy or patience with the bellowings of the multitude, but he may not ostentatiously refuse all community of ideas with simple people. His magnificence is not defended by scruples about everything low. It would not have mattered to Odysseus if he had been seen travelling in a cart, like Lancelot; though for Lancelot it was a great misfortune and anxiety. The art and pursuits of a gentleman in the heroic age are different from those of the churl, but not so far different as to keep them in different spheres. There is a community of prosaic interests. The great man is a good judge of cattle; he sails his own ship.

A gentleman adventurer on board his own ship,

following out his own ideas, carrying his men with him by his own power of mind and temper, and not by means of any system of naval discipline to which he as well as they must be subordinate ; surpassing his men in skill, knowledge, and ambition, but taking part with them and allowing them to take part in the enterprise, is a good representative of the heroic age. This relation between captain and men may be found, accidentally and exceptionally, in later and more sophisticated forms of society. In the heroic age a relation between a great man and his followers similar to that between an Elizabethan captain and his crew is found to be the most important and fundamental relation in society. In later times it is only by a special favour of circumstances, as for example by the isolation of shipboard from all larger monarchies, that the heroic relation between the leader and the followers can be repeated. As society becomes more complex and conventional, this relation ceases. The homeliness of conversation between Odysseus and his vassals, or between Njal and Thord Freedman's son, is discouraged by the rules of courtly behaviour as gentlefolk become more idle and ostentatious, and their vassals more sordid and dependent. The secrets also of political intrigue and dexterity made a difference between noble and villain, in later and more complex medieval politics, such as is unknown in the earlier days and the more homely forms of Society. An heroic age may be full of all kinds of nonsense and superstition, but its motives of action are mainly positive and sensible,—cattle, sheep, piracy, abduction, merchandise, recovery of stolen goods, revenge. The narrative poetry of an heroic age, whatever dignity it may obtain either by its dramatic force of imagination, or by the aid of its mythology, will keep its hold upon such common matters, simply because it cannot do without the essential practical interests, and has nothing to put in their place, if kings and chiefs are to be represented at all. The heroic age cannot dress up ideas or sentiments to play the part of characters. If its characters are not men they are nothing, not even thoughts or allegories; they cannot go on talking unless they have something to do; and so the whole business of life comes bodily into the epic poem.

How much the matter of the Northern heroic literature resembles the Homeric, may be felt and recognised at every turn in a survey of the ground. In both there are the *ashen spears*; there are the *shepherds of the people*; the retainers bound by loyalty to the prince who gives them meat and drink; the great hall with its minstrelsy, its boasting and bickering; the battles which are a number of single combats, while "physiology supplies the author with images"[1] for the same; the heroic rule of conduct (ἴομεν)[2]; the eminence of the hero, and at the same time his community of occupation and interest with those who are less distinguished.

There are other resemblances also, but some of these are miraculous, and perhaps irrelevant. By what magic is it that the cry of Odysseus, wounded and hard bestead in his retreat before the Trojans, comes over us like the three blasts of the horn of Roland?

> Thrice he shouted, as loud as the head of a man will bear; and three times Menelaus heard the sound thereof, and quickly he turned and spake to Ajax: "Ajax, there is come about me the cry of Odysseus slow to yield; and it is like as though the Trojans had come hard upon him by himself alone, closing him round in the battle."[3]

---

[1] Johnson on the Epic Poem (*Life of Milton*). [2] *Il.* xii. 328.
[3] *Il.* xi. 462.

It is reported as a discovery made by Mephistopheles in Thessaly, in the classical *Walpurgisnacht*, that the company there was very much like his old acquaintances on the Brocken. A similar discovery, in regard to more honourable personages and other scenes, may be made by other Gothic travellers in a "south-eastward" journey to heroic Greece. The classical reader of the Northern heroics may be frequently disgusted by their failures; he may also be bribed, if not to applaud, at least to continue his study, by the glimmerings and "shadowy recollections," the affinities and correspondences between the Homeric and the Northern heroic world.

Beowulf and his companions sail across the sea to Denmark on an errand of deliverance,—to cleanse the land of monsters. They are welcomed by Hrothgar, king of the Danes, and by his gentle queen, in a house less fortunate than the house of Alcinous, for it is exposed to the attacks of the lumpish ogre that Beowulf has to kill, but recalling in its splendour, in the manner of its entertainment, and the bearing of its gracious lord and lady, the house where Odysseus told his story. Beowulf, like Odysseus, is assailed by an envious person with discourteous words. Hunferth, the Danish courtier, is irritated by Beowulf's presence; "he could not endure that any one should be counted worthier than himself"; he speaks enviously, a biting speech—θυμοδακὴς γὰρ μῦθος—and is answered in the tone of Odysseus to Euryalus.[1] Beowulf has a story to tell of his former perils among the creatures of the sea. It is differently introduced from that of Odysseus, and has not the same importance, but it increases the likeness between the two adventurers.

In the shadowy halls of the Danish king a minstrel

[1] *Od.* viii. 165.

sings of the famous deeds of men, and his song is given as an interlude in the main action. It is a poem on that same tragedy of Finnesburh, which is the theme of a separate poem in the Old English heroic cycle; so Demodocus took his subjects from the heroic cycle of Achaea. The leisure of the Danish king's house is filled in the same manner as the leisure of Phaeacia. In spite of the difference of the climate, it is impossible to mistake the likeness between the Greek and the Northern conceptions of a dignified and reasonable way of life. The magnificence of the Homeric great man is like the magnificence of the Northern lord, in so far as both are equally marked off from the pusillanimity and cheapness of popular morality on the one hand, and from the ostentation of Oriental or chivalrous society on the other. The likeness here is not purely in the historical details, but much more in the spirit that informs the poetry.

If this part of *Beowulf* is a Northern *Odyssey*, there is nothing in the whole range of English literature so like a scene from the *Iliad* as the narrative of Maldon. It is a battle in which the separate deeds of the fighters are described, with not quite so much anatomy as in Homer. The fighting about the body of Byrhtnoth is described as strongly, as "the Fighting at the Wall" in the twelfth book of the *Iliad*, and essentially in the same way, with the interchange of blows clearly noted, together with the speeches and thoughts of the combatants. Even the most heroic speech in Homer, even the power of Sarpedon's address to Glaucus in the twelfth book of the *Iliad*, cannot discredit, by comparison, the heroism and the sublimity of the speech of the "old companion" at the end of *Maldon*. The language is simple, but it is not less adequate in its own way than the simplicity of Sarpedon's argument. It states, perhaps more clearly and absolutely than anything in Greek, the Northern principle of resistance to all odds, and defiance of ruin. In the North the individual spirit asserts itself more absolutely against the bodily enemies than in Greece; the defiance is made wholly independent of any vestige of prudent consideration; the contradiction, "Thought the harder, Heart the keener, Mood the more, as our Might lessens," is stated in the most extreme terms. This does not destroy the resemblance between the Greek and the Northern ideal, or between the respective forms of representation.

The creed of Maldon is that of Achilles:[1] "Xanthus, what need is there to prophesy of death? Well do I know that it is my doom to perish here, far from my father and mother; but for all that I will not turn back, until I give the Trojans their fill of war." The difference is that in the English case the strain is greater, the irony deeper, the antithesis between the spirit and the body more paradoxical.

Where the centre of life is a great man's house, and where the most brilliant society is that which is gathered at his feast, where competitive boasting, story-telling, and minstrelsy are the principal intellectual amusements, it is inevitable that these should find their way into a kind of literature which has no foundation except experience and tradition. Where fighting is more important than anything else in active life, and at the same time is carried on without organisation or skilled combinations, it is inevitable that it should be described as it is in the *Iliad*, the *Song of Maldon* and *Song of Roland*, and the Icelandic Sagas, as a series of personal encounters, in

[1] *Il.* xix. 420.

which every stroke is remembered. From this early aristocratic form of society, there is derived in one age the narrative of life at Ithaca or of the navigation of Odysseus, in another the representation of the household of Njal or of Olaf the Peacock, and of the rovings of Olaf Tryggvason and other captains. There is an affinity between these histories in virtue of something over and above the likeness in the conditions of things they describe. There is a community of literary sense as well as of historical conditions, in the record of Achilles and Kjartan Olafsson, of Odysseus and Njal.

The circumstances of an heroic age may be found in numberless times and places, in the history of the world. Among its accompaniments will be generally found some sort of literary record of sentiments and imaginations; but to find an heroic literature of the highest order is not so easy. Many nations instead of an *Iliad* or an *Odyssey* have had to make shift with conventional repetitions of the praise of chieftains, without any story; many have had to accept from their story-tellers all sorts of monstrous adventures in place of the humanities of debate and argument. Epic literature is not common; it is brought to perfection by a slow process through many generations. The growth of Epic out of the older and commoner forms of poetry, hymns, dirges, or panegyrics, is a progress towards intellectual and imaginative freedom. Few nations have attained, at the close of their heroic age, to a form of poetical art in which men are represented freely in action and conversation. The labour and meditation of all the world has not discovered, for the purposes of narrative, any essential modification of the procedure of Homer. Those who are considered reformers and discoverers in later times—Chaucer, Cervantes, Fielding—are discoverers merely of the old devices of dramatic narration which were understood by Homer and described after him by Aristotle.

The growth of Epic, in the beginning of the history of the modern nations, has been generally thwarted and stunted. It cannot be said of many of the languages of the North and West of Europe that in them the epic form has come fully to its own, or has realised its proper nature. Many of them, however, have at least made a beginning. The history of the older German literature, and of old French, is the history of a great number of experiments in Epic; of attempts, that is, to represent great actions in narrative, with the personages well defined. These experiments are begun in the right way. They are not merely barbarous nor fantastic. They are different also from such traditional legends and romances as may survive among simple people long after the day of their old glories and their old kings. The poems of *Beowulf* and *Waldere*, of *Roland* and *William of Orange*, are intelligible and reasonable works, determined in the main by the same essential principles of narrative art, and of dramatic conversation within the narrative, as are observed in the practice of Homer. Further, these are poems in which, as in the Homeric poems, the ideas of their time are conveyed and expressed in a noble manner: they are high-spirited poems. They have got themselves clear of the confusion and extravagance of early civilisation, and have hit upon a way of telling a story clearly and in proportion, and with dignity. They are epic in virtue of their superiority to the more fantastic motives of interest, and in virtue of their study of human character. They are heroic in the nobility of their temper and their style. If at any time they indulge in heroic commonplaces of sentiment, they do so without insincerity or affectation, as the expression of the general temper or opinion of their own time. They are not separated widely from the matters of which they treat; they are not antiquarian revivals of past forms, nor traditional vestiges of things utterly remote and separate from the actual world. What art they may possess is different from the "rude sweetness" of popular ballads, and from the unconscious grace of popular tales. They have in different degrees and manners the form of epic poetry, in their own right. There are recognisable qualities that serve to distinguish even a fragment of heroic poetry from the ballads and romances of a lower order, however near these latter forms may approach at times to the epic dignity.

II

EPIC AND ROMANCE

It is the nature of epic poetry to be at ease in regard to its subject matter, to be free from the strain and excitement of weaker and more abstract forms of poetry in dealing with heroic subjects. The heroic ideal of epic is not attained by a process of abstraction and separation from the meannesses of familiar things. The magnificence and aristocratic dignity of epic is conformable to the practical and ethical standards of the heroic age; that is to say, it tolerates a number of things that may be found mean and trivial by academicians. Epic poetry is one of the complex and comprehensive kinds of literature, in which most of the other kinds may be included—romance, history, comedy; *tragical*, *comical*, *historical*, *pastoral* are terms not sufficiently various to denote the variety of the *Iliad* and the *Odyssey*.

The "common life" of the Homeric poems may appeal to modern pedantic theorists, and be used by them in support of Euripidean or Wordsworthian receipts for literature. But the comprehensiveness of the greater kinds of poetry, of Homer and Shakespeare, is a different thing from the premeditated and self-assertive realism of the authors who take viciously to common life by way of protest against the romantic extreme. It has its origin, not in a critical theory about the proper matter of literature, but in dramatic imagination. In an epic poem where the characters are vividly imagined, it follows naturally that their various moods and problems involve a variety of scenery and properties, and so the whole business of life comes into the story.

The success of epic poetry depends on the author's power of imagining and representing characters. A kind of success and a kind of magnificence may be attained in stories, professing to be epic, in which there is no dramatic virtue, in which every new scene and new adventure merely goes to accumulate, in immortal verse, the proofs of the hero's nullity and insignificance. This is not the epic poetry of the heroic ages.

Aristotle, in his discussion of tragedy, chose to lay stress upon the plot, the story. On the other hand, to complete the paradox, in the epic he makes the characters all-important, not the story. Without the tragic plot or fable, the tragedy becomes a series of moral essays or monologues; the life of the drama is derived from the original idea of the fable which is its subject. Without dramatic representation of the characters, epic is mere history or romance; the variety and life of epic are to be found in the drama that springs up at every encounter of the personages.

"Homer is the only poet who knows the right proportions of epic narrative; when to narrate, and when to let the characters speak for themselves. Other poets for the most part tell their story straight on, with scanty passages of drama and far between. Homer, with little prelude, leaves the stage to his personages, men and women, all with characters of their own."[1]

[1] Ὅμηρος δὲ ἄλλα τε πολλὰ ἄξιος ἐπαινεῖσθαι καὶ δὴ καὶ ὅτι

Aristotle wrote with very little consideration for the people who were to come after him, and gives little countenance to such theories of epic as have at various times been prevalent among the critics, in which the dignity of the subject is insisted on. He does not imagine it the chief duty of an epic poet to choose a lofty argument for historical rhetoric. He does not say a word about the national or the ecumenical importance of the themes of the epic poet. His analysis of the plot of the *Odyssey*, but for the reference to Poseidon, might have been the description of a modern realistic story.

"A man is abroad for many years, persecuted by Poseidon and alone; meantime the suitors of his wife are wasting his estate and plotting against his son; after many perils by sea he returns to his own country and discovers himself to his friends. He falls on his enemies and destroys them, and so comes to his own again."

The *Iliad* has more likeness than the *Odyssey* to the common pattern of later sophisticated epics. But the war of Troy is not the subject of the *Iliad* in the same way as the siege of Jerusalem is the subject of Tasso's poem. The story of the *Aeneid* can hardly be told in the simplest form without some reference to the destiny of Rome, or the story of *Paradise Lost* without the feud of heaven and hell. But in the *Iliad*, the assistance of the Olympians, or even the presence of the whole of Greece, is not in the same degree essential to the plot of the story of Achilles. In the form of Aristotle's summary of the *Odyssey*,

μόνος τῶν ποιητῶν οὐκ ἀγνοεῖ ὃ δεῖ ποιεῖν αὐτόν. αὐτὸν γὰρ δεῖ τὸν ποιητὴν ἐλάχιστα λέγειν· οὐ γάρ ἐστι κατὰ ταῦτα μιμητής. οἱ μὲν οὖν ἄλλοι αὐτοὶ μὲν δι' ὅλου ἀγωνίζονται, μιμοῦνται δὲ ὀλίγα καὶ ὀλιγάκις· ὁ δὲ ὀλίγα φροιμιασάμενος εὐθὺς εἰσάγει ἄνδρα ἢ γυναῖκα ἢ ἄλλο τι ἦθος καὶ οὐδέν' ἀήθη ἀλλ' ἔχοντα ἤθη.—ARIST. *Poet.* 1460 a 5.

reduced to "the cool element of prose," the *Iliad* may be proved to be something quite different from the common fashion of literary epics. It might go in something like this way :—

"A certain man taking part in a siege is slighted by the general, and in his resentment withdraws from the war, though his own side is in great need of his help. His dearest friend having been killed by the enemy, he comes back into the action and takes vengeance for his friend, and allows himself to be reconciled."

It is the debate among the characters, and not the onset of Hera and Athena in the chariot of Heaven, that gives its greatest power to the *Iliad*. The *Iliad*, with its "machines," its catalogue of the forces, its funeral games, has contributed more than the *Odyssey* to the common pattern of manufactured epics. But the essence of the poem is not to be found among the Olympians. Achilles refusing the embassy or yielding to Priam has no need of the Olympian background. The poem is in a great degree independent of "machines"; its life is in the drama of the characters. The source of all its variety is the imagination by which the characters are distinguished; the liveliness and variety of the characters bring with them all the other kinds of variety.

It is impossible for the author who knows his personages intimately to keep to any one exclusive mode of sentiment or one kind of scene. He cannot be merely tragical and heroic, or merely comical and pastoral; these are points of view to which those authors are confined who are possessed by one kind of sentiment or sensibility, and who wish to find expression for their own prevailing mood. The author who is interested primarily in his characters will not allow them to be obliterated by the story or by its diffused impersonal sentiment. The action of an heroic poem must be "of a certain magnitude," but the accessories need not be all heroic and magnificent; the heroes do not derive their magnificence from the scenery, the properties, and the author's rhetoric, but contrariwise: the dramatic force and self-consistency of the *dramatis personae* give poetic value to any accessories of scenery or sentiment which may be required by the action. They are not figures "animating" a landscape; what the landscape means for the poet's audience is determined by the character of his personages.

All the variety of epic is explained by Aristotle's remark on Homer. Where the characters are true, and dramatically represented, there can be no monotony.

In the different kinds of Northern epic literature—German, English, French, and Norse—belonging to the Northern heroic ages, there will be found in different degrees this epic quality of drama. Whatever magnificence they may possess comes mainly from the dramatic strength of the heroes, and in a much less degree from the historic dignity or importance of the issues of the story, or from its mythological decorations.

The place of history in the heroic poems belonging to an heroic age is sometimes misconceived. Early epic poetry may be concerned with great historic events. It does not necessarily emphasise—by preference it does not emphasise—the historic importance or the historic results of the events with which it deals. Heroic poetry implies an heroic age, an age of pride and courage, in which there is not any extreme organisation of politics to hinder the individual talent and its achievements, nor on the other hand too much isolation of the hero through the absence of any national or popular consciousness. There must be some unity of sentiment, some common standard of appreciation, among the people to whom the heroes belong, if they are to escape oblivion. But this common sentiment must not be such as to make the idea of the community and its life predominant over the individual genius of its members. In such a case there may be a Roman history, but not anything approaching the nature of the Homeric poems.

In some epic poems belonging to an heroic age, and not to a time of self-conscious and reflective literature, there may be found general conceptions that seem to resemble those of the *Aeneid* rather than those of the *Iliad.* In many of the old French *Chansons de Geste*, the war against the infidels is made the general subject of the story, and the general idea of the Holy War is expressed as fully as by Tasso. Here, however, the circumstances are exceptional. The French epic with all its Homeric analogies is not as sincere as Homer. It is exposed to the touch of influences from another world, and though many of the French poems, or great part of many of them, may tell of heroes who would be content with the simple and positive rules of the heroic life, this is not allowed them. They are brought within the sphere of other ideas, of another civilisation, and lose their independence.

Most of the old German heroic poetry is clearly to be traced, as far as its subjects are concerned, to the most exciting periods in early German history, between the fourth and the sixth centuries. The names that seem to have been most commonly known to the poets are the names that are most important to the historian—Ermanaric, Attila, Theodoric. In the wars of the great migration the spirit of each of the German families was quickened, and at the same time the spirit of the whole of Germany, so that each part sympathised with all the rest, and the fame of the heroes went abroad beyond the limits of their own kindred. Ermanaric, Attila, and Theodoric, Sigfred the Frank, and Gundahari the Burgundian, are heroes over all the region occupied by all forms of Teutonic language. But although the most important period of early German history may be said to have produced the old German heroic poetry, by giving a number of heroes to the poets, at the same time that the imagination was stirred to appreciate great things and make the most of them, still the result is nothing like the patriotic epic in twelve books, the *Aeneid* or the *Lusiad*, which chooses, of set purpose, the theme of the national glory. Nor is it like those old French epics in which there often appears a contradiction between the story of individual heroes, pursuing their own fortunes, and the idea of a common cause to which their own fortunes ought to be, but are not always, subordinate. The great historical names which appear in the old German heroic poetry are seldom found there in anything like their historical character, and not once in their chief historical aspect as adversaries of the Roman Empire. Ermanaric, Attila, and Theodoric are all brought into the same Niblung story, a story widely known in different forms, though it was never adequately written out. The true history of the war between the Burgundians and the Huns in the fifth century is forgotten. In place of it, there is associated with the life and death of Gundahari the Burgundian king a story which may have been vastly older, and may have passed through many different forms before it became the story of the Niblung treasure, of Sigfred and Brynhild. This, which has made free with so many great historical names, the name of Attila, the name of Theodoric, has little to do with history. In this heroic story coming out of the heroic age, there is not much that can be traced to historical as distinct from mythical tradition. The tragedy of the death of Attila, as told in the *Atlakviða* and the *Atlamál*, may indeed owe something to the facts recorded by historians, and something more to vaguer historical tradition of the vengeance of Rosamund on Alboin the Lombard. But, in the main, the story of the Niblungs is independent of history, in respect of its matter; in its meaning and effect as a poetical story it is absolutely free from history. It is a drama of personal encounters and rivalries. This also, like the story of Achilles, is fit for a stage in which the characters are left free to declare themselves in their own way, unhampered by any burden of history, any purpose or moral apart from the events that are played out in the dramatic clashing of one will against another.

It is not vanity in an historian to look for the historical origin of the tale of Troy or of the vengeance of Gudrun; but no result in either case can greatly affect the intrinsic relations of the various elements within the poems. The relations of Achilles to his surroundings in the *Iliad*, of Attila and Ermanaric to theirs, are freely conceived by the several poets, and are intelligible at once, without reference to anything outside the poems. To require of the poetry of an heroic age that it shall recognise the historical meaning and importance of the events in which it originates, and the persons whose names it uses, is entirely to mistake the nature of it. Its nature is to find or make some drama played by kings and heroes, and to let the historical framework take care of itself The connexion of epic poetry with history is real, and it is a fitting subject for historical inquiry, but it lies behind the scene. The epic poem is cut loose and set free from history, and goes on a way of its own.

Epic magnificence and the dignity of heroic poetry may thus be only indirectly derived from such greatness or magnificence as is known to true prosaic history. The heroes, even if they can be identified as historical, may retain in epic nothing of their historical character, except such qualities as fit them for great actions. Their conduct in epic poetry may be very far unlike their actual demeanour in true history; their greatest works may be thrust into a corner of the epic, or barely alluded to, or left out altogether. Their greatness in epic may be quite a different kind of greatness from that of their true history; and where there are many poems belonging to the same cycle there may be the greatest discrepancy among the views taken of the same hero by different authors, and all the views may be alike remote from the prosaic or scientific view. There is no constant or self-consistent opinion about the character of Charles the Emperor in old French poetry: there is one view in the *Chanson de Roland*, another in the *Pèlerinage*, another in the *Coronemenz Loois*: none of the opinions is anything like an elaborate or detailed historical judgment. Attila, though he loses his political importance and most of his historical acquisitions in the Teutonic heroic poems in which he appears, may retain in some of them his ruthlessness and strength; at other times he may be a wise and peaceful king. All that is constant, or common, in the different poetical reports of him, is that he was great. What touches the mind of the poet out of the depths of the past is nothing but the tradition, undefined, of something lordly. This vagueness of tradition does not imply that tradition is impotent or barren; only that it leaves all the execution, the growth of detail, to the freedom of the poet. He is bound to the past, in one way; it is laid upon him to tell the stories of the great men of his own race. But in those stories, as they come to him, what is most lively is not a set and established series of incidents, true or false, but something to which the standards of truth and falsehood are scarcely applicable; something stirring him up to admiration, a compulsion or influence upon him requiring him to make the story again in his own way; not to interpret history, but to make a drama of his own, filled somehow with passion and strength of mind. It does not matter in what particular form it may be represented, so long as in some form or other the power of the national glory is allowed to pass into his work.

This vagueness and generality in the relation of heroic poetry to the historical events and persons of an heroic age is of course quite a different thing from vagueness in the poetry itself. Gunther and Attila, Roland and Charlemagne, in poetry, are very vaguely connected with their antitypes in history; but that does not prevent them from being characterised minutely, if it should agree with the poet's taste or lie within his powers to have it so. The strange thing is that this vague relation should be so necessary to heroic poetry; that it should be impossible at any stage of literature or in any way by taking thought to make up for the want of it.

The place of Gunther the Burgundian, Sigfred the Frank, and Attila the Hun, in the poetical stories of the Niblung treasure may be in one sense accidental. The fables of the treasure with a curse upon it, the killing of the dragon, the sleeping princess, the wavering flame, are not limited to this particular course of tradition, and, further, the traditional motives of the Niblung story have varied enormously not only in different countries, but in one and the same language at the same time. The story is never told alike by two narrators; what is common and essential in it is nothing palpable or fixed, but goes from poet to poet "like a shadow from dream to dream." And the historical names are apparently unessential; yet they remain. To look for the details of the Niblung story in the sober history of the Goths and Huns, Burgundians and Franks, is like the vanity confessed by the author of the *Roman de Rou*, when he went on a sentimental journey to Broceliande, and was disappointed to find there only the common daylight and nothing of the Faerie. Nevertheless it is the historical names, and the vague associations about them, that give to the Niblung story, not indeed the whole of its plot, but its temper, its pride and glory, its heroic and epic character.

Heroic poetry is not, as a rule, greatly indebted to historical fact for its material. The epic poet does not keep record of the great victories or the great disasters. He cannot, however, live without the ideas and sentiments of heroism that spring up naturally in periods like those of the Teutonic migrations. In this sense the historic Gunther and Attila are necessary to the Niblung story. The wars and fightings of generation on generation went to create the heroism, the loftiness of spirit, expressed in the Teutonic epic verse. The plots of the stories may be commonplace, the common property of all popular tales. The temper is such as is not found everywhere, but only in historical periods of great energy. The names of Ermanaric and Attila correspond to hardly anything of literal history in the heroic poems; but they are the sign of conquests and great exploits that have gone to form character, though their details are forgotten.

It may be difficult to appreciate and understand in detail this vague relation of epic poetry to the national life and to the renown of the national heroes, but the general fact is not less positive or less capable of verification than the date of the battle of Châlons, or the series of the Gothic vowels. All that is needed to prove this is to compare the poetry of a national cycle with the poetry that comes in its place when the national cycle is deserted for other heroes.

The secondary or adopted themes may be treated with so much of the manner of the original poetry as to keep little of their foreign character. The rhetoric, the poetical habit, of the original epic may be retained. As in the Saxon poem on the Gospel history, the *Hêliand*, the twelve disciples may be represented as Thanes owing loyalty to their Prince, in common poetic terms befitting the men of Beowulf or Byrhtnoth. As in the French poems on Alexander the Great, Alexander may become a feudal king, and take over completely all that belongs to such a rank. There may be no consciousness of any need for a new vocabulary or a new mode of expression to fit the foreign themes. In France, it is true, there is a general distinction of form between the *Chansons de Geste* and the romances; though to this there are exceptions, themes not French, and themes not purely heroic, being represented in the epic form. In the early Teutonic poetry there is no distinction of versification, vocabulary, or rhetoric between the original and the secondary narrative poems; the alliterative verse belongs to both kinds equally. Nor is it always the case that subjects derived from books or from abroad are handled with less firmness than the original and traditional plots. Though sometimes a prevailing affection for imported stories, for Celtic or Oriental legend, may be accompanied by a relaxation in the style, the superiority of national to foreign subjects is not always proved by greater strength or eloquence. Can it be said that the Anglo-Saxon *Judith*, for instance, is less heroic, less strong and sound, than the somewhat damaged and motley accoutrements of Beowulf?

The difference is this, that the more original and native kind of epic has immediate association with all that the people know about themselves, with all their customs, all that part of their experience which no one can account for or refer to any particular source. A poem like *Beowulf* can play directly on a thousand chords of association; the range of its appeal to the minds of an audience is almost unlimited; on no side is the poet debarred from freedom of movement, if only he remember first of all what is due to the hero. He has all the life of his people to strengthen him.

A poem like the *Hêliand* is under an obligation to a literary original, and cannot escape from this restriction. It makes what use it can of the native associations, but with whatever perseverance the author may try to bend his story into harmony with the laws of his own country, there is an untranslated residue of foreign ideas.

Whatever the defects or excesses of *Beowulf* may be, the characters are not distressed by any such unsolved contradiction as in the Saxon *Hêliand*, or in the old English *Exodus*, or *Andreas*, or the other poems taken from the Bible or the lives of saints. They have not, like the personages of the second order of poems, been translated from one realm of ideas to another, and made to take up burdens and offices not their own. They have grown naturally in the mind of a poet, out of the poet's knowledge of human nature, and the traditional ethical judgments of which he is possessed.

The comparative freedom of *Beowulf* in its relation to historical tradition and traditional ethics, and the comparative limitation of the *Hêliand*, are not in themselves conditions of either advantage or inferiority. They simply mark the difference between two types of narrative poem. To be free and comprehensive in relation to history, to summarise and represent in epic characters the traditional experience of an heroic age, is not the proper virtue of every kind of poetry, though it is proper to the Homeric kind. The freedom that belongs to the *Iliad* and the *Odyssey* is also shared by many a dismal and interminable poem of the Middle Ages. That foreign or literary subjects impose certain limitations, and interfere with the direct use of matter of experience in poetry, is nothing against them. The Anglo-Saxon *Judith*, which is thus restricted as compared with *Beowulf*, may be more like Milton for these restrictions, if it be less like Homer. Exemption from them is not a privilege, except that it gives room for the attainment of a certain kind of excellence, the Homeric kind; as, on the other hand, it excludes the possibility of the literary art of Virgil or Milton.

The relation of epic poetry to its heroic age is not to be found in the observance of any strict historical duty. It lies rather in the epic capacity for bringing together all manner of lively passages from the general experience of the age, in a story about famous heroic characters. The plot of the story gives unity and harmony to the composition, while the variety of its matter is permitted and justified by the dramatic variety of the characters and their interests.

By its comprehensiveness and the variety of its substance, which are the signs and products of its dramatic imagination, epic poetry of the heroic age is distinguished from the more abstract kinds of narrative, such as the artificial epic, and from all kinds of imagination or fancy that are limited in their scope.

In times when "the Epic Poem" was a more attractive, if not more perilous theme of debate than it now is, there was a strong controversy about the proper place and the proper kind of miraculous details to be admitted. The question was debated by Tasso in his critical writings, against the strict and pedantic imitators of classical models, and with a strong partiality for Ariosto against Trissino. Tasso made less of a distinction between romance and epic than was agreeable to some of his successors in criticism; and the controversy went on for generations, always more or less concerned with the great Italian heroic poems, *Orlando* and *Jerusalem*. Some record of it will be found in Dr. Hurd's *Letters on Chivalry and Romance* (1762). If the controversy has any interest now, it must be because it provided the most extreme statements of abstract literary principles, which on account of their thoroughness are interesting. From the documents it can be ascertained how near some of the critics came to that worship of the Faultless Hero with which Dryden in his heroic plays occasionally conformed, while he guarded himself against misinterpretation in his prefaces.

The epic poetry of the more austere critics was devised according to the strictest principles of dignity and sublimity, with a precise exclusion of everything "Gothic" and romantic. Davenant's Preface to *Gondibert*—"the Author's Preface to his much

Honour'd friend, Mr Hobs"—may show how the canon of epic was understood by poets who took things seriously; "for I will yield to their opinion, who permit not *Ariosto*, no, not *Du Bartas*, in this eminent rank of the *Heroicks*; rather than to make way by their admission for *Dante*, *Marino*, and others."

It is somewhat difficult to find a common measure for these names, but it is clear that what is most distasteful to the writer, in theory at any rate, is variety. Epic is the most solemn, stately, and frigid of all kinds of composition. This was the result attained by the perverse following of precepts supposed to be classical. The critics of the seventeenth and eighteenth centuries were generally right in distinguishing between Epic and Romance, and generally wrong in separating the one kind from the other as opposite and mutually exclusive forms, instead of seeing with Tasso, in his critical discourses, that romance may be included in epic. Against the manifold perils of the Gothic fantasy they set up the image of the Abstract Hero, and recited the formulas of the decorous and symmetrical abstract heroic poem. They were occasionally troubled by the "Gothic" elements in Homer, of which their adversaries were not slow to take advantage.

One of the most orthodox of all the formalists, who for some reason came to be very much quoted in England, Bossu, in his discourse on the Epic Poem, had serious difficulties with the adventures of Ulysses, and his stories told in Phaeacia. The episodes of Circe, of the Sirens, and of Polyphemus, are *machines*; they are also not quite easy to understand. "They are necessary to the action, and yet they are not humanly probable." But see how Homer gets over the difficulty and brings back these *machines* to the region of human probability. "Homère les fait adroitement rentrer dans la Vraisemblance humaine par la simplicité de ceux devant qui il fait faire ses récits fabuleux. Il dit assez plaisamment que les Phéaques habitoient dans une Isle éloignée des lieux où demeurent les hommes qui ont de l'esprit. *εἶσεν δ' ἐν Σχερίῃ ἕκας ἀνδρῶν ἀλφηστάων.* Ulysses les avoit connus avant que de se faire connoître à eux· et aiant observé qu'ils avoient toutes les qualités de ces fainéans qui n'admirent rien avec plus de plaisir que les aventures Romanesques: il les satisfait par ces récits accommodez à leur humeur. Mais le Poëte n'y a pas oublié les Lecteurs raisonnables. Il leur a donné en ces Fables tout le plaisir que l'on peut tirer des véritez Morales, si agréablement déguisées sous ces miraculeuses allégories. C'est ainsi qu'il a réduit ces Machines dans la vérité et dans la Vraisemblance Poëtique."[1]

Although the world has fallen away from the severity of this critic, there is still a meaning at the bottom of his theory of machines. He has at any rate called attention to one of the most interesting parts of Epic, and has found the right word for the episodes of the Phaeacian story of Odysseus. Romance is the word for them, and Romance is at the same time one of the constituent parts and one of the enemies of epic poetry. That it was dangerous was seen by the academical critics. They provided against it, generally, by treating it with contempt and proscribing it, as was done by those French critics who were offended by Ariosto and perplexed by much of the Gothic machinery of Tasso. They did not readily admit that epic poetry is as complex as the plays of Shakespeare, and as incongruous as these in its

[1] *Traité du Poëme Épique*, par le R. P. Le Bossu, Chanoine Régulier de Sainte Geneviève ; MDCLXXV (t. ii. p. 166).

composition, if the different constituents be taken out separately in the laboratory and then compared.

Romance by itself is a kind of literature that does not allow the full exercise of dramatic imagination; a limited and abstract form, as compared with the fulness and variety of Epic; though episodes of romance, and romantic moods and digressions, may have their place, along with all other human things, in the epic scheme.

The difference between the greater and the lesser kinds of narrative literature is vital and essential, whatever names may be assigned to them. In the one kind, of which Aristotle knew no other examples than the *Iliad* and the *Odyssey*, the personages are made individual through their dramatic conduct and their speeches in varying circumstances; in the other kind, in place of the moods and sentiments of a multitude of different people entering into the story and working it out, there is the sentiment of the author in his own person; there is one voice, the voice of the story-teller, and his theory of the characters is made to do duty for the characters themselves. There may be every poetic grace, except that of dramatic variety; and wherever, in narrative, the independence of the characters is merged in the sequence of adventures, or in the beauty of the landscape, or in the effusion of poetic sentiment, the narrative falls below the highest order, though the art be the art of Ovid or of Spenser.

The romance of Odysseus is indeed "brought into conformity with poetic verisimilitude," but in a different way from that of Bossu *On the Epic Poem*. It is not because the Phaeacians are romantic in their tastes, but because it belongs to Odysseus, that the Phaeacian night's entertainment has its place in the *Odyssey*. The *Odyssey* is the story of his home-coming, his recovery of his own. The great action of the drama of Odysseus is in his dealings with Penelope, Eumaeus, Telemachus, the suitors. The Phaeacian story is indeed episodic; the interest of those adventures is different from that of the meeting with Penelope. Nevertheless it is all kept in harmony with the stronger part of the poem. It is not pure fantasy and "Faerie," like the voyage of Maelduin or the vigil in the castle of Busirane. Odysseus in the house of Alcinous is not different from Odysseus of the return to Ithaca. The story is not pure romance, it is a dramatic monologue; and the character of the speaker has more part than the wonders of the story in the silence that falls on the listeners when the story comes to an end.

In all early literature it is hard to keep the story within limits, to observe the proportion of the *Odyssey* between strong drama and romance. The history of the early heroic literature of the Teutonic tongues, and of the epics of old France, comes to an end in the victory of various romantic schools, and of various restricted and one-sided forms of narrative. From within and without, from the resources of native mythology and superstition and from the fascination of Welsh and Arabian stories, there came the temptation to forget the study of character, and to part with an inheritance of tragic fables, for the sake of vanities, wonders, and splendours among which character and the tragic motives lost their pre-eminent interest and their old authority over poets and audience.

III

ROMANTIC MYTHOLOGY

BETWEEN the dramatic qualities of epic poetry and the myths and fancies of popular tradition there must inevitably be a conflict and a discrepancy. The greatest scenes of the *Iliad* and the *Odyssey* have little to do with myth. Where the characters are most vividly realised there is no room for the lighter kinds of fable; the epic "machines" are superfluous. Where all the character of Achilles is displayed in the interview with Priam, all his generosity, all his passion and unreason, the imagination refuses to be led away by anything else from looking on and listening. The presence of Hermes, Priam's guide, is forgotten. Olympus cannot stand against the spell of words like those of Priam and Achilles; it vanishes like a parched scroll. In the great scene in the other poem where the disguised Odysseus talks with Penelope, but will not make himself known to her for fear of spoiling his plot, there is just as little opportunity for any intervention of the Olympians. "Odysseus pitied his wife as she wept, but his eyes were firm as horn or steel, unwavering in his eyelids, and with art he concealed his tears.[1]"

[1] *αὐτὰρ' Οδυσσεὺς*
θυμῷ μὲν γοόωσαν ἑὴν ἐλέαιρε γυναῖκα,
ὀφθαλμοὶ δ' ὡς εἰ κέρα ἕστασαν ἠὲ σίδηρος
ἀτρέμας ἐν βλεφάροισι· δόλῳ δ' ὅ γε δάκρυα κεῦθεν.
Od. xix. 209.

In passages like these the epic poet gets clear away from the cumbrous inheritance of traditional fancies and stories. In other places he is inevitably less strong and self-sustained; he has to speak of the gods of the nation, or to work into his large composition some popular and improbable histories. The result in Homer is something like the result in Shakespeare, when he has a more than usually childish or old-fashioned fable to work upon. A story like that of the *Three Caskets* or the *Pound of Flesh* is perfectly consistent with itself in its original popular form. It is inconsistent with the form of elaborate drama, and with the lives of people who have souls of their own, like Portia or Shylock. Hence in the drama which uses the popular story as its ground-plan, the story is never entirely reduced into conformity with the spirit of the chief characters. The caskets and the pound of flesh, in despite of all the author's pains with them, are imperfectly harmonised; the primitive and barbarous imagination in them retains an inconvenient power of asserting its discordance with the principal parts of the drama. Their unreason is of no great consequence, yet it is something; it is not quite kept out of sight.

The epic poet, at an earlier stage of literature than Shakespeare, is even more exposed to this difficulty. Shakespeare was free to take his plots where he chose, and took these old wives' tales at his own risk. The epic poet has matter of this sort forced upon him. In his treatment of it, it will be found that ingenuity does not fail him, and that the transition from the unreasonable or old-fashioned part of his work to the modern and dramatic part is cunningly worked out. "He gets over the unreason by the grace and skill of his handling,"[1] says Aristotle

[1] *νῦν δὲ τοῖς ἄλλοις ἀγαθοῖς ἀφανίζει ἡδύνων τὸ ἄτοπον.*
ARISTOT. *Poet.* 1460 b.

of a critical point in the "machinery" of the *Odyssey*, where Odysseus is carried ashore on Ithaca in his sleep. There is a continual play in the *Iliad* and *Odyssey* between the wonders of mythology and the spirit of the drama. In this, as in other things, the Homeric poems observe the mean: the extremes may be found in the heroic literature of other nations; the extreme of marvellous fable in the old Irish heroic legends, for example; the extreme of plainness and "soothfastness" in the old English lay of *Maldon*. In some medieval compositions, as in *Huon of Bordeaux*, the two extremes are brought together clumsily and without harmony. In other medieval works again it is possible to find something like the Homeric proportion—the drama of strong characters, taking up and transforming the fanciful products of an earlier world, the inventions of minds not deeply or especially interested in character.

The defining and shaping of myths in epic poetry is a process that cannot go on in a wholly simple and unreflecting society. On the contrary, this process means that the earlier stages of religious legend have been succeeded by a time of criticism and selection. It is hard on the old stories of the gods when men come to appreciate the characters of Achilles and Odysseus. The old stories are not all of equal value and authority; they cannot all be made to fit in with the human story; they have to be tested, and some have to be rejected as inconvenient. The character of the gods is modified under the influence of the chief actors in the drama. Agamemnon, Diomede, Odysseus, Ajax, and Achilles set the standard by which the gods are judged. The Homeric view of the gods is already more than half-way to the view of a modern poet. The gods lose their old tyranny and their right to the steam of sacrifice as they gain their new poetical empire, from which they need not fear to be banished; not, at any rate, for any theological reasons.

In Shakespearean drama, where each man is himself, with his own character and his own fortune to make, there is small scope for any obvious Divine interposition in the scene. The story of human actions and characters, the more fully it is developed, leaves the less opportunity for the gods to interfere in it. Something of this sort was felt by certain medieval historians; they found it necessary to begin with an apologetic preface explaining the long-suffering of God, who has given freedom to the will of man to do good or evil. It was felt to be on the verge of impiety to think of men as left to themselves and doing what they pleased. Those who listen to a story might be tempted to think of the people in it as self-sufficient and independent powers, trespassing on the domain of Providence. A pious exculpation was required to clear the author of blame.[1]

In the *Iliad* this scrupulous conscience has less need to deliver itself. The gods are not far away;

[1] "In the events of this history may be proved the great long-suffering of God Almighty towards us every day; and the freedom of will which He has given to every man, that each may do what he will, good or evil."—*Hrafns Saga*, Prologue (*Sturlunga Saga* Oxford, 1878, II. p. 275).

"As all good things are the work of God, so valour is made by Him and placed in the heart of stout champions, and freedom therewithal to use it as they will, for good or evil."—*Fóstbræðra Saga* (1852), p. 12: one of the sophistical additions to the story: see below p. 275.

The moral is different in the following passage:—

"And inasmuch as the Providence of God hath ordained, and it is His pleasure, that the seven planets should have influence on the world, and bear dominion over man's nature, giving him divers inclinations to sin and naughtiness of life: nevertheless the Universal Creator has not taken from him the free will, which, as it is well governed, may subdue and abolish these temptations by virtuous living, if men will use discretion."—*Tirant lo Blanch* (1460), c. i.

the heroes are not left alone. But the poet has already done much to reduce the immediate power of the gods, not by excluding them from the action, certainly, nor by any attenuation of their characters into allegory, but by magnifying and developing the characters of men. In many occasional references it would seem that an approach was being made to that condition of mind, at ease concerning the gods, so common in the North, in Norway and Iceland, in the last days of heathendom. There is the great speech of Hector to Polydamas—"we defy augury"[1]—there is the speech of Apollo himself to Aeneas[2] about those who stand up for their own side, putting trust in their own strength. But passages like these do not touch closely on the relations of gods and men as they are depicted in the story. As so depicted, the gods are not shadowy or feeble abstractions and personifications; yet they are not of the first value to the poem, they do not set the tone of it.

They are subsidiary, like some other of the most beautiful things in the poem; like the similes of clouds and winds, like the pictures on the Shield. They are there because the whole world is included in epic poetry; the heroes, strong in themselves as they could be if they were left alone in the common day, acquire an additional strength and beauty from their fellowship with the gods. Achilles talking with the Embassy is great; he is great in another way when he stands at the trench with the flame of Athena on his head. These two scenes belong to two different kinds of imagination. It is because the first is there that the second takes effect. It is the hero that gives meaning and glory to the light of the goddess. It is of some importance that it is Achilles, and not

[1] *Il.* xii. 241. [2] *Il.* xvii. 227.

another, that here is crowned with the light of heaven and made terrible to his enemies.

There is a double way of escape for young nations from their outgrown fables and mythologies. They start with enormous, monstrous, and inhuman beliefs and stories. Either they may work their way out of them, by gradual rejection of the grosser ingredients, to something more or less positive and rational; or else they may take up the myths and transmute them into poetry.

The two processes are not independent of one another. Both are found together in the greater artists of early times, in Homer most notably; and also in artists less than Homer; in the poem of *Beowulf*, in the stories of Sigfred and Brynhild.

There are further, under the second mode, two chief ways of operation by which the fables of the gods may be brought into poetry.

It is possible to take them in a light-hearted way and weave them into poetical stories, without much substance or solemnity; enhancing the beauty that may be inherent in any part of the national legend, and either rejecting the scandalous chronicle of Olympus or Asgard altogether, or giving it over to the comic graces of levity and irony, as in the Phaeacian story of Ares and Aphrodite, wherein the Phaeacian poet digressed from his tales of war in the spirit of Ariosto, and with an equally accomplished and elusive defiance of censure.[1]

There is another way in which poetry may find room for fable.

It may treat the myths of the gods as material for

[1] The censure is not wanting :—

"L'on doit considérer que ce n'est ni le Poëte, ni son Héros, ni un honnête homme qui fait ce récit : mais que les Phéaques, peuples mols et effeminez, se le font chanter pendant leur festin." —BOSSU, *op. cit.* p. 152.

the religious or the ethical imagination, and out of them create ideal characters, analogous in poetry to the ideal divine or heroic figures of painting and sculpture. This is the kind of imagination in virtue of which modern poets are best able to appropriate the classical mythology; but this modern imagination is already familiar to Homer, and that not only in direct description, as in the description of the majesty of Zeus, but also, more subtly, in passages where the character of the divinity is suggested by comparison with one of the human personages, as when Nausicaa is compared to Artemis,[1] a comparison that redounds not less to the honour of the goddess than of Nausicaa.

In Icelandic literature there are many instances of the trouble arising from inconsiderate stories of the gods, in the minds of people who had got beyond the more barbarous kind of mythology. They took the boldest and most conclusive way out of the difficulty; they made the barbarous stories into comedy. The *Lokasenna*, a poem whose author has been called the Aristophanes of the Western Islands, is a dramatic piece in which Loki, the Northern Satan, appearing in the house of the gods, is allowed to bring his railing accusations against them and remind them of their doings in the "old days." One of his victims tells him to "let bygones be bygones." The gods are the subject of many stories that are here raked up against them, stories of another order of belief and of civilisation than those in which Odin appears as the wise and sleepless counsellor. This poem implies a great amount of independence in the author of it. It is not a satire on the gods; it is pure comedy; that is, it belongs to a type of literature which has risen above prejudices and which has an air of levity

[1] *Od.* vi. 151.

because it is pure sport—or pure art—and therefore is freed from bondage to the matter which it handles. This kind of invention is one that tests the wit of its audience. A serious-minded heathen of an older school would no doubt have been shocked by the levity of the author's manner. Not much otherwise would the poem have affected a serious adversary of heathendom, or any one whose education had been entirely outside of the circle of heathen or mythological tradition. An Englishman of the tenth century, familiar with the heroic poetry of his own tongue, would have thought it indecent. If chance had brought such an one to hear this *Lokasenna* recited at some entertainment in a great house of the Western Islands, he might very well have conceived the same opinion of his company and their tastes in literature as is ascribed by Bossu to Ulysses among the Phaeacians.

This genius for comedy is shown in other Icelandic poems. As soon as the monstrosities of the old traditions were felt to be monstrous, they were overcome (as Mr. Carlyle has shown) by an appreciation of the fun of them, and so they ceased to be burdensome. It is something of this sort that has preserved old myths, for amusement, in popular tales all over the world. The Icelandic poets went further, however, than most people in their elaborate artistic treatment of their myths. There is with them more art and more self-consciousness, and they give a satisfactory and final poetical shape to these things, extracting pure comedy from them.

The perfection of this ironical method is to be found in the *Edda*, a handbook of the Art of Poetry, written in the thirteenth century by a man of liberal genius, for whom the Æsir were friends of the imagination, without any prejudice to the claims of the Church or of his religion. In the view of Snorri Sturluson, the old gods are exempt from any touch of controversy. Belief has nothing to do with them; they are free. It may be remembered that some of the greatest English writers of the seventeenth century have come short of this security of view, and have not scrupled to repeat the calumny of the missionaries and the disputants against the ancient gods, that Jupiter and Apollo were angels of the bottomless pit, given over to their own devices for a season, and masking as Olympians.

In this freedom from embarrassing and irrelevant considerations in dealing with myth, the author of the *Edda* follows in his prose the spirit of mythological poems three centuries older, in which, even before the change of faith in the North, the gods were welcomed without fear as sharing in many humorous adventures.

And at the same time, along with this detached and ironical way of thinking there is to be found in the Northern poetry the other, more reverent mode of shaping the inherited fancies; the mode of Pindar, rejecting the vain things fabled about the gods, and holding fast to the more honourable things. The humours of Thor in the fishing for the serpent and the winning of the hammer may be fairly likened to the humours of Hermes in the Greek hymn. The *Lokasenna* has some likeness to the Homeric description of the brawls in heaven. But in the poems that refer to the death of Balder and the sorrow of the gods there is another tone; and the greatest of them all, the *Sibyl's Prophecy*, is comparable, not indeed in volume of sound, but in loftiness of imagination, to the poems in which Pindar has taken up the myths of most inexhaustible value and significance—the Happy Islands, the Birth of Athena.

The poet who lives in anything like an heroic or Homeric age has it in his power to mingle the elements of mythology and of human story—Phaeacia and Ithaca—in any proportion he pleases. As a matter of fact, all varieties of proportion are to be found in medieval documents. At the one extreme is the mythological romance and fantasy of Celtic epic, and at the other extreme the plain narrative of human encounters, in the old English battle poetry or the Icelandic family histories. As far as one can judge from the extant poems, the old English and old German poetry did not make such brilliant romance out of mythological legend as was produced by the Northern poets. These alone, and not the poets of England or Saxony, seem to have appropriated for literature, in an Homeric way, the histories of the gods. Myth is not wanting in old English or German poetry, but it does not show itself in the same clear and delightful manner as in the Northern poems of Thor, or in the wooing of Frey.

Thus in different places there are different modes in which an inheritance of mythical ideas may be appreciated and used. It may become a treasury for self-possessed and sure-handed artists, as in Greece, and so be preserved long after it has ceased to be adequate to all the intellectual desires. It may, by the fascination of its wealth, detain the minds of poets in its enchanted ground, and prevent them from ever working their way through from myth to dramatic imagination, as in Ireland.

The early literature, and therewith the intellectual character and aptitudes, of a nation may be judged by their literary use of mythology. They may neglect it, like the Romans; they may neglect all things for the sake of it, like the Celts; they may harmonise it, as the Greeks did, in a system of imaginative creations where the harmony is such that myth need never be felt as an encumbrance or an absurdity, however high or far the reason may go beyond it in any direction of art or science.

At the beginning of modern literature there are to be found the attempts of Irish and Welsh, of English and Germans, Danes and Northmen, to give shape to myth, and make it available for literature. Together with that, and as part of the same process, there is found the beginning of historical literature in an heroic or epic form. The results are various; but one thing may be taken as certain, that progress in literature is most assured when the mythology is so far under control as to leave room for the drama of epic characters; for epic, as distinguished from romance.

Now the fortunes of these people were such as to make this self-command exceedingly difficult for them, and to let in an enormous extraneous force, encouraging the native mythopoetic tendencies, and unfavourable to the growth of epic. They had to come to an understanding with themselves about their own heathen traditions, to bring the extravagances of them into some order, so as to let the epic heroes have free play. But they were not left to themselves in this labour of bringing mythology within bounds; even before they had fairly escaped from barbarism, before they had made a fair beginning of civilisation and of reflective literature on their own account, they were drawn within the Empire, into Christendom. Before their imaginations had fully wakened out of the primeval dream, the cosmogonies and theogonies, gross and monstrous, of their national infancy, they were asked to have an opinion about the classical mythology, as represented by the Latin poets; they were made acquainted with the miracles of the lives of saints.

More than all this, even, their minds were charmed away from the labour of epic invention, by the spell of the preacher. The task of representing characters —Waldere or Theodoric or Attila—was forgotten in the lyrical rapture of devotion, in effusion of pathos. The fascination of religious symbolism crept over minds that had hardly yet begun to see and understand things as they are; and in all their reading the "moral," "anagogical," and "tropological" significations prevailed against the literal sense.

One part of medieval history is concerned with the progress of the Teutonic nations, in so far as they were left to themselves, and in so far as their civilisation is home-made. The *Germania* of Tacitus, for instance, is used by historians to interpret the later development of Teutonic institutions. But this inquiry involves a good deal of abstraction and an artificial limitation of view. In reality, the people of Germania were never left to themselves at all, were never beyond the influence of Southern ideas; and the history of the influence of Southern ideas on the Northern races takes up a larger field than the isolated history of the North. Nothing in the world is more fantastic. The logic of Aristotle and the art of Virgil are recommended to people whose chief men, barons and earls, are commonly in their tastes and acquirements not very different from the suitors in the *Odyssey*. Gentlemen much interested in raids and forays, and the profits of such business, are confronted with a literature into which the labours of all past centuries have been distilled. In a society that in its native elements is closely analogous to Homer's Achaeans, men are found engaged in the study of Boethius *On the Consolation of Philosophy*, a book that sums up the whole course of Greek philosophical speculation. Ulysses quoting Aristotle is an anachronism; but King Alfred's translation of Boethius is almost as much of a paradox. It is not easy to remain unmoved at the thought of the medieval industry bestowed on authors like Martianus Capella *de Nuptiis Philologiae*, or Macrobius *de Somnio Scipionis*. What is to be said of the solemnity with which, in their pursuit of authoritative doctrine, they applied themselves to extract the spiritual meaning of Ovid's *Metamorphoses*, and appropriate the didactic system of the *Art of Love*?

In medieval literature, whatever there is of the Homeric kind has an utterly different relation to popular standards of appreciation from that of the Homeric poems in Greece. Here and there some care may be taken, as by Charlemagne and Alfred, to preserve the national heroic poetry. But such regard for it is rare; and even where it is found, it comes far short of the honour paid to Homer by Alexander. English Epic is not first, but one of the least, among the intellectual and literary interests of King Alfred. Heroic literature is only one thread in the weft of medieval literature.

There are some curious documents illustrative of its comparative value, and of the variety and complexity of medieval literature.

Hauk Erlendsson, an Icelander of distinction in the fourteenth century, made a collection of treatises in one volume for his own amusement and behoof. It contains the *Volospá*, the most famous of all the Northern mythical poems, the Sibyl's song of the doom of the gods; it contains also the *Landnámabók*, the history of the colonisation of Iceland; *Kristni Saga*, the history of the conversion to Christianity; the history of *Eric the Red*, and *Fóstbræðra Saga*, the story of the two sworn brethren, Thorgeir and

Thormod the poet. Besides these records of the history and the family traditions of Iceland and Greenland, there are some mythical stories of later date, dealing with old mythical themes, such as the life of Ragnar Lodbrok. In one of them, the *Heidreks Saga*, are embedded some of the most memorable verses, after *Volospá*, in the old style of Northern poetry—the poem of the *Waking of Angantyr*. The other contents of the book are as follows: geographical, physical, and theological pieces; extracts from St. Augustine; the *History of the Cross*; the *Description of Jerusalem*; the *Debate of Body and Soul*; *Algorismus* (by Hauk himself, who was an arithmetician); a version of the *Brut* and of *Merlin's Prophecy*; *Lucidarium*, the most popular medieval handbook of popular science. This is the collection, to which all the ends of the earth have contributed, and it is in strange and far-fetched company like this that the Northern documents are found. In Greece, whatever early transactions there may have been with the wisdom of Egypt or Phoenicia, there is no such medley as this.

Another illustration of the literary chaos is presented, even more vividly than in the contents of Hauk's book, by the whalebone casket in the British Museum. Weland the smith (whom Alfred introduced into his *Boethius*) is here put side by side with the Adoration of the Magi; on another side are Romulus and Remus; on another, Titus at Jerusalem; on the lid of the casket is the defence of a house by one who is shooting arrows at his assailants; his name is written over him, and his name is *Ægili*,—Egil the master-bowman, as Weland is the master-smith, of the Northern mythology. Round the two companion pictures, Weland on the left and the Three Kings on the right, side by side, there go wandering runes, with some old English verses about the "whale," or walrus, from which the ivory for these engravings was obtained. The artist plainly had no more suspicion than the author of *Lycidas* that there was anything incorrect or unnatural in his combinations. It is under these conditions that the heroic poetry of Germania has been preserved; never as anything more than an accident among an infinity of miscellaneous notions, the ruins of ancient empires, out of which the commonplaces of European literature and popular philosophy have been gradually collected.

The fate of epic poetry was the same as that of the primitive German forms of society. In both there was a progress towards independent perfection, an evolution of the possibilities inherent in them, independent of foreign influences. But both in Teutonic society, and in the poetry belonging to it and reflecting it, this independent course of life is thwarted and interfered with. Instead of independent strong Teutonic national powers, there are the more or less Romanised and blended nationalities possessing the lands that had been conquered by Goths and Burgundians, Lombards and Franks; instead of Germania, the Holy Roman Empire; instead of Epic, Romance; not the old-fashioned romance of native mythology, not the natural spontaneous romance of the Irish legends or the Icelandic stories of gods and giants, but the composite far-fetched romance of the age of chivalry, imported from all countries and literatures to satisfy the medieval appetite for novel and wonderful things.

Nevertheless, the stronger kind of poetry had still something to show, before all things were overgrown with imported legend, and before the strong enunciation of the older manner was put out of fashion by the medieval clerks and rhetoricians.

IV

THE THREE SCHOOLS—TEUTONIC EPIC—FRENCH EPIC—THE ICELANDIC HISTORIES

THE Teutonic heroic poetry was menaced on all hands from the earliest times; it was turned aside from the national heroes by saints and missionaries, and charmed out of its sterner moods by the spell ot wistful and regretful meditation. In continental Germany it appears to have been early vanquished. In England, where the epic poetry was further developed than on the Continent, it was not less exposed to the rivalry of the ideas and subjects that belonged to the Church.

The Anglo-Saxon histories of St. Andrew and St. Helen are as full of romantic passages as those poems of the fourteenth century in which the old alliterative verse is revived to tell the tale of Troy or of the *Mort Arthur*. The national subjects themselves are not proof against the ideas of the Church; even in the fragments of *Waldere* they are to be found; and the poem of *Beowulf* has been filled, like so much of the old English poetry, with the melancholy of the preacher, and the sense of the vanity of earthly things. But the influence of fantasy and pathos could not dissolve the strength of epic beyond recovery, or not until it had done something to show what it was worth. Not all the subjects are treated in the romantic manner of Cynewulf and his imitators. The poem of *Maldon*, written at the very end of the tenth century, is firm and unaffected in its style, and of its style there can be no question that it is heroic.

The old Norse poetry was beyond the influence of most of the tendencies and examples that corrupted the heroic poetry of the Germans, and changed the course of poetry in England. It was not till the day of its glory was past that it took to subjects like those of Cynewulf and his imitators. But it was hindered in other ways from representing the lives of heroes in a consistent epic form. If it knew less of the miracles of saints, it knew more of the old mythology; and though it was not, like English and German poetry, taken captive by the preachers, it was stirred and thrilled by the beauty of its own stories in a way that inclined to the lyrical rather than the epic tone. Yet here also there are passages of graver epic, where the tone is more assured and the composition more stately.

The relation of the French epics to French romance is on the one side a relation of antagonism, in which the older form gives way to the newer, because "the newer song is sweeter in the ears of men." The *Chanson de Geste* is driven out by poems that differ from it in almost every possible respect; in the character of their original subject-matter, in their verse, their rhetoric, and all their gear of commonplaces, and all the devices of their art. But from another point of view there may be detected in the *Chansons de Geste* no small amount of the very qualities that were fatal to them, when the elements were compounded anew in the poems of *Erec* and *Lancelot*.

The French epics have many points of likeness

with the Teutonic poetry of *Beowulf* or *Finnesburh*, or of the Norse heroic songs. They are epic in substance, having historical traditions at the back of them, and owing the materials of their picture to no deliberate study of authorities. They differ from *Beowulf* in this respect, among others, that they are the poems of feudal society, not of the simpler and earlier communities. The difference ought not to be exaggerated. As far as heroic poetry is concerned, the difference lies chiefly in the larger frame of the story. The kingdom of France in the French epics is wider than the kingdom of Hrothgar or Hygelac. The scale is nearer that of the *Iliad* than of the *Odyssey*. The "Catalogue of the Armies sent into the Field" is longer, the mass of fighting-men is more considerable, than in the epic of the older school. There is also, frequently, a much fuller sense of the national greatness and the importance of the defence of the land against its enemies, a consciousness of the dignity of the general history, unlike the carelessness with which the Teutonic poets fling themselves into the story of individual lives, and disregard the historical background. Generally, however, the Teutonic freedom and rebellious spirit is found as unmistakably in the *Chansons de Geste* as in the alliterative poems. Feudalism appears in heroic poetry, and indeed in prosaic history, as a more elaborate form of that anarchy which is the necessary condition of an heroic age. It does not deprive the poet of his old subjects, his family enmities, and his adventures of private war. Feudalism did not invent, neither did it take away, the virtue of loyalty that has so large a place in all true epic, along with its counterpart of defiance and rebellion, no less essential to the story. It intensified the poetical value of both motives, but they are older than the

Iliad. It provided new examples of the "wrath" of injured or insulted barons; it glorified to the utmost, it honoured as martyrs, those who died fighting for their lord.[1]

In all this it did nothing to change the essence of heroic poetry. The details were changed, the scene was enlarged, and so was the number of the combatants. But the details of feudalism that make a difference between Beowulf, or the men of Attila, and the epic paladins of Charlemagne in the French poems of the eleventh and twelfth centuries, need not obscure the essential resemblance between one heroic period and another.

On the other hand, it is plain from the beginning that French epic had to keep its ground with some difficulty against the challenge of romantic skirmishers. In one of the earliest of the poems about Charlemagne, the Emperor and his paladins are taken to the East by a poet whom Bossu would hardly have counted "honest." In the poem of *Huon of Bordeaux*, much later, the story of Oberon and the magic horn has been added to the plot of a feudal tragedy, which in itself is compact and free from extravagance. Between those extreme cases there are countless examples of the mingling of the graver epic with more or less incongruous strains. Sometimes there is magic, sometimes the appearance of a Paynim giant, often the repetition of long prayers with allusions to the lives of saints and martyrs, and throughout there is the constant presence of ideas derived from homilies and the common teaching of the Church. In some of these respects

[1] Lor autres mors ont toz en terre mis :
Crois font sor aus, qu'il erent droit martir :
Por lor seignor orent esté ocis.

Garin le Loherain, tom. ii. p. 88.

the French epics are in the same case as the old English poems which, like *Beowulf*, show the mingling of a softer mood with the stronger; of new conventions with old. In some respects they show a further encroachment of the alien spirit.

The English poem of *Maldon* has some considerable likeness in the matter of its story, and not a little in its ideal of courage, with the *Song of Roland.* A comparison of the two poems, in those respects in which they are commensurable, will show the English poem to be wanting in certain elements of mystery that are potent in the other.

The *Song of Maldon* and the *Song of Roncesvalles* both narrate the history of a lost battle, of a realm defended against its enemies by a captain whose pride and self-reliance lead to disaster, by refusing to take fair advantage of the enemy and put forth all his available strength. Byrhtnoth, fighting the Northmen on the shore of the Essex river, allows them of his own free will to cross the ford and come to close quarters. "He gave ground too much to the adversary; he called across the cold river and the warriors listened: 'Now is space granted to you; come speedily hither and fight; God alone can tell who will hold the place of battle.' Then the wolves of blood, the rovers, waded west over Panta."

This unnecessary magnanimity has for the battle of Maldon the effect of Roland's refusal to sound the horn at the battle of Roncesvalles; it is the tragic error or transgression of limit that brings down the crash and ruin at the end of the day.

In both poems there is a like spirit of indomitable resistance. The close of the battle of Maldon finds the loyal companions of Byrhtnoth fighting round his body, abandoned by the cowards who have run away, but themselves convinced of their absolute strength to resist to the end.

Byrhtwold spoke and grasped his shield—he was an old companion—he shook his ashen spear, and taught courage to them that fought:—

"Thought shall be the harder, heart the keener, mood shall be the more, as our might lessens. Here our prince lies low, they have hewn him to death! Grief and sorrow for ever on the man that leaves this war-play! I am old of years, but hence I will not go; I think to lay me down by the side of my lord, by the side of the man I cherished."

The story of Roncesvalles tells of an agony equally hopeless and equally secure from every touch of fear.

The *Song of Maldon* is a strange poem to have been written in the reign of Ethelred the Unready. But for a few phrases it might, as far as the matter is concerned, have been written before the conversion of England, and although it is a battle in defence of the country, and not a mere incident of private war, the motive chiefly used is not patriotism, but private loyalty to the captain. Roland is full of the spirit of militant Christendom, and there is no more constant thought in the poem than that of the glory of France. The virtue of the English heroes is the old Teutonic virtue. The events of the battle are told plainly and clearly; nothing adventitious is brought in to disturb the effect of the plain story; the poetical value lies in the contrast between the grey landscape (which is barely indicated), the severe and restrained description of the fighters, on the one hand, and on the other the sublimity of the spirit expressed in the last words of the "old companion." In the narrative of events there are no extraneous beauties to break the overwhelming strength of the eloquence in which the meaning of the whole thing is concentrated. With Roland at Roncesvalles the case is different. He is not shown in the grey light of the Essex battlefield. The background is more majestic. There is a mysterious half-lyrical refrain throughout the tale of the battle: "high are the mountains and dark the valleys" about the combatants in the pass; they are not left to themselves like the warriors of the poem of *Maldon*. It is romance, rather than epic or tragedy, which in this way recognises the impersonal power of the scene; the strength of the hills under which the fight goes on. In the first part of the *Odyssey* the spell of the mystery of the sea is all about the story of Odysseus; in the later and more dramatic part the hero loses this, and all the strength is concentrated in his own character. In the story of Roland there is a vastness and vagueness throughout, coming partly from the numbers of the hosts engaged, partly from the author's sense of the mystery of the Pyrenean valleys, and, in a very large measure, from the heavenly aid accorded to the champion of Christendom. The earth trembles, there is darkness over all the realm of France even to the Mount St. Michael:

C'est la dulur pur la mort de Rollant.

St. Gabriel descends to take from the hand of Roland the glove that he offers with his last confession; and the three great angels of the Lord are there to carry his soul to Paradise.

There is nothing like this in the English poem. The battle is fought in the light of an ordinary day; there is nothing to greet the eyes of Byrhtnoth and his men except the faces of their enemies.

It is not hard to find in old English poetry descriptions less austere than that of *Maldon*; there may be found in the French *Chansons de Geste* great spaces in which there is little of the majestic light and darkness of Roncesvalles. But it is hard to escape the conviction that the poem of *Maldon*, late as it is, has uttered the spirit and essence of the Northern heroic literature in its reserved and simple story, and its invincible profession of heroic faith; while the poem of Roncesvalles is equally representative of the French epic spirit, and of the French poems in which the ideas common to every heroic age are expressed with all the circumstances of the feudal society of Christendom, immediately before the intellectual and literary revolutions of the twelfth century. The French epics are full of omens of the coming victory of romance, though they have not yet given way. They still retain, in spite of their anticipations of the Kingdom of the Grail, an alliance in spirit with the older Teutonic poetry, and with those Icelandic histories that are the highest literary expression of the Northern spirit in its independence of feudalism.

The heroic age of the ancient Germans may be said to culminate, and end, in Iceland in the thirteenth century. The Icelandic *Sagas*—the prose histories of the fortunes of the great Icelandic houses—are the last and also the finest expression and record of the spirit and the ideas belonging properly to the Germanic race in its own right, and not derived from Rome or Christendom. Those of the German nations who stayed longest at home had by several centuries the advantage of the Goths and Franks, and had time to complete their native education before going into foreign subjects. The English were less exposed to Southern influences than the continental Germans; the Scandinavian nations less than the Angles and Saxons. In Norway particularly, the common German ideas were developed in a way that produced a code of honour, a consciousness of duty, and a strength of will, such as had been unknown in the German nations who were earlier called upon to match themselves against Rome. Iceland was colonised by a picked lot of Norwegians; by precisely those Norwegians who had this strength of will in its highest degree.

Political progress in the Middle Ages was by way of monarchy; but strong monarchy was contrary to the traditions of Germania, and in Norway, a country of great extent and great difficulties of communication, the ambition of Harold Fairhair was resisted by numbers of chieftains who had their own local following and their own family dignity to maintain, in their firths and dales. Those men found Norway intolerable through the tyranny of King Harold, and it was by them that Iceland was colonised through the earlier colonies in the west—in Scotland, in Ireland, in Shetland and the other islands.

The ideas that took the Northern colonists to Iceland were the ideas of Germania,—the love of an independent life the ideal of the old-fashioned Northern gentleman, who was accustomed to consideration and respect from the freemen, his neighbours, who had authority by his birth and fortune to look after the affairs of his countryside, who would not make himself the tenant, vassal, or steward of any king. In the new country these ideas were intensified and defined. The ideal of the Icelandic Commonwealth was something more than a vague motive, it was present to the minds of the first settlers in a clear and definite form. The most singular thing in the heroic age of Iceland is that the heroes knew what they were about. The heroic age of Iceland begins in a commonwealth founded by a social contract. The society that is established there is an association of individuals coming to an agreement with one another to invent a set of laws and observe them. Thus while Iceland on the one hand is a reactionary state, founded by men who were turning their backs on the only possible means of political progress, cutting themselves off from the world, and adhering obstinately to forms of life with no future before them, on the other hand this reactionary commonwealth, this fanatical representative of early Germanic use and wont, is possessed of a clearness of self-consciousness, a hard and positive clearness of understanding, such as is to be found nowhere else in the Middle Ages and very rarely at all in any polity.

The prose literature of Iceland displays the same two contradictory characters throughout. The actions described, and the customs, are those of an early heroic age, with rather more than the common amount of enmity and vengeance, and an unequalled power of resistance and rebellion in the individual wills of the personages. The record of all this anarchy is a prose history, rational and unaffected, seeing all things in a dry light; a kind of literature that has not much to learn from any humanism or rationalism, in regard to its own proper subjects at any rate.

The people of Iceland were not cut off from the ordinary European learning and its commonplaces. They read the same books as were read in England or Germany. They read St. Gregory *de Cura Pastorali*, they read *Ovidius Epistolarum*, and all the other popular books of the Middle Ages. In time those books and the world to which they belonged were able to obtain a victory over the purity of the Northern tradition and manners, but not until the Northern tradition had exhausted itself, and the Icelandic polity began to break up. The literature of the maturity of Iceland just before the fall of the Commonwealth is a literature belonging wholly and purely to Iceland, in a style unmodified by Latin syntax and derived from the colloquial idiom. The matter is the same in kind as the common matter of heroic poetry. The history represents the lives of adventurers, the rivalries and private wars of men who are not ignorant of right and honour, but who acknowledge little authority over them, and are given to choose their right and wrong for themselves, and abide the consequences. This common matter is presented in a form which may be judged on its own merits, and there is no need to ask concessions from any one in respect of the hard or unfavourable conditions under which this literature was produced. One at least of the Icelandic Sagas is one of the great prose works of the world—the story of Njal and his sons.

The most perfect heroic literature of the Northern nations is to be found in the country where the heroic polity and society had most room and leisure; and in Iceland the heroic ideals of life had conditions more favourable than are to be discovered anywhere else in history. Iceland was a world divided from the rest, outside the orbit of all the states of Europe; what went on there had little more than an ideal relation to the course of the great world; it had no influence on Europe, it was kept separate as much as might be from the European storms and revolutions. What went on in Iceland was the progress in seclusion of the old Germanic life—a life that in the rest of the world had been blended and immersed in other floods and currents. Iceland had no need of the great movements of European history.

They had a humanism of their own, a rationalism of their own, gained quite apart from the great

European tumults, and gained prematurely, in comparison with the rest of Europe. Without the labour of the Middle Ages, without the storm and stress of the reform of learning, they had the faculty of seeing things clearly and judging their values reasonably, without superstition. They had to pay the penalty of their opposition to the forces of the world; there was no cohesion in their society, and when once the balance of power in the island was disturbed, the Commonwealth broke up. But before that, they accomplished what had been ineffectually tried by the poet of *Beowulf*, the poet of *Roland*; they found an adequate form of heroic narrative. Also in their use of this instrument they were led at last to a kind of work that has been made nowhere else in the world, for nowhere else does the form of heroic narrative come to be adapted to contemporary events, as it was in Iceland, by historians who were themselves partakers in the actions they described. Epic, if the Sagas are epic, here coincides with autobiography. In the *Sturlunga Saga*, written by Sturla, Snorri's nephew, the methods of heroic literature are applied by an eye-witness to the events of his own time, and there is no discrepancy or incongruity between form and matter. The age itself takes voice and speaks in it; there is no interval between actors and author. This work is the end of the heroic age, both in politics and in literature. After the loss of Icelandic freedom there is no more left of Germania, and the *Sturlunga Saga* which tells the story of the last days of freedom is the last word of the Teutonic heroic age. It is not a decrepit or imitative or secondary thing; it is a masterpiece; and with this true history, this adaptation of an heroic style to contemporary realities, the sequence of German heroic tradition comes to an end.

CHAPTER II

THE TEUTONIC EPIC

I

THE TRAGIC CONCEPTION

OF the heroic poetry in the Teutonic alliterative verse, the history must be largely conjectural. The early stages of it are known merely through casual references like those of Tacitus. We know that to the mind of the Emperor Julian, the songs of the Germans resembled the croaking of noisy birds ; but this criticism is not satisfactory, though it is interesting. The heroes of the old time before Ermanaric and Attila were not without their poets, but of what sort the poems were in which their praises were sung, we can only vaguely guess. Even of the poems that actually remain it is difficult to ascertain the history and the conditions of their production. The variety of styles discoverable in the extant documents is enough to prevent the easy conclusion that the German poetry of the first century was already a fixed type, repeated by successive generations of poets down to the extinction of alliterative verse as a living form.

After the sixth century things become a little clearer, and it is possible to speak with more certainty. One thing at any rate of the highest importance may be regarded as beyond a doubt. The passages in which Jordanes tells of Suanihilda trampled to death by the horses of Ermanaric, and of the vengeance taken by her brothers Sarus and Ammius, are enough to prove that the subjects of heroic poetry had already in the sixth century, if not earlier, formed themselves compactly in the imagination. If Jordanes knew a Gothic poem on Ermanaric and the brothers of Suanihilda, that was doubtless very different from the Northern poem of Sorli and Hamther, which is a later version of the same story. But even if the existence of a Gothic ballad of Swanhild were doubted,—and the balance of probabilities is against the doubter,—it follows indisputably from the evidence that in the time of Jordanes people were accustomed to select and dwell upon dramatic incidents in what was accepted as history; the appreciation of tragedy was there, the talent to understand a tragic situation, to shape a tragic plot, to bring out the essential matter in relief and get rid of irrelevant particulars.

In this respect at any rate, and it is one of the most important, there is continuity in the ancient poetry, onward from this early date. The stories of Alboin in the Lombard history of Paulus Diaconus, the meaning of which for the history of poetry is explained so admirably in the Introduction to *Corpus Poeticum Boreale*, by Dr. Vigfusson and Mr. York Powell, are further and more vivid illustrations of the same thing. In the story of the youth of Alboin, and the story of his death, there is matter of the same amount as would suffice for one of the short epics of the kind we know,—a poem of the same length as the Northern lay of the death of Ermanaric, of the same compass as *Waltharius*,—or, to take another standard of measurement, matter for a single tragedy with the unities preserved. Further, there is in both of them exactly that resolute comprehension and exposition of tragic meaning which is the virtue of the short epics. The tragic contradiction in them could not be outdone by Victor Hugo. It is no wonder that the story of Rosamond and Albovine king of the Lombards became a favourite with dramatists of different schools, from the first essays of the modern drama in the *Rosmunda* of Rucellai, passing by the common way of the novels of Bandello to the Elizabethan stage. The earlier story of Alboin's youth, if less valuable for emphatic tragedy, being without the baleful figure of a Rosamond or a Clytemnestra, is even more perfect as an example of tragic complication. Here again is the old sorrow of Priam; the slayer of the son face to face with the slain man's father, and not in enmity. In beauty of original conception the story is not finer than that of Priam and Achilles; and it is impossible to compare the stories in any other respect than that of the abstract plot. But in one quality of the plot the Lombard drama excels or exceeds the story of the last book of the *Iliad*. The contradiction is strained with a greater tension; the point of honour is more nearly absolute. This does not make it a better story, but it proves that the man who told the story could understand the requirements of a tragic plot, could imagine clearly a strong dramatic situation, could refrain from wasting or obliterating the outline of a great story.

The Lombards and the Gepidae were at war. Alboin, son of the Lombard king Audoin, and Thurismund, son of the Gepid king Thurisvend, met in battle, and Alboin killed Thurismund. After the battle, the Lombards asked King Audoin to knight his son. But Audoin answered that he would not break the Lombard custom, according to which it was necessary for the young man to receive arms first from the king of some other people. Alboin when he heard this set out with forty of the Lombards, and went to Thurisvend, whose son he had killed, to ask this honour from him. Thurisvend welcomed him, and set him down at his right hand in the place where his son used to sit.

Then follows the critical point of the action. The contradiction is extreme; the reconciliation also, the solution of the case, is perfect. Things are stretched to the breaking-point before the release comes; nothing is spared that can possibly aggravate the hatred between the two sides, which is kept from breaking out purely by the honour of the king. The man from whom an infinite debt of vengeance is owing, comes of his own will to throw himself on the generosity of his adversary. This, to begin with, is hardly fair to simple-minded people like the Gepid warriors; they may fairly think that their king is going too far in his reading of the law of honour:

> And it came to pass while the servants were serving at the tables, that Thurisvend, remembering how his son had been lately slain, and calling to mind his death, and beholding his slayer there beside him in his very seat, began to draw deep sighs, for he could not withhold himself any longer, and at last his grief burst forth in words. "Very pleasant to me," quoth he, "is the seat, but sad enough it is to see him that is sitting therein."[1]

By his confession of his thoughts the king gives an opening to those who are waiting for it, and it is taken at once. Insult and rejoinder break out, and it is within a hair's breadth of the irretrievable plunge that the king speaks his mind. He is lord in that house, and his voice allays the tumult; he takes the weapons of his son Thurismund, and gives them to Alboin and sends him back in peace and safety to

[1] *C.P.B.*, Introduction, p. lii.

his father's kingdom. It is a great story, even in a prose abstract, and the strength of its tragic problem is invincible. It is with strength like that, with a knowledge not too elaborate or minute, but sound and clear, of some of the possibilities of mental conflict and tragic contradiction, that heroic poetry first reveals itself among the Germans. It is this that gives strength to the story of the combat between Hildebrand and his son, of the flight of Walter and Hildegund, of the death of Brynhild, of Attila and Gudrun. Some of the heroic poems and plots are more simple than these. The battle of Maldon is a fair fight without any such distressful circumstances as in the case of Hildebrand or of Walter of Aquitaine. The adventures of Beowulf are simple, also; there is suspense when he waits the attack of the monster, but there is nothing of the deadly crossing of passions that there is in other stories. Even in *Maldon*, however, there is the tragic error; the fall and defeat of the English is brought about by the over-confidence and over-generosity of Byrhtnoth, in allowing the enemy to come to close quarters. In *Beowulf*, though the adventures of the hero are simple, other less simple stories are referred to by the way. One of these is a counterpart to the story of the youth of Alboin and the magnanimity of Thurisvend. One of the most famous of all the old subjects of heroic poetry was the vengeance of Ingeld for the death of his father, King Froda. The form of this story in *Beowulf* agrees with that of Saxo Grammaticus in preserving the same kind of opposition as in the story of Alboin, only in this case there is a different solution. Here a deadly feud has been put to rest by a marriage, and the daughter of Froda's slayer is married to Froda's son. But as in the Lombard history and in so many of the stories of Iceland, this reconciliation is felt to be intolerable and spurious; the need of vengeance is real, and it finds a spokesman in an old warrior, who cannot forget his dead lord, nor endure the sight of the new bride's kinsmen going free and wearing the spoils of their victory. So Ingeld has to choose between his wife, wedded to him out of his enemy's house, and his father, whom that enemy has killed. And so everywhere in the remains, not too voluminous, of the literature of the heroic age, one encounters this sort of tragic scheme. One of those ancient plots, abstracted and written out fair by Saxo, is the plot of *Hamlet*.

There is not one of the old Northern heroic poems, as distinct from the didactic and mythological pieces, that is without this tragic contradiction; sometimes expressed with the extreme of severity, as in the lay of the death of Ermanaric; sometimes with lyrical effusiveness, as in the lament of Gudrun; sometimes with a mystery upon it from the under-world and the kingdom of the dead, as in the poems of Helgi, and of the daughter of Angantyr.

The poem of the death of Ermanaric is a version of the story told by Jordanes, which since his time had come to be attached to the cycle of the Niblungs.

Swanhild, the daughter of Sigurd and Gudrun, was wedded to Ermanaric, king of the Goths. The king's counsellor wrought on his mind with calumnies against the queen, and he ordered her to be trampled to death under horses' feet, and so she died, though the horses were afraid of the brightness of her eyes and held back until her eyes were covered. Gudrun stirred up her sons, Sorli and Hamther, to go and avenge their sister. As they set out, they quarrelled with their base-born brother Erp, and killed him,—the tragic error in this history, for it was the want of a third man that ruined them, and Erp would have helped them if they had let him. In the hall of the Goths they defy their enemy and hew down his men; no iron will bite in their armour; they cut off the hands and feet of Ermanaric. Then, as happens so often in old stories, they go too far, and a last insult alters the balance against them, as Odysseus alters it at the leave-taking with Polyphemus. The last gibe at Ermanaric stirs him as he lies, and he calls on the remnant of the Goths to stone the men that neither sword nor spear nor arrow will bring down. And that was the end of them.

"We have fought a good fight; we stand on slain Goths that have had their fill of war. We have gotten a good report, though we die to-day or to-morrow. No man can live over the evening, when the word of the Fates has gone forth."

There fell Sorli at the gable of the hall, and Hamther was brought low at the end of the house.

Among the Norse poems it is this one, the *Hamðismál*, that comes nearest to the severity of the English *Maldon* poem. It is wilder and more cruel, but the end attains to simplicity.

The gap in *Codex Regius*, the "Elder" or "Poetic Edda," has destroyed the poems midway between the beginning and end of the tragedy of Sigfred and Brynhild, and among them the poem of their last meeting. There is nothing but the prose paraphrase to tell what that was, but the poor substitute brings out all the more clearly the strength of the original conception, the tragic problem.

After the gap in the manuscript there are various poems of Brynhild and Gudrun, in which different views of the story are taken, and in all of them the tragic contradiction is extreme: in Brynhild's vengeance on Sigurd, in Gudrun's lament for her husband slain by her brothers, and in the later fortunes of Gudrun. In some of these poems the tragedy becomes lyrical, and two kinds of imagination, epic and elegiac, are found in harmony.

The story of Helgi and Sigrun displays this rivalry of moods—a tragic story, carried beyond the tragic stress into the mournful quiet of the shadows.

Helgi is called upon by Sigrun to help her against Hodbrodd, and save her from a hateful marriage. Helgi kills Hodbrodd, and wins Sigrun; but he has also killed Sigrun's father Hogni and her elder brother. The younger brother Dag takes an oath to put away enmity, but breaks his oath and kills Helgi.

It is a story like all the others in which there is a conflict of duties, between friendship and the duty of vengeance, a plot of the same kind as that of Froda and Ingeld. Sigrun's brother is tried in the same way as Ingeld in the story told by Saxo and mentioned in *Beowulf*. But it does not end with the death of Helgi. Sigrun looks for Helgi to come back in the hour of the "Assembly of Dreams," and Helgi comes and calls her, and she follows him :—

"Thy hair is thick with rime, thou art wet with the dew of death, thy hands are cold and dank."

"It is thine own doing, Sigrun from Sevafell, that Helgi is drenched with deadly dew ; thou weepest cruel tears, thou gold-dight, sunbright lady of the South, before thou goest to sleep ; every one of them falls with blood, wet and chill, upon my breast. Yet precious are the draughts that are poured for us, though we have lost both love and land, and no man shall sing a song of lamentation though he see the wounds on my breast, for kings' daughters have come among the dead."

"I have made thee a bed, Helgi, a painless bed, thou son of the Wolfings. I shall sleep in thine arms, O king, as I should if thou wert alive."

This is something different from epic or tragedy, but it does not interfere with the tragedy of which it is the end.

The poem of the *Waking of Angantyr* is so filled with mystery and terror that it is hard to find in it anything else. After the *Volospá* it is the most wonderful of all the Northern poems.

Hervor, daughter of Angantyr, is left alone to avenge her father and her eleven brothers, killed by Arrow Odd before her birth. In her father's grave is the sword of the Dwarfs that never is drawn in vain, and she comes to his grave to find it. The island where he lies is full of death-fires, and the dead are astir, but Hervor goes on. She calls on her father and her brothers to help her:

"Awake, Angantyr! It is Hervor that bids thee awake. Give me the sword of the Dwarfs! Hervard! Hiorvard! Rani! Angantyr! I bid you all awake!"

Her father answers from the grave; he will not give up the sword, for the forgers of it when it was taken from them put a curse on those who wear it. But Hervor will not leave him until he has yielded to her prayers, and at last she receives the sword from her father's hands.[1]

Although the poem of Hervor lies in this way "between the worlds" of Life and Death,—the phrase is Hervor's own,—although the action is so strange and so strangely encompassed with unearthly fire and darkness, its root is not set in the dim borderland where the dialogue is carried on. The root is tragic, and not fantastic, nor is there any excess, nor

[1] This poem has been followed by M. Leconte de Lisle in *L'Épée d'Angantyr* (*Poèmes Barbares*). It was among the first of the Northern poems to be translated into English, in Hickes's *Thesaurus* (1705), i. p. 193. It is also included in Percy's *Five Pieces of Runic Poetry* (1763).

anything strained beyond the limit of tragedy, in the passion of Hervor.

Definite imagination of a tragic plot, and sure comprehension of the value of dramatic problems, are not enough in themselves to make a perfect poem. They may go along with various degrees of imperfection in particular respects; faults of diction, either tenuity or extravagance of phrasing may accompany this central imaginative power. Strength of plot is partly independent of style; it bears translation, it can be explained, it is something that can be abstracted from the body of a poem and still make itself impressive. The dramatic value of the story of the death of Alboin is recognisable even when it is stated in the most general terms, as a mere formula; the story of *Waltharius* retains its life, even in the Latin hexameters; the plot of *Hamlet* is interesting, even in Saxo; the story of the Niblungs, even in the mechanical prose paraphrase. This gift of shaping a plot and letting it explain itself without encumbrances is not to be mistaken for the whole secret of the highest kind of poetry. But, if not the whole, it is the spring of the whole. All the other gifts may be there, but without this, though all but the highest kind of epic or tragic art may be attainable, the very highest will not be attained.

Aristotle may be referred to again. As he found it convenient in his description of epic to insist on its dramatic nature, in his description of tragedy it pleased him to lay emphasis on that part of the work which is common to tragedy and epic—the story, the plot. It may be remarked how well the barbarous poetry conforms to the pattern laid down in Aristotle's description. The old German epic, in *Hildebrand*, *Waldere*, *Finnesburh*, *Byrhtnoth*, besides all the Northern lays of Sigurd, Brynhild, and Gudrun, is dramatic in its method, letting the persons speak for themselves as much as may be. So far it complies with Aristotle's delineation of epic. And further, all this dramatic bent may be seen clearly to have its origin in the mere story,—in the dramatic situation, in fables that might be acted by puppets or in a dumb show, and yet be tragical. No analytic or psychological interest in varieties of character—in ἤθη—could have uttered the passion of Brynhild or of Gudrun. Aristotle knew that psychological analysis and moral rhetoric were not the authors of Clytemnestra or Oedipus. The barbarian poets are on a much lower and more archaic level than the poets with whom Aristotle is concerned, but here, where comparison is not meaningless nor valueless, their imaginations are seen to work in the same sound and productive way as the minds of Aeschylus or Sophocles, letting the seed—the story in its abstract form, the mere plot—develop itself and spring naturally into the fuller presentation of the characters that are implied in it. It is another kind of art that studies character in detail, one by one, and then sets them playing at chance medley, and trusts to luck that the result will be entertaining.

That Aristotle is confirmed by these barbarian auxiliaries is of no great importance to Aristotle, but it is worth arguing that the barbarous German imagination at an earlier stage, relatively, than the Homeric, is found already possessed of something like the sanity of judgment, the discrimination of essentials from accidents, which is commonly indicated by the term classical. Compared with Homer these German songs are prentice work; but they are begun in the right way, and therefore to compare them with a masterpiece in which the same way is carried out to its end is not unjustifiable.

II

SCALE OF THE POEMS

THE following are the extant poems on native heroic themes, written in one or other of the dialects of the Teutonic group, and in unrhymed alliterative measures.

(1) *Continental.*—The *Lay of Hildebrand* (*c.* A.D. 800), a Low German poem, copied by High German clerks, is the only remnant of the heroic poetry of the continental Germans in which, together with the national metre, there is a national theme.

(2) *English.*—The poems of this order in old English are *Beowulf*, *Finnesburh*, *Waldere*, and *Byrhtnoth*, or the *Lay of Maldon.* Besides these there are poems on historical themes preserved in the Chronicle, of which *Brunanburh* is the most important, and two dramatic lyrics, *Widsith* and *Deor*, in which there are many allusions to the mythical and heroic cycles.

(3) *Scandinavian and Icelandic.* — The largest number of heroic poems in alliterative verse is found in the old Northern language, and in manuscripts written in Iceland. The poems themselves may have come from other places in which the old language of Norway was spoken, some of them perhaps from Norway itself, many of them probably from those

islands round Britain to which a multitude of Norwegian settlers were attracted, — Shetland, the Orkneys, the Western Islands of Scotland.[1]

The principal collection is that of the manuscript in the King's Library at Copenhagen (2365, 4°) generally referred to as *Codex Regius* (R); it is this book, discovered in the seventeenth century, that has received the inaccurate but convenient names of *Elder Edda*, or *Poetic Edda*, or *Edda of Sæmund the Wise*, by a series of miscalculations fully described in the preface to the *Corpus Poeticum Boreale.* Properly, the name *Edda* belongs only to the prose treatise by Snorri Sturluson.

The chief contents of *Codex Regius* are a series of independent poems on the Volsung story, beginning with the tragedies of *Helgi and Swava* and *Helgi and Sigrun* (originally unconnected with the Volsung legend), and going on in the order of events.

The series is broken by a gap in which the poems dealing with some of the most important parts of the story have been lost. The matter of their contents is known from the prose paraphrase called *Volsunga Saga.* Before the Volsung series comes a number of poems chiefly mythological: the *Sibyl's Prophecy*, (Volospá); *the Wooing of Frey*, or the *Errand of Skirnir*; the *Flyting of Thor and Woden* (Harbarzlióð); *Thor's Fishing for the Midgarth Serpent* (Hymiskviða); the *Railing of Loki* (Lokasenna); the *Winning of Thor's Hammer* (Þrymskviða); the *Lay of Weland.* There are also some didactic poems, chief among them being the gnomic miscellany under the title *Hávamál*; while besides this there are others, like *Vafþrúðnismál*, treating of mythical subjects in

[1] Cf. G. Vigfusson, Prolegomena to *Sturlunga* (Oxford, 1878); (*Corpus Poeticum Boreale* (*ibid.* 1883); *Grimm Centenary Papers* 1886); Sophus Bugge, *Helgedigtene* (1896; trans. Schofield, 1899).

a more or less didactic and mechanical way. There are a number of prose passages introducing or linking the poems. The confusion in some parts of the book is great.

Codex Regius is not the only source; other mythic and heroic poems are found in other manuscripts. The famous poem of the *Doom of Balder* (Gray's "Descent of Odin"); the poem of the *Rescue of Menglad*, the enchanted princess; the verses preserved in the *Heiðreks Saga*, belonging to the story of Angantyr; besides the poem of the *Magic Mill* (Grottasöngr) and the *Song of the Dart* (Gray's "Fatal Sisters"). There are many fragmentary verses, among them some from the *Biarkamál*, a poem with some curious points of likeness to the English *Lay of Finnesburh.* A Swedish inscription has preserved four verses of an old poem on Theodoric.

Thus there is some variety in the original documents now extant out of the host of poems that have been lost. One conclusion at least is irresistible—that, in guessing at the amount of epic poetry of this order which has been lost, one is justified in making a liberal estimate. Fragments are all that we possess. The extant poems have escaped the deadliest risks; the fire at Copenhagen in 1728, the bombardment in 1807, the fire in the Cotton Library in 1731, in which *Beowulf* was scorched but not burned. The manuscripts of *Finnesburh* and *Maldon* have been mislaid; but for the transcripts taken in time by Hickes and Hearne they would have been as little known as the songs that the Sirens sang. The poor remnants of *Waldere* were found by Stephens in two scraps of bookbinders' parchment.

When it is seen what hazards have been escaped by those bits of wreckage, and at the same time how distinct in character the several poems are, it is plain that one may use some freedom in thinking of the amount of this old poetry that has perished.

The loss is partly made good in different ways: in the Latin of the historians, Jordanes, Paulus Diaconus, and most of all in the paraphrases, prose and verse, by Saxo Grammaticus; in Ekkehard's Latin poem of *Waltharius* (*c.* A.D. 930); in the *Volsunga Saga*, which has kept the matter of the lost poems of *Codex Regius* and something of their spirit; in the *Thidreks Saga*, a prose story made up by a Norwegian in the thirteenth century from current North German ballads of the Niblungs; in the German poems of the twelfth and thirteenth centuries, which, in a later form of the language and in rhyming verse, have preserved at any rate some matters of tradition, some plots of stories, if little of the peculiar manner and imagination of the older poetry.

The casual references to Teutonic heroic subjects in a vast number of authors have been brought together in a monumental work, *die deutsche Heldensage*, by Wilhelm Grimm (1829).

The Western Group

Hildebrand, *Finnesburh*, *Waldere*, *Beowulf*, *Byrhtnoth*

The Western group of poems includes all those that are not Scandinavian; there is only one among them which is not English, the poem of *Hildebrand*. They do not afford any very copious material for inferences as to the whole course and progress of poetry in the regions to which they belong. A comparison of the fragmentary *Hildebrand* with the fragments of *Waldere* shows a remarkable difference in compass and fulness; but, at the same time, the vocabulary and phrases of *Hildebrand* declare that poem unmistakably to belong to the same family as the more elaborate *Waldere*. *Finnesburh*, the fragmentary poem of the lost Lambeth MS., seems almost as far removed as *Hildebrand* from the more expansive and leisurely method of *Waldere*; while *Waldere*, *Beowulf*, and the poem of *Maldon* resemble one another in their greater ease and fluency, as compared with the brevity and abruptness of *Hildebrand* or *Finnesburh*. The documents, as far as they go, bear out the view that in the Western German tongues, or at any rate in England, there was a development of heroic poetry tending to a greater amplitude of narration. This progress falls a long way short of the fulness of Homer, not to speak of the extreme diffuseness of some of the French *Chansons de Geste*. It is such, however, as to distinguish the English poems, *Waldere*, *Beowulf*, and *Byrhtnoth*, very obviously from the poem of *Hildebrand*. While, at the same time, the brevity of *Hildebrand* is not like the brevity of the Northern poems. *Hildebrand* is a poem capable of expansion. It is easy enough to see in what manner its outlines might be filled up and brought into the proportions of *Waldere* or *Beowulf*. In the Northern poems, on the other hand, there is a lyrical conciseness, and a broken emphatic manner of exposition, which from first to last prevented any such increase of volume as seems to have taken place in the old English poetry; though there are some poems, the *Atlamál* particularly, which indicate that some of the Northern poets wished to go to work on a larger scale than was generally allowed them by their traditions.

In the Northern group there is a great variety in respect of the amount of incident that goes to a single poem; some poems deal with a single adventure, while others give an abstract of a whole heroic history. In the Western poems this variety is not to be found. There is a difference in this respect between *Hildebrand* and *Waldere*, and still more, at least on the surface, between *Hildebrand* and *Beowulf*; but nothing like the difference between the *Lay of the Hammer* (Þrymskviða), which is an episode of Thor, and the *Lay of Weland* or the *Lay of Brynhild*, which give in a summary way a whole history from beginning to end.

Hildebrand tells of the encounter of father and son, Hildebrand and Hadubrand, with a few references to the past of Hildebrand and his relations to Odoacer and Theodoric. It is one adventure, a tragedy in one scene.

Finnesburh, being incomplete at the beginning and end, is not good evidence. What remains of it presents a single adventure, the fight in the hall between Danes and Frisians. There is another version of the story of *Finnesburh*, which, as reported in *Beowulf* (ll. 1068-1154) gives a good deal more of the story than is given in the separate *Finnesburh Lay*. This episode in *Beowulf*, where a poem of *Finnesburh* is chanted by the Danish minstrel, is not to be taken as contributing another independent poem to the scanty stock; the minstrel's story is reported, not quoted at full length. It has been reduced by the poet of *Beowulf*, so as not to take up too large a place of its own in the composition. Such as it is, it may very well count as direct evidence of the way in which epic poems were produced and set before an audience; and it may prove that it was possible for an old English epic to deal with almost the whole of a tragic history in one sitting. In this case the tragedy is far less complex than the tale of the Niblungs, whatever interpretation may be given to the obscure allusions in which it is preserved.

Finn, son of Folcwalda, king of the Frisians, entertained Hnæf the Dane, along with the Danish warriors, in the castle of Finnesburh. There, for reasons of his own, he attacked the Danes; who kept the hall against him, losing their own leader Hnæf, but making a great slaughter of the Frisians.

The *Beowulf* episode takes up the story at this point.

Hnæf was slain in the place of blood. His sister Hildeburg, Finn's wife, had to mourn for brother and son.

Hengest succeeded Hnæf in command of the Danes and still kept the hall against the Frisians. Finn was compelled to make terms with the Danes. Hengest and his men were to live among the Frisians with a place of their own, and share alike with Finn's household in all the gifts of the king. Finn bound himself by an oath that Hengest and his men should be free of blame and reproach, and that he would hold any Frisian guilty who should cast it up against the Danes that they had followed their lord's slayer.[1] Then, after the oaths, was held the funeral of the Danish and the Frisian prince, brother and son of Hildeburg the queen.

Then they went home to Friesland, where Hengest stayed with Finn through the winter. With the spring he set out, meaning vengeance; but he dissembled and rendered homage, and accepted the sword the lord gives his liegeman. Death came upon

[1] Compare *Cynewulf and Cyneheard* in the Chronicle (A.D. 755); also the outbreak of enmity, through recollection of old wrongs, in the stories of Alboin, and of the vengeance for Froda (*supra*, pp. 68-70).

Finn in his house; for the Danes came back and slew him, and the hall was made red with the Frisian blood. The Danes took Hildeburg and the treasure of Finn and carried the queen and the treasure to Denmark.

The whole story, with the exception of the original grievance or grudge of the Frisian king, which is not explained, and the first battle, which is taken as understood, is given in *Beowulf* as the contents of one poem, delivered in one evening by a harper. It is more complicated than the story of *Hildebrand*, more even than *Waldere*; and more than either of the two chief sections of *Beowulf* taken singly—"Beowulf in Denmark" and the "Fight with the Dragon." It is far less than the plot of the long *Lay of Brynhild*, in which the whole Niblung history is contained. In its distribution of the action, it corresponds very closely to the story of the death of the Niblungs as given by the *Atlakviða* and the *Atlamál* The discrepancies between these latter poems need not be taken into account here. In each of them and in the *Finnesburh* story there is a double climax; first the wrong, then the vengeance. *Finnesburh* might also be compared, as far as the arrangement goes, with the *Song of Roland*; the first part gives the treacherous attack and the death of the hero; then comes a pause between the two centres of interest, followed in the second part by expiation of the wrong.

The story of *Finnesburh* is obscure in many respects; the tradition of it has failed to preserve the motive for Finn's attack on his wife's brother, without which the story loses half its value. Something remains, nevertheless, and it is possible to recognise in this episode a greater regard for unity and symmetry of narrative than is to be found in *Beowulf* taken as a whole.

The Lambeth poem of *Finnesburh* most probably confined itself to the battle in the hall. There is no absolute proof of this, apart from the intensity of its tone, in the extant fragment, which would agree best with a short story limited, like *Hildebrand*, to one adventure. It has all the appearance of a short lay, a single episode. Such a poem might end with the truce of Finn and Hengest, and an anticipation of the Danes' vengeance:

> It is marvel an the red blood run not, as the rain
> does in the street.

Yet the stress of this adventure is not greater than that of Roland, which does not end at Roncesvalles; it may be that the *Finnesburh* poem went on to some of the later events, as told in the *Finnesburh* abridgment in *Beowulf.*

The story of Walter of Aquitaine as represented by the two fragments of old English verse is not greatly inconsistent with the same story in its Latin form of *Waltharius.* The Latin verses of *Waltharius* tell the story of the flight of Walter and Hildegund from the house of Attila, and of the treacherous attack on Walter by Gunther, king of the Franks, against the advice, but with the unwilling consent, of Hagen, his liegeman and Walter's friend. Hagen, Hildegund, and Walter were hostages with Attila from the Franks, Burgundians, and Aquitanians. They grew up together at the Court of Attila till Gunther, son of Gibicho, became king of the Franks and refused tribute to the Huns. Then Hagen escaped and went home. Walter and Hildegund were lovers, and they, too, thought of flight, and escaped into the forests, westward, with a great load of treasure, and some fowling and fishing gear for the journey.

After they had crossed the Rhine, they were discovered by Hagen; and Gunther, with twelve of the Franks, went after them to take the Hunnish treasure: Hagen followed reluctantly. The pursuers came up with Walter as he was asleep in a hold among the hills, a narrow green place with overhanging cliffs all round, and a narrow path leading up to it. Hildegund awakened Walter, and he went and looked down at his adversaries. Walter offered terms, through the mediation of Hagen, but Gunther would have none of them, and the fight began. The Latin poem describes with great spirit how one after another the Franks went up against Walter: Camelo (ll. 664-685), Scaramundus (686-724), Werinhardus the bowman (725-755), Ekevrid the Saxon (756-780), who went out jeering at Walter; Hadavartus (781-845), Patavrid (846-913), Hagen's sister's son, whose story is embellished with a diatribe on avarice; Gerwicus (914-940), fighting to avenge his companions and restore their honour—

> Is furit ut caesos mundet vindicta sodales;

but he, too, fell—

> Exitiumque dolens, pulsabat calcibus arvum.

Then there was a breathing-space, before Randolf, the eighth of them, made trial of Walter's defence (962-981). After him came Eleuther, whose other name was Helmnod, with a harpoon and a line, and the line was held by Trogus, Tanastus, and the king; Hagen still keeping aloof, though he had seen his nephew killed. The harpoon failed; three Frankish warriors were added to the slain; the king and Hagen were left (l. 1060).

Gunther tried to draw Hagen into the fight. Hagen refused at first, but gave way at last, on account of the slaying of his nephew. He advised a retreat for the night, and an attack on Walter when he should have left the fastness. And so the day ended.

Walter and Hildegund took turns to watch, Hildegund singing to awaken Walter when his turn came. They left their hold in the morning; but they had not gone a mile when Hildegund, looking behind, saw two men coming down a hill after them. These were Gunther and Hagen, and they had come for Walter's life. Walter sent Hildegund with the horse and its burden into the wood for safety, while he took his stand on rising ground. Gunther jeered at him as he came up; Walter made no answer to him, but reproached Hagen, his old friend. Hagen defended himself by reason of the vengeance due for his nephew; and so they fought, with more words of scorn. Hagen lost his eye, and Gunther his leg, and Walter's right hand was cut off by Hagen; and "this was their sharing of the rings of Attila!"—

Sic, sic, armillas partiti sunt Avarenses (l. 1404).

Walter and Hildegund were king and queen of Aquitaine, but of his later wars and victories the tale has no more to tell.

Of the two old English fragments of this story the first contains part of a speech of Hildegund[1] encouraging Walter.

Its place appears to be in the pause of the fight, when the Frankish champions have been killed, and Gunther and Hagen are alone. The speech is rhetorical: "Thou hast the sword Mimming, the work of Weland, that fails not them that wield it. Be of good courage, captain of Attila; never didst thou draw back to thy hold for all the strokes of the

[1] Hildegyth, her English name, is unfortunately not preserved in either of the fragmentary leaves. It is found (Hildigið) in the *Liber Vitae* (Sweet, *Oldest English Texts*, p. 155).

foeman; nay, my heart was afraid because of thy rashness. Thou shalt break the boast of Gunther; he came on without a cause, he refused the offered gifts; he shall return home empty-handed, if he return at all." That is the purport of it.

The second fragment is a debate between Gunther and Walter. It begins with the close of a speech of Gunther (Guðhere) in which there are allusions to other parts of the heroic cycle, such as are common in *Beowulf*.

The allusion here is to one of the adventures of Widia, Weland's son; how he delivered Theodoric from captivity, and of Theodoric's gratitude. The connexion is obscure, but the reference is of great value as proving the resemblance of narrative method in *Waldere* and *Beowulf*, not to speak of the likeness to the Homeric way of quoting old stories. Waldere answers, and this is the substance of his argument: "Lo, now, Lord of the Burgundians, it was thy thought that Hagena's hand should end my fighting. Come then and win my corselet, my father's heirloom, from the shoulders weary of war." [1]

The fragment closes with a pious utterance of submission to heaven, by which the poem is shown to be of the same order as *Beowulf* in this respect also, as well as others, that it is affected by a turn for

[1] The resemblance to Hildebrand, l. 58, is pointed out by Sophus Bugge: "Doh maht du nu aodlihho, ibu dir din ellen taoc, In sus heremo man hrusti giwinnan." (Hildebrand speaks): "Easily now mayest thou win the spoils of so old a man, if thy strength avail thee." It is remarkable as evidence of the strong conventional character of the Teutonic poetry, and of the community of the different nations in the poetical convention, that two short passages like *Hildebrand* and *Waldere* should present so many points of likeness to other poems, in details of style. Thus the two lines quoted from *Hildebrand* as a parallel to *Waldere* contain also the equivalent of the Anglo-Saxon phrase, *Þonne his ellen deah*, a familiar part of the Teutonic *Gradus*.

edification, and cannot stand as anything like a pure example of the older kind of heroic poetry. The phrasing here is that of the Anglo-Saxon secondary poems; the common religious phrasing that came into vogue and supplemented the old heathen poetical catch-words.

The style of *Waldere* makes it probable that the action of the story was not hurried unduly. If the author kept the same proportion throughout, his poem may have been almost as long as *Waltharius*. It is probable that the fight among the rocks was described in detail; the *Maldon* poem may show how such a subject could be managed in old English verse, and how the matter of *Waltharius* may have been expressed in *Waldere*. Roughly speaking, there is about as much fighting in the three hundred and twenty-five lines of *Maldon* as in double the number of hexameters in *Waltharius*; but the *Maldon* poem is more concise than the extant fragments of *Waldere*. *Waldere* may easily have taken up more than a thousand lines.

The Latin and the English poems are not in absolute agreement. The English poet knew that Guðhere, Guntharius, was Burgundian, not Frank; and an expression in the speech of Hildegyth suggests that the fight in the narrow pass was not so exact a succession of single combats as in *Waltharius*.

The poem of *Maldon* is more nearly related in its style to *Waldere* and *Beowulf* than to the *Finnesburh* fragment. The story of the battle has considerable likeness to the story of the fight at Finnesburh. The details, however, are given in a fuller and more capable way, at greater length.

Beowulf has been commonly regarded as exceptional, on account of its length and complexity, among the remains of the old Teutonic poetry. This view is hardly consistent with a right reading of *Waldere*, or of *Maldon* either, for that matter. It is not easy to make any great distinction between *Beowulf* and *Waldere* in respect of the proportions of the story. The main action of *Beowulf* is comparable in extent with the action of *Waltharius*. The later adventure of *Beowulf* has the character of a sequel, which extends the poem, to the detriment of its proportions, but without adding any new element of complexity to the epic form. Almost all the points in which the manner of *Beowulf* differs from that of *Finnesburh* may be found in *Waldere* also, and are common to *Waldere* and *Beowulf* in distinction from *Hildebrand* and *Finnesburh*. The two poems, the poem of *Beowulf* and the fragments of *Waldere*, seem to be alike in the proportion they allow to dramatic argument, and in their manner of alluding to heroic matters outside of their own proper stories, not to speak of their affinities of ethical tone and sentiment.

The time of the whole action of *Beowulf* is long. The poem, however, falls naturally into two main divisions—*Beowulf in Denmark*, and the *Death of Beowulf*. If it is permissible to consider these for the present as two separate stories, then it may be affirmed that in none of the stories preserved in the old poetic form of England and the German Continent is there any great length or complexity. *Hildebrand*, a combat; *Finnesburh*, a defence of a house; *Waldere*, a champion beset by his enemies; *Beowulf in Denmark*, the hero as a deliverer from pests; *Beowulf's Death* in one action; *Maldon* the last battle of an English captain; these are the themes, and they are all simple. There is more complexity in the story of *Finnesburh*, as reported in *Beowulf*, than in all the rest; but even that story appears to have observed as much as possible the unity of action. The epic singer at the court of the Dane appears to have begun, not with the narrative of the first contest, but immediately after that, assuming that part of the story as known, in order to concentrate attention on the vengeance, on the penalty exacted from Finn the Frisian for his treachery to his guests.

Some of the themes may have less in them than others, but there is no such variety of scale among them as will be found in the Northern poems. There seems to be a general agreement of taste among the Western German poets and audiences, English and Saxon, as to the right compass of an heroic lay. When the subject was a foreign one, as in the *Hêliand*, in the poems of *Genesis* and *Exodus*, in *Andreas*, or *Elene*, there might be room for the complexity and variety of the foreign model. The poem of *Judith* may be considered as a happy instance in which the foreign document has of itself, by a pre-established harmony, conformed to an old German fashion. In the original story of *Judith* the unities are observed in the very degree that was suited to the ways of the Anglo-Saxon poetry. It is hazardous to speak generally of a body of poetry so imperfectly represented in extant literature, but it is at any rate permissible to say that the extant heroic poems, saved out of the wreck of the Western Teutonic poetry, show a strong regard for unity of action, in every case except that of *Beowulf*; while in that case there are two stories—a story and a sequel—each observing a unity within its own limit.

Considered apart from the Northern poems, the poems of England and Germany give indication of a progress in style from a more archaic and repressed, to a more developed and more prolix kind of narrative. The difference is considerable between

Hildebrand and *Waldere*, between *Finnesburh* and *Beowulf*.

It is the change and development in style, rather than any increase in the complexity of the themes, that accounts for the difference in scale between the shorter and the longer poems.

For the natural history of poetical forms this point is of the highest importance. The Teutonic poetry shows that epic may be developed out of short lays through a gradual increase of ambition and of eloquence in the poets who deal with common themes. There is no question here of the process of agglutination and contamination whereby a number of short lays are supposed to be compounded into an epic poem. Of that process it may be possible to find traces in *Beowulf* and elsewhere. But quite apart from that, there is the process by which an archaic stiff manner is replaced by greater freedom, without any loss of unity in the plot. The story of Walter of Aquitaine is as simple as the story of Hildebrand. The difference between *Hildebrand* and *Waldere* is the difference between an archaic and an accomplished mode of narrative, and this difference is made by a change in spirit and imagination, not by a process of agglutination. To make the epic of *Waldere* it was not necessary to cobble together a number of older lays on separate episodes. It was possible to keep the original plan of the old story in its simplest irreducible form, and still give it the force and magnificence of a lofty and eloquent style. It was for the attainment of this pitch of style that the heroic poetry laboured in *Waldere* and *Beowulf*, with at least enough success to make these poems distinct from the rest in this group.

With all the differences among them, the continental and English poems, *Hildebrand*, *Waldere*, and the rest, form a group by themselves, with certain specific qualities of style distinguishing them from the Scandinavian heroic poetry. The history of the Scandinavian poetry is the converse of the English development. Epic poetry in the North becomes more and more hopeless as time goes on, and with some exceptions tends further and further away from the original type which was common to all the Germans, and from which those common forms and phrases have been derived that are found in the "Poetic Edda" as well as in *Beowulf* or the *Hêliand*.[1]

In England before the old poetry died out altogether there was attained a certain magnitude and fulness of narrative by which the English poems are distinguished, and in virtue of which they may claim the title *epic* in no transferred or distorted sense of the term. In the North a different course is taken. There seems indeed, in the *Atlamál* especially, a poem of exceptional compass and weight among those of the North, to have been something like the Western desire for a larger scale of narrative poem. But the rhetorical expansion of the older forms into an equable and deliberate narrative was counteracted by the still stronger affection for lyrical modes of speech, for impassioned, abrupt, and heightened utterance. No epic solidity or composure could be obtained in the fiery Northern verse; the poets could not bring themselves into the frame of mind required for long recitals; they had no patience for the intervals necessary, in epic as in dramatic poetry, between the critical moments. They would have everything equally full of energy, everything must be emphatic and telling. But with all this, the Northern heroic poems are in some of their elements strongly allied to the more equable and duller poems of the West; there is a strong element of epic in their lyrical dialogues and monologues, and in their composition and arrangement of plots.

THE NORTHERN GROUP

In comparing the English and the Northern poems, it should be borne in mind that the documents of the Northern poetry are hardly sufficient evidence of the condition of Northern epic at its best. The English documents are fragmentary, indeed, but at least they belong to a time in which the heroic poetry was attractive and well appreciated; as is proved by the wonderful freshness of the *Maldon* poem, late though it is. The Northern poems seem to have lost their vogue and freshness before they came to be collected and written down. They were imperfectly remembered and reported; the text of them is broken and confused, and the gaps are made up with prose explanations. The fortunate preservation of a second copy of *Volospá*, in Hauk's book, has further multiplied labours and perplexities by a palpable demonstration of the vanity of copiers, and of the casual way in which the strophes of a poem might be shuffled at random in different texts; while the chief manuscript of the poems itself has in some cases double and incongruous versions of the same passage.[1]

The *Codex Regius* contains a number of poems that can only be called *epic* in the widest and loosest sense of the term, and some that are not *epic* in any sense at all. The gnomic verses, the mythological

[1] Cf. *C.P.B.*, i. p. 375, for double versions of part of *Hamðismál*, and of the *Lay of Helgi*. On pp. 377-379, parts of the two texts of *Volospá*—R and H—are printed side by side for comparison.

summaries, may be passed over for the present; whatever illustrations they afford of early beliefs and ideas, they have no evidence to give concerning the proportions of stories. Other poems in the collection come under the denomination of epic only by a rather liberal extension of the term to include poems which are no more epic than dramatic, and just as much the one as the other, like the poems of *Frey's Wooing* and of the earlier exploits of Sigurd, which tell their story altogether by means of dialogue, without any narrative passages at all. The links and explanations are supplied, in prose, in the manuscript. Further, among the poems which come nearer to the English form of narrative poetry there is the very greatest variety of scale. The amount of story told in the Northern poems may vary indefinitely within the widest limits. Some poems contain little more than an idyll of a single scene; others may give an abstract of a whole history, as the whole Volsung story is summarised, for instance, in the *Prophecy of Gripir.*

Some of the poems are found in such a confused and fragmentary form, with interruptions and interpolations, that, although it is possible to make out the story, it is hardly possible to give any confident judgment about the original proportions of the poems. This is particularly the case with the poems in which the hero bears the name of Helgi. The difficulties of these were partly appreciated, but not solved, by the original editor.

The differences of scale may be illustrated by the following summary description, which aims at little more than a rough measurement of the stories, for purposes of comparison with *Beowulf* and *Waldere.*

The *Lay of Weland* gives a whole mythical history. How Weland and his brother met with the swan-maidens, how the swan-brides left them in the ninth year, how Weland Smith was taken prisoner by King Nidad, and hamstrung, and set to work for the king; and of the vengeance of Weland. There are one hundred and fifty-nine lines, but in the text there are many defective places. The *Lay* is a ballad history, beginning at the beginning, and ending, not with the end of the life of Weland, nor with the adventures of his son Widia, but with the escape of Weland from the king, his enemy, after he had killed the king's sons and put shame on the king's daughter Bodvild.

In plan, the *Lay of Weland* is quite different from the lays of the adventures of Thor, the *Þrymskviða* and the *Hymiskviða*, the songs of the Hammer and the Cauldron. These are chapters, episodes, in the history of Thor, not summaries of the whole matter, such as is the poem of *Weland*.

The stories of Helgi Hundingsbane, and of his namesakes, as has been already remarked, are given in a more than usually complicated and tangled form.

At first everything is simple enough. A poem of the life of Helgi begins in a way that promises a mode of narrative fuller and less abrupt than the *Lay of Weland*. It tells of the birth of Helgi, son of Sigmund; of the coming of the Norns to make fast the threads of his destiny; of the gladness and the good hopes with which his birth was welcomed. Then the *Lay of Helgi* tells, very briefly, how he slew King Hunding, how the sons of Hunding made claims for recompense. "But the prince would make no payment of amends; he bade them look for no payment, but for the strong storm, for the grey spears, and for the rage of Odin."[1] And the

[1] Cf. *Maldon*, l. 45 *sq.*, "Hearest thou what this people answer? They will pay you, for tribute, spears, the deadly point, the old swords, the weapons of war that profit you not," etc.

sons of Hunding were slain as their father had been.

Then the main interest begins, the story of Helgi and Sigrun.

"A light shone forth from the Mountains of Flame, and lightnings followed." There appeared to Helgi, in the air, a company of armed maidens riding across the field of heaven; "their armour was stained with blood, and light went forth from their spears." Sigrun from among the other "ladies of the South" answered Helgi, and called on him for help; her father Hogni had betrothed her, against her will, to Hodbrodd, son of Granmar. Helgi summoned his men to save her from this loathed wedding. The battle in which Helgi slew his enemies and won the lady of the air is told very shortly, while disproportionate length is given to an interlude of vituperative dialogue between two heroes, Sinfiotli, Helgi's brother, and Gudmund, son of Granmar, the warden of the enemy's coast; this passage of *Vetus Comoedia* takes up fifty lines, while only six are given to the battle, and thirteen to the meeting of Helgi and Sigrun afterwards. Here ends the poem which is described in *Codex Regius* as the *Lay of Helgi* (*Helgakviða*). The story is continued in the next section in a disorderly way, by means of ill-connected quotations. The original editor, whether rightly or wrongly, is quite certain that the *Lay of Helgi*, which ends with the victory of Helgi over the unamiable bridegroom, is a different poem from that which he proceeds to quote as the *Old Lay of the Volsungs*, in which the same story is told. In this second version there is at least one interpolation from a third; a stanza from a poem in the "dialogue measure," which is not the measure in which the rest of the story is told. It is uncertain what application was meant to be given to the title *Old Lay of the Volsungs*, and whether the editor included under that title the whole of his second version of Helgi and Sigrun. For instance, he gives another version of the railing verses of Sinfiotli, which he may or may not have regarded as forming an essential part of his *Old Volsung Lay*. He distinguishes it at any rate from the other "Flyting," which he definitely and by name ascribes to *Helgakviða*.

It is in this second version of the story of Helgi that the tragedy is worked out. Helgi slays the father of Sigrun in his battle against the bridegroom's kindred: Sigrun's brother takes vengeance. The space is scant enough for all that is told in it; scant, that is to say, in comparison with the space of the story of Beowulf; though whether the poem loses, as poetry, by this compression is another matter.

It is here, in connexion with the second version, that the tragedy is followed by the verses of the grief of Sigrun, and the return of Helgi from the dead; the passage of mystery, the musical close, in which the tragic idea is changed into something less distinct than tragedy, yet without detriment to the main action.

Whatever may be the critical solution of the textual problems of these *Lays*, it is impossible to get out of the text any form of narrative that shall resemble the English mode. Even where the story of Helgi is slowest, it is quicker, more abrupt, and more lyrical even than the *Lay of Finnesburh*, which is the quickest in movement of the English poems.

The story of Helgi and Sigrun is intelligible, and though incomplete, not yet so maimed as to have lost its proportions altogether. Along with it, however, in the manuscript there are other, even more difficult fragments of poems about another Helgi, son of

Hiorvard, and his love for another Valkyria, Swava. And yet again there are traces of a third Helgi, with a history of his own. The editors of *Corpus Poeticum Boreale* have accepted the view of the three Helgis that is indicated by the prose passages of the manuscript here; namely, that the different stories are really of the same persons born anew, "to go through the same life-story, though with varying incidents."[1] "Helgi and Swava, it is said, were born again," is the note in the manuscript. "There was a king named Hogni, and his daughter was Sigrun. She was a Valkyria and rode over air and sea; *she was Swava born again.*" And, after the close of the story of Sigrun, "it was a belief in the old days that men were born again, but that is now reckoned old wives' fables. Helgi and Sigrun, it is reported, were born anew, and then he was Helgi Haddingjaskati, and she Kara, Halfdan's daughter, as is told in the songs of Kara, and she was a Valkyria."

It is still possible to regard the "old wives' fable" (which is a common element in Celtic legend and elsewhere) as something unessential in the poems of Helgi; as a popular explanation intended to reconcile different myths attaching to the name. However that may be, the poems of *Helgi and Swava* are so fragmentary and confused, and so much has to be eked out with prose, that it is impossible to say what the complete form and scale of the poetical story may have been, and even difficult to be certain that it was ever anything else than fragments. As they stand, the remains are like those of the story of Angantyr; prominent passages quoted by a chronicler, who gives the less important part of the story in prose, either because he has forgotten the rest of the poem, or because the poem was made in that way to begin with.

[1] *C.P.B.*, i. p. 130.

Of the poem of *Kara*, mentioned in the manuscript, there is nothing left except what can be restored by a conjectural transference of some verses, given under the name of Helgi and Sigrun, to this third mysterious plot. The conjectures are supported by the reference to the third story in the manuscript, and by the fact that certain passages which do not fit in well to the story of Helgi and Sigrun, where they are placed by the collector, correspond with prose passages in the late Icelandic romance of *Hromund Greipsson*,[1] in which Kara is introduced.

The story of Helgi and Swava is one that covers a large period of time, though the actual remnants of the story are small. It is a tragedy of the early Elizabethan type described by Sir Philip Sidney, which begins with the wooing of the hero's father and mother. The hero is dumb and nameless from his birth, until the Valkyria, Swava, meets him and gives him his name, Helgi; and tells him of a magic sword in an island, that will bring him victory.

The tragedy is brought about by a witch who drives Hedin, the brother of Helgi, to make a foolish boast, an oath on the Boar's head (like the vows of the Heron or the Peacock, and the *gabs* of the Paladins of France) that he will wed his brother's bride. Hedin confesses his vanity to Helgi, and is forgiven, Helgi saying, "Who knows but the oath may be fulfilled? I am on my way to meet a challenge."

Helgi is wounded mortally, and sends a message to Swava to come to him, and prays her after his death to take Hedin for her lord. The poem ends with two short energetic speeches: of Swava refusing to have any love but Helgi's; and of Hedin bidding farewell to Swava as he goes to make amends, and avenge his brother.

[1] *C.P.B.*, Introduction, p. lxxviii.

These fragments, though their evidence tells little regarding epic scale or proportions, are, at least, illustrations of the nature of the stories chosen for epic narrative. The character of Hedin, his folly and magnanimity, is in strong contrast to that of Dag, the brother of Sigrun, who makes mischief in the other poem. The character of Swava is a fainter repetition of Sigrun.

Nothing very definite can be made out of any of the Helgi poems with regard to the conventions of scale in narrative; except that the collector of the poems was himself in difficulties in this part of his work, and that he knew he had no complete poem to offer his readers, except perhaps the *Helgakviða.*

The poem named by the Oxford editors "The Long Lay of Brunhild" (i. p. 293) is headed in the manuscript "Qviða Sigurþar," *Lay of Sigurd*, and referred to, in the prose gloss of *Codex Regius*, as "The Short Lay of Sigurd."[1] This is one of the most important of the Northern heroic lays, in every respect; and, among other reasons, as an example of definite artistic calculation and study, a finished piece of work. It shows the difference between the Northern and the Western standards of epic measurement. The poem is one that gives the whole of the tragedy in no longer space than is used in the poem of *Maldon* for the adventures of a few hours of battle. There are 288 lines, not all complete.

There are many various modes of representation in the poem. The beginning tells the earlier story of Sigurd and Brynhild in twenty lines :—

It was in the days of old that Sigurd, the young Volsung, the slayer of Fafni, came to the house of Giuki. He took the troth-plight of two brothers ; the doughty

[1] The "Long Lay of Sigurd" has disappeared. Cf. Heusler, *Die Lieder der Lücke im Codex Regius der Edda*, 1902.

heroes gave oaths one to another. They offered him the maid Gudrun, Giuki's daughter, and store of treasure; they drank and took counsel together many a day, Child Sigurd and the sons of Giuki; until they went to woo Brynhild, and Sigurd the Volsung rode in their company; he was to win her if he could get her. The Southern hero laid a naked sword, a falchion graven, between them twain; nor did the Hunnish king ever kiss her, neither take her into his arms; he handed the young maiden over to Giuki's son.

She knew no guilt in her life, nor was any evil found in her when she died, no blame in deed or thought. The grim Fates came between.[1]

"It was the Fates that worked them ill." This sententious close of the prologue introduces the main story, chiefly dramatic in form, in which Brynhild persuades Gunnar to plan the death of Sigurd, and Gunnar persuades Hogni. It is love for Sigurd, and jealousy of Gudrun, that form the motive of Brynhild. Gunnar's conduct is barely intelligible; there is no explanation of his compliance with Brynhild, except the mere strength of her importunity. Hogni is reluctant, and remembers the oaths sworn to Sigurd. Gothorm, their younger brother, is made their instrument,—he was "outside the oaths." The slaying of Sigurd by Gothorm, and Sigurd's dying stroke that cuts his slayer in two, are told in the brief manner of the prologue to the poem; likewise the grief of Gudrun. Then comes Sigurd's speech to Gudrun before his death.

The principal part of the poem, from line 118 to the end, is filled by the storm in the mind of Brynhild: her laughter at the grief of Gudrun, her confession of her own sorrows, and her preparation for death; the expostulations of Gunnar, the bitter

[1] From *C.P.B.*, i. pp. 293, 294, with some modifications.

speech of Hogni,—"Let no man stay her from her long journey"; the stroke of the sword with which Brynhild gives herself the death wound; her dying prophecy. In this last speech of Brynhild, with all its vehemence, there is manifest care on the part of the author to bring out clearly his knowledge of the later fortunes of Gudrun and Gunnar. The prophecy includes the birth of Swanhild, the marriage of Attila and Gudrun, the death of Gunnar at the hands of Attila, by reason of the love between Gudrun and Oddrun; the vengeance of Gudrun on Attila, the third marriage of Gudrun, the death of Swanhild among the Goths. With all this, and carrying all this burden of history, there is the passion of Brynhild, not wholly obscured or quenched by the rhetorical ingenuity of the poet. For it is plain that the poet was an artist capable of more than one thing at a time. He was stirred by the tragic personage of Brynhild; he was also pleased, intellectually and dispassionately, with his design of grouping together in one composition all the events of the tragic history.

The poem is followed by the short separate Lay (forty-four lines) of the *Hell-ride of Brynhild*, which looks as if it might have been composed by the same or another poet, to supply some of the history wanting at the beginning of the *Lay of Brynhild*. Brynhild, riding Hell-ward with Sigurd, from the funeral pile where she and Sigurd had been laid by the Giuking lords, is encountered by a giantess who forbids her to pass through her "rock-built courts," and cries shame upon her for her guilt. Brynhild answers with the story of her evil fate, how she was a Valkyria, punished by Odin for disobedience, set in the ring of flame, to be released by none but the slayer of Fafni; how she had been beguiled in Gunnar's wooing, and how Gudrun cast it in her teeth. This supplies the motive for the anger of Brynhild against Sigurd, not clearly expressed in the *Lay*, and also for Gunnar's compliance with her jealous appeal, and Hogni's consent to the death of Sigurd. While, in the same manner as in the *Lay*, the formalism and pedantry of the historical poet are burnt up in the passion of the heroine. "Sorrow is the portion of the life of all men and women born: we two, I and Sigurd, shall be parted no more for ever." The latter part of the *Lay*, the long monologue of Brynhild, is in form like the *Lamentation of Oddrun* and the idyll of Gudrun and Theodoric; though, unlike those poems, it has a fuller narrative introduction: the monologue does not begin until the situation has been explained.

On the same subject, but in strong contrast with the *Lay of Brynhild*, is the poem that has lost its beginning in the great gap in *Codex Regius*. It is commonly referred to in the editions as the *Fragmentary Lay of Sigurd* ("Brot af Sigurðarkviðu"); in the Oxford edition it is styled the "Fragment of a short Brunhild Lay." There are seventy-six lines (incomplete) beginning with the colloquy of Gunnar and Hogni. Here also the character of Brynhild is the inspiration of the poet. But there does not seem to have been in his mind anything like the historical anxiety of the other poet to account for every incident, or at least to show that, if he wished, he could account for every incident, in the whole story. It is much stronger in expression, and the conception of Brynhild is more dramatic and more imaginative, though less eloquent, than in the longer poem. The phrasing is short and emphatic:—

Gudrun, Giuki's daughter, stood without, and this was the first word she spoke: "Where is Sigurd, the king of men, that my brothers are riding in the van?" Hogni made answer to her words: "We have hewn

Sigurd asunder with the sword; ever the grey horse droops his head over the dead king."

Then spake Brynhild, Budli's daughter: "Have great joy of your weapons and hands. Sigurd would have ruled everything as he chose, if he had kept his life a little longer. It was not meet that he should so rule over the host of the Goths and the heritage of Giuki, who begat five sons that delighted in war and in the havoc of battle."

Brynhild laughed, the whole house rang: "Have long joy of your hands and weapons, since ye have slain the valiant king."[1]

The mood of Brynhild is altered later, and she "weeps at that she had laughed at." She wakens before the day, chilled by evil dreams. "It was cold in the hall, and cold in the bed," and she had seen in her sleep the end of the Niblungs, and woke, and reproached Gunnar with the treason to his friend.

It is difficult to estimate the original full compass of this fragmentary poem, but the scale of its narrative and its drama can be pretty clearly understood from what remains. It is a poem with nothing superfluous in it. The death of Sigurd does not seem to have been given in any detail, except for the commentary spoken by the eagle and the raven, prophetic of the doom of the Niblungs. The mystery of Brynhild's character is curiously recognised by a sort of informal chorus. It is said that "they were stricken silent as she spoke, and none could understand her bearing, that she should weep to speak of that for which she had besought them laughing." It is one of the simplest forms in narrative; but in this case the simplicity of the rhetoric goes along with some variety and subtlety of dramatic imagination. The character of the heroine is rightly imagined and strongly ren-

[1] From *C.P.B.*, i. p. 307, with some changes.

dered, and her change of mind is impressive, as the author plainly meant it to be.

The *Lay of Attila* (*Atlakviða*) and the Greenland poem of *Attila* (*Atlamál*) are two poems which have a common subject and the same amount of story: how Attila sent for Gunnar and Hogni, the brothers of Gudrun, and had them put to death, and how Gudrun took vengeance on Attila.

In the *Atlakviða* there are 174 lines, and some broken places; in *Atlamál* there are 384 lines; its narrative is more copious than in most of the Norse Lays. There are some curious discrepancies in the matter of the two poems, but these hardly affect the scale of the story. The difference between them in this respect is fairly represented by the difference in the number of their lines. The scenes of the history are kept in similar proportions in both poems.

The story of Gudrun's vengeance has been seen (p. 83) to correspond, as far as the amount of action is concerned, pretty closely with the story of Hengest and Finn. The epic unity is preserved; and, as in the *Finnesburh* story, there is a distribution of interest between the *wrong* and the *vengeance*,—(1) the death of Hnæf, the death of Gunnar and Hogni; (2) the vengeance of Hengest, the vengeance of Gudrun, with an interval of dissimulation in each case.

The plot of the death of Attila, under all its manifold variations, is never without a certain natural fitness for consistent and well-proportioned narrative.

None of the Northern poems take any account of the theory that the murder of Sigfred was avenged by his wife upon her brothers. That theory belongs to the *Nibelungenlied*; in some form or other it was known to Saxo; it is found in the Danish ballad of *Grimild's Revenge*, a translation or adaptation from the German. That other conception of the story may be more full of tragic meaning; the Northern versions, which agree in making Attila the slayer of the Niblung kings, have the advantage of greater concentration. The motive of Attila, which is different in each of the poems on this subject, is in no case equal to the tragic motive of Kriemhild in the *Nibelungen.* On the other hand, the present interest of the story is not distracted by reference to the long previous history of Sigfred; a new start is made when the Niblungs are invited to Attila's Court. The situation is intelligible at once, without any long preliminary explanation.

In the *Lay of Attila* the hoard of the Niblungs comes into the story; its fatal significance is recognised; it is the "metal of discord" that is left in the Rhine for ever. But the situation can be understood without any long preliminary history of the Niblung treasure and its fate. Just as the story of *Waldere* explains itself at once,—a man defending his bride and his worldly wealth against a number of enemies, in a place where he is able to take them one by one, as they come on,—so the story of *Attila* can begin without long preliminaries; though the previous history is to be found, in tradition, in common stories, if any one cares to ask for it. The plot is intelligible in a moment: the brothers inveigled away and killed by their sister's husband (for reasons of his own, as to which the versions do not agree); their sister's vengeance by the sacrifice of her own children and the death of her husband.

In the *Atlamál* there is very much less recognition of the previous history than in *Atlakviða.* The story begins at once with the invitation to the Niblung brothers and with their sister's warning. Attila's motive is not emphasised; he has a grudge against them on account of the death of Brynhild his sister, but his motive is not very necessary for the story, as the story is managed here. The present scene and the present passion are not complicated with too much reference to the former history of the personages. This mode of procedure will be found to have given some trouble to the author, but the result at any rate is a complete and rounded work.

There is great difference of treatment between *Atlakviða* and the Greenland poem *Atlamál*, a difference which is worth some further consideration.[1] There is, however, no very great difference of scale; at any rate, the difference between them becomes unimportant when they are compared with *Beowulf*. Even the more prolix of the two, which in some respects is the fullest and most elaborate of the Northern heroic poems, yet comes short of the English scale. *Atlamál* takes up very little more than the space of the English poem of *Maldon*, which is a simple narrative of a battle, with nothing like the tragic complexity and variety of the story of the vengeance of Gudrun.

There is yet another version of the death of Gunnar the Giuking to compare with the two poems of *Attila*—the *Lament of Oddrun* (*Oddrúnargrátr*), which precedes the *Atlakviða* in the manuscript. The form of this, as well as the plot of it, is wonderfully different from either of the other two poems. This is one of the epic or tragic idylls in which a passage of heroic legend is told dramatically by one who had a share in it. Here the death of Gunnar is told by Oddrun his mistress, the sister of Attila.

This form of indirect narration, by giving so great a dramatic value to the person of the narrator, before the beginning of her story, of course tends to depreciate or to exclude the vivid dramatic scenes that

[1] See pp. 150-156 below.

are common everywhere else in the Northern poems. The character of the speaker leaves too little independence to the other characters. But in none of the poems is the tragic plot more strongly drawn out than in the seventy lines of Oddrun's story to Borgny.

The father of Oddrun, Brynhild, and Attila had destined Oddrun to be the bride of Gunnar, but it was Brynhild that he married. Then came the anger of Brynhild against Sigurd, the death of Sigurd, the death of Brynhild that is renowned over all the world. Gunnar sought the hand of Oddrun from her brother Attila, but Attila would not accept the price of the bride from the son of Giuki. The love of Oddrun was given to Gunnar. "I gave my love to Gunnar as Brynhild should have loved him. We could not withstand our love: I kept troth with Gunnar." The lovers were betrayed to Attila, who would not believe the accusation against his sister; "yet no man should pledge his honour for the innocence of another, when it is a matter of love." At last he was persuaded, and laid a plot to take vengeance on the Niblungs; Gudrun knew nothing of what was intended.

The death of Gunnar and Hogni is told in five-and-twenty lines:—

There was din of the hoofs of gold when the sons of Giuki rode into the Court. The heart was cut out of the body of Hogni; his brother they set in the pit of snakes. The wise king smote on his harp, for he thought that I should come to his help. Howbeit I was gone to the banquet at the house of Geirmund. From Hlessey I heard how the strings rang loud. I called to my handmaidens to rise and go; I sought to save the life of the prince; we sailed across the sound, till we saw the halls of Attila. But the accursed serpent crept to the heart of Gunnar, so that I might not save the life of the king.

Full oft I wonder how I keep my life after him, for I thought I loved him like myself.

Thou hast sat and listened while I have told thee many evils of my lot and theirs. The life of a man is as his thoughts are.

The Lamentation of Oddrun is finished.

The *Hamðismál*, the poem of the death of Ermanaric, is one that, in its proportions, is not unlike the *Atlakviða*: the plot has been already described (pp. 70-71). The poem of 130 lines as it stands has suffered a good deal. This also is like the story of Hengest and the story of Gudrun in the way the action is proportioned. It began with the slaying of Swanhild, the wrong to Gudrun—this part is lost. It goes on to the speech of Gudrun to her sons, Sorli and Hamther, and their expedition to the hall of the Goth; it ends with their death. In this case, also, the action must have begun at once and intelligibly, as soon as the motive of the Gothic treachery and cruelty was explained, or even without that explanation, in the more immediate sense of the treachery and cruelty, in the story of Swanhild trampled to death, and of the news brought to Gudrun. Here, also, there is much less expansion of the story than in the English poems; everything is surcharged with meaning.

The *Old Lay of Gudrun* (*Guðrúnarkviða in forna*), or the tale of Gudrun to Theodoric, an idyll like the story of Oddrun, goes quickly over the event of the killing of Sigurd, and the return of Grani, masterless. Unlike the *Lament of Oddrun*, this monologue of Gudrun introduces dramatic passages. The meeting of Gudrun and her brother is not merely told by Gudrun in indirect narration; the speeches of Hogni and Gudrun are reported directly, as they might have been in a poem of the form of *Atlakviða*, or the *Lay of Sigurd*, or any other in which the poet tells the story himself, without the introduction of an imaginary narrator. The main part of the poem is an account of the way in which Gudrun's mother, Grimhild, compelled her, by a potion of forgetfulness, to lose the thought of Sigurd and of all her woes, and consent to become the wife of Attila. This part is well prefaced by the quiet account of the life of Gudrun in her widowhood, before Grimhild began her schemes; how Gudrun lived in the house of Half, with Thora, daughter of Hakon, in Denmark, and how the ladies spent their time at the tapestry frame, working pictures of the heroes, the ships of Sigmund, the ranks of Hunnish warriors.

In the manuscript there are found at the end of the *Old Lay of Gudrun*, as if they were part of it, some verses which have been separated from it by the editors (*C.P.B.*, i. 347) as a "Fragment of an Atli Lay." They came from a poem of which the design, at any rate, was the same as that of the *Old Lay*, and Gudrun is the speaker. She tells how, after the death of Gunnar and Hogni, she was wakened by Atli, to listen to his evil dreams, foreboding his doom, and how she interpreted them in a way to comfort him and put him off his guard.

In English poetry there are instances of stories introduced dramatically, long before the pilgrimage to Canterbury. In *Beowulf* there are various episodes where a story is told by one of the persons engaged. Besides the poem of Hengest chanted in Heorot, there is Beowulf's own narrative of his adventures, after his return to his own people in the kingdom of the Gauts, and passages still nearer in form to the *Lament of Oddrun* and the *Confession of Gudrun* are the last speech of Beowulf before his death (2426-2537), and the long speech of Wiglaf (2900-

3027) telling of the enmity of the Gauts and the Swedes. But those are not filled with dramatic pathos to the same degree as these Northern *Heroides*, the monologues of Oddrun and Gudrun.

The *Lay of Gudrun* (*Gudrúnarkviða*) which comes in the manuscript immediately before the *Lay of Sigurd*, is a pure heroic idyll. Unlike most of its companions, it leaves the details of the Volsung story very much in neglect, and brings all its force to bear on the representation of the grief of the queen, contrasted with the stormy passion of Brynhild. It is rightly honoured for its pathetic imagination of the dumb grief of Gudrun, broken up and dissolved when her sister draws away the covering from the face of Sigurd. "But fire was kindled in the eyes of Brynhild, daughter of Budli, when she looked upon his wounds."

The refrain of the poem increases its resemblance to the form of a Greek idyll. The verse is that of narrative poetry; the refrain is not purely lyrical and does not come in at regular intervals.

The *Tregrof Guðrúnar*, or *Chain of Woe*, restored by the Oxford editors out of the most confused part of the original text, is pure lamentation, spoken by Gudrun before her death, recounting all her sorrows: the bright hair of Swanhild trampled in the mire; Sigurd slain in his bed, despoiled of victory; Gunnar in the court of the serpents; the heart of Hogni cut out of his living body—"Saddle thy white steed and come to me, Sigurd; remember what we promised to one another, that thou wouldst come from Hell to seek me, and I would come to thee from the living world."

The short poem entitled *Qviða Guðrúnar* in the manuscript, the *Ordeal of Gudrun* in the English edition, has a simple plot. The subject is the calumny which was brought against Gudrun by Herkja, the cast-off mistress of Attila (that "she had seen

Gudrun and Theodoric together") and the ordeal of water by which Gudrun proved her innocence, while the falsehood was brought home to Herkja, the bondwoman. The theme is slighter than all the rest, and this poem, at least, might be reckoned not unfit to be taken up as a single scene in a long epic.

Some of the Northern poems in the epic measure are almost wholly made up of dialogue. The story of *Balder's Doom* is a dialogue between Odin and the witch whom he raises from the dead. The earlier part of the story of Sigurd in the "Elder Edda" is almost all dialogue, even where the narrative measure is employed.

There is hardly any mere narrative in the poems remaining of the cycle of Angantyr. In several other cases, the writer has only given, perhaps has only remembered clearly, the dramatic part of the poems in which he was interested; the intervals of the story he fills up with prose. It is difficult to tell where this want of narrative connexion in the poetry is original, and where it is due to forgetfulness or ignorance; where the prose of the manuscripts is to be taken as standing in the place of lost narrative verses, and where it fills a gap that was never intended to be filled with verse, but was always left to the reciter, to be supplied in his own way by passages of story-telling, between his chantings of the poetic dialogue of Hervor and the Shepherd, for instance, or of Hervor and Angantyr.

The poems just mentioned are composed in narrative measure. There are also other dialogue poems in a measure different from this, and peculiarly adapted to dialogues, the measure of the gnomic *Hávamál* and of the didactic mythological poems, *Vafþrúðnismál*, *Alvíssmál*, *Grímnismál*. These pieces are some distance removed from epic or ballad poetry

But there are others in this gnomic measure which it is not easy to keep far apart from such dialogue poems as *Balder's Doom*, though their verse is different. By their peculiar verse they are distinguished from the English and Saxon heroic poetry; but they retain, for all their peculiar metre and their want of direct narrative, some of the characteristics of Teutonic epic.

The *Lokasenna* has a plot, and represents dramatically an incident in the history of the gods. The chief business is Loki's shameless rehearsal of accusations against the gods, and their helpless rejoinders. It is a masque of the gods, and not a ballad like the *Winning of Thor's Hammer*. It is not, however, a mere string of "flytings" without a plot; there is some plot and action. It is the absence of Thor that gives Loki courage to browbeat the gods; the return of Thor at the end of the poem avenges the gods on their accuser.

In the strange poem of the *Railing of Thor and Harbard*, and in a very rough and irregular kind of verse, there is a similar kind of plot.

The *Contention of Atli and Rimgerd the Giantess* is a short comic dialogue, interposed among the fragments of the poem of Helgi Hiorvard's son, and marked off from them by its use of the dialogue verse, as well as by its episodic plot.

Helgi Hiorvard's son had killed the giant Hati, and the giant's daughter comes at night where Helgi's ships are moored in the firth, and stands on a rock over them, challenging Helgi and his men. Atli, keeping watch on deck, answers the giantess, and there is an exchange of gibes in the old style between them. Helgi is awakened and joins in the argument. It is good comedy of its kind, and there is poetry in the giantess's description of the company of armed maidens of the air whom she has seen keeping guard over Helgi's ships—"three nines of maids, but one rode foremost, a white maid, enhelmed. Their rearing horses shook dew from their manes into the deep dales, and hail upon the lofty woods; thence come fair seasons among men. But the whole sight was hateful to me" (*C.P.B.*, i. p. 154).

The giantess is kept there by the gibes of Atli till the daybreak. "Look eastward, now, Rimgerd!" And the giantess is turned into stone, a great harbour mark, to be laughed at.

In some other poems there is much more action, and much more need for an interpreter to act as chorus in the intervals between the dialogues. The story of the wooing of Gerd is in this form: how Frey sat in the seat of Odin and saw a fair maid in Jotunheim, and got great sickness of thought, till his swain Skirnir found the cause of his languishing, and went to woo Gerd for him in Gymi's Garth. Another love-story, and a story not unlike that of Frey and Gerd, is contained in two poems *Grógaldr* and *Fiölsvinnsmál*, that tell of the winning of Menglad by her destined lover.

These two latter poems are not in *Codex Regius*, and it was only gradually that their relation to one another was worked out, chiefly by means of the Danish ballad which contains the story of both together in the right order.

In the first, Svipdag the hero comes to his mother's grave to call on her for counsel. He has been laid under a mysterious charge, to go on a quest which he cannot understand, "to find out Menglad," and Menglad he has never heard of, and does not know where she is to be found.

The second poem, also in dialogue, and in the dialogue measure, gives the coming of Svipdag to the mysterious castle, and his debate with the giant who keeps the gate. For Menglad is the princess whose story is told everywhere, and under a thousand names, —the lady of a strange country, kept under a spell in a witch's castle till the deliverer comes. The wooing of Gerd out of Jotunheim is another version of the same story, which in different forms is one of the oldest and most universal everywhere,—the fairy story of the princess beyond the sea.

The second dialogue is very much encumbered by the pedantries of the giant who keeps the gate; it ends, however, in the recognition of Svipdag and Menglad. Menglad says: "Long have I sat waiting for thee, many a day; but now is that befallen that I have sought for, and thou art come to my bower. Great was the sorrow of my waiting; great was thine, waiting for the gladness of love. Now it is very truth for us: the days of our life shall not be sundered."

The same form is used in the older poems of Sigurd, those that come before the hiatus of the great manuscript, and have been gathered together in the Oxford edition under the title of the *Old Play of the Wolsungs.* They touch briefly on all the chief points of the story of the Niblung hoard, from the capture and ransom of Andvari to the winning of the warrior maiden Sigrdrifa by Sigurd.

All these last-mentioned dialogue poems, in spite of their lyric or elegiac measure, are like the narrative poems in their dependence upon traditional, mythic, or heroic stories, from which they choose their themes. They are not like the lyrical heroic poems of *Widsith* and *Deor* in Anglo-Saxon literature, which survey a large tract of heroic legend from a point of vantage. Something of this sort is done by some of the Norse dialogue poems, *Vafþrúðnismál*, etc., but in the poems of Frey and Gerd, of Svipdag and

Menglad, and of the Niblung treasure, though this reflective and comparative method occasionally makes itself evident, the interest is that of the story. They have a story to represent, just as much as the narrative poems, though they are debarred from the use of narrative.

It must be confessed that there is an easily detected ambiguity in the use of the term epic in application to the poems, whether German, English, or Northern, here reviewed. That they are heroic poems cannot be questioned, but that they are epic in any save the most general sense of the term is not quite clear. They may be epic in character, in a general way, but how many of them have a claim to the title in its eminent and special sense? Most of them are short poems; most of them seem to be wanting in the breadth of treatment, in the amplitude of substance, that are proper to epic poetry.

Beowulf, it may be admitted, is epic in the sense that distinguishes between the longer narrative poem and the shorter ballad. The fragments of *Waldere* are the fragments of a poem that is not cramped for room, and that moves easily and with sufficient eloquence in the representation of action. The narrative of the *Maldon* poem is not pinched nor meagre in its proportions. Hardly any of the other poems, however, can be compared with these in this respect. These are the most liberal in scale of all the old Teutonic poems; the largest epic works of which we know anything directly. These are the fullest in composition, the least abstract or elliptical; and they still want something of the scale of the *Iliad*. The poem of *Maldon*, for instance, corresponds not to the *Iliad*, but to the action of a single book, such as the twelfth, with which it has been already compared.

If the story of the English *Waldere*, when complete, was not more elaborate than the extant Latin *Waltharius*, it must have come far short of the proportions of Homer. It is a story for a single recitation, like the story of Finnesburh in *Beowulf*. The poem of *Beowulf* may have more in it than the story of Walter and Hildegund, but this advantage would seem to be gained at the expense of the unity of the poem. It is lengthened out by a sequel, by the addition of a new adventure which requires the poet to make a new start. In the poem of *Hildebrand* there is a single tragedy contained in a single scene. It is briefly rendered, in a style evidently more primitive, less expansive and eloquent, than the style of *Beowulf* or *Waldere*. Even if it had been given in a fuller form, the story would still have been essentially a short one; it could not well have been longer than the poem of *Sohrab and Rustum*, where the theme is almost the same, while the scale is that of the classical epic.

If the old English epic poetry falls short of the Homeric magnitude, it almost equally exceeds the scale of the Northern heroic poems. If *Beowulf* and *Waldere* seem inadequate in size, the defect will not be made good out of the Northern lays of *Helgi* or *Sigfred*.

The Northern poems are exceedingly varied in their plan and disposition, but none of them is long, and many of them are in the form of *dramatic lyric*, with no place for pure narrative at all; such are the poems of *Frey's Wooing*, of *Svipdag and Menglad*, and others, in which there is a definite plot worked out by means of lyric dialogue. None of them is of anything like the same scale as *Beowulf*, which is a complex epic poem, or *Byrhtnoth*, which is an episodic poem liberally dealt with and of considerable length.

The Teutonic poetry presents itself, at a first view, as the complement of Homer. Here are to be found many of the things that are wanting at the beginning of Greek literary history. Here are single epic lays, or clusters of them, in every form. Here, in place of the two great poems, rounded and complete, there is the nebulous expanse of heroic tradition, the outline of an heroic cycle, together with a number of episodic poems taking their origin from one point or another of the cycle, according as the different parts of the story happen to catch the imagination of a poet. Instead of the Homeric scale of epic there are a number of brief epic tragedies, the plots of which are chosen from the multitude of stories current in tradition.

Among these shorter epic poems, if such they may be called, there are to be distinguished great varieties of procedure in regard to the amount of action represented in the poem.

There is one class of poem that represents a single action with some detail; there is another that represents a long and complex story in a summary and allusive way. The first kind may be called *episodic* in the sense that it takes up about the same quantity of story as might make an act in a play; or perhaps, with a little straining of the term, as much as might serve for one play in a trilogy.

The second kind is not episodic; it does not seem fitted for a place in a larger composition. It is a kind of short and summary epic, taking as large a province of history as the *Iliad* or the *Odyssey.*

Hildebrand, the *Fight at Finnesburh*, *Waldere*, *Byrhtnoth*, the *Winning of the Hammer*, *Thor's Fishing*, the *Death of the Niblungs* (in any of the Northern versions), the *Death of Ermanaric*, might all be fairly regarded as belonging to the first kind of story; while the *Lay of Weland* and the *Lay of Brynhild* cover a much larger extent of story, though not of actual space, than any of those.

It is not quite easy to find a common measure for these and for the Homeric poems. One can tell perhaps from Mr. Arnold's poem of *Sohrab and Rustum* how much is wanting to the *Lay of Hildebrand*, and on what scale the story of Hildebrand might have been told if it had been told in the Homeric instead of the archaic German manner. The story of Walter of Aquitaine in the Latin hexameters of *Waltharius* takes up 1456 lines. Although the author of this Latin poem is something short of Homer, "a little overparted" by the comparison, still his work is designed on the scale of classical epic, and gives approximately the right extent of the story in classical form. But while those stories are comparatively short, even in their most expanded forms, the story of Weland and the story of Helgi each contains as much as would suffice for the plot of an *Odyssey*, or more. The *Lay of Brynhild* is not an episodic poem of the vengeance and the passion of Brynhild, though that is the principal theme. It begins in a summary manner with Sigurd's coming to the house of the Niblungs, the wedding of Sigurd and Gudrun, the wooing of Brynhild for Gunnar; all these earlier matters are taken up and touched on before the story comes to the searchings of heart when the kings are persuaded to kill Sigurd. Then the death of Sigurd is told of, and the rest of the poem is filled with the tragedy of Brynhild and Gudrun; the future history of Gudrun is spoken of prophetically by Brynhild before she throws herself on the funeral pile. Plainly this cannot be considered in the same sense "episodic" as the poem of Thor's fishing for the Midgarth snake. The poems of Thor's fishing and the recovery of the hammer are distinctly fragments of a legendary cycle. The *Lay of Brynhild* makes an attempt to complete the whole Volsung story from beginning to end, while giving special importance to one particular incident of it,—the passion of Brynhild after the death of Sigurd. The poems of *Attila* and the *Lay of the Death of Ermanaric* are more restricted.

It remains true that the great story of the Niblung tragedy was never told at length in the poetical measure used for episodes of it, and for the summary form of the *Lay of Brynhild.* It should be remembered, however, that a poem of the scale of the *Nibelungenlied*, taking up the whole matter, must go as far beyond the Homeric limit as the *Lay of Brynhild* falls short of it. From one point of view the shorter episodic poems are more Homeric in their plots than either the summary epics which cover the whole ground, as the *Lay of Brynhild* attempts to cover it, or the longer works in prose that begin at the beginning and go on to the end, like the *Volsunga Saga.* The *Iliad* and the *Odyssey* are themselves episodic poems; neither of them has the reach of the *Nibelungenlied.* It should not be forgotten, either, that Aristotle found the *Iliad* and the *Odyssey* rather long. The Teutonic poems are not to be despised because they have a narrower orbit than the *Iliad.* Those among them that contain matter enough for a single tragedy, and there are few that have not as much as this in them, may be considered not to fall far short of the standard fixed by Aristotle for the right amount of action to be contained in an heroic poem. They are too hurried, they are wanting in the classical breadth and ease of narrative; but at any rate they are comprehensible, they observe an epic unity. They do not, like certain of the endless French poetical histories, remind one of the picture of incomprehensible bulk in Aristotle's *Poetics*, the animal 10,000 stadia long.

Thus, though it is natural at first to imagine that in the old Teutonic poetry one is possessed of such separate lays or ballads as might be the original materials of a larger epic, an epic of the Homeric scale, this impression will hardly remain long after a closer criticism of the workmanship of the poems. Very few of them correspond in the amount of their story to the episodes of the Homeric poems. Many of them contain in a short space the matter of stories more complicated, more tragical, than the story of Achilles. Most of them by their unity and self-consistency make it difficult to think of them as absorbed in a longer epic. This is the case not only with those that take in a whole history, like the *Lay of Brynhild*, but also with those whose plot is comparatively simple, like *Hildebrand* or *Waldere*. It is possible to think of the story of Walter and Hildegund as forming part of a larger story of the fortunes of the Huns. It has this subordinate place in the *Thidreks Saga*. But it is not easy to believe that in such a case it preserves its value. *Thidreks Saga* is not an epic, though it is made by an agglutination of ballads. In like manner the tragedy of *Hildebrand* gains by its isolation from the stories of the other chiefs, Theodoric and Odoacer. The stories of Walter and of Hildebrand, like the story of Hamlet the Dane, are too strong in themselves to form part of a larger composition, without detriment to its unity and harmony. They might be brought in allusively and in a subordinate way, like the story of Thebes and other stories in the *Iliad*; but that is not the same thing as making an epic poem out of separate lays. So that on all grounds the first impression of the Teutonic epic poetry has to be modified. If ever epic poetry was made by a conglomeration of ballads, it must have had other kinds of material than this. Some of the poems are episodic; others are rather to be described as abridgments of epic than as separate epic scenes. But neither in the one case nor in the other is there to be found the kind of poetry that is required by the hypothesis of composite epic. There are short epics that might conceivably have served as the framework, or the ground-plan, of a more elaborate work, containing, like the *Lay of Helgi* or the *Lay of Brynhild*, incidents enough and hints of character enough for a history fully worked out, as large as the Homeric poems. If it should be asked why there is so little evidence of any Teutonic attempt to weave together separate lays into an epic work, the answer might be, first, that the separate lays we know are too much separate and individual, too strong in themselves, to be satisfactorily cobbled into a more expansive fabric; and, secondly, that it has not yet been proved that epic poems can be made by process of cobbling. The need of a comprehensive epic of the Niblungs was not imperative. Neither was there any demand in Athens, in the time of Sophocles and Euripides, for a comprehensive work—a *Thebaid*, a *Roman de Thèbes*—to include the plots of all the tragedies of the house of Cadmus. It was not a poet, but a prose journeyman, who did this sort of work in the North, and it was not till the old school of poetry had passed away that the composite prose history of the Volsungs and Niblungs, of Sigmund and Sinfiotli, Sigurd, Brynhild, Gudrun, and Atli, was put together out of the old poems. The old lays, Northern and Western, whatever their value, have all strong individual characters of their own, and do not easily submit to be regarded as merely the unused materials, waiting for an epic composer who never was born.

III

EPIC AND BALLAD POETRY

THE ballads of a later age have many points of likeness to such poems as *Hildebrand*, *Finnesburh*, *Maldon*, and the poems of the Northern collection. The two orders of poetry are, however, not to be confounded. Their affinity indeed is clear. But the older poems in alliterative verse have a character not possessed by the ballads which followed them, and which often repeated the same stories in the later Middle Ages. Even the simplest of the older poems, which is the *Lay of Hildebrand*, is distinguished by evident signs of dignity from even the most ambitious of the rhyming ballads in any of the tongues. Its rhetoric is of a different order.

This is not a question of preferences, but of distinction of kinds. The claim of an epic or heroic rank for the older poems need not be forced into a denial of all the other excellences of the rhyming ballads.

Ballad, as the term is commonly used, implies a certain degree of simplicity, and an absence of high poetical ambition. Ballads are for the market-place and the "blind crowder," or for the rustic chorus that sings the ballad burden. The wonderful poetical beauty of some of the popular ballads of Scotland and

Denmark, not to speak of other lands, is a kind of beauty that is never attained by the great poetical artists; an unconscious grace. The ballads of the Scottish Border, from their first invention to the publication of the *Border Minstrelsy*, lie far away from the great streams of poetical inspiration. They have little or nothing to do with the triumphs of the poets; the "progress of poesy" leaves them untouched; they learn neither from Milton nor from Pope, but keep a life of their own that has its sources far remote in the past, in quite another tradition of art than that to which the great authors and their works belong.

The Teutonic epic poems, the Northern poems at any rate, are ballads in respect of their management of the plots. The scale of them is not to be distinguished from the scale of a ballad: the ballads have the same way of indicating and alluding to things and events without direct narrative, without continuity, going rapidly from critical point to point, in their survey of the fable.

But there is this great difference, that the style of the earlier epics is ambitious and self-conscious, an aristocratic and accomplished style. The ballads of *Clerk Saunders* or *Sir Patrick Spens* tell about things that have been generally forgotten, in the great houses of the country, by the great people who have other things to think about, and, if they take to literature, other models of style. The lay of the fight at Finnesburh, the lays of the death of Attila, were in their time the poems of the king's or the earl's hall; they were at the height of literary accomplishment in their generation, and their style displays the consciousness of rank. The ballads never had anything like the honour that was given to the older lays.

The difference between epic and ballad style comes out most obviously when, as frequently has happened, in Denmark, Iceland, and the Faroes, the poems of the old school have been translated from their epic verse into the "eights and sixes" or some other favourite measure of the common ballads. This has been the case, for instance, with the poem of Thor's Hammer, and the poem of the journey of Svipdag in search of Menglad. In other cases, as in that of the return of Helgi from the dead, it is less certain, though it is probable, that there is a direct relation between the two kinds of poetry, between the old Northern poem of Helgi and the Danish ballad of Sir Aage which has the same story to tell; but a comparison of the two styles, in a case like this, is none the less possible and justifiable.

The poems in the older form and diction, however remote they may be from modern fashions, assert themselves unmistakably to be of an aristocratic and not a popular tradition. The ballads have many things in common with the other poems, but they have lost the grand style, and the pride and solemnity of language. One thing they have retained almost invariably. Ballad poetry may be trusted to preserve the sense of the tragic situation. If some ballads are less strong than others in their rendering of a traditional story, their failure is not peculiar to that kind of composition. Not every ballad-singer, and not every tragic poet, has the same success in the development of his fable. As a rule, however, it holds good that the ballads are sound in their conception of a story; if some are constitutionally weak or unshapely, and others have suffered from the infirmity of reciters and transcribers, these accidents are not to be counted against the class of poetry to which they belong Yet, however well the ballads may give the story, they cannot give it with the power of epic; and that this power belongs to the older kind of verse, the verse of the *Lay of Brynhild*, may be proved with all the demonstration that this kind of argument allows. It is open to any one to say that the grand style is less attractive than the charm of the ballad burdens, that the airy music of the ballads is more appealing and more mysterious than all the eloquence of heroic poetry; but that does not touch the question. The rhetoric of the older poems merely claims to be acknowledged for what it is worth.

The Danish ballad of *Ungen Sveidal*, "Child Sveidal,"[1] does not spoil the ancient story which had been given in the older language and older verse of *Svipdag and Menglad*. But there are different ways of describing how the adventurer comes to the dark tower to rescue the unknown maiden. The ballad uses the common ballad forms, the common easy rhymes and assonances:—

> Out they cast their anchor
> All on the white sea sand,
> And who was that but the Child Sveidal
> Was first upon the land?
>
> His heart is sore with deadly pain
> For her that he never saw,
> His name is the Child Sveidal;
> So the story goes.

This sort of story need not be despised, and it is peculiarly valuable when it appears in the middle of one of the least refreshing seasons of literature, like this ballad in the age of the Lutheran Reformation in Denmark. In such an age and among theological tracts and controversies, the simple ballad measures may bring relief from oppression and desolation; and call for thanks to the Danish ladies by whose care this ballad and so many others were written

[1] Grundtvig, *Danmarks gamle Folkeviser*, No. 70. See above, p. 114.

down. But gratitude need not conceal the truth, that the style of the ballad is unlike the style of an heroic poem. The older poem from which *Child Sveidal* is derived may have left many poetical opportunities unemployed; it comes short in many things, and makes up for them by mythological irrelevances. But it is composed in a style of which it is impossible to mistake the gravity; it has all the advantage of established forms that have been tested and are able to bear the weight of the poetical matter. There is a vast difference between the simplicity of the ballad and the stately measure and rhetorical pomp of the original :—

> Svipdag is my name ; Sunbright was my Father's name
> The winds have driven me far, along cold ways ;
> No one can gainsay the word of Fate,
> Though it be spoken to his own destruction.

The difference is as great as the difference between the ballad of the *Marriage of Gawayne* and the same story as told in the *Canterbury Tales*; or the difference between Homer's way of describing the recovery of lifted cattle and the ballad of *Jamie Telfer of the Fair Dodheid.*

It happens fortunately that one of the Danish ballads, *Sivard og Brynild*, which tells of the death of Sigurd (*Danmarks gamle Folkeviser*, No. 3), is one of the best of the ballads, in all the virtues of that style, so that a comparison with the *Lay of Brynhild*, one of the best poems of the old collection, is not unfair to either of them.

The ballad of *Sivard*, like the *Lay of Brynhild*, includes much more than an episode; it is a complete tragic poem, indicating all the chief points of the story. The tragic idea is different from that of any of the other versions of the Volsung story, but quite as distinct and strong as any.

SIVARD

(O the King's Sons of Denmark!)

Sivard has a horse that is fleet, and he has stolen Brynild from the Mountain of Glass, all by the light of day. From the Mountain of Glass he has stolen proud Brynild, and given her to Hagen, his brother-in-arms. Brynild and Signild went to the river shore to wash their silken gowns. "Signild, my sister, where got you the golden rings on your hand?"—"The gold rings on my hand I got from Sivard, my own true love; they are his pledge of troth: and you are given to Hagen." When Brynild heard this she went into the upper room and lay there sick: there she lay sick and Hagen came to her. "Tell me, maiden Brynild, my own true love, what is there in the world to heal you; tell me, and I will bring it, though it cost all the world's red gold." —"Nothing in the world you can bring me, unless you bring me, into my hands, the head of Sivard."—"And how shall I bring to your hands the head of Sivard? There is not the sword in all the world that will bite upon him: no sword but his own, and that I cannot get."— "Go to his room, and bid him lend you his sword, for his honour, and say, 'I have vowed an adventure for the sake of my true love.' When first he hands you over his sword, I pray you remember me, in the Lord God's name." It is Hagen that has swept his mantle round him, and goes into the upper room to Sivard. "Here you sit, Sivard, my foster-brother; will you lend me your good sword for your honour? for I have vowed a vow for the sake of my love."— "And if I lend you my good sword Adelbring, you will never come in battle where it will fail you. My good sword Adelbring you may have, indeed, but keep you well from the tears of blood that are under the hilt, keep you from the tears of blood that are so red.[1] If they run down upon your fingers, it will be your death."

Hagen got the sword, and it was his own sworn brother he slew there in the room. He took up the bloody head under his cloak of furs and brought it to proud Brynild. "Here you have the head for which you sought; for the sake of you I have slain my brother to my undoing."—"Take away the head and let me not see it; nor will I pledge you my troth to make you glad."—"Never will I pledge troth to you, and nought is the gladness; for the sake of you I have slain my brother; sorrow is on me, sore and great." It was Hagen drew his sword and took the proud Brynild and hewed her asunder. He set the sword against a stone, and the point was deadly in the King's son's heart. He set the sword in the black earth, and the point was death in the King's son's heart. Ill was the day that maiden was born. For her were spilt the lives of two King's sons. (*O the King's Sons of Denmark!*)

This is a consistent tragic story, and it is well told. It has the peculiar virtue of the ballad, to make things impressive by the sudden manner in which they are spoken of and passed by; in this abrupt mode of narrative the ballads, as has been noted already, are not much different from the earlier poems. The *Lay of Brynhild* is not much more diffuse than the ballad of *Sivard* in what relates to the slaying of the hero. Both are alike distinct from the method of Homer; compared with Homer both the lays and the ballads are hurried in their action, over-emphatic, cramped in a narrow space. But when the style and temper are considered, apart from the incidents of the story, then it will appear that the lay belongs to a totally different order of literature

[1] Compare the warning of Angantyr to Hervor when he gives her the sword Tyrfing—"Keep the sword sheathed, the slayer of Hialmar; touch not the edges, there is venom upon them"—and the magic sword Skofnung in *Kormaks Saga*.

from the ballad. The ballad tells of things dimly discerned by the poet; king's sons and daughters are no more to him than they are to the story-tellers of the market-place—forms of a shadowy grandeur, different from ordinary people, swayed by strange motives, not irrationally, nor altogether in a way beyond the calculation of simple audiences, yet in ways for which there is no adequate mode of explanation known to the reciter. The ballad keeps instinctively a right outline for its tragic story, but to develop the characters is beyond its power. In the epic *Lay of Brynhild*, on the other hand, the poet is concerned with passions which he feels himself able to comprehend and to set forth dramatically; so that, while the story of the poem is not very much larger in scale than that of the ballad, the dramatic speeches are greatly elaborated. Brynhild in the lay is not a mere tragic symbol, as in the ballad, but a tragic character. The ballad has the seed of tragedy in it, but in the lay the seed has sprung up in the dramatic eloquence of Brynhild's utterances before her death. The ballad is tragical, but in an abstract manner. The plot of the slighted woman and her vengeance, with the remorse of Hagen, is all true, and not exaggerated in motive. But while the motives are appreciated, it is not in the power of the poet to develop the exposition of them, to make them dramatically characteristic, as well as right in their general nature. It is just this dramatic ideal which is the ambition and inspiration of the other poet; the character of Brynhild has taken possession of his imagination, and requires to be expressed in characteristic speech. A whole poetical world is open to the poet of Brynhild, and to the other poets of the Northern heroic cycle. They have taken the first day's journey into the empire of Homer and Shakespeare; the forms of poetry that they employ are varied and developed by them so as to express as fully as possible the poetical conception of different individual characters. It is not easy to leave them without the impression that their poetry was capable of infinitely greater progress in this direction; that some at least of the poets of the North were "bearers of the torch" in their generation, not less than the poets of Provence or France who came after them and led the imagination of Christendom into another way. That is, it is possible to think of the poets of Sigurd and Brynhild as holding among the Northern nations of the tenth or eleventh century the place that is held in every generation by some set of authors who, for the time, are at the head of intellectual and literary adventure, who hold authority, from Odin or the Muses, to teach their contemporaries one particular kind of song, till the time comes when their vogue is exhausted, and they are succeeded by other masters and other schools. This commission has been held by various kinds of author since the beginning of history, and manifold are the lessons that have been recommended to the world by their authority; now epic, now courtly and idealist lyric, romantic drama, pedantic tragedy, funeral orations, analytical novels. They are not all amusing, and not all their prices are more than the rate of an old song. But they all have a value as trophies, as monuments of what was most important in their time, of the things in which the generations, wise and foolish, have put their trust and their whole soul. The ballads have not this kind of importance; the ballad poets are remote from the lists where the great champions overthrow one another, where poet takes the crown from poet. The ballads, by their very nature, are secluded and apart from the great literary enterprises; it is the beauty of them that they are exempt from the proclamations and the arguments, the shouting and the tumult, the dust and heat, that accompany the great literary triumphs and make epochs for the historians, as in the day of *Cléopatre*, or the day of *Hernani.* The ballad has no weight of responsibility upon it; it does not carry the intellectual light of its century; its authors are easily satisfied. In the various examples of the Teutonic alliterative poetry there is recognisable the effort and anxiety of poets who are not content with old forms, who have a poetical vocation to go on and find out new forms, who are on the search for the "one grace above the rest," by which all the chief poets are led. The remains of this poetry are so many experiments, which, in whatever respects they may have failed, yet show the work and energy of authors who are proud of their art, as well as the dignity of men who are familiar with greatness and great actions: in both which respects they differ from the ballad poets. The spell of the popular story, the popular ballad, is not quite the same as theirs. Theirs is more commanding; they are nearer to the strenuous life of the world than are the simple people who remember, over their fires of peat, the ancient stories of the wanderings of kings' sons. They have outgrown the stage of life for which the fables and old wives' tales are all-sufficient; they have begun to make a difference between fable and characters; they have entered on a way by which the highest poetical victories are attainable. The poetry of the old lays of the Volsungs, as compared with popular ballads and tales, is "weighty and philosophical"—full of the results of reflection on character. Nor have they with all this lost the inexplicable magic of popular poetry, as the poems of Helgi and Sigrun, and of the daughter of Angantyr, and others, may easily prove.

IV

THE STYLE OF THE POEMS

THE style of the poems, in what concerns their verse and diction, is not less distinctly noble than their spirit and temper. The alliterative verse, wherever it is found, declares itself as belonging to an elaborate poetical tradition. The alliterative line is rhetorically capable of a great amount of emphasis; it lends itself as readily as the "drumming decasyllabon" of the Elizabethan style to pompous declamation. Parallelism of phrases, the favourite rhetorical device, especially with the old English poets, is incompatible with tenuity of style; while the weight of the verse, as a rule, prevents the richness of phrasing from becoming too extravagant and frivolous.[1]

The style of alliterative verse is not monotonous. Without reckoning the forms that deviate from the common epic measure, such as the Northern lyrical staves, there may be found in it as many varieties of style as in English blank verse from the days of *Gorboduc* onward.

In its oldest common form it may be supposed that the verse was not distinctly epic or lyric; lyric rather than epic, lyric with such amount of epic as is proper for psalms of triumph, or for the praise of

[1] Examples in Appendix, Note A.

a king, the kind of verse that might be used for any sort of *carmina*, such as for marking authorship and ownership on a sword or a horn, for epitaphs or spells, or for vituperative epigrams.

In England and the Continent the verse was early adapted for continuous history. The lyrical and gnomic usages were not abandoned. The poems of *Widsith* and *Deor's Lament* show how the allusive and lyrical manner of referring to heroic legend was kept up in England. The general tendency, however, seems to have favoured a different kind of poetry. The common form of old English verse is fitted for narrative. The ideal of the poets is one that would have the sense "variously drawn out from one verse to another." When the verse is lyrical in tone, as in the *Dream of the Rood*, or the *Wanderer*, the lyrical passion is commonly that of mourning or regret, and the expression is elegiac and diffuse, not abrupt or varied. The verse, whether narrative or elegiac, runs in rhythmical periods; the sense is not "concluded in the couplet." The lines are mortised into one another; by preference, the sentences begin in the middle of a line. The parallelism of the old poetry, and its wealth of paraphrase, encourage deliberation in the sentences, though they are often interrupted by a short sentence, generally introduced to point a moral.

The old Norse poetry, with many likenesses to the old English, had a different taste in rhetorical syntax. Instead of the long-drawn phrases of the English poetry, and an arrangement of sentences by which the metrical limits of the line were generally disguised, the Norse alliterative poetry adopted a mode of speech that allowed the line to ring out clearly, and gave full force to the natural emphasis of the rhythm.

These two opposite rhetorical tendencies are illustrated also by the several variations upon the common rhythm that found favour in one region and the other. Where an English or a German alliterative poet wishes to vary from the common metre, he uses the lengthened line, an expansion of the simple line, which, from its volume, is less suitable for pointed expression, and more capable of pathos or solemnity, than the ordinary form of verse. The long line of the Saxon and English poets is not used in the Norse poetry; there the favourite verse, where the ordinary narrative line is discarded, is in the form of gnomic couplets, in which, as in the classical elegiac measure, a full line is succeeded by a truncated or broken rhythm, and with the same effect of clinching the meaning of the first line as is commonly given by the Greek or Latin pentameter. Of this favourite Northern measure there are only one or two casual and sporadic instances in English poetry; in the short dramatic lyric of the *Exeter Book*, interpreted so ingeniously by Mr. Bradley and Mr. Gollancz, and in the gnomic verses of the same collection.

This difference of taste goes very far to explain the difference between English and Norse epic; to appreciate the difference of style is to understand the history of the early poetry. It was natural that the more equable form of the English and the Continental German narrative poetry should prove itself fit for extended and continuous epic narrative; it was inevitable that the Norse intolerance of tame expression, and of everything unimpassioned or unemphatic, should prevent the growth of any of the larger and slower kinds of poetry.

The triumphs of alliterative poetry in the first or English kind are the long swelling passages of tragic monologue, of which the greatest is in the

Saxon *Genesis*,—the speech of Satan after the fall from heaven. The best of the Northern poetry is all but lyrical; the poem of the Sibyl, the poems of Sigrun, Gudrun, Hervor.

The nature of the two forms of poetry is revealed in their respective manners of going wrong. The decline of the old English poetry is shown by an increase of diffuseness and insipidity. The old Norse poetry was attacked by an evil of a different sort, the malady of false wit and over-decoration. The English poetry, when it loses strength and self-control, is prone to monotonous lamentation; the Norse poetry is tempted to overload itself with conceits.

In the one there is excess of sentiment, in the other the contrary vice of frigidity, and a premeditated and ostentatious use of figurative expressions.

The poem of *Beowulf* has known the insidious approach and temptation of diffuse poetic melancholy. The Northern poems are corrupted by the vanity of metaphor. To evade the right term for everything has been the aim of many poetic schools; it has seldom been attained more effectually than in the poetry of the Norwegian tongue.

Periphrastic epithets are part of the original and common stock of the Teutonic poetry. They form a large part of the vocabulary of common phrases which bear witness to the affinity existing among the remains of this poetry in all the dialects.[1]

But this common device was differently applied in the end, by the two literatures, English and Icelandic, in which the old forms of verse held their

[1] Compare the index to Sievers's edition of the *Hêliand* for illustrations of this community of poetical diction in old Saxon, English, Norse, and High German; and J. Grimm, *Andreas und Elene* (1840), pp. xxv.-xliv.

ground longest against the rhyming forms. The tendency in England was to make use of the well-worn epithets, to ply the *Gradus*: the duller kind of Anglo-Saxon poetry is put together as Latin verses are made in school,—an old-fashioned metaphor is all the more esteemed for its age. The poets, and presumably their hearers, are best content with familiar phrases. In Iceland, on the other hand, there was an impatience of the old vocabulary, and a curiosity and search for new figures, that in the complexity and absurdity of its results is not approached by any school of "false wit" in the whole range of literature.

Already in the older forms of Northern poetry it is plain that there is a tendency to lyrical emphasis which is unfavourable to the chances of long narrative in verse. Very early, also, there are symptoms of the familiar literary plague, the corruption of metaphor. Both these tendencies have for their result the new school of poetry peculiar to the North and the courts of the Northern kings and earls,—the Court poetry, or poetry of the Scalds, which in its rise and progress involved the failure of true epic. The German and English epic failed by exhaustion in the competition with Latin and Romance literature, though not without something to boast of before it went under. The Northern epic failed, because of the premature development of lyrical forms, first of all within itself, and then in the independent and rival modes of the Scaldic poetry.

The Scaldic poetry, though later in kind than the poems of *Codex Regius*, is at least as old as the tenth century;[1] the latest of the epic poems, *Atlamál* (the Greenland poem of Attila), and others,

[1] See *Bidrag til den ældste Skaldedigtnings Historie*, by Dr Sophus Bugge (1894).

show marks of the influence of Court poetry, and are considerably later in date than the earliest of the Scalds.

The Court poetry is lyric, not epic. The aim of the Court poets was not the narrative or the dramatic presentation of the greater heroic legends; it was the elaborate decoration of commonplace themes, such as the praise of a king, by every possible artifice of rhyme and alliteration, of hard and exact construction of verse, and, above all, of far-sought metaphorical allusions. In this kind of work, in the praise of kings alive or dead, the poet was compelled to betake himself to mythology and mythical history, like the learned poets of other nations with their mythology of Olympus. In the mythology of Asgard were contained the stores of precious names and epithets by means of which the poems might be made to glitter and blaze.[1] It was for the sake of poets like these that Snorri wrote his *Edda*, and explained the mythical references available for the modern poetry of his time, though fortunately his spirit and talent were not limited to this didactic end, nor to the pedantries and deadly brilliance of fashionable verse. By the time of Snorri the older kind of poetry had become very much what Chaucer was to the Elizabethan sonneteers, or Spenser to the contemporaries of Pope. It was regarded with some amount of honour, and some condescension, but it had ceased to be the right kind of poetry for a "courtly maker."

The Northern poetry appears to have run through some of the same stages as the poetry of Greece, though with insufficient results in most of them. The epic poetry is incomplete, with all its nobility.

[1] Compare *C.P.B.*, ii. 447, Excursus on the Figures and Metaphors of old Northern Poetry.

The best things of the old poetry are dramatic—lyrical monologues, like the song of the Sibyl, and Gudrun's story to Theodoric, or dialogues like those of Helgi and Sigrun, Hervor and Angantyr. Before any adequate large rendering had been accorded to those tragic histories, the Northern poetry, in its impatience of length, had discovered the idyllic mode of expression and the dramatic monologue, in which there was no excuse for weakness and tameness, and, on the contrary, great temptation to excess in emphatic and figurative language. Instead of taking a larger scene and a more complex and longer story, the poets seem to have been drawn more and more to cut short the story and to intensify the lyrical passion of their dialogue or monologue. Almost as if they had known the horror of infinite flatness that is all about the literature of the Middle Ages, as if there had fallen upon them, in that Aleïan plain, the shadow of the enormous beast out of Aristotle's *Poetics*, they chose to renounce all superfluity, and throw away the make-shift wedges and supports by which an epic is held up. In this way they did great things, and *Volospá* (the *Sibyl's Prophecy*) is their reward. To write out in full the story of the Volsungs and Niblungs was left to the prose compilers of the *Volsunga Saga*, and to the Austrian poet of the *Nibelungenlied.*

The *Volospá* is as far removed from the courtly odes and their manner and ingenuity as the *Marriage Hymn* of Catullus from the *Coma Berenices.* The *Volospá*, however, has this in common with the mechanical odes, that equally with these it stands apart from epic, that equally with these it fuses epic material into an alien form. The sublimity of this great poem of the *Doom* is not like the majesty or strength of epic. The voice is not the voice of a teller of stories. And it is here, not in true epic verse, that the Northern poetry attains its height.

It is no ignoble form of poetry that is represented by the *Sibyl's Song* and the *Lament of Gudrun.* But it was not enough for the ambition of the poets. They preferred the composition of correct and elaborate poems in honour of great men, with much expenditure of mythology and without passion;[1] one of the forms of poetry which may be truly said to leave nothing to be desired, the most artificial and mechanical poetry in the world, except possibly the closely-related kinds in the traditional elaborate verse of Ireland or of Wales.

It was still possible to use this modern and difficult rhetoric, occasionally, for subjects like those of the freer epic; to choose a subject from heroic tradition and render it in the fashionable style. The *Death-Song of Ragnar Lodbrok*[2] is the chief of those secondary dramatic idylls. It is marked off by difference of verse, for one thing, from the *Hamðismál* and the *Atlakviða*; and, besides this, it has the characteristic of imitative and conventional heroic literature—the unpersuasive and unconvincing force of the heroic romance, the rhetoric of Almanzor. The end of the poem is fine, but it does not ring quite true:—

> The gods will welcome me; there is nothing to bewail in death. I am ready to go; they are calling me home, the maidens whom Odin has sent to call me. With gladness will I drink the ale, set high among the gods. The hours of life are gone over; laughing will I die.

It is not like the end of the sons of Gudrun; it is not of the same kind as the last words of Sorli,

[1] These may be found in the second volume of the *Corpus Poeticum Boreale.* [2] *C.P.B.*, ii. 339.

which are simpler, and infinitely more imaginative and true :—

> We have fought ; if we die to-day, if we die to-morrow, there is little to choose. No man may speak when once the Fates have spoken (*Hamðismál*, s.f.).

It is natural that the *Song of Ragnar Lodbrok* should be appreciated by modern authors. It is one of the documents responsible for the conventional Valkyria and Valhalla of the Romantic School, and for other stage properties, no longer new. The poem itself is in spirit rather more nearly related to the work of Tegnér or Oehlenschläger than to the *Volospá*. It is a secondary and literary version, a "romantic" version of ideas and images belonging to a past time, and studied by an antiquarian poet with an eye for historical subjects.[1]

The progress of epic was not at an end in the rise of the new Court poetry that sounded sweeter in the ears of mortals than the old poems of *Sigurd* and *Brynhild*. The conceits and the hard correctness of the Scalds did not satisfy all the curiosity or the imaginative appetite of their patrons. There still remained a desire for epic, or at least for a larger and freer kind of historical discourse. This was satisfied by the prose histories of the great men of Iceland, of the kings of Norway and the lords of the Isles; histories the nearest to true epic of all that have ever been spoken without verse. That the chief of all the masters of this art should have been Snorri Sturluson, the exponent and practitioner of the mystery of the Court poets, is among the pleasantest of historical paradoxes.

The development of the Court poetry to all

[1] Translated in Percy's *Runic Poetry* (1763), p. 27, and often since.

extremes of "false wit," and of glaring pretence and artificiality of style, makes the contrast all the more vivid between its brocaded stiffness and the ease and freedom of the Sagas. But even apart from the Court poetry, it is clear that there was little chance for any development of the Northern heroic poetry into an Homeric fulness of detail. In the Norse poetry, as in Greek, the primitive forms of heroic dirges or hymns give place to narrative poetry; and that again is succeeded by a new kind of lyric, in which the ancient themes of the *Lament* and the *Song of Praise* are adorned with the new ideas and the new diction of poets who have come to study novelty, and have entered, though with far other arms and accoutrements, on the same course as the Greek lyric authors of dithyrambs and panegyrical odes. In this progress of poetry from the unknown older songs, like those of which Tacitus speaks, to the epic form as it is preserved in the "Elder Edda," and from the epic form to the lyrical form of the Scalds, the second stage is incomplete; the epic form is uncertain and half-developed. The rise of the Court poetry is the most obvious explanation of this failure. The Court poetry, with all its faults, is a completed form which had its day of glory, and even rather more than its share of good fortune. It is the characteristic and successful kind of poetry in Iceland and Norway, just as other kinds of elaborate lyric were cultivated, to the depreciation of epic, in Provence and in Italy. It was to the Court poet that the prizes were given; the epic form was put out of favour, generations before the fragments of it were gathered together and preserved by the collector from whose books they have descended to the extant manuscripts and the editions of the "Elder Edda."

But at the same time it may be represented that

the Court poetry was as much effect as cause of the depreciation of epic. The lyrical strain declared itself in the Northern epic poetry too strongly for any such epic work as either *Beowulf* or the *Hêliand*. The bent was given too early, and there was no recovery possible. The Court poetry, in its rhetorical brilliance and its allusive phrases, as well as in the hardness and correctness of its verse, is carrying out to completion certain tastes and principles whose influence is manifest throughout the other orders of old Northern poetry; and there is no need to go to the Court poetry to explain the difference between the history of Northern and of English alliterative verse, though it is by means of the Court poetry that this difference may be brought into the strongest light. The contrast between the English liking for continuous discourse and the Norse liking for abrupt emphasis is already to be discerned in the oldest literary documents of the two nations.

V

THE PROGRESS OF EPIC

VARIOUS RENDERINGS OF THE SAME STORY

Due (1) to accidents of tradition and impersonal causes:
(2) to calculation and selection of motives by the poets, and intentional modification of traditional matter.

BEOWULF, as the poem stands, is quite a different sort of thing from the poems in the Copenhagen manuscript. It is given out by its scribes in all the glory of a large poem, handsomely furnished with a prelude, a conclusion, and divisions into several books. It has the look of a substantial epic poem. It was evidently regarded as something considerable, as a work of eminent virtue and respectability. The Northern poems, treasured and highly valued as they evidently were, belong to a different fashion. In the *Beowulf* of the existing manuscript the fluctuation and variation of the older epic tradition has been controlled by editors who have done their best to establish a text of the poem. The book has an appearance of authority. There is little of this in the Icelandic manuscript. The Northern poems have evidently been taken as they were found. Imperfections of tradition, which in *Beowulf* would have been glossed over by an editorial process, are here left staring at the reader. The English poem pretends to be a literary work of importance—a book, in short; while the Icelandic verses are plainly gathered from all quarters, and in such a condition as to defy the best intentions of the editor, who did his best to understand what he heard, but had no consistent policy of improvement or alteration, to correct the accidental errors and discrepancies of the oral communications.

Further, and apart from the accidents of this particular book, there is in the poems, even when they are best preserved, a character of fluctuation and uncertainty, belonging to an older and less literary fashion of poetry than that of *Beowulf*.

Beowulf has been regarded by some as a composite epic poem made out of older and shorter poems. *Codex Regius* shows that this hypothesis is dealing with an undoubted *vera causa* when it talks of short lays on heroic subjects, and of the variations of treatment to be found in different lays on one and the same theme, and of the possibilities of contamination.

Thus, in considering the story of Beowulf's descent under water, and the difficulties and contradictions of that story as it stands, Ten Brink has been led to suppose that the present text is made up of two independent versions, run together by an editor in a hazardous way without regard to the differences in points of detail, which still remain to the annoyance of the careful reader.

There is no great risk in the assumption that there were different versions of the fight with Grendel's mother, which may have been carelessly put together into one version in spite of their contradictions. In the *Codex Regius* there are three different versions of the death of the Niblungs, the

Atlakviða, *Atlamál*, and the *Lament of Oddrun*. The *Lament of Oddrun* is vitally different from the other two poems, and these differ from one another, with regard to the motive of Atli's feud with Gunnar. It is possible for the human mind to imagine an editor, a literary man, capable of blending the poems in order to make a larger book. This would be something like the process which Ten Brink has suspected in the composition of this part of *Beowulf*. It is one thing, however, to detect the possibility of such misdemeanours; and quite another thing to suppose that it is by methods such as these that the bulk of the larger epic is swollen beyond the size of common lays or ballads. It is impossible, at any rate, by any reduction or analysis of *Beowulf*, to get rid of its stateliness of narrative; it would be impossible by any fusion or aggregation of the Eddic lays to get rid of their essential brevity. No accumulation of lays can alter the style from its trick of detached and abrupt suggestions to the slower and more equable mode.

That there was a growth of epic among the Teutonic nations is what is proved by all the documents. This growth was of the same general kind as the progress of any of the great forms of literature —the Drama, the Novel. Successive generations of men, speaking the same or similar forms of language, made poetical experiments in a common subject-manner, trying different ways of putting things, and changing their forms of poetry according to local and personal variations of taste; so that the same story might be told over and over again, in different times, with different circumstances.

In one region the taste might be all for compression, for increase of the tension, for suppression of the tamer intervals in the story. In another it might run to greater length and ease, and favour a gradual explication of the plot.

The "Elder Edda" shows that contamination was possible. It shows that there might be frequent independent variations on the same theme, and that, apart from any editorial work, these versions might occasionally be shuffled and jumbled by mere accidents of recollection.

Thus there is nothing contrary to the evidence in the theory that a redactor of *Beowulf* may have had before him different versions of different parts of the poem, corresponding to one another, more or less, as *Atlamál* corresponds to the *Atlakviða*. This hypothesis, however, does not account for the difference in form between the English and the Northern poems. No handling of the *Atlamál* or the *Atlakviða* could produce anything like the appearance of *Beowulf*. The contaminating editor may be useful as an hypothesis in certain particular cases. But the heroic poetry got on very well without him, generally speaking. It grew by a free and natural growth into a variety of forms, through the ambitions and experiments of poets.

Variety is evident in the poems that lie outside the Northern group; *Finnesburh* is of a different order from *Waldere*. It is in the Northern collection, however, that the variety is most evident. There the independent versions of the same story are brought together, side by side. The experiments of the old school are ranged there; and the fact that experiments were made, that the old school was not satisfied with its conventions, is perhaps the most legitimate inference, and one of the most significant, to be made by a reader of the poems.

Variations on similar themes are found in all popular poetry; here again the poems of the *Edda* present themselves as akin to ballads. Here again they are distinguished from ballads by their greater degree of ambition and self-consciousness. For it will not do to dismiss the Northern poems on the Volsung story as a mere set of popular variations on common themes. The more carefully they are examined, the less will be the part assigned to chance and imperfect recollection in producing the variety of the poems. The variation, where there are different presentations of the same subject, is not produced by accident or the casual and faulty repetition of a conventional type of poem, but by a poetical ambition for new forms. *Codex Regius* is an imperfect monument of a time of poetical energy in which old forms were displaced by new, and old subjects refashioned by successive poets. As in the Athenian or the English drama the story of Oedipus or of Lear might be taken up by one playwright after another, so in the North the Northern stories were made to pass through changes in the minds of different poets.

The analogy to the Greek and the English drama need not be forced. Without any straining of comparisons, it may be argued that the relation of the *Atlamál* and *Atlakviða* is like the relation of Euripides to Aeschylus, and not so much like the variations of ballad tradition, in this respect, that the *Atlamál* is a careful, deliberate, and somewhat conceited attempt to do better in a new way what has been done before by an older poet. The idylls of the heroines, Brynhild, Gudrun, Oddrun, are not random and unskilled variations; they are considerate and studied poems, expressing new conceptions and imaginations.

It is true that this poetry is still, in many respects, in the condition of popular poetry and popular traditional stories. The difference of plot in some versions of the same subject appears to be due to the ordinary causes that produce the variants of popular tales,—defective memory, accidental loss of one point in the story, and change of emphasis in another. To causes such as these, to the common impersonal accidents of tradition, may perhaps be referred one of the strangest of all the alterations in the bearing of a story—the variation of plot in the tradition of the Niblungs.

In the "Elder Edda" the death of the Niblungs is laid to the charge of Attila; their sister Gudrun does her best to save them; when she fails in this, she takes vengeance for them on her husband.

In the German tradition, as in the version known to Saxo, in the *Nibelungenlied*, in the Danish ballad of *Grimild's Revenge* (which is borrowed from the German), the lines are laid quite differently. There it is their sister who brings about the death of the kings; it is the wife of Sigfred, of Sigfred whom they have killed, that exacts vengeance from her brothers Gunther and Hagene. Attila is here put aside. Gudrun's slaughter of her children is unrecorded; there is no motive for it when all her anger is turned against her brothers. This shifting of the centre of a story is not easy to explain. But, whatever the explanation may be, it seems probable that it lies somewhere within the range of popular tradition, that the change is due to some of the common causes of the transformation of stories, and not to a definite and calculated poetical modification. The tragical complications are so many in the story of the Niblungs that there could not fail to be variations in the traditional interpretation of motives, even without the assistance of the poets and their new readings of character.

In some of the literary documents there may be found two kinds of variation from an original form of story,—variation due to those popular and indefinite causes, the variation of failing memory, on the one hand; and on the other, variation due to the ambition or conceit of an author with ideas of his own.

A comparison of the *Atlakviða*, the *Atlamál*, and the *Lamentation of Oddrun* may at first suggest that we have here to deal with just such variants as are common wherever stories are handed on by oral tradition. Further consideration will more and more reduce the part allotted to oral maltreatment, and increase the part of intentional and artistic modification, in the variations of story to be found in these poems.

All three poems are agreed in their ignorance of the variation which makes the wife of Sigfred into the avenger of his death. In all three it is Attila who brings about the death of the brothers of Gudrun.

It seems to have been a constant part of the traditional story, as known to the authors of these three poems, that Attila, when he had the brothers of Gudrun in his power, gave order to cut out the heart of Hogni, and thereafter to throw Gunnar into the serpents' den.

The *Atlakviða* presents an intelligible explanation of this; the other two poems leave this part of the action rather vague.

In the *Atlakviða* the motive of Attila's original hatred is left at first unexplained, but comes out in the circumstances of the death of the Niblungs. When the Burgundian kings are seized and bound, they are called upon to buy themselves off with gold. It is understood in Gunnar's reply, that the gold of the Niblung treasure is what is sought for.

He asks that the heart of Hogni may be brought to him. They bring him, instead, the heart of Hialli, which Gunnar detects at once as the heart of a coward. Then at last the heart of Hogni is cut out and brought to Gunnar; and then he defies the Huns, and keeps his secret.

Now is the hoard of the Niblungs all in my keeping alone, for Hogni is dead: there was doubt while we two lived, but now there is doubt no more. Rhine shall bear rule over the gold of jealousy, the eager river over the Niblung's heritage; the goodly rings shall gleam in the whirling water, they shall not pass to the children of the Huns.

Gunnar was thrown among the snakes, and there he harped upon his harp before his death came on him. The end of Gunnar is not told explicitly; the story goes on to the vengeance of Gudrun.

In the *Oddrúnargrátr* there is another motive for Attila's enmity to Gunnar: not the gold of the Niblungs, but the love that was between Gunnar and Oddrun (Oddrun was the sister of Attila and Brynhild). The death of Brynhild is alluded to, but that is not the chief motive. The gold of the Niblungs is not mentioned. Still, however, the death of Hogni precedes the death of Gunnar,—"They cut out the heart of Hogni, and his brother they set in the serpents' close." Gunnar played upon his harp among the serpents, and for a long time escaped them; but the old serpent came out at last and crawled to his heart. It is implied that the sound of his music is a charm for the serpents; but another motive is given by Oddrun, as she tells the story: Gunnar played on his harp for Oddrun, to be heard by her, so that she could come to help him. But she came too late.

It might be inferred from this poem that the original story of the death of Hogni has been imperfectly recollected by the poet who touches lightly on it and gives no explanation here. It is fairer to suppose that it was passed over because it was irrelevant. The poet had chosen for his idyll the love of Gunnar and Oddrun, a part of the story which is elsewhere referred to among these poems, namely in the *Long Lay of Brynhild* (l. 58). By his choice of this, and his rendering of it in dramatic monologue, he debarred himself from any emphatic use of the motive for Hogni's death. It cannot be inferred from his explanation of Gunnar's harp-playing that the common explanation was unknown to him. On the contrary, it is implied here, just as much as in *Atlakviða*, that the serpents are kept from him by the music, until the old sleepless one gives him his death. But the poet, while he keeps this incident of the traditional version, is not particularly interested in it, except as it affords him a new occasion to return to his main theme of the love story. Gunnar's music is a message to Oddrun. This is an imaginative and dramatic adaptation of old material, not a mere lapse of memory, not a mere loss of the traditional bearings of the story.

The third of these poems, the *Atlamál*, is in some respects the most remarkable of them all. In its plot it has more than the others, at the first reading, the appearance of a faulty recollection; for, while it makes a good deal of play with the circumstances of the death of Hogni, it misses, or appears to miss, the point of the story; the motive of Gunnar, which is evident and satisfactory in the *Atlakviða*, is here suppressed or dropped. The gold of the Niblungs is not in the story at all; the motive of Attila appears to be anger at the death of his sister Brynhild,

Gunnar's wife, but his motive is not much dwelt on. It is as if the author had forgotten the run of events, like a blundering minstrel.

On the other hand, the poem in its style is further from all the manners of popular poetry, more affected and rhetorical, than any of the other pieces in the book. It is written in the *málaháttr*, a variety of the common epic measure, with a monotonous cadence; the sort of measure that commends itself to an ambitious and rhetorical poet with a fancy for correctness and regularity. The poem has its origin in an admiration for the character of Gudrun, and a desire to bring out more fully than in the older poems the tragic thoughts and passion of the heroine. Gudrun's anxiety for her brothers' safety, and her warning message to them not to come to the Court of the Huns, had been part of the old story. In the *Atlakviða* she sends them a token, a ring with a wolf's hair twisted round it, which is noticed by Hogni but not accepted by Gunnar. In the *Atlamál* something more is made of this; her message here is written in runes, and these are falsified on the way by Attila's messenger, so that the warning is at first unread. But the confusion of the runes is detected by the wife of Hogni, and so the story opens with suspense and forebodings of the doom. The death of Hogni and Gunnar is explained in a new way, and always with the passion of Gudrun as the chief theme. In this story the fight of the Niblungs and the Huns is begun outside the doors of the hall. Gudrun hears the alarm and rushes out with a welcome to her brothers,—"that was their last greeting,"—and a cry of lamentation over their neglect of her runes. Then she tries to make peace, and when she fails in that, takes up a sword and fights for her brothers. It is out of rage and spite against Gudrun, and in order to tame her spirit, that Attila has the heart of Hogni cut out of him, and sends Gunnar to the serpents.

All this change in the story is the result of meditation and not of forgetfulness. Right or wrong, the poet has devised his story in his own way, and his motives are easily discovered. He felt that the vengeance of Gudrun required to be more carefully and fully explained. Her traditional character was not quite consistent with the horrors of her revenge. In the *Atlamál* the character of Gudrun is so conceived as to explain her revenge,—the killing of her children follows close upon her fury in the battle, and the cruelty of Attila is here a direct challenge to Gudrun, not, as in the *Atlakviða*, a mere incident in Attila's search for the Niblung treasure. The cruelty of the death of Hogni in the *Atlakviða* is purely a matter of business; it is not of Attila's choosing, and apparently he favours the attempt to save Hogni by the sacrifice of Hialli the feeble man. In the *Atlamál* it is to save Hogni from Attila that Hialli the cook is chased into a corner and held under the knife. This comic interlude is one of the liveliest passages of the poem. It serves to increase the strength of Hogni. Hogni begs them to let the creature go,—"Why should we have to put up with his squalling?" It may be observed that in this way the poet gets out of a difficulty. It is not in his design to have the coward's heart offered to Gunnar; he has dropped that part of the story entirely. Gunnar is not asked to give up the treasure, and has no reason to protect his secret by asking for the death of his brother; and there would be no point in keeping the incident for the benefit of Attila. That Gunnar should first detect the imposture, and should then recognise the heart of his brother, is a fine piece of heroic imagination of a primitive kind.

It would have been wholly inept and spiritless to transfer this from Gunnar to Attila. The poet of *Atlamál* shows that he understands what he is about. The more his work is scrutinised, the more evident becomes the sobriety of his judgment. His dexterity in the disposing of his incidents is proved in every particular. While a first reading of the poem and a first comparison with the story of *Atlakviða* may suggest the blundering and irresponsible ways of popular reciters, a very little attention will serve to bring out the difference and to justify this poet. He is not an improviser; his temptations are of another sort. He is the poet of a second generation, one of those who make up by energy of intelligence for their want of original and spontaneous imagination. It is not that he is cold or dull; but there is something wanting in the translation of his thoughts into speech. His metres are hammered out; the precision of his verse is out of keeping with the fury of his tragic purport. The faults are the faults of overstudy, the faults of correctness and maturity.

The significance of the *Atlamál* is considerable in the history of the Northern poetry. It may stand for the furthest mark in one particular direction; the epic poetry of the North never got further than this. If *Beowulf* or *Waldere* may perhaps represent the highest accomplishment of epic in old English verse, the *Atlamál* has, at least, as good a claim in the other language. The *Atlamál* is not the finest of the old poems. That place belongs, without any question, to the *Volospá*, the Sibyl's Song of the judgment; and among the others there are many that surpass the *Atlamál* in beauty. But the *Atlamál* is complete; it is a work of some compass, diligently planned and elaborated. Further, although it has many of the marks of the new rhetoric, these do not change its character as a narrative poem. It is a narrative poem, not a poem of lyrical allusions, not an heroic ode. It is at once the largest and the most harmonious in construction of all the poems. It proves that the change of the Northern poetry, from narrative to the courtly lyric, was a change not made without fair opportunity to the older school to show what it was worth. The variety of the three poems of Attila, ending in the careful rhetoric of the *Atlamál*, is proof sufficient of the labour bestowed by different poets in their use of the epic inheritance. Great part of the history of the North is misread, unless account is taken of the artistic study, the invention, the ingenuity, that went to the making of those poems. This variety is not the confusion of barbarous tradition, or the shifts and experiments of improvisers. The prosody and the rhetorical furniture of the poems might prevent that misinterpretation. It might be prevented also by an observation of the way the matter is dealt with, even apart from the details of the language and the style. The proof from these two quarters, from the matter and from the style, is not easily impugned.

So the first impression is discredited, and so it appears that the "Elder Edda," for all its appearance of disorder, haste, and hazard, really contains a number of specimens of art, not merely a heap of casual and rudimentary variants. The poems of the Icelandic manuscript assert themselves as individual and separate works. They are not the mere makings of an epic, the mere materials ready to the hand of an editor. It still remains true that they are defective, but it is true also that they are the work of artists, and of a number of artists with different aims and ideals. The earliest of them is long past the stage of popular improvisation, and the latest has the qualities of a school that has learned more art than is good for it.

The defect of the Northern epic is that it allowed itself to be too soon restricted in its scope. It became too minute, too emphatic, too intolerant of the comfortable dilutions, the level intervals, between the critical moments.[1] It was too much affected by the vanities of the rival Scaldic poetry; it was overcome by rhetoric. But it cannot be said that it went out tamely.

[1] There is a natural affinity to Gray's poetry in the Icelandic poetry that he translated—compressed, emphatic, incapable of laxity.

VI

BEOWULF

THE poem of *Beowulf* has been sorely tried; critics have long been at work on the body of it, to discover how it is made. It gives many openings for theories of agglutination and adulteration. Many things in it are plainly incongruous. The pedigree of Grendel is not authentic; the Christian sentiments and morals are not in keeping with the heroic or the mythical substance of the poem; the conduct of the narrative is not always clear or easy to follow. These difficulties and contradictions have to be explained; the composition of the poem has to be analysed; what is old has to be separated from what is new and adventitious; and the various senses and degrees of "old" and "new" have to be determined, in the criticism of the poem. With all this, however, the poem continues to possess at least an apparent and external unity. It is an extant book, whatever the history of its composition may have been; the book of the adventures of Beowulf, written out fair by two scribes in the tenth century; an epic poem, with a prologue at the beginning, and a judgment pronounced on the life of the hero at the end; a single book, considered as such by its transcribers, and making a claim to be so considered.

Before any process of disintegration is begun, this

claim should be taken into account; the poem deserves to be appreciated as it stands. Whatever may be the secrets of its authorship, it exists as a single continuous narrative poem; and whatever its faults may be, it holds a position by itself, and a place of some honour, as the one extant poem of considerable length in the group to which it belongs. It has a meaning and value apart from the questions of its origin and its mode of production. Its present value as a poem is not affected by proofs or arguments regarding the way in which it may have been patched or edited. The patchwork theory has no power to make new faults in the poem; it can only point out what faults exist, and draw inferences from them. It does not take away from any dignity the book may possess in its present form, that it has been subjected to the same kind of examination as the *Iliad*. The poem may be reviewed as it stands, in order to find out what sort of thing passed for heroic poetry with the English at the time the present copy of the poem was written. However the result was obtained, *Beowulf* is, at any rate, the specimen by which the Teutonic epic poetry must be judged. It is the largest monument extant. There is nothing beyond it, in that kind, in respect of size and completeness. If the old Teutonic epic is judged to have failed, it must be because *Beowulf* is a failure.

Taking the most cursory view of the story of *Beowulf*, it is easy to recognise that the unity of the plot is not like the unity of the *Iliad* or the *Odyssey*. One is inclined at first to reckon *Beowulf* along with those epics of which Aristotle speaks, the *Heracleids* and *Theseids*, the authors of which "imagined that because Heracles was one person the story of his life could not fail to have unity."[1]

[1] *Poet.* 1451 a.

It is impossible to reduce the poem of *Beowulf* to the scale of Aristotle's *Odyssey* without revealing the faults of structure in the English poem :—

> A man in want of work goes abroad to the house of a certain king troubled by Harpies, and having accomplished the purification of the house returns home with honour. Long afterwards, having become king in his own country, he kills a dragon, but is at the same time choked by the venom of it. His people lament for him and build his tomb.

Aristotle made a summary of the Homeric poem, because he wished to show how simple its construction really was, apart from the episodes. It is impossible, by any process of reduction and simplification, to get rid of the duality in *Beowulf*. It has many episodes, quite consistent with a general unity of action, but there is something more than episodes, there is a sequel. It is as if to the *Odyssey* there had been added some later books telling in full of the old age of Odysseus, far from the sea, and his death at the hands of his son Telegonus. The adventure with the dragon is separate from the earlier adventures. It is only connected with them because the same person is involved in both.

It is plain from Aristotle's words that the *Iliad* and the *Odyssey* were in this, as in all respects, above and beyond the other Greek epics known to Aristotle. Homer had not to wait for *Beowulf* to serve as a foil to his excellence. That was provided in the other epic poems of Greece, in the cycle of Troy, in the epic stories of Theseus and Heracles. It seems probable that the poem of *Beowulf* may be at least as well knit as the *Little Iliad*, the Greek cyclic poem of which Aristotle names the principal incidents, contrasting its variety with the simplicity of the *Iliad* and *Odyssey*.[1]

Indeed it is clear that the plan of *Beowulf* might easily have been much worse, that is, more lax and diffuse, than it is. This meagre amount of praise will be allowed by the most grudging critics, if they will only think of the masses of French epic, and imagine the extent to which a French company of poets might have prolonged the narrative of the hero's life—the *Enfances*, the *Chevalerie*—before reaching the *Death of Beowulf*.

At line 2200 in *Beowulf* comes the long interval of time, the fifty years between the adventure at Heorot and the fight between Beowulf and the dragon. Two thousand lines are given to the first story, a thousand to the *Death of Beowulf*. Two thousand lines are occupied with the narrative of Beowulf's expedition, his voyage to Denmark, his fight with Grendel and Grendel's mother, his return to the land of the Gauts and his report of the whole matter to King Hygelac. In this part of the poem, taken by itself, there is no defect of unity. The action is one, with different parts all easily and naturally included between the first voyage and the return. It is amplified and complicated with details, but none of these introduce any new main interests. *Beowulf* is not like the *Heracleids* and *Theseids*. It transgresses the limits of the Homeric unity, by adding a sequel; but for all that it is not a mere string of adventures, like the bad epic in Horace's *Art of Poetry*, or the innocent plays described by Sir Philip Sidney and Cervantes. A third of the whole poem is detached, a separate

[1] τοιγαροῦν ἐκ μὲν Ἰλιάδος καὶ Ὀδυσσείας μία τραγῳδία ποιεῖται ἑκατέρας ἢ δύο μόναι· ἐκ δὲ Κυπρίων πολλαὶ καὶ τῆς μικρᾶς Ἰλιάδος πλέον ὀκτώ, οἷον ὅπλων κρίσις, Φιλοκτήτης, Νεοπτόλεμος, Εὐρύπυλος, πτωχεία, Λάκαιναι, Ἰλίου πέρσις, καὶ ἀπόπλους καὶ Σίνων καὶ Τρῳάδες (1459 b).

adventure. The first two-thirds taken by themselves form a complete poem, with a single action; while, in the orthodox epic manner, various allusions and explanations are introduced regarding the past history of the personages involved, and the history of other people famous in tradition. The adventure at Heorot, taken by itself, would pass the scrutiny of Aristotle or Horace, as far as concerns the lines of its composition.

There is variety in it, but the variety is kept in order and not allowed to interfere or compete with the main story. The past history is disclosed, and the subordinate novels are interpolated, as in the *Odyssey*, in the course of an evening's conversation in hall, or in some other interval in the action. In the introduction of accessory matter, standing in different degrees of relevance to the main plot, the practice of *Beowulf* is not essentially different from that of classical epic.

In the *Iliad* we are allowed to catch something of the story of the old time before Agamemnon,—the war of Thebes, Lycurgus, Jason, Heracles,—and even of things less widely notable, less of a concern to the world than the voyage of Argo, such as, for instance, the business of Nestor in his youth. In *Beowulf*, in a similar way, the inexhaustible world outside the story is partly represented by means of allusions and digressions. The tragedy of Finnesburh is sung by the harper, and his song is reported at some length, not merely referred to in passing. The stories of Thrytho, of Heremod, of Sigemund the Wælsing and Fitela his son (Sigmund and Sinfiotli), are introduced like the stories of Lycurgus or of Jason in Homer. They are illustrations of the action, taken from other cycles. The fortunes of the Danish and Gautish kings, the fall of Hygelac, the feuds with Sweden, these matters come into closer relation with the story. They are not so much illustrations taken in from without, as points of attachment between the history of *Beowulf* and the untold history all round it, the history of the persons concerned, along with Beowulf himself, in the vicissitudes of the Danish and Gautish kingdoms.

In the fragments of *Waldere*, also, there are allusions to other stories. In *Waldere* there has been lost a poem much longer and fuller than the *Lay of Hildebrand*, or any of the poems of the "Elder Edda"—a poem more like *Beowulf* than any of those now extant. The references to Weland, to Widia Weland's son, to Hama and Theodoric, are of the same sort as the references in *Beowulf* to the story of Froda and Ingeld, or the references in the *Iliad* to the adventures of Tydeus.

In the episodic passages of *Beowulf* there are, curiously, the same degrees of relevance as in the *Iliad* and *Odyssey*.

Some of them are necessary to the proper fulness of the story, though not essential parts of the plot. Such are the references to Beowulf's swimming-match; and such, in the *Odyssey*, is the tale told to Alcinous.

The allusions to the wars of Hygelac have the same value as the references in the *Iliad* and the *Odyssey* to such portions of the tale of Troy, and of the return of the Greek lords, as are not immediately connected with the anger of Achilles, or the return of Odysseus. The tale of *Finnesburh* in *Beowulf* is purely an interlude, as much as the ballad of *Ares and Aphrodite* in the *Odyssey*.

Many of the references to other legends in the *Iliad* are illustrative and comparative, like the passages about Heremod or Thrytho in *Beowulf*.

"Ares suffered when Otus and Ephialtes kept him in a brazen vat, Hera suffered and Hades suffered, and were shot with the arrows of the son of Amphitryon" (*Il.* v. 385). The long parenthetical story of Heracles in a speech of Agamemnon (*Il.* xx. 98) has the same irrelevance of association, and has incurred the same critical suspicions, as the contrast of Hygd and Thrytho, a fairly long passage out of a wholly different story, introduced in *Beowulf* on the very slightest of suggestions.

Thus in *Beowulf* and in the Homeric poems there are episodes that are strictly relevant and consistent, filling up the epic plan, opening out the perspective of the story; also episodes that without being strictly relevant are rightly proportioned and subordinated, like the interlude of Finnesburh, decoration added to the structure, but not overloading it, nor interfering with the design; and, thirdly, episodes that seem to be irrelevant, and may possibly be interpolations. All these kinds have the effect of increasing the mass as well as the variety of the work, and they give to *Beowulf* the character of a poem which, in dealing with one action out of an heroic cycle, is able, by the way, to hint at and partially represent a great number of other stories.

It is not in the episodes alone that *Beowulf* has an advantage over the shorter and more summary poems. The frequent episodes are only part of the general liberality of the narrative.

The narrative is far more cramped than in *Homer*; but when compared with the short method of the Northern poems, not to speak of the ballads, it comes out as itself Homeric by contrast. It succeeds in representing pretty fully and continuously, not by mere allusions and implications, certain portions of heroic life and action.

The principal actions in *Beowulf* are curiously trivial, taken by themselves. All around them are the rumours of great heroic and tragic events, and the scene and the personages are heroic and magnificent. But the plot in itself has no very great poetical value; as compared with the tragic themes of the Niblung legend, with the tale of Finnesburh, or even with the historical seriousness of the *Maldon* poem, it lacks weight. The largest of the extant poems of this school has the least important subject-matter; while things essentially and in the abstract more important, like the tragedy of Froda and Ingeld, are thrust away into the corners of the poem.

In the killing of a monster like Grendel, or in the killing of a dragon, there is nothing particularly interesting; no complication to make a fit subject for epic. *Beowulf* is defective from the first in respect of plot.

The story of Grendel and his mother is one that has been told in myriads of ways; there is nothing commoner, except dragons. The killing of dragons and other monsters is the regular occupation of the heroes of old wives' tales; and it is difficult to give individuality or epic dignity to commonplaces of this sort. This, however, is accomplished in the poem of *Beowulf*. Nothing can make the story of Grendel dramatic like the story of Waldere or of Finnesburh. But the poet has, at any rate, in connexion with this simple theme, given a rendering, consistent, adequate, and well-proportioned, of certain aspects of life and certain representative characters in an heroic age.

The characters in *Beowulf* are not much more than types; not much more clearly individual than the persons of a comedy of Terence. In the shorter Northern poems there are the characters of Brynhild and Gudrun; there is nothing in *Beowulf* to compare with them, although in *Beowulf* the personages are consistent with themselves, and intelligible.

Hrothgar is the generous king whose qualities were in Northern history transferred to his nephew Hrothulf (Hrolf Kraki), the type of peaceful strength, a man of war living quietly in the intervals of war.

Beowulf is like him in magnanimity, but his character is less uniform. He is not one of the more cruel adventurers, like Starkad in the myth, or some of the men of the Icelandic Sagas. But he is an adventurer with something strange and not altogether safe in his disposition. His youth was like that of the lubberly younger sons in the fairy stories. "They said that he was slack." Though he does not swagger like a Berserk, nor "gab" like the Paladins of Charlemagne, he is ready on provocation to boast of what he has done. The pathetic sentiment of his farewell to Hrothgar is possibly to be ascribed, in the details of its rhetoric, to the common affection of Anglo-Saxon poetry for the elegiac mood; but the softer passages are not out of keeping with the wilder moments of *Beowulf*, and they add greatly to the interest of his character. He is more variable, more dramatic, than the king and queen of the Danes, or any of the secondary personages.

Wealhtheo, the queen, represents the poetical idea of a noble lady. There is nothing complex or strongly dramatic in her character.

Hunferth, the envious man, brought in as a foil to Beowulf, is not caricatured or exaggerated. His sourness is that of a critic and a politician, disinclined to accept newcomers on their own valuation. He is not a figure of envy in a moral allegory.

In the latter part of the poem it is impossible to find in the character of Wiglaf more than the general and abstract qualities of the "loyal servitor."

Yet all those abstract and typical characters are introduced in such a way as to complete and fill up the picture. The general impression is one of variety and complexity, though the elements of it are simple enough.

With a plot like that of *Beowulf* it might seem that there was danger of a lapse from the more serious kind of heroic composition into a more trivial kind. Certainly there is nothing in the plain story to give much help to the author; nothing in Grendel to fascinate or tempt a poet with a story made to his hand.

The plot of *Beowulf* is not more serious than that of a thousand easy-going romances of chivalry, and of fairy tales beyond all number.

The strength of what may be called an epic tradition is shown in the superiority of *Beowulf* to the temptations of cheap romantic commonplace. Beowulf, the hero, is, after all, something different from the giant-killer of popular stories, the dragon-slayer of the romantic schools. It is the virtue and the triumph of the poet of *Beowulf* that when all is done the characters of the poem remain distinct in the memory, that the thoughts and sentiments of the poem are remembered as significant, in a way that is not the way of the common romance. Although the incidents that take up the principal part of the scene of *Beowulf* are among the commonest in popular stories, it is impossible to mistake the poem for one of the ordinary tales of terror and wonder. The essential part of the poem is the drama of characters; though the plot happens to be such that the characters are never made to undergo a tragic ordeal like that of so many of the other Teutonic stories. It is not incorrect to say of the poem of *Beowulf* that the main story is really less important to the imagination than the accessories by which the characters are defined and distinguished. It is the defect of the poem this should be so. There is a constitutional weakness in it.

Although the two stories of *Beowulf* are both commonplace, there is a difference between the story of Grendel and the story of the dragon.

The story of the dragon is more of a commonplace than the other. Almost every one of any distinction, and many quite ordinary people in certain periods of history have killed dragons; from Hercules and Bellerophon to Gawain, who, on different occasions, narrowly escaped the fate of Beowulf; from Harald Hardrada (who killed two at least) to More of More Hall who killed the dragon of Wantley.

The latter part of *Beowulf* is a tissue oi commonplaces of every kind: the dragon and its treasure; the devastation of the land; the hero against the dragon; the defection of his companions; the loyalty of one of them; the fight with the dragon; the dragon killed, and the hero dying from the flame and the venom of it; these are commonplaces of the story, and in addition to these there are commonplaces of sentiment, the old theme of this transitory life that "fareth as a fantasy," the lament for the glory passed away; and the equally common theme of loyalty and treason in contrast. Everything is commonplace, while everything is also magnificent in its way, and set forth in the right epic style, with elegiac passages here and there. Everything is commonplace except the allusions to matters of historical tradition, such as the death of Ongentheow, the death of Hygelac. With these exceptions, there is nothing in the latter part of *Beowulf* that might not have been taken at almost any time from the common stock of fables and appropriate sentiments, familiar to every maker cr hearer of poetry from the days of the English conquest of Britain, and long before that. It is not to be denied that the commonplaces here are handled with some discretion; though commonplace, they are not mean or dull.[1]

The story of Grendel and his mother is also common, but not as common as the dragon. The function of this story is considerably different from the other, and the class to which it belongs is differently distributed in literature. Both are stories of the killing of monsters, both belong naturally to legends of heroes like Theseus or Hercules. But for literature there is this difference between them, that dragons belong more appropriately to the more fantastic kinds of narrative, while stories of the deliverance of a house from a pestilent goblin are much more capable of sober treatment and verisimilitude. Dragons are more easily distinguished and set aside as fabulous monsters than is the family of Grendel. Thus the story of Grendel is much better fitted than the dragon story for a composition like *Beowulf*, which includes a considerable amount of the detail of common experience and ordinary life. Dragons are easily scared from the neighbourhood of sober experience; they have to be looked for in the mountains and caverns of romance or fable. Whereas Grendel remains a possibility in the middle of common life, long after the last dragon has been disposed of.

The people who tell fairy stories like the *Well of the World's End*, the *Knight of the Red Shield*, the *Castle East o' the Sun and West o' the Moon*, have

[1] It has been shown recently by Dr. Edward Sievers that Beowulf's dragon corresponds in many points to the dragon killed by Frotho, father of Haldanus, in Saxo, Book II. The dragon is not wholly commonplace, but has some particular distinctive traits. See *Berichte der Königl. Sächs. Gesellschaft der Wissenschaften*, 6 Juli 1895.

no belief, have neither belief nor disbelief, in the adventures of them. But the same people have other stories of which they take a different view, stories of wonderful things more near to their own experience. Many a man to whom the *Well of the World's End* is an idea, a fancy, has in his mind a story like that of Grendel which he believes, which makes him afraid. The bogle that comes to a house at night and throttles the goodman is a creature more hardy than the dragon, and more persevering. Stories like that of Beowulf and Grendel are to be found along with other popular stories in collections; but they are to be distinguished from them. There are popular heroes of tradition to this day who are called to do for lonely houses the service done by Beowulf for the house of Hrothgar.

Peer Gynt (not Ibsen's Peer Gynt, who is sophisticated, but the original Peter) is a lonely deer-stalker on the fells, who is asked by his neighbour to come and keep his house for him, which is infested with trolls. Peer Gynt clears them out,[1] and goes back to his deer-stalking. The story is plainly one that touches the facts of life more nearly than stories of *Shortshanks* or the *Blue Belt*. The trolls are a possibility.

The story of Uistean Mor mac Ghille Phadrig is another of the same sort.[2] It is not, like the *Battle of the Birds* or *Conal Gulban*, a thing of pure fantasy. It is a story that may pass for true when the others have lost everything but their pure imaginative value as stories. Here, again, in the West Highlands, the champion is called upon like Beowulf and Peer Gynt to save his neighbours from a warlock. And it is matter of history that Bishop Gudmund Arason of

[1] Asbjörnsen, *Norske Huldre-Eventyr og Folkesagn*. *At renske Huset* is the phrase—"to cleanse the house." Cf. *Heorot is gefælsod*, "Heorot is cleansed," in *Beowulf*.

[2] J. F. Campbell, *Tales of the West Highlands*, ii. p. 99. The reference to this story in *Catriona* (p. 174) will be remembered.

Holar in Iceland had to suppress a creature with a seal's head, Selkolla, that played the game of Grendel.[1]

There are people, no doubt, for whom Peer Gynt and the trolls, Uistean Mor and the warlock, even Selkolla that Bishop Gudmund killed, are as impossible as the dragon in the end of the poem of *Beowulf*. But it is certain that stories like those of Grendel are commonly believed in many places where dragons are extinct. The story of Beowulf and Grendel is not wildly fantastic or improbable; it agrees with the conditions of real life, as they have been commonly understood at all times except those of peculiar enlightenment and rationalism. It is not to be compared with the Phaeacian stories of the adventures of Odysseus. Those stories in the *Odyssey* are plainly and intentionally in a different order of imagination from the story of the killing of the suitors. They are pure romance, and if any hearer of the *Odyssey* in ancient times was led to go in search of the island of Calypso, he might come back with the same confession as the seeker for the wonders of Broceliande,—*fol i alai*. But there are other wonderful things in the *Iliad* and the *Odyssey* which are equally improbable to the modern rationalist and sceptic; yet by no means of the same kind of wonder as Calypso or the Sirens. Probably few of the earliest hearers of the *Odyssey* thought of the Sirens or of Calypso as anywhere near them, while many of them must have had their grandmothers' testimony for things like the portents before the death of the suitors. Grendel in the poem of *Beowulf* is in the same order of existence as these portents. If they are superstitions, they are among the most persistent; and they are superstitions, rather than creatures of romance. The fight with Grendel is not of the same kind of

[1] *Biskupa Sögur*, i. p. 604.

adventure as Sigurd at the hedge of flame, or Svipdag at the enchanted castle. And the episode of Grendel's mother is further from matter of fact than the story of Grendel himself. The description of the desolate water is justly recognised as one of the masterpieces of the old English poetry ; it deserves all that has been said of it as a passage of romance in the middle of epic. Beowulf's descent under the water, his fight with the warlock's mother, the darkness of that "sea dingle," the light of the mysterious sword, all this, if less admirably worked out than the first description of the dolorous mere, is quite as far from Heorot and the report of the table-talk of Hrothgar, Beowulf, and Hunferth. It is also a different sort of thing from the fight with Grendel. There is more of supernatural incident, more romantic ornament, less of that concentration in the struggle which makes the fight with Grendel almost as good in its way as its Icelandic counterpart, the wrestling of Grettir and Glam.

The story of *Beowulf*, which in the fight with Grendel has analogies with the plainer kind of goblin story, rather alters its tone in the fight with Grendel's mother. There are parallels in *Grettis Saga*, and elsewhere, to encounters like this, with a hag or ogress under water; stories of this sort have been found no less credible than stories of haunting warlocks like Grendel. But this second story is not told in the same way as the first. It has more of the fashion and temper of mythical fable or romance, and less of matter of fact. More particularly, the old sword, the sword of light, in the possession of Grendel's dam in her house under the water, makes one think of other legends of mysterious swords, like that of Helgi, and the "glaives of light" that are in the keeping of divers "gyre carlines" in the *West Highland Tales*.

Further, the whole scheme is a common one in popular stories, especially in Celtic stories of giants; after the giant is killed his mother comes to avenge him.

Nevertheless, the controlling power in the story of *Beowulf* is not that of any kind of romance or fantastic invention; neither the original fantasy of popular stories nor the literary embellishments of romantic schools of poetry. There are things in *Beowulf* that may be compared to things in the fairy tales; and, again, there are passages of high value for their use of the motive of pure awe and mystery. But the poem is made what it is by the power with which the characters are kept in right relation to their circumstances. The hero is not lost or carried away in his adventures. The introduction, the arrival in Heorot, and the conclusion, the return of Beowulf to his own country, are quite unlike the manner of pure romance; and these are the parts of the work by which it is most accurately to be judged.

The adventure of Grendel is put in its right proportion when it is related by Beowulf to Hygelac. The repetition of the story, in a shorter form, and in the mouth of the hero himself, gives strength and body to a theme that was in danger of appearing trivial and fantastic. The popular story-teller has done his work when he has told the adventures of the giant-killer; the epic poet has failed, if he has done no more than this.

The character and personage of Beowulf must be brought out and impressed on the audience; it is the poet's hero that they are bound to admire. He appeals to them, not directly, but with unmistakable force and emphasis, to say that they have beheld ("as may unworthiness define") the nature of the hero, and to give him their praises.

The beauty and the strength of the poem of

Beowulf, as of all true epic, depend mainly upon its comprehensive power, its inclusion of various aspects, its faculty of changing the mood of the story. The fight with Grendel is an adventure of one sort, grim, unrelieved, touching close upon the springs of mortal terror, the recollection or the apprehension of real adversaries possibly to be met with in the darkness. The fight with Grendel's mother touches on other motives; the terror is further away from human habitations, and it is accompanied with a charm and a beauty, the beauty of the Gorgon, such as is absent from the first adventure. It would have loosened the tension and broken the unity of the scene, if any such irrelevances had been admitted into the story of the fight with Grendel. The fight with Grendel's mother is fought under other conditions; the stress is not the same; the hero goes out to conquer, he is beset by no such apprehension as in the case of the night attack. The poet is at this point free to make use of a new set of motives, and here it is rather the scene than the action that is made vivid to the mind. But after this excursion the story comes back to its heroic beginning; and the conversation of Beowulf with his hosts in Denmark, and the report that he gives to his kin in Gautland, are enough to reduce to its right episodic dimensions the fantasy of the adventure under the sea. In the latter part of the poem there is still another distribution of interest. The conversation of the personages is still to be found occasionally carried on in the steady tones of people who have lives of their own, and belong to a world where the tunes are not all in one key. At the same time, it cannot be denied that the story of the *Death of Beowulf* is inclined to monotony. The epic variety and independence are obliterated by the too obviously pathetic intention. The character of this part of the poem is that of a late school of heroic poetry attempting, and with some success, to extract the spirit of an older kind of poetry, and to represent in one scene an heroic ideal or example, with emphasis and with concentration of all the available matter. But while the end of the poem may lose in some things by comparison with the stronger earlier parts, it is not so wholly lost in the charms of pathetic meditation as to forget the martial tone and the more resolute air altogether. There was a danger that Beowulf should be transformed into a sort of Amadis, a mirror of the earlier chivalry; with a loyal servitor attending upon his death, and uttering the rhetorical panegyric of an abstract ideal. But this danger is avoided, at least in part. Beowulf is still, in his death, a sharer in the fortunes of the Northern houses; he keeps his history. The fight with the dragon is shot through with reminiscences of the Gautish wars: Wiglaf speaks his sorrow for the champion of the Gauts; the virtues of Beowulf are not those of a fictitious paragon king, but of a man who would be missed in the day when the enemies of the Gauts should come upon them.

The epic keeps its hold upon what went before, and on what is to come. Its construction is solid, not flat. It is exposed to the attractions of all kinds of subordinate and partial literature,—the fairy story, the conventional romance, the pathetic legend,—and it escapes them all by taking them all up as moments, as episodes and points of view, governed by the conception, or the comprehension, of some of the possibilities of human character in a certain form of society. It does not impose any one view on the reader; it gives what it is the proper task of the higher kind of fiction to give—the play of life in different moods and under different aspects.

CHAPTER III

THE ICELANDIC SAGAS

I

ICELAND AND THE HEROIC AGE

The epic poetry of the Germans came to an end in different ways and at different seasons among the several nations of that stock. In England and the Continent it had to compete with the new romantic subjects and new forms of verse. In Germany the rhyming measures prevailed very early, but the themes of German tradition were not surrendered at the same time. The rhyming verse of Germany, foreign in its origin, continued to be applied for centuries in the rendering of German myths and heroic stories, sometimes in a style with more or less pretence to courtliness, as in the *Nibelungenlied* and *Kudrun*; sometimes in open parade of the travelling minstrel's "public manners" and simple appetites. England had exactly the opposite fortune in regard to verse and subject-matter. In England the alliterative verse survived the changes of inflexion and pronunciation for more than five hundred years after *Maldon*, and uttered its last words in a poem written like the *Song of Byrhtnoth* on a contemporary battle,—the poem of *Scottish Field*.[1]

[1] Ed. Robson, Chetham Society, 1855, from the Lyme MS.; ed. Furnivall and Hales, *Percy Folio Manuscript*, 1867.

There was girding forth of guns, with many great stones;
Archers uttered out their arrows and eagerly they shotten;
They proched us with spears and put many over;
That the blood outbrast at their broken harness.
There was swinging out of swords, and swapping of heads,
We blanked them with bills through all their bright armour,
That all the dale dinned of the derf strokes.

But while this poem of Flodden corresponds in its subject to the poem of *Maldon*, there is no such likeness between any other late alliterative poem and the older poems of the older language. The alliterative verse is applied in the fourteenth and fifteenth centuries to every kind of subject except those of Germanic tradition. England, however, has the advantage over Germany, that while Germany lost the old verse, England did not lose the English heroic subjects, though, as it happens, the story of King Horn and the story of Havelock the Dane are not told in the verse that was used for King Arthur and Gawain, for the tale of Troy and the wars of Alexander. The recent discovery of a fragment of the *Song of Wade* is an admonition to be cautious in making the extant works of Middle English literature into a standard for all that has ceased to exist. But no new discovery, even of a Middle English alliterative poem of Beowulf or of Walter of Aquitaine, would alter the fact that the alliterative measure of English poetry in the fourteenth and fifteenth centuries, like the ancient themes of the German rhyming poems, is a survival in an age when the chief honours go to other kinds of poetry. The author of *Piers Plowman* is a notable writer, and so are the poets of *Gawain*, and of the *Mort Arthure*, and of the *Destruction of Troy*; but Chaucer and not Langland is the poetical master of that age. The poems of the *Nibelungen* and of *Kudrun* are rightly honoured, but it was to the author of *Parzival*, and to the courtly lyrics of

Walther von der Vogelweide, that the higher rank was given in the age of the Hohenstaufen, and the common fame is justified by history, so often as history chooses to have any concern with such things.

In the lands of the old Northern speech the old heroic poetry was displaced by the new Court poetry of the Scalds. The heroic subjects were not, however, allowed to pass out of memory. The new poetry could not do without them, and required, and obtained, its heroic dictionary in the *Edda*. The old subjects hold their own, or something of their own, with every change of fashion. They were made into prose stories, when prose was in favour; they were the subjects of *Rímur*, rhyming Icelandic romances, when that form came later into vogue.[1] In Denmark they were paraphrased, many of them, by Saxo in his *History*; many of them became the subjects of ballads, in Denmark, Norway, Sweden, and the Faroes.

In this way some of the inheritance of the old German world was saved in different countries and languages, for the most part in ballads and chap-books, apart from the main roads of literature. But these heirlooms were not the whole stock of the heroic age. After the failure and decline of the old poetry there remained an unexhausted piece of ground; and the great imaginative triumph of the Teutonic heroic age was won in Iceland with the creation of a new epic tradition, a new form applied to new subjects.

Iceland did something more than merely preserve the forms of an antiquated life whose day was over. It was something more than an island of refuge for muddled and blundering souls that had found the

[1] See below, p. 283.

career of the great world too much for them. The ideas of an old-fashioned society migrated to Iceland, but they did not remain there unmodified. The paradox of the history of Iceland is that the unsuccessful old ideas were there maintained by a community of people who were intensely self-conscious and exceptionally clear in mind. Their political ideas were too primitive for the common life of medieval Christendom. The material life of Iceland in the Middle Ages was barbarous when compared with the life of London or Paris, not to speak of Provence or Italy, in the same centuries. At the same time, the modes of thought in Iceland, as is proved by its historical literature, were distinguished by their freedom from extravagances,—from the extravagance of medieval enthusiasm as well as from the superstitions of barbarism. The life of an heroic age—that is, of an older stage of civilisation than the common European medieval form—was interpreted and represented by the men of that age themselves with a clearness of understanding that appears to be quite unaffected by the common medieval fallacies and "idolisms." This clear self-consciousness is the distinction of Icelandic civilisation and literature. It is not vanity or conceit. It does not make the Icelandic writers anxious about their own fame or merits. It is simply clear intelligence, applied under a dry light to subjects that in themselves are primitive, such as never before or since have been represented in the same way. The life is their own life; the record is that of a dispassionate observer.

While the life represented in the Sagas is more primitive, less civilised, than the life of the great Southern nations in the Middle Ages, the record of that life is by a still greater interval in advance of all the common modes of narrative then known to the more fortunate or more luxurious parts of Europe. The conventional form of the Saga has none of the common medieval restrictions of view. It is accepted at once by modern readers without deduction or apology on the score of antique fashion, because it is in essentials the form with which modern readers are acquainted in modern story-telling; and more especially because the language is unaffected and idiomatic, not "quaint" in any way, and because the conversations are like the talk of living people. The Sagas are stories of characters who speak for themselves, and who are interesting on their own merits. There are good and bad Sagas, and the good ones are not all equally good throughout. The mistakes and misuses of the inferior parts of the literature do not, however, detract from the sufficiency of the common form, as represented at its best. The invention of the common form of the Saga is an achievement which deserves to be judged by the best in its kind. That kind was not exempt, any more than the Elizabethan drama or the modern novel, from the impertinences and superfluities of trivial authors. Further, there were certain conditions and circumstances about its origin that sometimes hindered in one way, while they gave help in another. The Saga is a compromise between opposite temptations, and the compromise is not always equitable.

II

MATTER AND FORM

It is no small part of the force of the Sagas, and at the same time a difficulty and an embarrassment, that they have so much of reality behind them. The element of history in them, and their close relation to the lives of those for whom they were made, have given them a substance and solidity beyond anything else in the imaginative stories of the Middle Ages. It may be that this advantage is gained rather unfairly. The art of the Sagas, which is so modern in many things, and so different from the medieval conventions in its selection of matter and its development of the plot, is largely indebted to circumstances outside of art. In its rudiments it was always held close to the real and material interests of the people; it was not like some other arts which in their beginning are fanciful, or dependent on myth or legend for their subject-matter, as in the medieval schools of painting or sculpture generally, or in the medieval drama. Its imaginative methods were formed through essays in the representation of actual life; its first artists were impelled by historical motives, and by personal and local interests. The art of the Sagas was from the first "immersed in matter"; it had from the first all the advantage that is given by interests stronger and more substantial than those of mere literature;

and, conversely, all the hindrance that such irrelevant interests provide, when "mere literature" attempts to disengage itself and govern its own course.

The local history, the pedigrees of notable families, are felt as a hindrance, in a greater or less degree, by all readers of the Sagas; as a preliminary obstacle to clear comprehension. The Sagas differ in value, according to their use and arrangement of these matters, in relation to a central or imaginative conception of the main story and the characters engaged in it. The best Sagas are not always those that give the least of their space to historical matters, to the genealogies and family memoirs. From these the original life of the Sagas is drawn, and when it is cut off from these the Saga withers into a conventional and insipid romance. Some of the best Sagas are among those which make most of the history, and, like *Njála* and *Laxdæla*, act out their tragedies in a commanding way that carries along with it the whole crowd of minor personages, yet so that their minor and particular existences do not interfere with the story, but help it and give it substantiality. The tragedy of *Njal*, or of the *Lovers of Gudrun*, may be read and judged, if one chooses, in abstraction from the common background of Icelandic history, and in forgetfulness of its bearing upon the common fortunes of the people of the land; but these Sagas are not rightly understood if they are taken only and exclusively in isolation. The tragedies gain a very distinct additional quality from the recurrence of personages familiar to the reader from other Sagas. The relation of the Sagas to actual past events, and to the whole range of Icelandic family tradition, was the initial difficulty in forming an adequate method of story-telling; the particulars were too many, and also too real. But the reality of them was, at the same time, the initial impulse of the Sagas; and the best of the Sagas have found a way of saving the particulars of the family and local histories, without injury to the imaginative and poetical order of their narratives.

The Sagas, with all the differences between them, have common features, but among these is not to be reckoned an equal consideration for the unity of action. The original matter of the oral traditions of Iceland, out of which the written Sagas were formed, was naturally very much made up of separate anecdotes, loosely strung together by associations with a district or a family. Some of the stories, no doubt, must have had by nature a greater unity and completeness than the rest:—history in the rough has very often the outlines of tragedy in it; it presents its authors with dramatic contrasts ready made (Richard II. and Bolingbroke, Lewis XI. and Charles the Bold, Elizabeth and Mary Queen of Scots); it provides real heroes. But there are many interesting things which are not well proportioned, and which have no respect for the unities; the hero is worth talking about whether his story is symmetrical or not. The simplest form of heroic narrative is that which puts together a number of adventures, such as may easily be detached and repeated separately, adventures like that of David and Goliath, Wallace with his fishing-rod, or Bruce in the robbers' house. Many of the Sagas are mere loose strings of adventures, of short stories, or idylls, which may easily be detached and remembered out of connexion with the rest of the series. In the case of many of these it is almost indifferent at what point they may be introduced in the Saga; they merely add some particulars without advancing the plot, if there be any plot. There are all varieties of texture in the Sagas, from the extreme laxity of those that look like mere collections of the anecdotes of a country-side (*Eyrbyggja*), to the definite structure of those in which all the particulars contribute to the main action (*Hrafnkels Saga*, *Bandamanna*, *Gísla Saga*).

The loose assemblage of stories current in Iceland before the Sagas were composed in writing must, of course, have been capable of all kinds of variation. The written Sagas gave a check to oral variations and rearrangements; but many of them in extant alternative versions keep the traces of the original story-teller's freedom of selection, while all the Sagas together in a body acknowledge themselves practically as a selection from traditional report. Each one, the most complete as well as the most disorderly, is taken out of a mass of traditional knowledge relating to certain recognisable persons, of whom any one may be chosen for a time as the centre of interest, and any one may become a subordinate character in some one else's adventures. One Saga plays into the others, and introduces people incidentally who may be the heroes of other stories. As a result of this selective practice of the Sagas, it sometimes happens that an important or an interesting part of the record may be dropped by one Saga and picked up casually by another. Thus in the written Sagas, one of the best stories of the two Foster-brothers (or rather "Brothers by oath," *fratres jurati*) Thorgeir and Thormod the poet, is preserved not by their own proper history, *Fóstbræðra Saga*, but in the story of Grettir the Strong; how they and Grettir lived a winter through in the same house without quarrelling, and how their courage was estimated by their host.[1]

This solidarity and interconnexion of the Sagas

[1] "Is it true, Thorgils, that you have entertained those three men this winter, that are held to be the most regardless and over-

needs no explanation. It could not be otherwise in a country like Iceland; a community of neighbours (in spite of distances and difficulties of travelling) where there was nothing much to think about or to know except other people's affairs. The effect in the written Sagas is to give them something like the system of the *Comédie Humaine.* There are new characters in each, but the old characters reappear. Sometimes there are discrepancies; the characters are not always treated from the same point of view. On the whole, however, there is agreement. The character of Gudmund the Great, for example, is well drawn, with zest, and some irony, in his own Saga (*Ljósvetninga*); he is the prosperous man, the "rich glutton," fond of praise and of influence, but not as sound as he looks, and not invulnerable. His many appearances in other Sagas all go to strengthen this impression of the full-blown great man and his ambiguous greatness. So also Snorri the Priest, whose rise and progress are related in *Eyrbyggja*, appears in many other Sagas, and is recognised whenever he appears with the same certainty and the same sort of interest as attaches to the name of Rastignac, when that politician is introduced in stories not properly his own. Each separate mention of Snorri the Priest finds its place along with all the rest; he is never unequal to himself.

bearing, and all of them outlaws, and you have handled them so that none has hurt another?" Yes, it was true, said Thorgils. Skapti said: "That is something for a man to be proud of; but what do you think of the three, and how are they each of them in courage?" Thorgils said: "They are all three bold men to the full; yet two of them, I think, may tell what fear is like. It is not in the same way with both; for Thormod fears God, and Grettir is so afraid of the dark that after dark he would never stir, if he had his own way; but I do not know that Thorgeir, my kinsman, is afraid of anything."—"You have read them well," says Skapti; and so their talk ended (*Grettis Saga*, c. 51).

It is in the short story, the episodic chapter, that the art of Icelandic narrative first defines itself. This is the original unity; it is here, in a limited, easily comprehensible subject-matter, that the lines are first clearly drawn. The Sagas that are least regular and connected are made up of definite and well-shaped single blocks. Many of the Sagas are much improved by being taken to pieces and regarded, not as continuous histories, but as collections of separate short stories. *Eyrbyggja*, *Vatnsdæla*, and *Ljósvetninga* are collections of this sort—"Tales of the Hall." There is a sort of unity in each of them, but the place of Snorri in *Eyrbyggja*, of Ingimund in *Vatnsdæla*, and of Gudmund the Great in the history of the House of Ljósavatn, is not that of a tragic or epic hero who compels the episodes to take their right subordinate rank in a larger story. These Sagas break up into separate chapters, losing thereby none of the minor interests of story-telling, but doing without the greater tragic or heroic interest of the fables that have one predominant motive.

Of more coherent forms of construction there are several different examples among the Sagas. In each of these cases it is the tragic conception, the tragic idea, of the kind long familiar to the Teutonic nations, that governs the separate passages of the traditional history.

Tragic situations are to be found all through the Icelandic literature, only they are not always enough to make a tragedy. There is Nemesis in the end of Gudmund the Great, when his murdered enemy haunts him; but this is not enough to make his Saga an organic thing. The tragic problem of Alboin recurs, as was pointed out by the editors of *Corpus Poeticum Boreale*, in the prelude to *Vatnsdæla Saga*; but it stands by itself as one of the separate chapters in that history, which contains the plots of other tragedies also, without adopting any one of them as its single and overruling motive. These are instances of the way in which tragic imagination, or at any rate the knowledge and partial appreciation of tragic plots, may come short of fulfilment, and may be employed in a comparatively futile and wasteful form of literature. In the greater works, where the idea is fully realised, there is no one formal type. The Icelandic Sagas have different forms of success in the greater works, as well as different degrees of approximation to success in the more desultory and miscellaneous histories.

Njála, which is the greatest of all the Sagas, does not make its effect by any reduction of the weight or number of its details. It carries an even greater burden of particulars than *Eyrbyggja*; it has taken up into itself the whole history of the south country of Iceland in the heroic age.

The unity of *Njála* is certainly not the unity of a restricted or emaciated heroic play. Yet with all its complexity it belongs to quite a different order of work from *Eyrbyggja*.

It falls into three divisions, each of these a story by itself, with all three combining to form one story, apart from which they are incomplete. The first, the story of Gunnar, which is a tragedy by itself, is a necessary part of the whole composition; for it is also the story of the wisdom of Njal and the dignity of Bergthora, without which the second part would be insipid, and the great act of the burning of Njal's house would lose its depth and significance. The third part is the payment of a debt to Njal, Bergthora, and Skarphedinn, for whom vengeance is required; but it is also due even more to Flosi their adversary. The essence of the tragic situation lies in this, that the good man is in the wrong, and his adversary in the right. The third part is required to restore the balance, in order that the original wrong, Skarphedinn's slaughter of the priest of Whiteness, should not be thought to be avoided in the death of its author. *Njála* is a work of large scale and liberal design; the beauty of all which, in the story, is that it allows time for the characters to assert themselves and claim their own, as they could not do in a shorter story, where they would be whirled along by the plot. The vengeance and reconciliation in the third part of *Njála* are brought about by something more than a summary poetical justice of fines and punishments for misdeeds. It is a more leisurely, as well as a more poetical justice, that allows the characters to assert themselves for what they really are; the son of Lambi "filthy still," and Flosi the Burner not less true in temper than Njal himself.

Njála and *Laxdæla* are examples of two different ways in which inconvenient or distracting particulars of history or tradition might be reduced to serve the ends of imagination and the heroic design. *Njála* keeps up, more or less, throughout, a continuous history of a number of people of importance, but always with a regard for the principal plot of the story. In *Laxdæla* there is, on the other hand, a gradual approach to the tragedy of Kjartan, Bolli, and Gudrun; an historical prologue of the founding of Laxdale, and the lives of Kjartan's father and grandfather, before the chief part of the story begins. In *Njála* the main story opens as soon as Njal appears; of prologue there is little more than is needed to prepare for the mischief of Hallgerda, who is the cause of the strain between the two houses of Lithend and Bergthorsknoll, and thereby the touchstone of the generosity of Njal. In *Laxdæla*, although the prologue is not irrelevant, there is a long delay before the principal personages are brought together. There is no mistake about the story when once it begins, and no question about the unity of the interest; Gudrun and Fate may divide it between them, if it be divisible. It is purely the stronger quality of this part of the book, in comparison with the earlier, that saves *Laxdœla* from the defects of its construction; by the energy of the story of Kjartan, the early story of Laxdale is thrown back and left behind as a mere prelude, in spite of its length.

The story of Egil Skallagrimsson, the longest of the biographical Sagas, shows exactly the opposite proportions to those of *Laxdœla*. The life of Egil is prefaced by the history of his grandfather, father, and uncle, Kveldulf, Skallagrim (Grim the Bald), and Thorolf. Unhappily for the general effect of the book, the life of Egil is told with less strength and coherence than the fate of his uncle. The most commanding and most tragic part of *Egla* is that which represents Skallagrim and Thorolf in their relations to the tyranny of Harald the king; how Thorolf's loyalty was ill paid, and how Skallagrim his brother went in defiance to speak to King Harald. This, though it is only a prelude to the story of Egil, is one of the finest imaginative passages in the whole literature. The Saga has here been able to express, in a dramatic and imaginative form, that conflict of principles between the new monarchy and the old liberty which led to the Icelandic migration. The whole political situation, it might be said the whole early history of Iceland and Norway, is here summed up and personified in the conflict of will between the three characters. Thorolf, Harald the king, and Skallagrim play the drama of the Norwegian monarchy, and the founding of the Icelandic Commonwealth. After this compact and splendid piece of work the adventures of Egil Skallagrimsson appear rather ineffectual and erratic, in spite of some brilliant episodes.

What was an author to do when his hero died in his bed, or survived all his feuds and enmities? or when a feud could not be wound up in one generation?

Vápnfirðinga Saga gives the history of two generations of feud, with a reconciliation at the end, thus obtaining a rounded unity, though at some cost of the personal interest in its transference from fathers to sons.

Víga-Glúms Saga is a story which, with the best intentions in the world, could not attain to tragedy like that of Gisli or of Grettir, because every one knew that Glum was a threatened man who lived long, and got through without any deadly injury. Glum is well enough fitted for the part of a tragic hero. He has the slow growth, the unpromising youth, the silence and the dangerous laughter, such as are recorded in the lives of other notable personages in heroic literature :—

> Glum turned homeward ; and a fit of laughing came on him. It took him in this way, that his face grew pale, and there ran tears from his eyes like hailstones : it was often so with him afterwards, when bloodshed was in his mind.

But although there are several feuds in the story of Glum or several incidents in a feud, somehow there is no tragedy. Glum dies quietly, aged and sightless. There is a thread of romantic destiny in his story ; he keeps his good luck till he parts with the gifts of his grandfather Vigfus—the cloak, the spear, and the sword that Vigfus had given him in Norway. The prayer for Glum's discomfiture, which one of his early adversaries had offered to Frey, then takes effect, when the protecting luck has been given away. The fall of Glum is, however, nothing incurable; the change in his fortune is merely that he has to give up the land which he had extorted from his adversary long before, and that he ceases to be the greatest man in Eyjafirth, though continuing to be a man of importance still. His honour and his family are not hard hit, after all.

The history of Glum, with its biographical unity, its interest of character, and its want of tragedy, is a form of story midway between the closer knit texture of *Gísla Saga* and the laxity of construction in the stories without a hero, or with more than one, such as *Ljósvetninga* or *Vatnsdæla*. It is a biography with no strong crisis in it; it might have been extended indefinitely. And, in fact, the existing form of the story looks as if it were rather carelessly put together, or perhaps abridged from a fuller version. The story in *Reykdæla* of Viga Skuta, Glum's son-in-law and enemy, contains a better and fuller account of their dealings than *Glúma*, without any discrepancy, though the *Reykdæla* version alludes to divergencies of tradition in certain points. The curious thing is that the *Reykdæla* version supplies information about Glum's character which supplements what is told more baldly in his own Saga. Both accounts agree about Glum's good nature, which is practised on by Skuta. Glum is constant and trustworthy whenever he is appealed to for help. The *Reykdæla* version gives a pretty confirmation of this view of Glum's character (c. 24), where Glum protects the old Gaberlunzie man, with the result that the old man goes and praises his kindness, and so lets his enemies know of his movements, and spoils his game for that time. This episode is related to *Glúma*, as the foster-brother episode of Grettir (c. 51), quoted above, is related to *Fóstbræðra Saga*.

If *Glúma* is interesting and even fairly compact, in spite of its want of any great dramatic moment, on the other hand the tragic ending is not always enough to save a story from dissipation of interest. In the story of Glum's antagonist, Viga Skuta, in the second part of *Reykdæla Saga*, there is no proportion or composition; his adventures follow one upon the other, without development, a series of hazards and escapes, till he is brought down at last. In the earlier part of the same Saga (the story of Vemund, Skuta's cousin, and Askel, Skuta's father) there is more continuity in the chronicle of wrongs and revenges, and, if this story be taken by itself, more form and definite design. The two rivals are well marked out and opposed to one another, while the mischief-making Vemund is well contrasted with his uncle Askel, the just man and the peacemaker, who at the end is killed in one of his nephew's feuds, in the fight by the frozen river from which Vemund escapes, while his enemy is drowned and his best friend gets a death wound.

There are two Sagas in which a biographical theme is treated in such a way that the story produces one single impressive and tragical effect, leaving the mind with a sense of definite and necessary movement towards a tragic conclusion,—the story of Grettir the Strong, and the story of Gisli the Outlaw. These stories have analogies to one another, though they are not cast in quite the same manner.

In the life of Grettir there are many detached episodes, giving room for theories of adulteration such as are only too inevitable and certain in regard to the imbecile continuation of the story after Grettir's death and his brother's vengeance. The episodes in the main story are, however, not to be dismissed quite so easily as the unnecessary romance of the Lady Spes (*Grettis Saga*, cc. 90-95). While many of the episodes do little to advance the story, and some of them seem to have been borrowed from other Sagas without sufficient reason (cc. 25-27, from the *Foster-brothers*), most of them serve to accentuate the character of Grettir, or to deepen the sense of the mystery surrounding his life.

The tragedy of Grettir is one of those which depend on Accident, interpreted by the author as Fate. The hero is a doomed man, like Gisli, who sees things clearly coming on, but is unable to get out of their way. In both *Gisli* and *Grettir* there is an accompaniment of mystery and fantasy—for Gisli in the songs of the dream woman, for Grettir in various touches unlike the common prose of the Sagas. The hopelessness of his ill fortune is brought out in a sober way in his dealings with the chiefs who are unable to protect him, and in the cheerless courage of his relations with the foster-brothers, when the three are all together in the house of Thorgils Arason. It is illustrated in a quite different and more fantastic way in the scenes of his wanderings among the mountains, in the mysterious quiet of Thorisdal, in his alliance with strange deliverers, outside of the common world and its society, in the curse of Glam under the moonlight. This last is one of the few scenes in the Sagas, though not the only one, when the effect depends on something more than the persons engaged in it. The moon with the clouds driving over counts for more than a mere indication of time or weather; it is essential to the story, and lends itself to the malignity of the adversary in casting the spell of fear upon Grettir's mind. The solitude of Drangey, in the concluding chapters of *Grettis Saga*, the cliffs, the sea and the storms are all much less exceptional; they are necessary parts of the action, more closely and organically related to the destiny of the hero. There, in the final scenes, although there is witchcraft practised against Grettir, it is not that, but the common and natural qualities of the foolishness of the thrall and the heroism of Grettir and his young brother on which the story turns. These are the humanities of Drangey, a strong contrast, in the art of narrative, to the moonlight spell of Glam. The notable thing is that the romantic and fantastic passages in Grettir are not obscurations of the tragedy, not irrelevant, but rather an expression by the way, and in an exceptional mood, of the author's own view of the story and his conviction that it is all one coherent piece. This certainly is the effect of the romantic interludes in *Gísli*, which is perhaps the most tragic of all the Sagas, or at any rate the most self-conscious of its tragic aim. In the story of Gisli there is an introduction and preparation, but there is no very great expense of historical preliminaries. The discrepancies here between the two extant redactions of the Saga seem to show that introductory chapters of this sort were regarded as fair openings for invention and decoration by editors, who had wits enough to leave the essential part of the story very much to itself. Here, when once the action has begun, it goes on to the end without a fault. The chief characters are presented at the beginning; Gisli and Thorkell his brother; Thorgrim the Priest and Vestein, their two brothers-in-law. A speech foretelling their disunion is reported to Gisli, and leads him to propose the oath of fellowship between the four; which proposal, meant to avert the omen, brings about its fulfilment. And so the story goes on logically and inevitably to the death of Gisli, who slew Thorgrim, and the passionate agony of Thordis, Thorgrim's wife and Gisli's sister.

Hrafnkels Saga is a tragic idyll, complete and rounded. It is different in its design from *Njála* or *Laxdæla*, from the stories of Grettir and Gisli. It is a short story, well concentrated. For mere symmetry of design it might compete with any of the greater Icelandic works, not to speak of any modern fiction.

Hrafnkel, the proud man, did a cruel thing "for his oath's sake"; killed his shepherd Einar for riding on Freyfaxi, the horse that belonged to Frey the god, and to Hrafnkel his priest. To the father of Einar he made offers of compensation which were not accepted. Then the story, with much admirable detail (especially in the scenes at the Althing), goes on to show how Hrafnkel's pride was humbled by Einar's cousin. All through, however, Hrafnkel is represented as guilty of tragic terror, not of wickedness; he is punished more than is due, and in the end the balance is redressed, and his arrogant conqueror is made to accept Hrafnkel's terms. It is a story clearly and symmetrically composed; it would be too neat, indeed, if it were not that it still leaves some accounts outstanding at the end: the original error is wasteful, and the life of an innocent man is sacrificed in the clearing of scores between Hrafnkel and his adversary.

The theory of a conglomerate epic may be applied to the Icelandic Sagas with some effect. It is plain on the face of them that they contain short stories from tradition which may correspond to the short lays of the epic theory, which do in fact resemble in many things certain of the lays of the "Elder Edda." Many of the Sagas, like *Eyrbyggja*, *Vatnsdæla*, *Svarfdæla*, are ill compacted, and easily broken up into separate short passages. On the other hand, these broken and variegated Sagas are wanting in dignity and impressiveness compared with some others, while those others have attained their dignity, not by choosing their episodic chapters merely, but by forcing their own original and commanding thought upon all their matter. This is the case, whether the form be that of the comprehensive, large, secure, and elaborate *Njála*; of *Laxdæla*, with its dilatory introduction changing to the eagerness and quickness of the story of Gudrun; of *Grettir* and *Gisli*, giving shape in their several ways to the traditional accumulation of a hero's adventures; or, not less remarkable, the precision of *Hrafnkels Saga* and *Bandamanna*,[1] which appear to have discovered and fixed for themselves the canons of good imaginative narrative in short compass, and to have freed themselves, in a more summary way than *Njála*, from the encumbrances of traditional history, and the distracting interests of the antiquarian and the genealogist. These two stories, with that of Howard of Icefirth[2] and some others, might perhaps be taken as corresponding in Icelandic prose to the short epic in verse, such as the *Atlakviða*. They show, at any rate, that the difficulties of reluctant subject-matter and of the manifold deliverances of tradition were not able, in all cases, to get the better of that sense of form which was revealed in the older poetic designs.

In their temper also, and in the quality of their heroic ideal, the Sagas are the inheritors of the older heroic poetry.

[1] See below, pp. 229 *sqq*. [2] p. 216.

III

THE HEROIC IDEAL

In the material conditions of Icelandic life in the "Saga Age" there was all the stuff that was required for heroic narrative. This was recognised by the story-tellers, and they made the most of it. It must be admitted that there is some monotony in the circumstances, but it may be contended that this is of no account in comparison with the results that are produced in the best Sagas out of trivial occasions. "Greatly to find quarrel in a straw" is the rule of their conduct. The tempers of the men are easily stirred; they have a general name[1] for the trial of a man's patience, applied to anything that puts a strain on him, or encroaches on his honour. The trial may come from anything—horses, sheep, hay, women, merchandise. From these follow any number of secondary or retaliatory insults, trespasses, and manslaughters. Anything almost is enough to set the play going. What the matter in dispute may be, is almost indifferent to the author of the story. Its value depends on the persons; it is what they choose to make it.

The Sagas differ from all other "heroic" literatures in the larger proportion that they give to the

[1] *Skapraun*, lit. *test of condition.*

meannesses of reality. Their historical character, and their attempts to preserve an accurate memory of the past, though often freely modified by imagination, yet oblige them to include a number of things, gross, common, and barbarous, because they are part of the story. The Sagas differ one from another in this respect. The characters are not all raised to the height of Gunnar, Njal, Skarphedinn, Flosi, Bolli, Kjartan, Gisli. In many of the Sagas, and in many scenes, the characters are dull and ungainly. At the same time their perversity, the naughtiness, for example, of Vemund in *Reykdæla*, or of Thorolf the crank old man in *Eyrbyggja*, belongs to the same world as the lives of the more heroic personages. The Sagas take an interest in misconduct, when there is nothing better to be had, and the heroic age is frequently represented by them rather according to the rules of modern unheroic story-telling than of Bossu *on the Epic Poem*. The inequitable persons (*újafnaðarmenn*) in the Sagas are not all of them as lordly as Agamemnon. For many readers this is an advantage; if the Sagas are thereby made inferior to Homer, they are all the closer to modern stories of "common life." The people of Iceland seem always to have been "at the auld work of the marches again," like Dandie Dinmont and Jock o' Dawstoncleugh, and many of their grievances and wrongs might with little change have been turned into subjects for Crabbe or Mr. Hardy. It requires no great stretch of fancy to see Crabbe at work on the story of Thorolf Bægifot and his neighbour in *Eyrbyggja*; the old Thorolf, "curst with age," driven frantic by his homely neighbour's greater skill in the weather, and taking it out in a vicious trespass on his neighbour's hay; the neighbour's recourse to Thorolf's more considerate son Arnkell; Arnkell's payment of the damage, and summary method of putting accounts square again by seizure of his father's oxen; with the consequences of all this, which perhaps are somewhat too violent to be translated literally into the modern language of Suffolk or Wessex. Episodes of this type are common in the Sagas, and it is to them in a great measure that the Sagas owe their distinction from the common run of medieval narrative. But no appreciation of this "common life" in the Sagas can be just, if it ignores the essentially "heroic" nature of the moral laws under which the Icelandic narratives are conducted. Whether with good results or bad, is another question; but there can be no doubt that the Sagas were composed under the direction of an heroic ideal, identical in most respects with that of the older heroic poetry. This ideal view is revealed in different ways, as the Sagas have different ways of bringing their characters before the audience. In the best passages, of course, which are the most dramatic, the presuppositions and private opinions of the author are not immediately disclosed in the speeches of the characters. But the Sagas are not without their chorus; the general judgment of people about their leaders is often expressed; and although the action of the Sagas is generally sufficient to make its own impression and explain itself, the author's reading of his characters is frequently added. From the action and the commentary together, the heroic ideal comes out clearly, and it is plain that its effect on the Sagas was not merely an implicit and unconscious influence. It had risen into the consciousness of the authors of the Sagas; it was not far from definite expression in abstract terms. In this lay the danger. An ideal, defined or described in set terms, is an ideal without any responsibility and without any privilege. It may be picked up and traded on by any fool or hypocrite. Undefined and undivulged, it belongs only to those who have some original strength of imagination or will, and with them it cannot go wrong. But a definite ideal, and the terms of its definition, may belong to any one and be turned to any use. So the ideal of Petrarch was formulated and abused by the Petrarchists. The formula of Amadis of Gaul is derived from generations of older unformulated heroes, and implies the exhaustion of the heroic strain, in that line of descent. The Sagas have not come as far as that, but the latter days, that have seen Amadis, and the mechanical repetitions of Amadis, may find in the Sagas some resemblances and anticipations of the formal hero, though not yet enough to be dangerous.

In all sound heroic literature there are passages that bring up the shadow of the sceptic,—passages of noble sentiment, whose phrases are capable of being imitated, whose ideas may make the fortune of imitators and pretenders. In the Teutonic epic poetry, as in Homer, there are many noble speeches of this sort, speeches of lofty rhetoric, about which the spirit of depreciation prompts a suspicion that perhaps they may be less weighty and more conventional than we think. False heroics are easy, and unhappily they have borrowed so much of the true, that the truth itself is sometimes put out of countenance by the likeness.

In the English and the Icelandic heroic poetry there is some ground for thinking that the process of decline and the evolution of the false heroic went to some length before it was stopped. The older poems laid emphasis on certain qualities, and made them an example and an edification. "So ought a man to do," is a phrase common to the English and the

Northern schools of epic. The point of honour comes to be only too well understood—too well, that is, for the work of the imagination. Possibly the latter part of *Beowulf* is more abstract than it ought to be; at any rate, there are many of the secondary Anglo-Saxon poems which, like the old Saxon *Hêliand*, show an excessive use of the poetic formulas of courage and loyalty. The Icelandic poetry had also its spurious heroic phrases, by which something is taken away from the force of their more authentic originals.

In the Sagas, as in the *Iliad*, in the *Song of Maldon*, in the *Death of Ermanaric*, there is a rhetorical element by which the ideas of absolute courage are expressed. Unhappily it is not always easy to be sure whether the phrases are of the first or the second growth; in most cases, the better opinion perhaps will be that they belong to a time not wholly unsophisticated, yet not in the stage of secondary and abstract heroic romance. The rhetoric of the Sagas, like the rhetoric of the "Poetic Edda," was taken too seriously and too greedily by the first modern discoverers of the old Northern literature. It is not, any more than the rhetoric of Homer, the immediate expression of the real life of an heroic age; for the good reason that it is literature, and literature just on the autumnal verge, and plainly capable of decay. The best of the Sagas were just in time to escape that touch of over-reflexion and self-consciousness which checks the dramatic life and turns it into matter of edification or sentiment. The best of them also give many indications to show how near they were to over-elaboration and refinement.

Kjartan, for example, in *Laxdæla* is represented in a way that sometimes brings him dangerously near the ideal hero. The story (like many of the other

Sagas) plays about between the two extremes, of strong imagination applied dramatically to the subject-matter, on the one hand, and abstract ethical reflexion on the other. In the scene of Kjartan's encounter with Olaf Tryggvason in Norway[1] there is a typical example of the two kinds of operation. The scene and the dialogue are fully adequate to the author's intention, about which there can be no mistake. What he wishes to express is there expressed, in the most lively way, with the least possible encumbrance of explanation or chorus: the pride of Kjartan, his respect for his unknown antagonist in the swimming-match, his anxiety to keep clear of any submission to the king, with the king's reciprocal sense of the Icelander's magnanimity; no stroke in all this is other than right. While also it may be perceived that the author has brought into his story an ingredient of rhetoric. In this place it has its use and its effect; and, nevertheless, it is recognisable as the dangerous essence of all that is most different from sound narrative or drama.

Then said the king, "It is well seen that Kjartan is used to put more trust in his own might than in the help of Thor and Odin."

This rings as true as the noble echo of it in the modern version of the *Lovers of Gudrun*:—

> If neither Christ nor Odin help, why then
> Still at the worst we are the sons of men.

No amount of hacking work can take away the eloquence of this phrasing. Yet it is beyond question, that these phrases, like that speech of Sarpedon which has been borrowed by many a hero since, are of a different stuff from pure drama, or any pure

[1] Translated in Appendix, Note B.

imaginative work. By taking thought, they may be more nearly imitated than is possible in the case of any strong dramatic scene. The words of the king about Kjartan are like the words that are used to Earl Hakon, by Sigmund of the Faroes;[1] they are on their way to become, or they have already become, an ethical commonplace. In the place where they are used, in the debate between Kjartan and King Olaf, they have received the strong life of the individual persons between whom they pass, just as an actor may give life and character to any words that are put in his mouth. Yet elsewhere the phrase may occur as a commonplace formula—*hann trúði á mátt sinn ok megin* (he trusted in his own might and main)—applied generally to those Northern pagans who were known to be *securi adversus Deos* at the time of the first preaching of Christendom in the North.

All is well, however, so long as this heroic ideal is kept in its right relation, as one element in a complex work, not permitted to walk about by itself as a personage. This right subordination is observed in the Sagas, whereby both the heroic characters are kept out of extravagance (for neither Gunnar, Kari, nor Kjartan is an abstract creature), and the less noble or the more complex characters are rightly estimated. The Sagas, which in many things are ironical or reticent, do not conceal their standard of measurement or value, in relation to which characters and actions are to be appraised. They do not, on the other hand, allow this ideal to usurp upon the rights of individual characters. They are imaginative, dealing in actions and characters; they are not ethical or sentimental treatises, or mirrors of chivalry.

[1] "Tell me what faith you are of," said the earl. "I believe in my own strength," said Sigmund (*Færeyinga Saga*).

IV

TRAGIC IMAGINATION

In their definite tragical situations and problems, the Sagas are akin to the older poetry of the Teutonic race. The tragical cases of the earlier heroic age are found repeated, with variations, in the Sagas. Some of the chief of these resemblances have been found and discussed by the editors of *Corpus Poeticum Boreale.* Also in many places where there is no need to look for any close resemblance in detail, there is to be seen the same mode of comprehending the tragical stress and contradiction as is manifested in the remains of the poetry. As in the older Germanic stories, so in the Sagas, the plot is often more than mere contest or adventure. As in *Finnesburh* and *Waldere*, so in *Gísla Saga* and *Njála* and many other Icelandic stories, the action turns upon a debate between opposite motives of loyalty, friendship, kindred. Gisli kills his sister's husband; it is his sister who begins the pursuit of Gisli, his sister who, after Gisli's death, tries to avenge him. Njal has to stand by his sons, who have killed his friend. Gunnlaug and Hrafn, Kjartan and Bolli, are friends estranged by "Fate and their own transgression," like Walter and Hagena.

The Sagas, being prose and having an historical

tradition to take care of, are unable to reach the same intensity of passion as some of the heroic poems, the poems of *Helgi* and of *Sigurd*. They are all the more epic, perhaps, on that account; more equable in their course, with this compensation for their quieter manner, that they have more room and more variety than the passionate heroic poems. These histories have also, as a rule, to do without the fantasies of such poetry as *Hervor and Angantyr*, or *Helgi and Sigrun*. The vision of the Queens of the Air, the return of Helgi from the dead, the chantings of Hervor "between the worlds," are too much for the plain texture of the Sagas. Though, as has already been seen in *Grettir* and *Gisli*, this element of fantastic beauty is not wholly absent; the less substantial graces of mythical romance, "fainter and flightier" than those of epic, are sometimes to be found even in the historical prose; the historical tragedies have their accompaniment of mystery. More particularly, the story of the *Death of Thidrandi whom the Goddesses slew*, is a prose counterpart to the poetry of Sigrun and Hervor.[1]

There are many other incidents in the Sagas which have the look of romance about them. But of a number of these the distinction holds good that has been already put forward in the case of *Beowulf*: they are not such wonders as lie outside the bounds of common experience, according to the estimate of those for whom the stories were told. Besides some wonderful passages that still retain the visionary and fantastic charm of myth and mythical romance, there are others in which the wonders are more gross and nearer to common life. Such is the story of the hauntings at Froda, in *Eyrbyggja*; the drowned man

[1] It is summarised in Dasent's *Njal*, i. p. xx., and translated in Sephton's *Olaf Tryggvason* (1895), pp. 339-341.

and his companions coming home night after night and sitting in their wet clothes till daybreak; such is the ghastly story of the funeral of Viga-Styrr in *Heiðarvíga Saga.* Things of that sort are no exceptions to common experience, according to the Icelandic judgment, and do not stand out from the history as something different in kind; they do not belong to the same order as the dream-poetry of Gisli or the vision of Thidrandi.

The self-denial of the Icelandic authors in regard to myth and pure romance has secured for them, in exchange, everything that is essential to strong dramatic stories, independent of mythological or romantic attractions.

Some of the Sagas are a reduction of heroic fable to the temper and conditions of modern prose. *Laxdæla* is an heroic epic, rewritten as a prose history under the conditions of actual life, and without the help of any supernatural "machinery." It is a modern prose version of the Niblung tragedy, with the personages chosen from the life of Iceland in the heroic age, and from the Icelandic family traditions. It is not the only work that has reduced the Niblung story to terms of matter of fact. The story of Sigurd and Brynhild has been presented as a drama by Ibsen in his *Warriors in Helgeland*, with the names changed, with new circumstances, and with nothing remaining of the mythical and legendary lights that play about the fortunes of Sigurd in the Northern poems. The play relies on the characters, without the mysteries of Odin and the Valkyria. An experiment of the same sort had been made long before. In *Laxdæla*, Kjartan stands for Sigurd: Gudrun daughter of Osvifr, wife of Bolli, is in the place of Brynhild wife of Gunnar, driving her husband to avenge her on her old lover. That the authors of the Sagas were conscious at least in some cases of their relation to the poems is proved by affinities in the details of their language. In *Gísla Saga*, Thordis, sister of Gisli, has to endure the same sorrow as the wife of Sigurd in the poems; her husband, like Sigurd, is killed by her brother. One of the verses put in the mouth of Gisli in the story contrasts her with Gudrun, daughter of Giuki, who killed her husband (Attila) to avenge her brothers; whereas Thordis was waking up the pursuers of her brother Gisli to avenge her husband. With this verse in his head, it is impossible that the writer of the Saga can have overlooked the resemblance which is no less striking than the contrast between the two cases.

The relation of the Sagas to the older poetry may be expressed in this way, perhaps, that they are the last stage in a progress from the earliest mythical imagination, and the earliest dirges and encomiums of the great men of a tribe, to a consistent and orderly form of narrative literature, attained by the direction of a critical faculty which kept out absurdities, without impairing the dramatic energy of the story. The Sagas are the great victory of the Humanities in the North, at the end of a long process of education. The Northern nations, like others, had to come to an understanding with themselves about their inherited myths, their traditional literary forms. One age after another helped in different ways to modify their beliefs, to change their literary taste. Practically, they had to find out what they were to think of the gods; poetically, what they were to put into their songs and stories. With problems of this sort, when a beginning has once been made, anything is possible, and there is no one kind of success. Every nation that has ever come to anything has had to go to school in this way. None has ever been successful right through; while, on the other hand, success does not mean the attainment of any definite end. There is a success for every stage in the progress, and one nation or literature differs from another, not by reason of an ultimate victory or defeat, but in the number of prizes taken by the way.

As far as can be made out, the people of the Northern tongue got the better of the Western Teutons, in making far more than they out of the store of primeval fancies about the gods and the worlds, and in giving to their heroic poems both an intenser passion of expression and a more mysterious grace and charm. The Western Teutons in their heroic poetry seem, on the other hand, to have been steadier and less flighty. They took earlier to the line of reasonable and dignified narrative, reducing the lyrical element, perhaps increasing the gnomic or reflective proportions of their work. So they succeeded in their own way, with whatever success belongs to *Beowulf*, *Waldere*, *Byrhtnoth*, not to speak of the new essays they made with themes taken from the Church, in the poems of *Andreas*, *Judith*, and all the rest. Meanwhile the Northerners were having their own difficulties and getting over them, or out of them. They knew far more about the gods, and made poems about them. They had no patience, so that they could not dilute and expand their stories in the Western way. They saw no good in the leisurely methods; they must have everything emphatic, everything full of poetical meaning; hence no large poetry, but a number of short poems with no slackness in them. With these they had good reason to be content, as a good day's work in their day. But whatever advantage the fiery Northern poems may have over the slower verse of the Anglo-Saxons, they do not correspond to the same intellectual wants, and they leave out something which seems to have been attained in the Western poetry. The North had still to find out what could be done with simpler materials, and without the magical light of the companions of Sigrun. The Icelandic prose histories are the solution of this new problem, a problem which the English had already tried and solved in their own manner in the quieter passages of their epic poetry, and, above all, in the severity of the poem of *Maldon*.

The Sagas are partly indebted to a spirit of negative criticism and restraint; a tendency not purely literary, corresponding, at any rate, to a similar tendency in practical life. The energy, the passion, the lamentation of the Northern poetry, the love of all the wonders of mythology, went along with practical and intellectual clearness of vision in matters that required cool judgment. The ironical correction of sentiment, the tone of the *advocatus diaboli*, is habitual with many of the Icelandic writers, and many of their heroes. "To see things as they really are," so that no incantation could transform them, was one of the gifts of an Icelandic hero,[1] and appears to have been shared by his countrymen when they set themselves to compose the Sagas.

The tone of the Sagas is generally kept as near as may be to that of the recital of true history. Nothing is allowed any preponderance over the story and the speeches in it. It is the kind of story furthest removed from the common pathetic fallacies of the Middle Ages. The rationalist mind has cleared away all the sentimental and most of the superstitious encumbrances and hindrances of strong narrative.

The history of the early Northern rationalism and its practical results is part of the general history of

[1] *Harðar Saga*, c. xi.

religion and politics. In some respects it may have been premature; in many cases it seems (as might be expected) to have gone along with hardness and sterility of mind, and to have left an inheritance of vacuity behind it. The curious and elaborate hardness of the Icelandic Court poetry may possibly be a sign of this same temper; in another way, the prevalent coolness of Northern piety, even before the Reformation, is scarcely to be dissociated from the coolness of the last days of heathendom. The spirited acuteness of Snorri the Priest and his contemporaries was succeeded by a moderate and unenthusiastic fashion of religion, for the most part equally remote from the extravagances and the glories of the medieval Church. But with these things the Sagas have little to do; where they are in relation to this common rationalist habit of mind, it is all to their good. The Sagas are not injured by any scepticism or coolness in the minds of their authors. The positive habit of mind in the Icelanders is enough to secure them against a good deal of the conventional dulness of the Middle Ages. It made them dissatisfied with anything that seemed wanting in vividness or immediate force; it led them to select, in their histories, such things as were interesting in themselves, and to present them definitely, without any drawling commonplaces, or any makeshift rhetorical substitutes for accurate vision and clear record. It did not hinder, but it directed and concentrated the imagination. The self-repression in the Sagas is bracing. It gives greater clearness, greater resonance; it does not cut out or renounce anything that is really worth keeping.

If not the greatest charm of the Sagas, at any rate that which is perhaps most generally appreciated by modern readers is their economy of phrasing in the critical passages, the brevity with which the incidents and speeches are conveyed, the restriction of all commentary to the least available compass. Single phrases in the great scenes of the Sagas are full-charged with meaning to a degree hardly surpassed in any literature, certainly not in the literatures of medieval Europe. Half a dozen words will carry all the force of the tragedy of the Sagas, or render all the suspense and terror of their adventurous moments, with an effect that is like nothing so much as the effect of some of the short repressed phrases of Shakespeare in *Hamlet* or *King Lear*. The effect is attained not by study of the central phrase so much as by the right arrangement and selection of the antecedents; that is, by right proportion in the narrative. It is in this way that the killing of Gunnar's dog, in the attack on Lithend, is made the occasion for one of the great strokes of narrative. The words of Gunnar, when he is roused by the dog's howl—"Sore art thou handled, Sam, my fosterling, and maybe it is meant that there is not to be long between thy death and mine!"—are a perfect dramatic indication of everything the author wishes to express—the coolness of Gunnar, and his contempt for his enemies, as well as his pity for his dog. They set everything in tune for the story of Gunnar's death which follows. It is in this way that the adventures of the Sagas are raised above the common form of mere reported "fightings and flockings," the common tedious story of raids and reprisals. This is one of the kinds of drama to be found in the Sagas, and not exclusively in the best of them. One of the conditions of this manner of composition and this device of phrasing is that the author shall be able to keep himself out of the story, and let things make their own impression. This is the result of the Icelandic habit of restraint. The intellectual coolness of the

Sagas is a pride that keeps them from pathetic effusions; it does not impede the dramatic passion, it merely gives a lesson to the sensibilities and sympathies, to keep them out of the way when they are not wanted.

This is one notable difference of temper and rhetoric between the Sagas and the old English poems. One of the great beauties of the old English poetry is its understanding of the moods of lamentation—the mood of Ossian it might be called, without much error in the name. The transience and uncertainty of the world, the memory of past good fortune, and of things lost,—with themes like these the Anglo-Saxon poets make some of their finest verse; and while this fashion of meditation may seem perhaps to have come too readily, it is not the worst poets who fall in with it. In the Icelandic poetry the notes of lamentation are not wanting, and it cannot be said that the Northern elegies are less sweet or less thrilling in their grief than those of England in the kindred forms of verse. It is enough to think of *Gudrun's Lament* in the "Elder Edda," or of *Sonatorrek*, Egil Skallagrimsson's elegy on the death of his two sons. It was not any congenital dulness or want of sense that made the Sagas generally averse to elegy. No mere writer of Sagas was made of stronger temper than Egil, and none of them need have been ashamed of lamentation after Egil had lamented. But they saw that it would not do, that the fabric of the Saga was not made for excessive decoration of any kind, and least of all for parenthesis of elegy. The English heroic poetry is more relenting. *Beowulf* is invaded by pathos in a way that often brings the old English verse very nearly to the tone of the great lament for Lancelot at the end of the *Morte d'Arthur*; which, no doubt, is justification enough for any lapse from the pure heroic. In the Sagas the sense of all the vanity of human wishes is expressed in a different way: the lament is turned into dramatic action; the author's sympathy is not shown in direct effusions, but in his rendering of the drama.[1] The best instance of this is the story of Howard of Icefirth.

Howard's son Olaf, a high-spirited and generous young man, comes under the spite of a domineering gentleman, all the more because he does some good offices of his own free will for this tyrannical person. Olaf is attacked and killed by the bully and his friends; then the story goes on to tell of the vengeance of his father and mother. The grief of the old man is described as a matter of fact; he was lame and feeble, and took to his bed for a long time after his son's death. Then he roused himself, and he and his wife went to look for help, and finally were able to bring down their enemy. In all this there is no reflexion or commentary by the author. The pathos is turned into narrative; it is conveyed by means of the form of the story, the relation of the incidents to one another. The passion of the old people turns into resolute action, and is revealed in the perseverance of Bjargey, Olaf's mother, tracking out her enemy and coming to her kinsmen to ask for help. She rows her boat round her enemy's ship and finds out his plans; then she goes to her brothers' houses, one after another, and "borrows" avengers for her son. The repression and irony of the Icelandic character are shown in the style of her address to her brothers. "I have come to borrow

[1] The pathos of Asdis, Grettir's mother, comes nearest to the tone of the old English laments, or of the Northern elegiac poetry, and may be taken as a contrast to the demeanour of Bjargey in *Hávarðar Saga*, and an exception to the general rule of the Sagas in this respect.

your nets," she says to one, and "I have come to borrow your turf-spade," to another; all which is interpreted aright by the brothers, who see what her meaning is. Then she goes home to her husband; and here comes in, not merely irony, but an intentional rebuke to sentiment. Her husband is lying helpless and moaning; and she asks him whether he has slept. To which he answers in a stave of the usual form in the Sagas, the purport of which is that he has never known sleep since the death of Olaf his son. "'Verily that is a great lie,' says she, 'that thou hast never slept once these three years. But now it is high time to be up and play the man, if thou wilt have revenge for Olaf thy son; because never in thy days will he be avenged, if it be not this day.' And when he heard his wife's reproof he sprang out of bed on to the floor, and sang this other stave,"—of which the substance is still lamentation, but greatly modified in its effect by the action with which it is accompanied. Howard seems to throw off his age and feebleness as time goes on, and the height of his passion is marked by a note of his cheerfulness and gladness after he has killed his enemy. This is different from the method of *Beowulf*, where the grief of a father for his son is rendered in an elegy, with some beauty and some irrelevance, as if the charm of melancholy were too much for the story-teller.

The hardness of the Sagas is sometimes carried too far for the taste of some readers, and there is room for some misgiving that in places the Sagas have been affected by the contrary vice from that of effusive pathos, namely, by a pretence of courage and endurance. In some of the Northern poetry, as in *Ragnar's Death-Song*,[1] there may be detected the same kind of

[1] *Vide supra*, p. 140, and *infra*, p. 295.

insincere and exaggerated heroism as in the modern romantic imitations of old Northern sentiment, now fortunately less common than in the great days of the Northern romantic movement at the beginning of this century. The old Northern poetry seems to have become at one stage too self-conscious of the literary effect of magnanimity, too quick to seize all the literary profit that was to be made out of the conventional Viking. The Viking of the modern romantic poets has been the affliction of many in the last hundred years; none of his patrons seem to have guessed that he had been discovered, and possibly had begun to be a bore, at a time when the historical "Viking Age" had scarcely come to its close. There is little in the Icelandic Sagas to show any affinity with his forced and ostentatious bravery; but it may be suspected that here and there the Sagas have made some use of the theatrical Viking, and have thrown their lights too strongly on their death scenes. Some of the most impressive passages of the Sagas are those in which a man receives a death-wound with a quaint remark, and dies forthwith, like Atli in the story of Grettir, who was thrust through as he stood at his door, and said, "Those broad spears are in fashion now," as he went down. This scene is one of the best of its kind; there is no fault to be found with it. But there are possibly too many scenes and speeches of the same sort; enough to raise the suspicion that the situation and the form of phrase were becoming a conventional device, like some of the "machines" in the secondary Sagas, and in the too-much-edited parts of the better ones. This suspicion is not one that need be scouted or choked off. The worser parts and baser parts of the literature are to be detected by any means and all means. It is well in criticism, however, to supplement this amputating practice by some regard for the valid substances that have no need of it, and in this present case to look away from the scenes where there is suspicion of journey work and mechanical processes to the masterpieces that set the standard ; more especially to the story of the burning of Njal, which more than any other is full of the peculiar strength and quality of the Sagas.

The beauty of *Njála*, and especially of the chapters about Njal's death, is the result of a harmony between two extremes of sentiment, each of which by itself was dangerous, and both of which have here been brought to terms with each other and with the whole design of the work. The ugliness of Skarphedinn's demeanour might have turned out to be as excessive as the brutalities of *Svarfdæla* or *Ljósvetninga Saga* ; the gentleness of Njal has some affinities with the gentleness of the martyrs. Some few passages have distinctly the homiletic or legendary tone about them :—

Then Flosi and his men made a great pile before each of the doors, and then the women-folk who were inside began to weep and to wail.

Njal spoke to them, and said : " Keep up your hearts, nor utter shrieks, for this is but a passing storm, and it will be long before you have another such ; and put your faith in God, and believe that He is so merciful that He will not let us burn both in this world and the next."

Such words of comfort had he for them all, and others still more strong (c. 128, Dasent's translation).

It is easy to see in what school the style of this was learned, and of this other passage, about Njal after his death :—

Then Hjallti said, " I shall speak what I say with all freedom of speech. The body of Bergthora looks as it was likely she would look, and still fair; but Njal's body and visage seem to me so bright that I have never seen any dead man's body so bright as this" (c. 131).

At the other extreme are the heathenish manners of Skarphedinn, who, in the scene at the Althing, uses all the bad language of the old "flytings" in the heroic poetry,[1] who "grins" at the attempts to make peace, who might easily, by a little exaggeration and change of emphasis, have been turned into one of the types of the false heroic.

Something like this has happened to Egil, in another Saga, through want of balance, want of comprehensive imagination in the author. In *Njála*, where no element is left to itself, the picture is complete and full of variety. The prevailing tone is neither that of the homily nor that of the robustious Viking; it is the tone of a narrative that has command of itself and its subject, and can play securely with everything that comes within its scope.

In the death of Njal the author's imagination has found room for everything,—for the severity and the nobility of the old Northern life, for the gentleness of the new religion, for the irony in which the temper of Skarphedinn is made to complement and illustrate the temper of Njal.

Then Flosi went to the door and called out to Njal, and said he would speak with him and Bergthora.

Now Njal does so, and Flosi said: "I will offer thee, master Njal, leave to go out, for it is unworthy that thou shouldst burn indoors."

"I will not go out," said Njal, "for I am an old man, and little fitted to avenge my sons, but I will not live in shame."

Then Flosi said to Bergthora: "Come thou out, housewife, for I will for no sake burn thee indoors."

---

[1] Pp. 96, 113, above.

"I was given away to Njal young," said Bergthora, "and I have promised him this, that we should both share the same fate."

After that they both went back into the house.

"What counsel shall we now take?" said Bergthora.

"We will go to our bed," says Njal, "and lay us down; I have long been eager for rest."

Then she said to the boy Thord, Kari's son: "Thee will I take out, and thou shalt not burn in here."

"Thou hast promised me this, grandmother," says the boy, "that we should never part so long as I wished to be with thee; but methinks it is much better to die with thee and Njal than to live after you."

Then she bore the boy to her bed, and Njal spoke to his steward and said:—

"Now shalt thou see where we lay us down, and how I lay us out, for I mean not to stir an inch hence, whether reek or burning smart me, and so thou wilt be able to guess where to look for our bones."

He said he would do so.

There had been an ox slaughtered, and the hide lay there. Njal told the steward to spread the hide over them, and he did so.

So there they lay down both of them in their bed, and put the boy between them. Then they signed themselves and the boy with the cross, and gave over their souls into God's hand, and that was the last word that men heard them utter.

Then the steward took the hide and spread it over them, and went out afterwards. Kettle of the Mark caught hold of him and dragged him out; he asked carefully after his father-in-law Njal, but the steward told him the whole truth. Then Kettle said:—

"Great grief hath been sent on us, when we have had to share such ill-luck together."

Skarphedinn saw how his father laid him down and how he laid himself out, and then he said:—

"Our father goes early to bed, and that is what was to be looked for, for he is an old man."

The harmonies of *Laxdæla* are somewhat different from those of the history of Njal, but here again the elements of grace and strength, of gentleness and terror, are combined in a variety of ways, and in such a way as to leave no preponderance to any one exclusively. Sometimes the story may seem to fall into the exemplary vein of the "antique poet historicall"; sometimes the portrait of Kjartan may look as if it were designed, like the portrait of Amadis or Tirant the White, "to fashion a gentleman or noble person in vertuous and gentle discipline." Sometimes the story is involved in the ordinary business of Icelandic life, and Kjartan and Bolli, the Sigurd and Gunnar of the tragedy, are seen engaged in common affairs, such as make the alloy of heroic narrative in the *Odyssey*. The hero is put to the proof in this way, and made to adapt himself to various circumstances. Sometimes the story touches on the barbarism and cruelty, which were part of the reality familiar to the whole of Iceland in the age of the Sturlungs, of which there is more in the authentic history of the Sturlungs than in the freer and more imaginative story of Kjartan. At one time the story uses the broad and fluent form of narrative, leaving scene after scene to speak for itself; at other times it allows itself to be condensed into a significant phrase. Of these emphatic phrases there are two especially, both of them speeches of Gudrun, and the one is the complement of the other: the one in the tone of irony, Gudrun's comment on the death of Kjartan, a repetition of Brynhild's phrase on the death of Sigurd;[1] the other Gudrun's confession to her son at the end of the whole matter.

[1] Then Brynhild laughed till the walls rang again: "Good luck to your hands and swords that have felled the goodly prince" (*Brot Sgkv.* 10; cf. p. 103 above).

Gudrun meets her husband coming back, and says: "A good day's work and a notable; I have spun twelve ells of yarn, and you have slain Kjartan Olaf's son."

Bolli answers: "That mischance would abide with me, without thy speaking of it."

Said Gudrun: "I reckon not that among mischances; it seemed to me thou hadst greater renown that winter Kjartan was in Norway, than when he came back to Iceland and trampled thee under foot. But the last is best, that Hrefna will not go laughing to bed this night."

Then said Bolli in great wrath: "I know not whether she will look paler at this news than thou, and I doubt thou mightest have taken it no worse if we had been left lying where we fought, and Kjartan had come to tell of it."

Gudrun saw that Bolli was angry, and said: "Nay, no need of words like these; for this work I thank thee; there is an earnest in it that thou wilt not thwart me after."

This is one of the crises of the story, in which the meaning of Gudrun is brought out in a short passage of dialogue, at the close of a section of narrative full of adventure and incident. In all that precedes, in the relations of Gudrun to Kjartan before and after her marriage with Bolli, as after the marriage of Kjartan and Hrefna, the motives are generally left to be inferred from the events and actions. Here it was time that Gudrun should speak her mind, or at least the half of her mind.

Her speech at the end of her life is equally required, and the two speeches are the complement of one another. Bolli her son comes to see her and sits with her.

The story tells that one day Bolli came to Helgafell; for Gudrun was always glad when he came to see her.

Bolli sat long with his mother, and there was much talk between them. At last Bolli said: "Mother, will you tell me one thing? It has been in my mind to ask you, who was the man you loved best?"

Gudrun answers: "Thorkell was a great man and a lordly; and no man was goodlier than Bolli, nor of gentler breeding; Thord Ingwin's son was the most discreet of them all, a wise man in the law. Of Thorvald I make no reckoning."

Then says Bolli: "All this is clear, all the condition of your husbands as you have told; but it has not yet been told whom you loved best. You must not keep it secret from me longer."

Gudrun answers: "You put me hard to it, my son; but if I am to tell any one, I will rather tell you than another."

Bolli besought her again to tell him. Then said Gudrun: "I did the worst to him, the man that I loved the most."

"Now may we believe," says Bolli, "that there is no more to say."

He said that she had done right in telling him what he asked.

Gudrun became an old woman, and it is said that she lost her sight. She died at Helgafell, and there she rests.

This is one of the passages which it is easy to quote, and also dangerous. The confession of Gudrun loses incalculably when detached from the whole story, as also her earlier answer fails, by itself, to represent the meaning and the art of the Saga. They are the two keys that the author has given; neither is of any use by itself, and both together are of service only in relation to the whole story and all its fabric of incident and situation and changing views of life.

V

COMEDY

THE Poetical Justice of Tragedy is observed, and rightly observed, in many of the Sagas and in the greater plots. Fate and Retribution preside over the stories of Njal and his sons, and the *Lovers of Gudrun*. The story of Gisli works itself out in accordance with the original forebodings, yet without any illicit process in the logic of acts and motives, or any intervention of the mysterious powers who accompany the life of Gisli in his dreams. Even in less consistent stories the same ideas have a part; the story of Gudmund the Mighty, which is a series of separate chapters, is brought to an end in the Nemesis for Gudmund's injustice to Thorkell Hake. But the Sagas claim exemption from the laws of Tragedy, when poetical Justice threatens to become tyrannical. Partly by the nature of their origin, no doubt, and their initial dependence on historical recollections of actual events,[1] they are driven to include a number of things that might disappoint a well-educated gallery of spectators; the drama is not always worked out, or it may be that the meaning of a chapter or episode lies precisely in the disappointment of conventional expectations.

[1] *Vide supra*, p. 193 (the want of tragedy in *Víga-Glúms Saga*).

There is only one comedy, or at most two, among the Sagas—the story of the Confederates (*Bandamanna Saga*) with an afterpiece, the short story of Alecap (*Olkofra Þáttr*). The composition of the Sagas, however, admits all sorts of comic passages and undignified characters, and it also quietly unravels many complications that seem to be working up for a tragic ending. The dissipation of the storm before it breaks is, indeed, so common an event that it almost becomes itself a convention of narrative in the Sagas, by opposition to the common devices of the feud and vengeance. There is a good instance of this paradoxical conclusion in *Arons Saga* (c. 12), an authentic biography, apparently narrating an actual event. The third chapter of *Glúma* gives another instance of threatened trouble passing away. Ivar, a Norwegian with a strong hatred of Icelanders, seems likely to quarrel with Eyolf, Glum's father, but being a gentleman is won over by Eyolf's bearing. This is a part of the Saga where one need not expect to meet with any authentic historical tradition. The story of Eyolf in Norway is probably mere literature, and shows the working of the common principles of the Saga, as applied by an author of fiction. The sojourn of Grettir with the two foster-brothers is another instance of a dangerous situation going off without result. The whole action of *Vápnfirðinga Saga* is wound up in a reconciliation, which is a sufficient close; but, on the other hand, the story of Glum ends in a mere exhaustion of the rivalries, a drawn game. One of the later more authentic histories, the story of Thorgils and Haflidi, dealing with the matters of the twelfth century and not with the days of Gunnar, Njal, and Snorri the Priest, is a story of rivalry passing away, and may help to show how the composers of the Sagas were influenced by their knowledge and observation of things near their own time in their treatment of matters of tradition.

Even more striking than this evasion of the conventional plot of the blood-feud, is the freedom and variety in respect of the minor characters, particularly shown in the way they are made to perplex the simple-minded spectator. To say that all the characters in the Sagas escape from the limitations of mere typical humours might be to say too much; but it is obvious that simple types are little in favour, and that the Icelandic authors had all of them some conception of the ticklish and dangerous variability of human dispositions, and knew that hardly any one was to be trusted to come up to his looks, for good or evil. Popular imagination has everywhere got at something of this sort in its views of the lubberly younger brother, the ash-raker and idler who carries off the princess. Many of the heroes of the Sagas are noted to have been slow in their growth and unpromising, like Glum, but there are many more cases of change of disposition in the Sagas than can be summed up under this old formula. There are stories of the quiet man roused to action, like Thorarin in *Eyrbyggja*, where it is plain that the quietness was strength from the first. A different kind of courage is shown by Atli, the poor-spirited prosperous man in *Hávarðar Saga*, who went into hiding to escape being dragged into the family troubles, but took heart and played the man later on. One of the most effective pieces of comedy in the Sagas is the description of his ill-temper when he is found out, and his gradual improvement. He comes from his den half-frozen, with his teeth chattering, and nothing but bad words for his wife and her inconvenient brother who wants his help. His wife puts him to bed, and he comes to think better of himself and the world; the change of his mind being represented in the unobtrusive manner which the Sagas employ in their larger scenes.

One of the most humorous and effective contradictions of the popular judgment is that episode in *Njála*, where Kari has to trust to the talkative person whose wife has a low opinion of him. It begins like farce: any one can see that Bjorn has all the manners of the swaggering captain; his wife is a shrew and does not take him at his own valuation. The comedy of Bjorn is that he proves to be something different both from his own Bjorn and his wife's Bjorn. He is the idealist of his own heroism, and believes in himself as a hero. His wife knows better; but the beauty of it all is that his wife is wrong. His courage, it is true, is not quite certain, but he stands his ground; there is a small particle of a hero in him, enough to save him. His backing of Kari in the fight is what many have longed to see, who have found little comfort in the discomfiture of Bobadil and Parolles, and who will stand to it that the chronicler has done less than justice to Sir John Falstaff both at Gadshill and Shrewsbury. Never before Bjorn of *Njála* was there seen on any theatre the person of the comfortable optimist, with a soul apparently damned from the first to a comic exposure and disgrace, but escaping this because his soul has just enough virtue to keep him steady. The ordeal of Bjorn contains more of the comic spirit than all the host of stage cowards from Pyrgopolinices to Bob Acres, precisely because it introduces something more than the simple humour, an essence more spiritual and capricious.

Further, the partnership of Kari and Bjorn, and Kari's appreciation of his idealist companion, go a long way to save Kari from a too exclusive and limited devotion to the purpose of vengeance. There is much to be said on behalf of this Bjorn. His relations with Kari prevent the hero of the latter part of the book from turning into a mere hero. The humorous character of the squire brings out something new in the character of the knight, a humorous response; all which goes to increase the variety of the story, and to widen the difference between this story and all the monotonous and abstract stories of chivalrous adventures.

The Sagas have comedy in them, comic incidents and characters, because they have no notion of the dignity of abstract and limited heroics; because they cannot understand the life of Iceland otherwise than in full, with all its elements together. The one intentionally comic history, *Bandamanna Saga*, "The Confederates," which is exceptional in tone and plot, is a piece of work in which what may be called the form or spirit or idea of the heroic Saga is brought fully within one's comprehension by means of contrast and parody. *Bandamanna Saga* is a complete work, successful in every detail; as an artistic piece of composition it will stand comparison with any of the Sagas. But it is comedy, not tragedy; it is a mock-heroic, following the lines of the heroic model, consistently and steadily, and serving as a touchstone for the vanity of the heroic age. It is worth study, for Comedy is later and therefore it would seem more difficult than Tragedy, and this is the first reasonable and modern comedy in the history of modern Europe. Further, the method of narrative, and everything in it except the irony, belong to all the Sagas in common; there is nothing particularly new or exceptional in the style or the arrangement of the scenes; it is not so much a parody or a mock-heroic, as an heroic work inspired with comic irony. It is not a new kind of

Saga, it is the old Saga itself put to the ordeal by the Comic Muse, and proving its temper under the severest of all strains.

This is the story of the Confederates.—There was a man named Ufeig who lived in Midfirth, a free-handed man, not rich, who had a son named Odd. The father and son disagreed, and Odd, the son, went off to make his own fortune, and made it, without taking any further notice of his father. The two men are contrasted; Ufeig being an unsuccessful man and a humorist, too generous and too careless to get on in the world, while Odd, his son, is born to be a prosperous man. The main plot of the story is the reconciliation of the respectable son and the prodigal father, which is brought about in the most perfect and admirable manner.

Odd got into trouble. He had a lawsuit against Uspak, a violent person whom he had formerly trusted, who had presumed too much, had been disgraced, and finally had killed the best friend of Odd in one of the ways usual in such business in the Sagas. In the course of the lawsuit a slight difficulty arose—one of Odd's jurymen died, and another had to be called in his place. This was informal, but no one at first made anything of it; till it occurred to a certain great man that Odd was becoming too strong and prosperous, and that it was time to put him down. Whereupon he went about and talked to another great man, and half persuaded him that this view was the right one; and then felt himself strong enough to step in and break down the prosecution by raising the point about the formation of the jury. Odd went out of the court without a word as soon as the challenge was made.

While he was thinking it over, and not making much of it, there appeared an old. bent, ragged man, with a flapping hat and a pikestaff; this was Ufeig, his father, to whom he had never spoken since he left his house. Ufeig now is the principal personage in the story. He asks his son about the case and pretends to be surprised at his failure. "Impossible! it is not like a gentleman to try to take in an old man like me; how could you be beaten?" Finally, after Odd had been made to go over all the several points of his humiliation, he is reduced to trust the whole thing to his father, who goes away with the comforting remark that Odd, by leaving the court when he did, before the case was finished, had made one good move in the game, though he did not know it. Ufeig gets a purse full of money from his son; goes back to the court, where (as the case is not yet closed) he makes an eloquent speech on the iniquity of such a plea as has been raised. "To let a man-slayer escape, gentlemen! where are your oaths that you swore? Will you prefer a paltry legal quibble to the plain open justice of the case?" and so on, impressively and emotionally, in the name of Equity, while all the time (equity + x) he plays with the purse under his cloak, and gets the eyes of the judges fixed upon it. Late in the day, Odd is brought back to hear the close of the case, and Uspak is outlawed.

Then the jealousy of the great men comes to a head, and a compact is formed among eight of them to make an end of Odd's brand-new prosperity. These eight are the Confederates from whom the Saga is named, and the story is the story of Ufeig's ingenuity and malice as applied to these noble Pillars of Society. To tell it rightly would be to repeat the Saga. The skill with which the humorist plays upon the strongest motives, and gets the conspirators to betray one another, is not less beautifully represented than the spite which the humorist provokes among the subjects of his experiments. The details are finished to the utmost; most curiously and subtly in some of the indications of character and disposition in the eight persons of quality. The details, however, are only the last perfection of a work which is organic from the beginning. Ufeig, the humorist, is the servant and deputy of the Comic Muse, and there can be no doubt of the validity of his credentials, or of the soundness of his procedure. He is the ironical critic and censor of the heroic age; his touch is infallible, as unerring as that of Figaro, in bringing out and making ridiculous the meanness of the nobility. The decline and fall of the noble houses is recorded in *Sturlunga Saga*; the essence of that history is preserved in the comedy of the *Banded Men*.

But, however the material of the heroic age may be handled in this comedy, the form of heroic narrative comes out unscathed. There is nothing for the comic spirit to fix upon in the form of the Sagas. The Icelandic heroes may be vulnerable, but Comedy cannot take advantage of them except by using the general form of heroic narrative in Iceland, a form which proves itself equally capable of Tragedy and Comedy. And as the more serious Icelandic histories are comprehensive and varied, so also is this comic history. It is not an artificial comedy, nor a comedy of humours, nor a purely satirical comedy. It is no more exclusive or abstract in its contents that *Njála*; its strict observance of limit and order is not the same thing as monotony; its unity of action is consistent with diversities of motive. Along with, and inseparable from, the satirical criticism of the great world, as represented by the eight discomfited noble Confederates, there is the even more satisfactory plot of the Nemesis of Respectability in the case of Odd;

while the successful malice and craft of Ufeig are inseparable from the humanity, the constancy, and the imaginative strength, which make him come out to help his prosaic son, and enable him, the bent and thriftless old man, to see all round the frontiers of his son's well-defined and uninteresting character. Also the variety of the Saga appears in the variety of incident, and that although the story is a short one. As the solemn histories admit of comic passages, so conversely this comic history touches upon the tragic. The death of Vali, slain by Uspak, is of a piece with the most heroic scenes in Icelandic literature. Vali the friend of Odd goes along with him to get satisfaction out of Uspak the mischief-maker. Vali is all for peace; he is killed through his good nature, and before his death forgives and helps his assailant.

And when with the spring the days of summons came on, Odd rode out with twenty men, till he came near by the garth of Svalastead. Then said Vali to Odd: "Now you shall stop here, and I will ride on and see Uspak, and find out if he will agree to settle the case now without more ado." So they stopped, and Vali went up to the house. There was no one outside; the doors were open and Vali went in. It was dark within, and suddenly there leapt a man out of the side-room and struck between the shoulders of Vali, so that he fell on the spot. Said Vali: "Look out for yourself, poor wretch! for Odd is coming, hard by, and means to have your life. Send your wife to him; let her say that we have made it up; and you have agreed to everything, and that I have gone on about my own gear down the valley!" Then said Uspak: "This is an ill piece of work; this was meant for Odd and not for you."

This short heroic scene in the comedy has an effect corresponding to that of the comic humours in the Icelandic tragedies; it redresses the balance, it qualifies and diversifies what would otherwise be monotonous. Simple and clear in outline as the best of the short Icelandic stories are, they are not satisfied unless they have introduced something, if only a suggestion, of worlds different from their own immediate interests, a touch to show where their proper story branches out into the history of other characters and fortunes. This same story of the Confederates is wound up at the end, after the reconciliation of the father and son, by a return to the adventures of Uspak and to the subordinate tragic element in the comedy. The poetical justice of the story leaves Uspak, the slayer of Vali, dead in a cave of the hills; discovered there, alone, by shepherds going their autumn rounds.

VI

THE ART OF NARRATIVE

THE art of the Sagas will bear to be tested in every way: not that every Saga or every part of one is flawless, far from it; but they all have, though in different measure, the essentials of the fine art of story-telling. Except analysis, it is hardly possible to require from a story anything which will not be found supplied in some form or other in the Sagas. The best of them have that sort of unity which can hardly be described, except as a unity of life—the organic unity that is felt in every particular detail. It is absurd to take separately the details of a great work like *Njála*, or of less magnificent but not less perfect achievements such as the story of Hrafnkel. There is no story in the world that can surpass the *Bandamanna Saga* in the liveliness with which each particular reveals itself as a moment in the whole story, inseparable from the whole, and yet in its own proper space appearing to resume and absorb the life of the whole. Where the work is elaborated in this way, where every particular is organic, it is not possible to do much by way of illustration, or to exhibit piecemeal what only exists as a complete thing, and can only be understood as such. It is of some importance in the history of literature that the rank and general character of these Icelandic works should be asserted and understood. It would be equally laborious and superfluous to follow each of them with an exposition of the value of each stroke in the work. There are difficulties enough in the language, and in the history, without any multiplication of commentaries on the obvious; and there is little in the art of the Sagas that is of doubtful import, however great may be the lasting miracle that such things, of such excellence, should have been written there and then.

There is one general quality or characteristic of the Sagas which has not yet been noticed, one which admits of explanation and illustration, while it represents very well the prevailing mode of imagination in the Sagas. The imaginative life of the Sagas (in the best of them) is intensely strong at each critical point of the story, with the result that all abstract, makeshift explanations are driven out; the light is too strong for them, and the events are made to appear in the order of their appearance, with their meaning gradually coming out as the tale rolls on. No imagination has ever been so consistently intolerant of anything that might betray the author's knowledge before the author's chosen time. That everything should present itself first of all as appearance, before it becomes appearance with a meaning, is a common rule of all good story-telling; but no historians have followed this rule with so complete and sound an instinct as the authors of the Sagas. No medieval writers, and few of the modern, have understood the point of view as well as the authors of the story of Njal or of Kjartan. The reserve of the narrator in the most exciting passages of the Sagas is not dulness or want of sensibility; it is a consistent mode of procedure, to allow things to make their own impression; and the result is attained by following the order of impressions in the mind of one of the actors, or of a looker-on. "To see things as they are" is an equivocal formula, which may be claimed as their own privilege by many schools and many different degrees of intelligence. "To see things as they become," the rule of Lessing's *Laocoon*, has not found so many adherents, but it is more certain in meaning, and more pertinent to the art of narrative. It is a fair description of the aim of the Icelandic authors and of their peculiar gift. The story for them is not a thing finished and done with; it is a series of pictures rising in the mind, succeeding, displacing, and correcting one another; all under the control of a steady imagination, which will not be hurried, and will not tell the bearing of things till the right time comes. The vivid effect of the Saga, if it be studied at all closely, will be found to be due to this steadiness of imagination which gives first the blurred and inaccurate impression, the possibility of danger, the matter for surmises and suspicions, and then the clearing up. Stated generally in this way, the rule is an elementary one, but it is followed in the Sagas with a singular consistency and success, and with something more than a compulsory obedience. That both the narrators and their audience in that country had their whole lives filled with momentous problems in the interpretation of appearances may well be understood. To identify a band of riders in the distance, or a single man seen hurrying on the other side of the valley, was a problem which might be a matter of life or death any day; but so it has been in many places where there is nothing like the narrative art of Iceland. The Icelandic historian is like no other in putting into his work the thrill of suspense at something indistinctly seen going on in the distance

—a crowd of men moving, not known whether friends or enemies. So it was in *Thorgils Saga* (one of the later more authentic histories, of the Sturlung cycle), when Thorgils and his men came down to the Althing, and Bard and Aron were sent on ahead to find out if the way was clear from the northern passes across the plain of the Thing. Bard and Aron, as they came down past Armannsfell, saw a number of horses and men on the plain below just where Haflidi, the enemy, might have been expected to block the way. They left some of their band to wait behind while they themselves went on. From that point a chapter and more is taken up with the confused impression and report brought back by the scouts to the main body. They saw Bard and Aron ride on to the other people, and saw the others get up to meet them, carrying weapons; and then Bard and Aron went out of sight in the crowd, but the bearers of the report had no doubt that they were prisoners. And further, they thought they made out a well-known horse, Dapplecheek, and a gold-mounted spear among the strangers, both of which had belonged to Thorgils, and had been given away by him to one of his friends. From which it is inferred that his friend has been robbed of the horse and the spear.

The use of all this, which turns out to be all made up of true eyesight and wrong judgment, is partly to bring out Thorgils; for his decision, against the wish of his companions, is to ride on in any event, so that the author gets a chapter of courage out of the mistake. Apart from that, there is something curiously spirited and attractive in the placing of the different views, with the near view last of all. In the play between them, between the apprehension of danger, the first report of an enemy in the way, the appearance of an indistinct crowd, the false inference, and the final truth of the matter, the Saga is faithful to its vital principle of variety and comprehensiveness; no one appearance, not even the truest, must be allowed too much room to itself.

This indirect description is really the most vivid of all narrative forms, because it gives the point of view that is wanting in an ordinary continuous history. It brings down the story-teller from his abstract and discursive freedom, and makes him limit himself to one thing at a time, with the greatest advantage to himself and all the rest of his story. In that way the important things of the story may be made to come with the stroke and flash of present reality, instead of being prosed away by the historian and his good grammar.

There is a very remarkable instance of the use of this method in the Book of Kings. Of Jehoram, son of Ahab, king of Israel, it is told formally that "he wrought evil in the sight of the Lord," with the qualification that his evil was not like that of Ahab and Jezebel. This is impressive in its formal and summary way. It is quite another mode of narrative, and it is one in which the spectator is introduced to vouch for the matter, that presents the king of Israel, once for all, in a sublime and tragic protest against the sentence of the historian himself, among the horrors of the famine of Samaria.

> So we boiled my son, and did eat him: and I said unto her on the next day, Give thy son, that we may eat him; and she hath hid her son.
>
> And it came to pass, when the king heard the words of the woman, that he rent his clothes; and he passed by upon the wall, and the people looked, and, behold, he had sackcloth within upon his flesh.

No more than this is told of the unavailing penance

of Jehoram the son of Ahab. There is no preparation; all the tragedy lies in this notice of something casually seen, and left without a commentary, for any one to make his own story about, if he chooses. There is perhaps nothing anywhere in narrative quite so sudden as this. The Northern writers, however, carry out consistently the same kind of principles, putting their facts or impressions forward in a right order and leaving them to take care of themselves; while in the presentation of events the spectator within the story has a good deal given him to do. Naturally, where the author does not make use of analysis and where he trusts to the reader's intellect to interpret things aright, the "facts" must be fairly given; in a lucid order, with a progressive clearness, from the point of view of those who are engaged in the action.

There is another and somewhat different function of the spectator in the Sagas. In some cases, where there is no problem, where the action is straightforward, the spectator and his evidence are introduced merely to give breadth and freedom to the presentment, to get a foreground for the scene. This is effected best of all, as it happens, in a passage that called for nothing less than the best of the author's power and wit; namely, the chapter of the death of Kjartan in *Laxdæla*.

And with this talk of Gudrun, Bolli was made to magnify his ill-will and his grievance against Kjartan; and took his weapons and went along with the others. They were nine altogether; five sons of Osvifr, that is to say, Ospak and Helgi, Vandrad, Torrad, and Thorolf; Bolli was the sixth, Gunnlaug the seventh, sister's son of Osvifr, a comely man; the other two were Odd and Stein, sons of Thorhalla the talkative. They rode to Svinadal and stopped at the gully called Hafragil; there they tied their horses and sat down. Bolli was silent all the day, and laid him down at the edge of the gully, above.

Kjartan and his companions had come south over the pass, and the dale was opening out, when Kjartan said that it was time for Thorkell and his brother to turn back. Thorkell said they would ride with him to the foot of the dale. And when they were come south as far as the bothies called the North Sheilings, Kjartan said to the brothers that they were not to ride further.

"Thorolf, the thief, shall not have this to laugh at, that I was afraid to ride on my way without a host of men."

Thorkell Whelp makes answer: "We will give in to you and ride no further; but sorry shall we be if we are not there and you are in want of men this day."

Then said Kjartan: "Bolli my kinsman will not try to have my life, and for the sons of Osvifr, if they lie in wait for me, it remains to be seen which of us shall tell the tale afterwards, for all that there may be odds against me."

After that the brothers and their men rode west again.

Now Kjartan rides southward down the valley, he and the two others, An the Swart and Thorarinn. At Hafratindr in Svinadal lived a man called Thorkell. There is no house there now. He had gone to look after his horses that day, and his shepherd along with him. They had a view of both companies; the sons of Osvifr lying in wait, and Kjartan's band of three coming down along the dale. Then said the herd lad that they should go and meet Kjartan; it would be great luck if they could clear away the mischief that was waiting for them.

"Hold your tongue," said Thorkell; "does the fool think he can give life to a man when his doom is set? It is but little I grudge them their good pleasure, though they choose to hurt one another to their hearts' content. No! but you and I, we will get to a place where there will be no risk, where we can see all their meeting and have good sport out of their play. They all say that Kjartan has more fighting in him than any man; maybe he will need it all, for you and I can see that the odds are something."

And so it had to be as Thorkell wished.

The tragic encounter that follows, the last meeting of the two friends, Kjartan throwing away his weapons when he sees Bolli coming against him, Bolli's repentance when he has killed his friend, when he sits with his knee under Kjartan's head,—all this is told as well as may be; it is one of the finest passages in all the Sagas. But even this passage has something to gain from the episode of the churl and his more generous servant who looked on at the fight. The scene opens out; the spaces of the valley are shown as they appear to a looker-on; the story, just before the critical moment, takes us aside from the two rival bands and gives us the relation between them, the gradually-increasing danger as the hero and his companions come down out of the distance and nearer to the ambush.

In this piece of composition, also, there goes along with the pictorial vividness of the right point of view a further advantage to the narrative in the character of the spectator. Two of the most notable peculiarities of the Icelandic workmanship are thus brought together,—the habit of presenting actions and events as they happen, from the point of view of an immediate witness; and the habit of correcting the heroic ideal by the ironical suggestion of the other side. Nothing is so deeply and essentially part of the nature of the Icelandic story, as its inability to give a limited or abstract rendering of life. It is from this glorious incapacity that there are derived both the habit of looking at events as appearances, before they are interpreted, and the habit of checking heroics by means of unheroic details, or, as here, by a suggestion of the way it strikes a vulgar contemporary. Without this average man and his commentary the story of the death of Kjartan would lose much. There is first of all the comic value of the meanness and envy in the mind of the boor, his complacency at the quarrels and mutual destruction of the magnificent people. His intrusion on the scene, his judgment of the situation, is proof of the variety of the life from which the Saga is drawn. More than that, there is here a rather cruel test of the heroics of *Laxdæla*, of the story itself; the notable thing about this spectator and critic is that his boorish judgment is partly right, as the judgment of Thersites is partly right—"too much blood and too little brains." He is vulgar common sense in the presence of heroism. In his own way a critic of the heroic ideals, his appearance in Svinadal as a negative and depreciatory chorus in the tragedy of Kjartan is a touch of something like the mood of *Bandamanna Saga* in its criticism of the nobles and their rivalries; although the author of *Laxdæla* is careful not to let this dangerous spirit penetrate too far. It is only enough to increase the sense of the tragic vanity of human wishes in the life and death of Kjartan Olafsson.

Everything in the Sagas tends to the same end; the preservation of the balance and completeness of the history, as far as it goes; the impartiality of the record. The different sides are not represented as fully as in *Clarissa Harlowe* or *The Ring and the Book*, but they are allowed their chance, according to the rules, which are not those of analytical psychology. The Icelandic imagination is content if the character is briefly indicated in a few dramatic speeches. The brevity and externality of the Saga method might easily provoke from admirers of

Richardson a condemnation like that of Dr. Johnson on those who know the dial-plate only and not the works. The psychology of the Sagas, however, brief and superficial as it may be, is yet of the sort that may be tested; the dials keep time, though the works are not exposed. It may be doubtful at any moment how Skarphedinn will act, but when his history is in progress, and when it is finished, the reader knows that Skarphedinn is rightly rendered, and furthermore that it is impossible to deal with him except as an individual character, impressing the mind through a variety of qualities and circumstances that are inexplicably consistent. It is impossible to take his character to pieces. The rendering is in one sense superficial, and open to the censures of the moralist —"from without inwards"—like the characters of Scott. But as in this latter case, the superficiality and slightness of the work are deceptive. The character is given in a few strokes and without elaboration, but it is given inevitably and indescribably; the various appearances of Skarphedinn, different at different times, are all consistent with one another in the unity of imagination, and have no need of psychological analysis to explain them.

The characters in the best of the Sagas grow upon the mind with each successive appearance, until they are known and recognised at a hint. In some cases it looks almost as if the author's dramatic imagination were stronger and more just than his deliberate moral opinions; as if his characters had taken the matter into their own hands, against his will. Or is it art, and art of the subtlest order, which in Kjartan Olafsson, the glorious hero, still leaves something of lightness, of fickleness, as compared both with the intensity of the passion of Gudrun and the dogged resolution of Bolli? There is another Saga in which a hero of the likeness of Kjartan is contrasted with a dark, malevolent, not ignoble figure,—the story of the Faroes, of Sigmund Brestisson and Thrond of Gata. There, at the end of the story, when Thrond of Gata has taken vengeance for the murder of his old enemy, it is not Sigmund, the glorious champion of King Olaf, who is most thought of, but Thrond the dark old man, his opponent and avenger. The character of Thrond is too strong to be suppressed, and breaks through the praise and blame of the chronicler, as, in another history, the character of Saul asserts itself against the party of David. The charge of superficiality or externality falls away to nothing in the mind of any one who knows by what slight touches of imagination a character may be brought home to an audience, if the character is there to begin with. It is not by elaborate, continuous analysis, but by a gesture here and a sentence there, that characters are expressed. The Sagas give the look of things and persons at the critical moments, getting as close as they can, by all devices, to the vividness of things as they appear, as they happen; brief and reserved in their phrasing, but the reverse of abstract or limited in their regard for the different modes and aspects of life, impartial in their acknowledgment of the claims of individual character, and unhesitating in their rejection of conventional ideals, of the conventional romantic hero as well as the conventional righteous man. The Sagas are more solid and more philosophical than any romance or legend.

VII

EPIC AND HISTORY

In the close of the heroic literature of Iceland a number of general causes are to be found at work. The period of the Sagas comes to an end partly by a natural progress, culmination, and exhaustion of a definite form of literary activity, partly through external influences by which the decline is hastened. After the material of the early heroic traditions had been all used up, after the writers of the thirteenth century had given their present shapes to the stories of the tenth and the eleventh centuries, two courses were open, and both courses were taken. On the one hand the form of the Saga was applied to historical matter near the writer's own time, or actually contemporary, on the other hand it was turned to pure fiction. The literature divides into history and romance. The authentic history, the Sturlung cycle in particular, is the true heir and successor of the heroic Saga. The romantic Sagas are less intimately related to the histories of Njal or Gisli, though those also are representative of some part of the essence of the Saga, and continue in a shadowy way something of its original life. The Northern literatures in the thirteenth century were invaded from abroad by the same romantic forces as had put an end to the epic literature of France; translations of French romances became popular, and helped to change the popular taste in Norway and Iceland. At the same time the victory of Romance was not entirely due to these foreigners; they found allies in the more fanciful parts of the native literature. The schools of Northern prose romance, which took the place of the older Sagas, were indebted almost as much to the older native literature as to Tristram or Perceval; they are the product of something that had all along been part, though hardly the most essential part, of the heroic Sagas. The romantic story of Frithiof and the others like it have disengaged from the complexity of the older Sagas an element which contributes not a little, though by no means everything, to the charm of *Njála* and *Laxdæla.*

The historical work contained in the *Sturlunga Saga* is a more comprehensive and thorough modification of the old form. Instead of detaching one of the elements and using it in separation from the rest, as was done by the author of *Frithiof*, for example, the historian of the Sturlungs kept everything that he was not compelled to drop by the exigencies of his subject. The biographical and historical work belonging to the *Sturlunga Saga* falls outside the order to which *Njal* and *Gisli* belong; it is epic, only in the sense that a history may be called epic. Nevertheless it is true that this historical work shows, even better than the heroic Sagas themselves, what the nature of the heroic literature really is. In dealing with a more stubborn and less profitable subject it brings out the virtues of the Icelandic form of narrative.

The relation of the Saga to authentic history had always been close. The first attempt to give shape, in writing, to the traditions of the heroic age was made by Ari Thorgilsson (*ob.* 1148), especially in his *Landnámabók*, a history exact and positive, a record in detail of all the first settlers of the island, with notes of the substance of the popular stories by which their fame was transmitted. This exact history, this positive work, precedes the freer and more imaginative stories, and supplies some of them with a good deal of their matter, which they work up in their own way. The fashion of writing, the example of a written form of narrative, was set by Ari; though the example was not followed closely nor in all points by the writers of the Sagas: his form is too strict for them.

It was too strict for his greatest successor in historical writing in Iceland. Snorri Sturluson is the author of *Lives of the Kings of Norway*, apparently founded upon Ari's *Book of Kings*, which has been lost as an independent work. Snorri's *Lives* themselves are extant in a shape very far from authentic; one has to choose between the abridged and inconvenient shape of *Heimskringla*, in which Snorri's work appears to have been cut down and trimmed, and the looser form presented by such compilations as the longer Saga of Olaf Tryggvason, where more of Snorri appears to have been retained than in *Heimskringla*, though it has to be extricated from all sorts of irrelevant additions and interpolations. But whatever problems may still remain unsolved, it is certain enough that Snorri worked on his historical material with no intention of keeping to the positive lines of Ari, and with the fullest intention of giving to his history of Norway all the imaginative force of which he was capable. This was considerable, as is proved by the stories of the gods in his *Edda*; and in the histories of Olaf Tryggvason and of Saint Olaf, kings of Norway, he has given companions to the very noblest of the

Sagas dealing with the Icelandic chiefs. Between the more scientific work of Ari and the more imaginative work of Snorri comes, half-way, the *Life of King Sverre* (*ob.* 1202), written at the king's own dictation by the Abbot Karl of Thingeyri.

Ari collected the historical materials, both for Iceland and Norway, and put them together in the extant *Landnámabók* and the lost *Kings' Lives.* Snorri Sturluson treated the *Kings' Lives* in the spirit of the greater Icelandic Sagas; his *Lives* belong to heroic literature, if there is any meaning in that name. The *Life of Sverre* is not so glorious as the *Life* of either Olaf. Abbot Karl had not the same interests or the same genius as Snorri, and his range was determined, in most of the work, by the king himself. King Sverre, though he could quote poetry to good effect when he liked, was mainly practical in his ideas.

The Sturlung history, which is the close of the heroic literature of Iceland, has resemblances to the work of all three of the historians just named. It is like Ari in its minuteness and accuracy; like *Sverris Saga*, it has a contemporary subject to treat of; and it shares with Snorri his spirit of vivid narrative and his sympathy with the methods of the greater Sagas of Iceland. If authors were to be judged by the difficulty of their undertakings, then Sturla, the writer of the Sturlung history, would certainly come out as the greatest of them all. For he was limited by known facts as much, or even more than Ari; while he has given to his record of factions, feuds, and anarchy almost as much spirit as Snorri gave to his lives of the heroic kings, and more than Abbot Karl could give to the history of Sverre and his political success. At the same time, however, the difficulty of Sturla's work had been a good deal reduced in the gradual progress of Icelandic literature. He had to represent modern history, the history of his own time, in the form and with the vividness of the imaginative Sagas. In undertaking this he was helped by some examples of the same sort of thing, in Sagas written before his time, and forming an intermediate stage between the group of which *Njála* is the head, and Sturla's history of his own family. The biographies of Icelanders in the twelfth century, like that of Thorgils and Haflidi quoted above, which form an introduction to the Sturlung history, are something more authentic than the heroic Sagas, but not much less spirited. It is difficult to draw a decided line anywhere between the different classes; or, except by the date of its subject, to mark off the story of the heroic age from the story of the rather less heroic age that followed it. There was apparently an accommodation of the Saga form to modern subjects, effected through a number of experiments, with a result, complete and admirable, in Sturla's history of the Sturlung fortunes.

It may be said, also, that something of the work was done ready to the author's hand; there was a natural fitness and correspondence between the Icelandic reality, even when looked at closely by contemporary eyes in the broad daylight, and the Icelandic form of representation. The statue was already part shapen in the block, and led the hand of the artist as he worked upon it. It is dangerous, no doubt, to say after the work has been done, after the artist has conquered his material and finished off his subject, that there was a natural affinity between the subject and the author's mind. In the case of Iceland, however, this pre-existent harmony is capable of being proved. The conditions of life in Iceland were, and still are, such as to exclude a number of the things that in other countries prevent the historian from writing epic. There were none of the large, abstract considerations and problems that turn the history into a dissertation on political forces, on monarchy, on democracy, on diplomacy; there were none of the large, vague multitudes of the people that impose themselves on the historian's attention, to the detriment of his individual characters. The public history of Iceland lies all in the lives of private characters; it is the life of a municipality, very much spread out, it is true, but much more like the life of a country town or a group of country neighbours, than the society of a complex state of any kind that has ever existed in Europe. Private interests and the lives of individual men were what they had to think about and talk about; and just in so far as they were involved in gossip, they were debarred from the achievements of political history, and equally inclined to that sort of record in which individual lives are everything. If their histories were to have any life at all, it must be the life of the drama or the dramatic narrative, and not that of the philosophical history, or even of those medieval chronicles, which, however unphilosophical, are still obliged by the greatness of their subject to dwarf the individual actors in comparison with the greatness of Kingdoms, Church, and Empire. Of those great impersonalities there was little known in Iceland; and if the story of Iceland was not to be (what it afterwards became) a mere string of trivial annals, it must be by a deepening of the personal interest, by making the personages act and talk, and by following intently the various threads of their individual lives.

So far the work was prepared for authors like Sturla, who had to enliven the contemporary record of life in Iceland; it was prepared to this extent, that any other kind of work was unpromising or even hopeless. The present life in Sturla's time was, like the life of the heroic age, a perpetual conflict of private wills, with occasional and provisional reconciliations. The mode of narrative that was suitable for the heroic stories could hardly fail to be the proper mode for the contemporary factions of chiefs, heroic more or less, and so it was proved by Sturla.

Sturlunga Saga contains some of the finest passages of narrative in the whole of Icelandic literature. The biographical Sagas, with which it is introduced or supported, are as good as all but the best of the heroic Sagas, while they are not out of all comparison even with *Njála* or *Gísla*, with *Hrafnkels Saga* or *Bandamanna*, in the qualities in which these excel.

The story of Thorgils and Haflidi has already been referred to in illustration of the Icelandic method of narrative at its best. It is a good story, well told, with the unities well preserved. The plot is one that is known to the heroic Sagas—the growth of mischief and ill-will between two honourable gentlemen, out of the villainy of a worthless beast who gets them into his quarrels. Haflidi has an ill-conditioned nephew whom, for his brother's sake, he is loth to cast off. Thorgils takes up one of many cases in which this nephew is concerned, and so is brought into disagreement with Haflidi. The end is reconciliation, effected by the intervention of Bishop Thorlak Runolfsson and Ketill the priest, aided by the good sense of the rivals at a point where the game may be handsomely drawn, with no dishonour to either side. The details are given with great liveliness. One of the best scenes is that which has already been referred to (p. 238); another may be quoted of a rather different sort from an earlier year.

In the year 1120 at the Althing, Thorgils was with difficulty dissuaded from breaking the peace as they stood, both parties, by the door of the Thingvalla church on St. Peter's Day. Thorgils' friend Bodvar had to use both arguments and unction to make him respect the sanctity of the Althing, of the Church, and of the Saint to whom the day belonged. Afterwards Thorgils said to his friend, "You are more pious than people think."

> Bodvar answered: "I saw that we were penned between two bands of them at the church door, and that if it broke into a fight we should be cut to pieces. But for that I should not have cared though Haflidi had been killed in spite of the peace of Church and Parliament."

The intervention at the end is very well given, particularly Ketill the priest's story of his own enemy.

Sturlu Saga, the story of the founder of the great Sturlung house, the father of the three great Sturlung brothers, of whom Snorri the historian was one, is longer and more important than the story of Thorgils and Haflidi. The plot is a simple one: the rivalry between Sturla and Einar, son of Thorgils. The contest is more deadly and more complicated than that of Thorgils himself against Haflidi; that was mainly a case of the point of honour, and the opponents were both of them honourable men, while in this contest Sturla is politic and unscrupulous, and his adversary "a ruffian by habit and repute." There is a considerable likeness between the characters of Sturla and of Snorri the priest, as that is presented in *Eyrbyggja* and elsewhere. A comparison of the rise of Snorri, as told in *Eyrbyggja*, with the life of Sturla will bring out the unaltered persistence of the old ways and the old standards, while the advantage lies with the later subject in regard to concentration of interest. The *Life of Sturla* is not so varied as *Eyrbyggja*, but it is a more orderly piece of writing, and at the same time more lively, through the unity of its plot. Nor are the details spoiled by any tameness. Notable is the company of rogues maintained by Einar; they and their ways are well described. There was Geir the thief, son of Thorgerda the liar; he was hanged by the priest Helgi. There was Vidcuth, son of stumpy Lina (these gentry have no father's name to them); he was a short man and a nimble. The third was Thorir the warlock, a little man from the North country. This introduction serves to bring on the story of a moonlight encounter with the robbers in snow; and in this sort of thing the history of Sturla is as good as the best. It is worth while to look at the account of the last decisive match with Einar—another snow piece. It may be discovered there that the closer adhesion to facts, and the nearer acquaintance with the persons, were no hindrance to the Icelandic author who knew his business. It was not the multitude and confusion of real details that could prevent him from making a good thing out of his subject, if only his subject contained some opportunity for passion and conflict, which it generally did.

In this scene of the midnight raid in which the position of the two rivals is decided, there is nothing at all heightened or exaggerated, yet the proportions are such, the relations of the incidents are given in such a way, as could not be bettered by any modern author dealing with a critical point in a drama of private life. The style is that of the best kind of subdued and sober narrative in which the excitement of the situations is not spent in rhetoric.

It fell at Hvamm in the winter nights (about

Hallowmass) of the year 1171 that a man passed through, an old retainer of Sturla's; and Sturla did not like his manner. As it turned out, this man went west to Stadarhol, the house of Sturla's enemy, and told Einar all the state of Sturla's house, how there were few men there.

There was dancing at Hvamm that night, and it was kept up late. The night was still, and every now and then some would look out and listen, but they could hear no one stirring.

The night after that Einar set out. He avoided Hvamm, but came down on another steading, the house of Sturla's son-in-law Ingjald, and drove off the cows and sheep, without any alarm; it was not till the morning that one of the women got up and found the beasts gone. The news was brought at once to Hvamm. Sturla had risen at daybreak and was looking to his haystacks; it was north wind, and freezing. Ingjald came up, and, "Now he is coming to ask me to buy his wethers," says Sturla; for Sturla had warned him that he was in danger of being raided, and had tried to get Ingjald to part with his sheep. Ingjald told him of the robbery. Sturla said nothing, but went in and took down his axe and shield. Gudny his wife was wakened, and asked what the news was. "Nothing so far; only Einar has driven all Ingjald's beasts." Then Gudny sprang up and shouted to the men: "Up, lads! Sturla is out, and his weapons with him, and Ingjald's gear is gone!"

Then follows the pursuit over the snow, and the fight, in which Ingjald is killed, and Einar wounded and driven to beg for quarter. After which it was the common saying that Einar's strength had gone over to Sturla.

It is a piece of clean and exact description, and

particularly of the succession of scenes and moods in life. The revels go on through the calm night with an accompaniment of suspense and anxiety. There is no better note in any chronicle of the anxieties of a lawless time, and the steady flow of common pleasures in spite of the troubles; all the manners of an heroic or a lawless time are summed up in the account of the dance and its intermittent listening for the sound of enemies. Sturla in the early light sees his son-in-law coming to him, and thinks he knows what his errand is,—the author here, as usual, putting the mistaken appearance first, and the true interpretation second. In the beginning of the pursuit there is the silence and the repression of a man in a rage, and the vehement call of his wife who knows what he is about, and finds words for his anger and his purpose. The weather of the whole story is just enough to play into the human life—the quiet night, the north wind, and the frosty, sunless morning. The snow is not all one surface; the drifts on the hill-sides, the hanging cornice over a gully, these have their place in the story, just enough to make the movements clear and intelligible. This is the way history was written when the themes were later by two centuries than those of the heroic Sagas. There is not much difference, except in the "soothfastness"; the author is closer to his subject, his imagination is confronted with something very near reality, and is not helped, as in the older stories, by traditional imaginative modifications of his subject.

It is the same kind of excellence that is found in the other subsidiary parts of *Sturlunga*, hardly less than in the main body of that work. There is no reason for depressing these histories below the level of any but the strongest work in the heroic Sagas. The history of Bishop Gudmund and the separate lives of his two friends, Hrafn and Aron, are not less vivid than the stories of the men of Eyre or the men of Vatzdal. The wanderings of Aron round Iceland are all but as thrilling as those of the outlaw Gisli or Grettir, whose adventures and difficulties are so like his own. It is not easy to specify any element in the one that is not in the other, while the handling of the more authentic stories is not weak or faltering in comparison with the others. No single incident in any of the Sagas is much better in its way, and few are more humane than the scene in which Eyjolf Karsson gets Aron to save himself, while he, Eyjolf, goes back into danger.[1]

The *Islendlinga* or *Sturlunga Saga* of Sturla Thordarson, which is the greatest of the pure historical works, is in some things inferior to stories like those of the older Sturla, or of Hrafn and Aron. There is no hero; perhaps least of all that hero, namely the nation itself, which gives something like unity to the Shakespearean plays of the Wars of the Roses. Historically there is much resemblance between the Wars of the Roses and the faction fights in Iceland in which the old constitution went to pieces and the old spirit was exhausted. But the Icelandic tragedy had no reconciliation at the end, and there was no national strength underneath the disorder, fit to be called out by a peacemaker or a "saviour of society" like Henry VII. There was nothing but the family interests of the great houses, and the *Sturlunga Saga* leaves it impossible to sympathise with either side in a contest that has no principles and no great reformer to distinguish it. The anarchy is worse than in the old days of the Northern rovers; the men are more formal and more vain. Yet the history of these tumults is not without its brightness of character. The generous and lawless Bishop Gudmund belongs

[1] Translated in Appendix, Note C.

to the story; so do his champions Eyjolf, Hrafn, and Aron. The figure of Snorri Sturluson is there, though he is rather disappointing in his nephew's view of him. His enemy, Gizur the earl, is a strong man, whose strength is felt in the course of the history; and there are others.

The beauty of *Sturlunga* is that it gives a more detailed and more rational account than is to be found elsewhere in the world of the heroic age going to the bad, without a hero. The kind of thing represented may be found in countless other places, but not Froissart has rendered it so fully or with such truth, nor the *Paston Letters* with more intimate knowledge and experience. It is a history and not an epic; the title of epic which may be claimed for *Njála* and *Laxdæla*, and even in a sense transferred to the later biographies, does not rightly belong to Sturla's history of Iceland. It is a record from year to year; it covers two generations; there is nothing in it but faction. But it is descended from the epic school; it has the gift of narrative and of vision. It represents, as no prosaic historian can, the suspense and the shock of events, the alarm in the night, the confusion of a house attacked, the encounter of enemies in the open, the demeanour of men going to their death. The scenes are epic at least, though the work as a whole is merely historical.

There is a return in this to the original nature of the Saga, in some respects. It was in the telling of adventures that the Sagas began, separate adventures attaching to great names of the early days. The separate adventures of Gisli were known and were told about before his history was brought into the form and unity which it now possesses, where the end is foreknown from the beginning. Many of the heroic Sagas have remained in what must be very like their old oral form—a string of episodes. *Eyrbyggia*, *Vatnsdæla*, *Flóamanna*, *Svarfdæla*, are of this sort. *Sturlunga*, has not more unity than *Eyrbyggja*, perhaps not as much, unless the rise of Gizur may be reckoned to do for it what is done for the older story by the rise of Snorri the Priest. But while the scenes thus fall apart in *Sturlunga*, they are more vivid than in any other Icelandic book. In no other is the art of description so nearly perfect.

The scenes of *Sturlunga* come into rivalry with the best of those in the heroic Sagas. No one will ever be able to say, much less to convince any one else, whether the burning of Njal's house or the burning of Flugumyri is the better told or the more impressive. There is no comparison between the personages in the two stories. But in pure art of language and in the certainty of its effect the story of Flugumyri is not less notable than the story of Bergthorsknoll. It may be repeated here, to stand as the last words of the great Icelandic school; the school which went out and had no successor till all its methods were invented again, independently, by the great novelists, after ages of fumbling and helpless experiments, after all the weariness of pedantic chronicles and the inflation of heroic romance.

Sturla had given his daughter Ingibjorg in marriage to Hall, son of Gizur, and had come to the wedding at Flugumyri, Gizur's house at the foot of the hills of Skagafjord, with steep slopes behind and the broad open valley in front, a place with no exceptional defences, no fortress. It was here, just after the bridal, and after the bride's father had gone away, that Gizur's enemy, Eyjolf, came upon him, as he had threatened openly in men's hearing. Sturla, who had left the house just before, tells the story with the details that came to him from the eye-witnesses, with exact particular descriptions. But there is no drag in the story, and nothing mean in the style, whatever may have been the brutal reality. It is, once again, the great scene of Epic poetry repeated, the defence of a man's life and of his own people against surrounding enemies; it is the drama of Gunnar or of Njal played out again at the very end of the Northern heroic age, and the prose history is quick to recognise the claims upon it.

This is the end of the wedding at Flugumyri, in October of the year 1253, as told by Sturla:—

THE BURNING OF FLUGUMYRI

Eyjolf saw that the attack was beginning to flag, and grew afraid that the countryside might be raised upon them; so they brought up the fire. John of Bakki had a tar-pin with him; they took the sheepskins from the frames that stood outside there, and tarred them and set them on fire. Some took hay and stuffed it into the windows and put fire to it; and soon there was a great smoke in the house and a choking heat. Gizur lay down in the hall by one of the rows of pillars, and kept his nose on the floor. Groa his wife was near him. Thorbjorn Neb was lying there too, and he and Gizur had their heads close together. Thorbjorn could hear Gizur praying to God in many ways and fervently, and thought he had never before heard praying like it. As for himself, he could not have opened his mouth for the smoke. After that Gizur stood up and Groa supported him, and he went to the south porch. He was much distressed by the smoke and heat, and thought to make his way out rather than be choked inside. Gizur Glad was standing at the door, talking to Kolbein Grön, and Kolbein was offering him quarter, for there was a pact between them, that if ever it came to that, they should give quarter to one another, whichever of them had it in his power. Gizur stood behind Gizur Glad, his namesake while they were talking, and got some coolness the while. Gizur Glad said to Kolbein, "I will take quarter for myself, if I may bring out another man along with me." Kolbein agreed to this at once, excepting only Gizur and his sons.

Then Ingibjorg, Sturla's daughter, came to Groa at the door; she was in her nightgown, and barefoot. She was then in her fourteenth year, and tall and comely to see. Her silver belt had tangled round her feet as she came from her bedroom. There was on it a purse with many gold rings of hers in it; she had it there with her. Groa was very glad to see her, and said that there should be one lot for both of them, whatever might befall.

When Gizur had got himself cooled a little, he gave up his thought of dashing out of the house. He was in linen clothes, with a mail-coat over them, and a steel cap on his head, and his sword *Corselet-biter* in his hand. Groa was in her nightgown only. Gizur went to Groa and took two gold rings out of his girdle-pocket and put them into her hand, because he thought that she would live through it, but not he himself. One ring had belonged to Bishop Magnus his uncle, and the other to his father Thorvald.

"I wish my friends to have the good of these," he says, "if things go as I would have them."

Gizur saw that Groa took their parting much to heart.

Then he felt his way through the house, and with him went Gudmund the Headstrong, his kinsman, who did not wish to lose sight of him. They came to the doors of the ladies' room; and Gizur was going to make his way out there. Then he heard outside the voices of men cursing and swearing, and turned back from there.

Now in the meantime Groa and Ingibjorg had gone to the door. Groa asked for freedom for Ingibjorg. Kolbein heard that, her kinsman, and asked Ingibjorg to come out to him. She would not, unless she got leave to take some one out along with her. Kolbein said that was too much to ask. Groa besought her to go.

"I have to look after the lad Thorlak, my sister's son," says she.

Thorlak was a boy of ten, the son of Thorleif the Noisy. He had jumped out of the house before this, and his linen clothes were all ablaze when he came down to the ground: he got safe to the church. Some men say that Thorstein Genja pushed Groa back into the fire; she was found in the porch afterwards. Kolbein dashed into the fire for Ingibjorg, and carried her out to the church.

Then the house began to blaze up. A little after, Hall Gizur's son [the bridegroom] came to the south door, and Arni the Bitter, his henchman, with him. They were both very hard put to it, and distressed by the heat. There was a board across the doorway, half-way up. Hall did not stop to look, but jumped straight out over the hatch. He had a sword in one hand, and no weapon besides. Einar Thorgrimsson was posted near where he leapt out, and hewed at his head with a sword, and that was his death-wound. As he fell, another man cut at his right leg below the knee and slashed it nearly off. Thorleif the monk from Thverá, the brewer, had got out before, and was in the yard; he took a sheepskin and put it under Hall when Einar and the others went away; then he rolled all together, Hall and the sheepskin, along to the church when they were not looking. Hall was lightly clad, and the cold struck deep into his wounds. The monk was barefoot, and his feet were frostbitten, but he brought himself and Hall to the church at last.

Arni leapt out straight after Hall; he struck his foot on the hatch (he was turning old) and fell as he came out. They asked who that might be, coming in such a hurry.

"Arni the Bitter is here," says he; "and I will not ask for quarter. I see one lying not far away makes me like it well enough if I travel the same road with him."

Then said Kolbein: "Is there no man here remembers Snorri Sturluson?" [1]

They both had a stroke at him, Kolbein and Ari Ingimund's son, and more of them besides hewed at him, and he came by his death there.

Then the hall fell in, beginning from the north side into the loft above the hall. Now all the buildings began to flare up, except that the guest-house did not burn, nor the ladies' room, nor the dairy.

Now to go back to Gizur: he made his way through the house to the dairy, with Gudmund, his kinsman, after him. Gizur asked him to go away, and said that one man might find a way of escape, if fate would have it so, that would not do for two. Then Parson John Haldorsson came up; and Gizur asked them both to leave him. He took off his coat of mail and his morion, but kept his sword in his hand. Parson John and Gudmund made their way from the dairy to the south door, and got quarter. Gizur went into the dairy and found a curd-tub standing on stocks; there he thrust the sword into the curds down over the hilts. He saw close by a vat sunk in the earth with whey in it, and the curd-tub stood over it and nearly hid the sunken vat altogether. There was room for Gizur to get into it, and he sat down in the whey in his linen clothes and nothing else, and the whey came up to his breast. It was cold in the whey. He had not been long there when he heard voices, and their talk went thus, that three men were meant to have the hewing of him; each man his stroke, and no hurry about it, so as to see how he took it. The three appointed were Hrani and Kolbein and Ari. And now they came into the dairy with a light, and searched about everywhere. They came to the vat

---

[1] Arni Beiskr (the Bitter) in company with Gizur murdered Snorri Sturluson the historian at his house of Reykholt, 22nd September 1241.

that Gizur was in, and thrust into it three or four times with spears. Then there was a wrangle among them; some said there was something in the vat, and others said no. Gizur kept his hand over his belly, moving gently, so that they might be as long as possible in finding out that there was anything there. He had grazes on his hands, and all down to his knees skin wounds, little and many. Gizur said afterwards that before they came in he was shaking with cold, so that it rippled in the vat, but after they came in he did not shiver at all. They made two searches through the dairy, and the second time was like the first. After that they went out and made ready to ride away. Those men that still had life in them were spared, to wit, Gudmund Falkason, Thord the Deacon, and Olaf, who was afterwards called Guest, whose life Einar Thorgrimsson had attempted before. By that time it was dawn.

There is one passage in the story of Flugumyri, before the scene of the burning, in which the narrative is heightened a little, as if the author were conscious that his subject was related to the matter of heroic poetry, or as if it had at once, like the battle of Maldon, begun to be magnified by the popular memory into the likeness of heroic battles. It is in the description of the defence of the hall (*skáli*) at Flugumyri, before the assailants were driven back and had to take to fire, as is told above.

Eyjolf and his companions made a hard assault on the hall. Now was there battle joined, and sharp onset, for the defence was of the stoutest. They kept at it far into the night, and struck so hard (say the men who were there) that fire flew, as it seemed, when the weapons came together. Thorstein Gudmund's son said afterwards that he had never been where men made a braver stand; and all are agreed to praise the defence of Flugumyri, both friends and enemies.

The fire of the swords which is here referred to by the way, and with something like an apology for exaggeration, is in the poem of *Finnesburh* brought out with emphasis, as a proper part of the composition :—

swurdléoma stód,
Swylce eall Finnesburh fýrenu wǽre.

The sword-light rose, as though all Finnsburgh were aflame.

It is characteristic of the Icelandic work that it should frequently seem to reflect the incidents of epic poetry in a modified way. The Sagas follow the outlines of heroic poetry, but they have to reduce the epic magnificence, or rather it would be truer to say that they present in plain language, and without extravagance, some of the favourite passages of experience that have been at different times selected and magnified by epic poets. Thus the death of Skarphedinn is like a prose rendering of the death of Roland; instead of the last stroke of the hero in his agony, cleaving the rock with Durendal, it is noted simply that Skarphedinn had driven his axe into the beam before him, in the place where he was penned in, and there the axe was found when they came to look for him after the burning. The moderation of the language here does not conceal the intention of the writer that Skarphedinn's last stroke is to be remembered. It is by touches such as these that the heroic nature of the Sagas is revealed. In spite of the common details and the prose statement, it is impossible to mistake their essential character. They are something loftier than history, and their authors knew it. When history came to be written as it was written by Sturla, it still retained this distinction. It is history governed by an heroic spirit; and while it is closely bound to the facts, it is at the same time controlled and directed by the forms of an imaginative literature that had grown up in greater freedom and at a greater distance from its historical matter. Sturla uses, for contemporary history, a kind of narrative created and perfected for another purpose, namely for the imaginative reconstruction and representation of tradition, in the stories of Njal, Grettir, and Gisli.

There is no distortion or perversion in this choice and use of his instrument, any more than in Fielding's adaptation of the method of *Joseph Andrews* to the matter of the *Voyage to Lisbon*. In the first place, the imaginative form of narrative obliges the author to take his subject seriously and treat it with dignity; he cannot leave it crude and unformed. In the second place, there is a real affinity, in Iceland, between the subject-matters of the true history and the heroic Saga; the events are of the same kind, the personages are not unlike.

The imaginative treatment of the stories of Njal and Gisli had been founded on real knowledge of life; in *Sturlunga* the history of real life is repaid for its loan. In Sturla's book, the contemporary alarms and excursions, the midnight raids, the perils and escapes, the death of the strong man, the painful ending of the poor-spirited, all the shocks and accidents of his own time, are comprehended by the author in the light of the traditional heroics, and of similar situations in the imaginative Sagas; and so these matters of real life, and of the writer's own experience, or near it, come to be co-ordinated, represented, and made intelligible through imagination. *Sturlunga* is something more than a bare diary, or a series of pieces of evidence. It has an author, and the author understands and appreciates the matter in hand, because it is illuminated for him by the example of the heroic literature. He carries an imaginative narrative design in his head, and things as they happen fall into the general scheme of his story as if he had invented them.

How much this imaginative kind of true history is bound and indebted to its native land, how little capable of transportation, is proved in a very striking and interesting way by Sturla's other work, his essay in foreign history, the *Life of King Hacon of Norway*. The *Hákonar Saga*, as compared with *Sturlunga*, is thin, grey, and abstract. It is a masterly book in its own kind; fluent and clear, and written in the inimitable Icelandic prose. The story is parallel to the history of Iceland, contemporary with *Sturlunga*. It tells of the agonies of Norway, a confusion no less violent and cruel than the anarchy of Iceland in the same sixty years; while the Norwegian history has the advantage that it comes to an end in remedy, not in exhaustion. There was no one in Iceland like King Hacon to break the heads of the disorderly great men, and thus make peace in an effective way. *Sturlunga*, in Iceland, is made up of mere anarchy; *Hákonar Saga* is the counterpart of *Sturlunga*, exhibiting the cure of anarchy in Norway under an active king. But while the political import of Sturia's *Hacon* is thus greater, the literary force is much less, in comparison with the strong work of *Sturlunga*. There is great dexterity in the management of the narrative, great lucidity; but the vivid imagination shown in the story of Flugumyri, and hardly less in other passages of *Sturlunga*, is replaced in the life of Hacon by a methodical exposition of facts, good enough as history, but seldom giving any hint of the author's reserve of imaginative force. It is not that Sturla does not understand his subject. The tragedy of Duke Skule does not escape him; he recognises the contradiction in the life of Hacon's greatest rival, between Skule's own nobility and generosity of temper, and the hopelessness of the old scrambling misrule of which he is the representative. But the tragedy of the *Rival Kings* (*Kongsemnerne*) is left for Ibsen to work out in full; the portraits of Skule and Hacon are only given in outline. In the part describing Hacon's childhood among the veterans of the Old Guard (Sverre's men, the "ancient Birchlegs"), and in a few other places, there is a lapse into the proper Icelandic manner. Elsewhere, and in the more important parts of the history especially, it would seem as if the author had gone out of his way to find a sober and colourless pattern of work, instead of the full and vivid sort of story that came natural to him.

After Sturla, and after the fall of the Commonwealth of Iceland, although there were still some interesting biographies to be written—the *Life of Bishop Arne*, the *Life of Bishop Laurence*—it may be reckoned that the heroic strain is exhausted. After that, it is a new world for Iceland, or rather it is the common medieval world, and not the peculiar Icelandic version of an heroic age. After the fourteenth century the historical schools die out into meagre annals; and even the glorious figure of Jón Arason, and the tragic end of the Catholic bishop, the poet, the ruler, who along with his sons was beheaded in the interests of the Reformed Religion and its adherents, must go without the honours that were freely paid in the thirteenth century to bishops and lords no more heroic, no more vehement and self-willed. The history of Jón Arason has to be made out and put together from documents; his Saga was left unwritten, though the facts of his life and death may seem to prove that the old spirit lived long after the failure of the old literature.

The thirteenth century, the century of Snorri Sturluson and of Sturla his nephew, is also the age of Villehardouin and Joinville. That is to say, the finished historical work of the Icelandic School is contemporary with the splendid improvisations and first essays of French historical prose. The fates of the two languages are an instance of "the way that things are shared" in this world, and may raise some grudges against the dispensing fortune that has ordered the *Life of St. Louis* to be praised, not beyond its deserts, by century after century, while the Northern masterpieces are left pretty much to their own island and to the antiquarian students of the Northern tongues. This, however, is a consideration which does not touch the merits of either side. It is part of the fate of Icelandic literature that it should not be influential in the great world, that it should fall out of time, and be neglected, in the march of the great nations. It is in this seclusion that its perfection is acquired, and there is nothing to complain of.

A comparison of the two contemporaries, Sturla and Joinville, brings out the difference between two admirable varieties of history, dealing with like subjects. The scenery of the *Life of St. Louis* is different from that of *Sturlunga*, but there is some resemblance in parts of their themes, in so far as both narrate the adventures of brave men in difficult places, and both are told by authors who were on the spot themselves, and saw with their own eyes, or heard directly from those who had seen. As a subject for literature there is not much to choose between St. Louis in Egypt in 1250 and the burning of Flugumyri three years later, though the one adventure had all the eyes of the world upon it, and the other was of no more practical interest to the world than floods or landslips or the grinding of rocks and stones in an undiscovered valley. Nor is there much to choose between the results of the two methods; neither Sturla nor Joinville has anything to fear from a comparison between them.

Sometimes, in details, there is a very close approximation of the French and the Icelandic methods. Joinville's story, for example, of the moonlight adventure of the clerk of Paris and the three robbers might go straight into Icelandic. Only, the seneschal's opening of the story is too personal, and does not agree with the Icelandic manner of telling a story:—

> As I went along I met with a wagon carrying three dead men that a clerk had slain, and I was told they were being brought for the king to see. When I heard this I sent my squire after them, to know how it had fallen out.

The difference between the two kinds is that Joinville, being mainly experimental and without much regard for the older precedents and models of historical writing, tells his story in his own way, as memoirs, in the order of events as they come within his view, revealing his own sentiments and policy, and keeping a distinction between the things he himself saw and the things he did not see. Whereas Sturla goes on the lines that had been laid down before him, and does not require to invent his own narrative scheme; and further, the scheme he receives from his masters is the opposite of Joinville's personal memories. Though Sturla in great part of his work is as near the reality as Joinville, he is obliged by the Icelandic custom to keep himself out of the story, except when he is necessary; and then he only appears in the third person on the same terms as the other actors, with nothing except perhaps a greater particularity in description to show that the author is there himself in the thick of it. To let the story take care of itself is the first rule of the Icelandic authors. If they have any emotion or sentiment of their own, it must go into the story impersonally; it must inform or enliven the characters and their speeches; it must quicken the style unobtrusively, or else it must be suppressed. The parts of the Sagas that are most touching, such as the death of Njal, and the parting of Grettir and his mother, though they give evidence of the author's sensibility, never allow him a word for himself. The method is the method of Homer—δόλῳ δ' ὅ γε δάκρυα κεῦθεν—"he would not confess that he wept."

In Joinville, on the contrary, all the epic matter of the story is surveyed and represented not as a drama for any one to come and look at, and make his own judgment about it, but as the life of himself, the Sire de Joinville, Seneschal of Champagne, known and interpreted to himself first of all. It is barely possible to conceive the *Life of St. Louis* transposed into the mood of the *Odyssey* or of *Njála*. It is hard to see who would be a gainer thereby—certainly not St. Louis himself. He would be deprived, for instance, of what is at once the most heroic and the most trifling of all the passages in his story, which belongs altogether to Joinville, and is worth nothing except as he tells it, and because he tells it. The story of Joinville's misunderstanding of the king, and the king's way of taking it, on occasion of the Council at Acre and the question whether to return or to stay and recover the prisoners from the Saracens, is not only the whole *Life of St. Louis* summed up and put into one chapter, but it is also one of those rarest passages of true history in which a character whom we thought we knew is presented with all his qualities intensified in a momentary act or speech. It is as if the dulness of custom were magically broken, and the familiar character stood out, not different from himself, but with a new expression. In this great scene the Barons were for returning home, and put forward Guy Malvoisin their foreman to state their opinion. Joinville took the other side, remembering the warning of a kinsman of his own not to return in a hurry and forget the Lord's poor servants (*le peuple menu Nostre Signour*). There was no one there but had friends in prison among the Saracens, "so they did not rebuke me," says Joinville; but only two ventured to speak on his side, and one of these was shouted at (*mout felonessement*) by his uncle, the good knight Sir Jehan de Beaumont, for so doing. The king adjourned the Council for a week. What follows is a kind of narrative impossible under the Homeric or the Icelandic conditions—no impersonal story, but a record of Joinville's own changes of mind as he was played upon by the mind of the king; an heroic incident, but represented in a way quite different from any epic manner. Joinville describes the breaking up of the Council, and how he was baited by them all: "The king is a fool, Sire de Joinville, if he does not take your advice against all the council of the realm of France"; how he sat beside the king at dinner, but the king did not speak to him; how he, Joinville, thought the king was displeased; and how he got up when the king was hearing grace, and went to a window in a recess and stuck his arms out through the bars, and leant there gazing out and brooding over the whole matter, making up his mind to stay, whatever happened to all the rest; till some one came behind him and put his hands on his head at the window and held him there, and Joinville thought it was one of the other side beginning to bother him again (*et je cuidai que ce fust mes sires Phelippes d'Anemos, qui trop d'ennui m'avoit fait le jour pour le consoil que je li avoie donnei*), till as he was trying to get free he saw, by a ring on the hand, that it was the king. Then the king asked him how it was that he, a young man, had been bold enough to set his opinion against all the wisdom of France; and before their talk ended, let him see that he was of the same mind as Joinville.

This personal kind of story, in which an heroic scene is rendered through its effect on one particular mind, is quite contrary to the principles of the Icelandic history, except that both kinds are heroic, and both are alive.

Joinville gives the succession of his own emotions; the Icelandic narrators give the succession of events, either as they might appear to an impartial spectator, or (on occasion) as they are viewed by some one in the story, but never as they merely affect the writer himself, though he may be as important a personage as Sturla was in the events of which he wrote the Chronicle. The subject-matter of the Icelandic historian (whether his own experience or not) is displayed as something in which he is not more nearly concerned than other people; his business is to render the successive moments of the history so that any one may form a judgment about them such as he might have formed if he had been there. Joinville, while giving his own changes of mind very clearly, is not as careful as the Icelandic writers are about the proper order of events. Thus an Icelander would not have written, as Joinville does, "the king came and put his hands on my head"; he would have said, "John found that his head was being held"; and the discovery by means of the ring would have been the first direct intimation who it was. The story as told by Joinville, though it is so much more intimate than any of the Sagas, is not as true to the natural order of impressions. He follows out his own train of sentiment; he is less careful of the order of perception, which the Icelanders generally observe, and sometimes with extraordinary effect.

Joinville's history is not one of a class, and there is nothing equal to it; but some of the qualities of his history are characteristic of the second medieval period, the age of romance. His prose, as compared with that of Iceland, is unstudied and simple, an apparently unreserved confession. The Icelandic prose, with its richness of contents and its capability of different moods, is by comparison resolute, secure, and impartial; its authors are among those who do not give their own opinion about their stories. Joinville, for all his exceptional genius in narrative, is yet like all the host of medieval writers except the Icelandic school, in his readiness to give his opinion, to improve the occasion, and to add to his plain story something like the intonation of the preacher. Inimitable as he is, to come from the Icelandic books to Joinville is to discover that he is "medieval" in a sense that does not apply to those; that his work, with all its sobriety and solidity, has also the incalculable and elusive touch of fantasy, of exaltation, that seems to claim in a special way the name of Romance.

VIII

THE NORTHERN PROSE ROMANCES

THE history of the Sturlungs is the last great work of the classical age of Icelandic literature, and after it the end comes pretty sharply, as far as masterpieces are concerned. There is, however, a continuation of the old literature in a lower degree and in degenerate forms, which if not intrinsically valuable, are yet significant, as bringing out by exaggeration some of the features and qualities of the older school, and also as showing in a peculiar way the encroachments of new "romantic" ideas and formulas.

One of the extant versions of the *Foster-brothers' Story* is remarkable for its patches of euphuistic rhetoric, which often appear suddenly in the course of plain, straightforward narrative. These ornamental additions are not all of the same kind. Some of them are of the alliterative antithetical kind which is frequently found in the old Northern ecclesiastical prose,[1] and which has an English counterpart in the

[1] *Fóstbr.* (1852) p. 8: Því at ekki var hjarta hans seen fóarn í fugli: ekki var þat blóðfullt svá at þat skylfi af hræzlu, heldr var þat herdt af enum hæsta höfuðsmið í öllum hvatleik." ("His heart was not fashioned like the crop in a fowl: it was not gorged with blood that it should flutter with fear, but was tempered by the High Headsmith in all alacrity.")

alliterative prose of Ælfric. Others are more unusual; they are borrowed not from the Latin ecclesiastical school of prose, but from the terms of the Northern poetry, and their effect is often very curious. For instance, on page 13 there is a sudden break from the common, unemphatic narrative of a storm at sea ("they were drenched through, and their clothes froze on them") into the incongruous statement that "the daughters of Ran (the sea-goddess) came and wooed them and offered them rest in their embraces,"—a conceit which might possibly be mistaken by a modern reader for the fancy of Hans Andersen, but which is really something quite different, not "pathetic fallacy," but an irruption of metaphorical rhetoric from the poetical dictionary. There is another metaphorical flare-up on the next page, equally amazing, in its plain context:—

> She gave orders to take their clothes and have them thawed. After that they had supper and were shown to bed. They were not long in falling asleep. Snow and frost held all the night through; *all that night the Dog (devourer) of the elder-tree howled with unwearying jaws and worried the earth with grim fangs of cold.* And when it began to grow light towards daybreak, a man got up to look out, and when he came in Thorgeir asked what sort of weather it was outside;

and so on in the ordinary sober way. It is not surprising that an editor should have been found to touch up the plain text of a Saga with a few ornamental phrases here and there. Considering the amount of bad taste and false wit in the contemporary poetry, the wonder is that there should be such a consistent exclusion of all such things from the prose of the Sagas. The *Fóstbræðra* variations show the beginning of a process of decay, in which the lines of separation between prose and poetry are cut through.

Except, however, as an indication of a general decline of taste, these diversions in *Fóstbræðra Saga* do not represent the later and secondary schools of Icelandic narrative. They remain as exceptional results of a common degeneracy of literature; the prevailing forms are not exactly of this special kind. Instead of embroidering poetical diction over the plain text of the old Sagas, the later authors preferred to invent new stories of their own, and to use in them the machinery and vocabulary of the old Sagas. Hence arose various orders of romantic Saga, cut off from the original sources of vitality, and imitating the old forms very much as a modern romanticist might intimate them. One of the best, and one of the most famous, of these romantic Sagas is the story of Frithiof the Bold, which was chosen by Tegnér as the ground-work of his elegant romantic poem, a brilliant example of one particular kind of modern medievalism. The significance of Tegnér's choice is that he went for his story to the secondary order of Sagas. The original *Frithiof* is almost as remote as Tegnér himself from the true heroic tradition; and, like Tegnér's poem, makes up for this want of a pedigree by a study and imitation of the great manner, and by a selection and combination of heroic traits from the older authentic literature. Hence Tegnér's work, an ingenious rhetorical adaptation of all the old heroic motives, is already half done for him by the earlier romanticist; the original prose Frithiof is the same romantic hero as in the Swedish poem, and no more like the men of the Icelandic histories than Raoul de Bragelonne is like D'Artagnan. At the same time, it is easy to see how the authentic histories have supplied materials for the romance; as has been shown already, there are passages in the older Sagas that contain some suggestions for the later kind of stories, and the fictitious hero is put together out of reminiscences of Gunnar and Kjartan.

The "romantic movement" in the old Northern literature was greatly helped by foreign encouragement from the thirteenth century onward, and particularly by a change of literary taste at the Court of Norway. King Sverre at the end of the twelfth century quotes from the old Volsung poem; he perhaps kept the Faroese memory for that kind of poetry from the days of his youth in the islands. Hakon Hakonsson, two generations later, had a different taste in literature and was fond of French romances. It was in his day that the work of translation from the French began; the results of which are still extant in *Strengleikar* (the Lays of Marie de France), in *Karlamagnus Saga*, in the Norwegian versions of Tristram, Perceval, Iwain, and other books of chivalry.[1] These cargoes of foreign romance found a ready market in the North; first of all in Norway, but in Iceland also. They came to Iceland just at the time when the native literature, or the highest form of it at any rate, was failing; the failure of the native literature let in these foreign competitors. The Norwegian translations of French romances are not the chief agents in the creation of the secondary Icelandic School, though they help. The foreigners have contributed something to the story of Frithiof and the story of Viglund.

[1] "The first romantic Sagas"— *i.e.* Sagas derived from French romance—"date from the reign of King Hakon Hakonsson (1217-1263), when the longest and best were composed, and they appear to cease at the death of King Hakon the Fifth (1319), who, we are expressly told, commanded many translations to be made" (G. Vigfusson, Prol. § 25).

The phrase *náttúra amorsins* (= *natura amoris*) in the latter work shows the intrusion even of the Romance vocabulary here, as under similar conditions in Germany and England. But while the old Northern literature in its decline is affected by the vogue of French romance, it still retains some independence. It went to the bad in its own way; and the later kinds of story in the old Northern tongue are not wholly spurious and surreptitious. They have some claim upon *Njála* and *Laxdæla*; there is a strain in them that distinguishes them from the ordinary professional medieval romance in French, English, or German.

When the Icelandic prose began to fail, and the slighter forms of Romance rose up in the place of Epic history, there were two modes in which the older literature might be turned to profit. For one thing, there was plenty of romantic stuff in the old heroic poetry, without going to the French books. For another thing, the prose stories of the old tradition had in them all kinds of romantic motives which were fit to be used again. So there came into existence the highly-interesting series of Mythical Romances on the themes of the old Northern mythical and heroic poetry, and another series besides, which worked up in its own way a number of themes and conventional motives from the older prose books.

Mythical sagas had their beginning in the classical age of the North. Snorri, with his stories of the adventures of the gods, is the leader in the work of getting pure romance, for pure amusement, out of what once was religious or heroic myth, mythological or heroic poetry. Even Ari the Wise, his great predecessor, had done something of the same sort, if the *Ynglinga Saga* be his, an historical abstract of Northern mythical history; though his aim, like that of Saxo Grammaticus, is more purely scientific than is the case with Snorri. The later mythical romances are of different kinds. The *Volsunga Saga* is the best known on account of its subject. The story of Heidrek, instead of paraphrasing throughout like the Volsung book, inserts the poems of Hervor and Angantyr, and of their descendants, in a consecutive prose narrative. *Halfs Saga* follows the same method. The story of *Hrolf Kraki*, full of interest from its connexion with the matter of *Beowulf* and of Saxo Grammaticus, is more like *Volsunga Saga* in its procedure.[1]

The other class [2] contains the Sagas of *Frithiof* and *Viglund*, and all the fictitious stories which copy the style of the proper Icelandic Sagas. Their matter is taken from the adventures of the heroic age; their personages are idealised romantic heroes; romantic formulas, without substance.

Among the original Sagas there are some that show the beginning of the process by which the substance was eliminated, and the romantic *eidolon* left to walk about by itself. The introductions of many of the older Sagas, of *Gisli* and *Grettir* for example, giving the adventures of the hero's ancestors, are made up in this way; and the best Sagas have many conventional passages—Viking exploits, discomfiture of berserkers, etc.—which the reader learns to take for granted, like the tournaments in the French books, and which have no more effect than simple adjectives to say that the hero is brave or strong. Besides these stock incidents, there are ethical passages (as has already been seen) in which the hero is in

[1] The Mythical Sagas are described and discussed by Vigfusson, Prol. § 34.

[2] *Ibid.* § 11, "Spurious Icelandic Sagas" (*Skrök-Sögur*). For *Frithiof*, see § 34.

some danger of turning into a figure of romance. Grettir, Gisli, Kjartan, Gunnlaug the Wormtongue, Gunnar of Lithend, are all in some degree and at some point or other in danger of romantic exaggeration, while Kari has to thank his humorous squire, more than anything in himself, for his preservation. Also in the original Sagas there are conventions of the main plot, as well as of the episodes, such as are repeated with more deliberation and less skill in the romantic Sagas.

The love-adventures of Viglund are like those of Frithiof, and they have a common likeness, except in their conclusion, to the adventures of Kormak and Steingerd in *Kormaks Saga.* Kormak was too rude and natural for romance, and the romancers had to make their heroes better-looking, and to provide a happy ending. But the story of the poet's unfortunate love had become a commonplace.

The plot of *Laxdæla*, the story of the *Lovers of Gudrun*, which is the Volsung story born again, became a commonplace of the same sort. It certainly had a good right to the favour it received. The plot of *Laxdæla* is repeated in the story of Gunnlaug and Helga, even to a repetition of the course of events by which Kjartan is defrauded. The true lover is left in Norway and comes back too late; the second lover, the dull, persistent man, contrasted with a more brilliant but less single-minded hero, keeps to his wooing and spreads false reports, and wins his bride without her goodwill. Compared with the story of Kjartan and Gudrun, the story of Gunnlaug and Helga is shallow and sentimental; the likeness to *Frithiof* is considerable.

The device of a false report, in order to carry off the bride of a man absent in Norway, is used again in the story of *Thorstein the White*, where the result is more summary and more in accordance with poetical justice than in *Laxdæla* or *Gunnlaug.* This is one of the best of the Icelandic short stories, firmly drawn, with plenty of life and variety in it. It is only in its use of what seems like a stock device for producing agony that it resembles the more pretentious romantic Sagas.

Another short story of the same class and the same family tradition (Vopnafjord), the story of *Thorstein Staffsmitten*, looks like a clever working-up of a stock theme—the quiet man roused.[1] The combat in it is less like the ordinary Icelandic fighting than the combats in the French poems, more especially that of Roland and Oliver in *Girart de Viane*; and on the whole there is no particular reason, except its use of well-known East-country names, to reckon this among the family histories rather than the romances.

Romantic Sagas of different kinds have been composed in Iceland, century after century, in a more or less mechanical way, by the repetition of old adventures, situations, phrases, characters, or pretences of character. What the worst of them are like may be seen by a reference to Mr. Ward's Catalogue of MS. Romances in the British Museum, which contains a number of specimens. There is fortunately no need to say anything more of them here. They are among the dreariest things ever made by human fancy. But the first and freshest of the romantic Sagas have still some reason in them and some beauty; they are at least the reflection of something living, either of the romance of the old mythology, or of the romantic grace by which the epic strength of *Njal* and *Gisli* is accompanied.

[1] Translated by Mr. William Morris and Mr. E. Magnússon, in the same volume as *Gunnlaug, Frithiof,* and *Viglund* (*Three Northern Love Stories*, etc., 1875).

There are some other romantic transformations of the old heroic matters to be noticed, before turning away from the Northern world and its "twilight of the gods" to the countries in which the course of modern literature first began to define itself as something distinct from the older unsuccessful fashions, Teutonic or Celtic.

The fictitious Sagas were not the most popular kind of literature in Iceland in the later Middle Ages. The successors of the old Sagas, as far as popularity goes, are to be found in the *Rímur*, narrative poems, of any length, in rhyming verse; not the ballad measures of Denmark, nor the short couplets of the French School such as were used in Denmark and Sweden, in England, and in High and Low Germany, but rhyming verse derived from the medieval Latin rhymes of the type best known from the works of Bishop Golias.[1] This rhyming poetry was very industrious, and turned out all kinds of stories; the native Sagas went through the mill in company with the more popular romances of chivalry.

They were transformed also in another way. The Icelandic Sagas went along with other books to feed the imagination of the ballad-singers of the Faroes. Those islands, where the singing of ballads has always had a larger share of importance among the literary and intellectual tastes of the people than anywhere else in the world, have relied comparatively little on their own traditions or inventions for their ballad themes. Natural and popular as it is, the ballad poetry of the Faroes is derived from Icelandic literary traditions. Even Sigmund Brestisson, the hero of the islands, might have been forgotten but

[1] Vigfusson, Prol. p. cxxxviii. *C.P.B.*, ii. 392. The forms of verse used in the *Rímur* are analysed in the preface to *Riddara Rímur*, by Theodor Wisén (1881).

for the *Færeyinga Saga*; and Icelandic books, possibly near relations of *Codex Regius*, have provided the islanders with what they sing of the exploits of Sigurd and his horse Grani, as other writings brought them the story of Roncesvalles. From Iceland also there passed to the Faroes, along with the older legends, the stories of Gunnar and of Kjartan; they have been turned into ballad measures, together with *Roland* and *Tristram*, in that refuge of the old songs of the world.

CHAPTER IV

THE OLD FRENCH EPIC

THE OLD FRENCH EPIC

(*Chansons de Geste*)

IT appears to be generally the case in all old epic literature, and it is not surprising, that the existing specimens come from the end of the period of its greatest excellence, and generally represent the epic fashion, not quite at its freshest and best, but after it has passed its culmination, and is already on the verge of decline. This condition of things is exemplified in *Beowulf*; and the Sagas also, here and there, show signs of over-refinement and exhaustion. In the extant mass of old French epic this condition is enormously exaggerated. The *Song of Roland* itself, even in its earliest extant form, is comparatively late and unoriginal; while the remainder of French epic poetry, in all its variety, is much less authentic than *Roland*, sensibly later, and getting rapidly and luxuriantly worse through all the stages of lethargy.

It is the misfortune of French epic that so much should have been preserved of its "dotages," so little of the same date and order as the *Song of Roland*, and nothing at all of the still earlier epic—the more original *Roland* of a previous generation. The exuberance, however, of the later stages of French epic, and its long persistence in living beyond its due time, are proof of a certain kind of vitality. The French epic in the twelfth century, long after its best days were over, came into the keenest and closest rivalry with the younger romantic schools in their first vigour. Fortune has to some extent made up for the loss of the older French poems by the preservation of endless later versions belonging in date to the exciting times of the great romantic revolution in literature. Feeble and drowsy as they often are, the late-born hosts of the French epic are nevertheless in the thick of a great European contest, matched not dishonourably against the forces of Romance. They were not the strongest possible champions of the heroic age, but they were *there*, in the field, and in view of all spectators. At this distance of time, we can see how much more fully the drift of the old Teutonic world was caught and rendered by the imagination of Iceland; how much more there is in Grettir or Skarphedinn than in Ogier the Dane, or Raoul de Cambrai, or even Roland and Oliver. But the Icelandic work lay outside of the consciousness of Europe, and the French epic was known everywhere. There are no such masterpieces in the French epic as in the Icelandic prose. The French epic, to make up for that, has an exciting history; it lived by antagonism, and one may look on and see how the *chansons de geste* were fighting for their life against the newer forms of narrative poetry. In all this there is the interest of watching one of the main currents of history, for it was nothing less than the whole future imaginative life of Europe that was involved in the debate between the stubborn old epic fashion and the new romantic adventurers.

The *chansons de geste* stand in a real, positive, ancestral relation to all modern literature; there is something of them in all the poetry of Europe. The

Icelandic histories can make no such claim. Their relation to modern life is slighter, in one sense; more spiritual, in another. They are not widely known, they have had no share in establishing the forms or giving vogue to the commonplaces of modern literature. Now that they are published and accessible to modern readers, their immediate and present worth, for the friends of Skarphedinn and Gunnar, is out of all proportion to their past historical influence. They have anticipated some of the literary methods which hardly became the common property of Europe till the nineteenth century; even now, when all the world reads and writes prose stories, their virtue is unexhausted and unimpaired. But this spiritual affinity with modern imaginations and conversations, across the interval of medieval romance and rhetoric, is not due to any direct or overt relation. The Sagas have had no influence; that is the plain historical fact about them.

The historical influence and importance of the *chansons de geste*, on the other hand, is equally plain and evident. Partly by their opposition to the new modes of fiction, and partly by compliance with their adversaries, they belong to the history of those great schools of literature in the twelfth and thirteenth centuries from which all modern imaginations in prose and rhyme are descended. The "dolorous rout" of Roncesvalles, and not the tragedy of the Niblungs, still less the history of Gunnar or of Njal, is the heroic origin of modern poetry; it is remembered and renowned, πᾶσι μέλουσα, among the poets who have given shape to modern imaginative literature, while the older heroics of the Teutonic migration are forgotten, and the things of Iceland are utterly unknown.

French epic has some great advantages in comparison with the epic experiments of Teutonic verse.

For one thing, it exists in great quantity; there is no want of specimens, though they are not all of the best sort or the best period. Further, it has no difficulty, only too much ease, in keeping a long regular course of narrative. Even *Beowulf* appears to have attained to its epic proportions by a succession of efforts, and with difficulty; it labours rather heavily over the longer epic course. *Maldon* is a poem that runs freely, but here the course is shorter, and it carries much less weight. The Northern poems of the "Elder Edda" never attain the right epic scale at all; their abrupt and lyrical manner is the opposite of the epic mode of narration. It is true that the *chansons de geste* are far from the perfect continuity of the Homeric narrative. *Roland* is described by M. Gaston Paris in terms not unlike those that are applied by Ten Brink in his criticism of *Beowulf*:—

On peut dire que la *Chanson de Roland* (ainsi que toutes nos plus anciennes chansons de geste) se développe non pas, comme les poèmes homériques, par un courant large et ininterrompu, non pas, comme le *Nibelungenlied*, par des battements d'ailes égaux et lents, mais par un suite d'explosions successives, toujours arrêteés court et toujours reprenant avec soudaineté" (*Litt. fr. au moyen âge*, p. 59).

Roland is a succession of separate scenes, with no gradation or transition between them. It still bears traces of the lyrical origins of epic. But the narrative, though broken, is neither stinted nor laboured; it does not, like *Beowulf*, give the impression that it has been expanded beyond the convenient limits, and that the author is scant of breath. And none of the later *chansons de geste* are so restricted and reserved in their design as *Roland*; most of them are diffuse and long. The French and the Teutonic epics are at opposite extremes of style.

The French epics are addressed to the largest conceivable audience.[1] They are plain and simple, as different as possible from the allusive brevity of the Northern poems. Even the plainest of the old English poems, even *Maldon*, has to employ the poetical diction, the unprosaic terms and figures of the Teutonic School. The alliterative poetry down to its last days has a vocabulary different from that of prose, and much richer. The French epic language is not distinguished and made difficult in this way; it is "not prismatic but diaphanous." Those who could understand anything could understand it, and the *chansons de geste* easily found currency in the market-place, when they were driven by the new romances from their old place of honour in "bower and hall." The Teutonic poetry, even at its simplest, must have required more attention in its hearers than the French, through the strangeness and the greater variety of its vocabulary. It is less familiar, less popular. Whatever dignity may be acquired by the French epic is not due to any special or elaborate convention of phrase. Where it is weak, its poverty is not disguised, as in the weaker portions of Teutonic poetry, by the ornaments and synonyms of the *Gradus*. The commonplaces of French epic are not imposing.[2] With this difference between the French and the Teutonic conventions, there is all the more interest in a comparison of the two kinds, where they come into comparison through any resemblance of their subjects or their thought, as in *Byrhtnoth* and *Roland*.

[1] G. Paris, Preface to *Histoire de la littérature française*, edited by L. Petit de Julleville.

[2] See the preface to *Raoul de Cambrai*, ed. Paul Meyer (Anc. Textes), for examples of such *chevilles*; and also *Aimeri de Narbonne*, p. civ.

The French epics have generally a larger political field, more numerous armies, and more magnificent kings, than the Teutonic. In the same degree, their heroism is different from that of the earlier heroic age. The general motives of patriotism and religion, France and Christendom, prevent the free use of the simpler and older motives of individual heroism. The hero of the older sort is still there, but his game is hindered by the larger and more complex political conditions of France; or if these are evaded, still the mere size of the country and numbers of the fighting-men tell against his importance; he is dwarfed by his surroundings. The limitation of the scenes in the poems of *Beowulf*, *Ermanaric*, and *Attila* throws out the figures in strong relief. The mere extent of the stage and the number of the supernumeraries required for the action of most of the French stories appear to have told against the definiteness of their characters; as, on the other hand, the personages in *Beowulf*, without much individual character of their own, seem to gain in precision and strength from the smallness of the scene in which they act. There is less strict economy in the *chansons de geste*.

Apart from this, there is real and essential vagueness in their characters; their drama is rudimentary. The simplicity of the French epic style, which is addressed to a large audience and easily intelligible, is not capable of much dramatic subtlety. It can be made to express a variety of actions and a variety of moods, but these are generally rendered by means of common formulas, without much dramatic insight or intention. While the fragments of Teutonic epic seem to give evidence of a growing dramatic imagination, and the Northern poems, especially, of a series of experiments in character, the French epic imagination appears to have remained content with its established and abstract formulas for different modes of sentiment and passion. It would not be easy to find anything in French epic that gives the same impression of discovery and innovation, of the search for dramatic form, of the absorption of the poet's mind in the pursuit of an imaginary character, as is given, again and again, by the Northern poems of the Volsung cycle. Yet the *chansons de geste* are often true and effective in their outlines of character, and include a quantity of "humours and observation," though their authors seem to have been unable to give solidity to their sketches.

The weakness of the drama in the French epics, even more than their compliance with foreign romance in the choice of incidents or machinery, is against their claim to be reckoned in the higher order of heroic narrative. They are romantic by the comparative levity of their imagination; the story, with them, is too much for the personages. But it is still the problem of heroic character that engages them, however feebly or conventionally they may deal with it. They rely, like the Teutonic epic and the Sagas, on situations that test the force of character, and they find those situations in the common conditions of an heroic age, subject of course to the modifications of the comparatively late period and late form of society to which they belong. *Roland* is a variation on the one perpetual heroic theme; it has a grander setting, a grander accompaniment, than *Byrhtnoth* or *Waldere*, but it is essentially the old story of the heroic age,—no knight-errantry, but the last resistance of a man driven into a corner.

The greatness of the poem of *Roland* is that of an author who knows his own mind, who has a certain mood of the heroic imagination to express, and is at no loss for his instrument or for the lines of his work.

The poem, as has been already noted, has a general likeness in its plan to the story of Finnesburh as told in *Beowulf*, and to the poems of the death of Attila. The plot falls into two parts, the second part being the vengeance and expiation.

Although the story is thus not absolutely simple, like the adventures of Beowulf, no epic has a more magnificent simplicity of effect. The other personages, Charlemagne, Ganelon, Oliver, King Marsile, have to Roland nothing like the importance of Agamemnon, Ajax, Diomede, or Hector, as compared with Achilles in the *Iliad*. The poem is almost wholly devoted to the praise and glorification of a single hero; it retains very much of the old manners of the earlier stages of epic poetry, before it ceased to be lyric. It is a poem in honour of a chieftain.

At the same time, this lyrical tone in *Roland* and this pathetic concentration of the interest on one personage do not interfere with the epic plan of the narrative, or disturb the lines of the composition. The central part of the poem is on the Homeric scale; the fighting, the separate combats, are rendered in an Homeric way. *Byrhtnoth* and *Roland* are the works that have given the best medieval counterpart to the battles of Homer. There is more of a crisis and a climax in *Roland* than in the several battles of the *Iliad*, and a different sort of climax from that of *Byrhtnoth*. Everything leads to the agony and heroic death of Roland, and to his glory as the unyielding champion of France and Christendom. It is not as in the *Iliad*, where different heroes have their day, or as at Maldon, where the fall of the captain leads to the more desperate defence and the more exalted heroism of his companions. Roland is the absolute master of the *Song of Roland*. No other heroic poetry conveys the same effect of pre-eminent simplicity and grandeur. There is hardly anything in the poem except the single mood; its simplicity is overpowering, a type of heroic resistance for all the later poets of Europe. This impressive effect is aided, it is true, by an infusion of the lyrical tone and by playing on the pathetic emotions. Roland is ideal and universal, and the story of his defeat, of the blast of his horn, and the last stroke of Durendal, is a kind of funeral march or "heroic symphony" into which a meaning may be read for every new hero, to the end of the world; for any one in any age whose *Mood is the more as the Might lessens.* Yet although Roland has this universal or symbolical or musical meaning—unlike the more individual personages in the Sagas, who would resent being made into allegories—the total effect is mainly due to legitimate epic means. There is no stinting of the epic proportions or suppression of the epic devices. The *Song of Roland* is narrative poetry, a model of narrative design, with the proper epic spaces well proportioned, well considered, and filled with action. It may be contrasted with the *Death-Song of Ragnar Lodbrok*, which is an attempt to get the same sort of moral effect by a process of lyrical distillation from heroic poetry; putting all the strongest heroic motives into the most intense and emphatic form. There is something lyrical in *Roland*, but the poem is not governed by lyrical principles; it requires the deliberation and the freedom of epic; it must have room to move in before it can come up to the height of its argument. The abruptness of its periods is not really an interruption of its even flight; it is an abruptness of detail, like a broken sea with a larger wave moving under it; it does not impair or disguise the grandeur of the movement as a whole.

There are other poems among the *chansons de*

geste which admit of comparison with *Roland*, though *Roland* is supreme; other epics in which the simple motives of heroism and loyalty are treated in a simple and noble way, without any very strong individual character among the personages. Of these rather abstract expositions of the heroic ideal, some of the finest are to be found in the cycle of William of Orange, more especially in the poems relating the exploits of William and his nephew Vivian, and the death of Vivian in the battle against the Moors—

> En icel jor que la dolor fu grans
> Et la bataille orible en Aliscans.

Like *Roland*, the poem of *Aliscans* is rather lyrical in its effect, reiterating and reinforcing the heroic motives, making an impression by repetition of one and the same mood; a poem of the glorification of France. It shows, at the same time, how this motive might be degraded by exaggeration and amplification. There are too many Moors in it (as also in *Roland*), and the sequel is reckless and extravagant, where William of Orange rides to the king's court for help and discovers an ally in the enormous scullion of the king's kitchen, Rainouart, the Morgante of French epic. Rainouart, along with William of Orange, was seen by Dante in Paradise. In his gigantic and discourteous way he was one of the champions of Christendom, and his manners are interesting as a variation from the conventional heroic standards. But he takes up too much room; he was not invented by the wide and comprehensive epic imagination which finds a place for many varieties of mankind in its story, but by some one who felt that the old epic forms were growing thin and unsatisfactory, and that there was need of some violent diversion to keep the audiences awake. This new device is not abandoned till Rainouart has been sent to Avalon—the epic form and spirit losing themselves in a misappropriation of Romance. These excursions are of course not to be ascribed to the central authors of the cycle of William of Orange; but already even in the most heroic parts of the cycle there are indications of the flagging imagination, the failure of the old motives, which gave an opening to these wild auxiliary forces. Where the epic came to trust too much to the mere heroic sentiment, to the moral of *Roland*, to the contrast of knight and infidel, there was nothing for it but either to have recourse to the formal heroics of Camoens or Tasso,—for which the time had not yet come,—or to be dissolved altogether in a medley of adventures, and to pass from its old station in the front of literature to those audiences of the market-place that even now, in some parts of the world, have a welcome for Charlemagne and his peers.[1]

Those of the French epics in which the motives of *Roland* are in some form or other repeated, in which the defence of Christendom is the burden, are rightly considered the best representatives of the whole body. But there are others in which with less dignity of theme there is more freedom, and in which an older epic type, more akin to the Teutonic, nearer in many ways to the Icelandic Sagas, is preserved, and for a long time maintains itself distinct from all the forms of romance and the romantic schools. It is not in *Roland* or in *Aliscans* that the epic interest in character is most pronounced and most effective. Those among the *chansons de geste* which make least of the adventures in comparison with the personages, which think more of the tragic situation than of rapid

[1] *Historia Verdadera de Carlo Magno y los doce Pares de Francia:* Madrid, 4to (1891), a chap-book of thirty-two pages.

changes of scene and incident, are generally those which represent the feuds and quarrels between the king and his vassals, or among the great houses themselves; the anarchy, in fact, which belongs to an heroic age and passes from experience into heroic literature. There is hardly any of the *chansons de geste* in which this element of heroic anarchy is not to be found in a greater or less degree. In *Roland*, for example, though the main action is between the French and the Moors, it is jealousy and rivalry that bring about the catastrophe, through the treason of Ganelon. This sort of jealousy, which is subordinate in *Roland*, forms the chief motive of some of the other epics. These depend for their chief interest on the vicissitudes of family quarrels almost as completely as the Sagas. These are the French counterparts of *Eyrbyggja*, and of the stories of Glum or Gisli. In France, as in Iceland, the effect of the story is produced as much by the energy of the characters as by the interest of adventures. Only in the French epic, while they play for larger stakes, the heroes are incomparably less impressive. The imagination which represents them is different in kind from the Icelandic, and puts up with a very indefinite and general way of denoting character. Though the extant poems are late, some of them have preserved a very elementary psychology and a very simple sort of ethics, the artistic formulas and devices of a rudimentary stage which has nothing to correspond to it in the extant Icelandic prose.

Raoul de Cambrai in its existing form is a late poem; it has gone through the process of translation from assonance into rhyme, and like *Huon of Bordeaux*, though by a different method, it has been fitted with a romantic continuation. But the first part of the poem apparently keeps the lines of an older and more original version. The story is not one of the later cyclic fabrications; it has an historical basis and is derived from the genuine epic tradition of that tenth-century school which unfortunately is only known through its descendants and its influence. *Raoul de Cambrai*, though in an altered verse and later style, may be taken as presenting an old story still recognisable in most of its original features, especially in its moral.

Raoul de Cambrai, a child at his father's death, is deprived of his inheritance. To make up for this he is promised, later, the first fief that falls vacant, and asserts his claim in a way that brings him into continual trouble,—a story with great opportunities for heroic contrasts and complications. The situation is well chosen; it is better than that of the story of Glum, which is rather like it[1]—the right is not all on one side. Raoul has a just cause, but cannot make it good; he is driven to be unjust in order to come by his own. Violence and excess in a just cause will make a tragic history; there is no fault to be found with the general scheme or principle in this case. It is in the details that the barbarous simplicity of the author comes out. For example, in the invasion of the lands on which he has a claim, Raoul attacks and burns a nunnery, and in it the mother of his best friend and former squire, Bernier. The injured man, his friend, is represented as taking it all in a helpless dull expostulatory way. The author has no language to express any imaginative passion; he can only repeat, in a muffled professional voice, that it was really a very painful and discreditable affair. The violent passions here are those of the heroic age in its most barbarous form; more sudden and uncontrolled even than the anger of Achilles. But

[1] Glum, like Raoul, is a widow's son deprived of his rights.

with all their vehemence and violence there is no real tragic force, and when the hero is killed by his friend, and the friend is sorry afterwards, there is nothing but the mere formal and abstract identity of the situation to recall to mind the tragedy of Kjartan and Bolli.

Garin le Loherain is a story with a similar plot,—the estrangement and enmity of old friends, "sworn companions." Though no earlier than *Raoul de Cambrai*, though belonging in date to the flourishing period of romance, it is a story of the older heroic age, and its contents are epic. Its heroes are unsophisticated, and the incidents, sentiments, and motives are primitive and not of the romantic school. The story is much superior to *Raoul de Cambrai* in speed and lightness; it does not drag at the critical moments; it has some humour and some grace. Among other things, its gnomic passages represent very fairly the dominant heroic ideas of courage and good temper; it may be appealed to for the humanities of the *chansons de geste*, expressed in a more fluent and less emphatic shape than *Roland*. The characters are taken very lightly, but at least they are not obtuse and awkward. If there is not much dramatic subtlety, there is a recognition and appreciation of different aspects of the same character. The story proceeds like an Icelandic Saga, through different phases of a long family quarrel, springing from a well-marked origin; foreshadowed and accompanied, as in many of the Sagas, by the hereditary felonious character of the one party, which yet is not blackened too much nor wholly unrelieved.

As in many of the Icelandic stories, there is a stronger dramatic interest in the adversary, the wrong side, than in the heroes. As with Kari and Flosi in *Njála*, as with Kjartan and Bolli in *Laxdæla*, and with Sigmund and Thrond of Gata in *Færeyinga*

Saga, so in the story of Garin it is Fromont the enemy whose case is followed with most attention, because it is less simple than that of the heroes, Garin of Lorraine and Begon his brother. The character of Fromont shows the true observation, as well as the inadequate and sketchy handling, of the French epic school. Fromont is in the wrong; all the trouble follows from his original misconduct, when he refused to stand by Garin in a war of defence against the Moors:—

Iluec comence li grans borroflemens.

But Fromont's demeanour afterwards is not that of a traitor and a felon, such as his father was. He belongs to a felonious house; he is the son of Hardré, one of the notorious traitors of French epic tradition; but he is less than half-hearted in his own cause, always lamentable, perplexed, and peevish, always trying to be just, and always dragged further into iniquity by the mischief-makers among his friends. This idea of a distracted character is worked out as well as was possible for a poet of that school, in a passage of narrative which represents more than one of the good qualities of French epic poetry,—the story of the death of Begon, and the vengeance exacted for him by his brother Garin. This episode shows how the French poets could deal with matter like that of the Sagas. The story is well told, fluently and clearly; it contains some fine expressions of heroic sentiment, and a good fight, as well as the ineffectual sorrows and good intentions of the anti-hero Fromont, with all the usual tissue of violence which goes along with a feud in heroic narrative, when the feud is regarded as something impersonal and fatal, outside the wishes of the agents in it.

It may be said here that although the story of

Garin and of the feud between the house of Lorraine and their enemies is long drawn out and copious in details, it is not confused, but falls into a few definite episodes of warfare, with intervals of truce and apparent reconciliation. Of these separate acts in the tragedy, the *Death of Begon* is the most complete in itself; the most varied, as well as the most compact. The previous action is for a modern taste too much occupied with the commonplaces of epic warfare, Homeric combats in the field, such as need the heroic motives of Maldon or Roncesvalles to make them interesting. In the story of the *Death of Begon* there is a change of scene from the common epic battlefield; the incidents are not taken from the common stock of battle-poetry, and the Homeric supernumeraries are dismissed.

This episode[1] begins after an interval in the feud, and tells how Begon one day thought of his brother Garin whom he had not seen for seven years and more (the business of the feud having been slack for so long), and how he set out for the East country to pay his brother a visit, with the chance of a big boar-hunt on the way. The opening passage is a very complete and lively selection from the experience and the sentiments of the heroic age; it represents the old heroic temper and the heroic standard of value, with, at the same time, a good deal of the gentler humanities.

One day Begon was in his castle of Belin; at his side was the Duchess Beatrice, and he kissed her on the mouth: he saw his two sons coming through the hall (so the story runs). The elder was named Gerin and the younger Hernaudin; the one was twelve and the

[1] *Garin le Loherain*, ed. Paulin Paris (1833-35), vol. ii. pp. 217-272.

other was ten years old, and with them went six noble youths, running and leaping with one another, playing and laughing and taking their sport.

The Duke saw them and began to sigh, and his lady questioned him :—

"Ah, my Lord Duke, why do you ponder thus? Gold and silver you have in your coffers; falcons on their perch, and furs of the vair and the grey, and mules and palfreys; and well have you trodden down your enemies: for six days' journey round you have no neighbour so stout but he will come to your levy."

Said the Duke: "Madame, you have spoken true, save in one thing. Riches are not in the vair and the grey, nor in money, nor in mules and horses, but riches are in kinsmen and friends: the heart of a man is worth all the gold in the land. Do you not remember how I was assailed and beset at our home-coming? and but for my friends how great had been my shame that day! Pepin has set me in these marches where I have none of my near friends save Rigaut and Hervi his father; I have no brother but one, Garin the Lothering, and full seven years are past and gone that I have not seen him, and for that I am grieved and vexed and ill at ease. Now I will set off to see my brother Garin, and the child Girbert his son that I have never seen. Of the woods of Vicogne and of St. Bertin I hear news that there is a boar there; I will run him down, please the Lord, and will bring the head to Garin, a wonder to look upon, for of its like never man heard tell."

Begon's combined motives are all alike honest, and his rhetoric is as sound as that of Sarpedon or of Gunnar. Nor is there any reason to suppose, any more than in the case of Byrhtnoth, that what is striking in the poem is due to its comparative lateness, and to its opportunities of borrowing from new discoveries in literature. If that were so, then we might find similar things among the newer fashions of the contemporary twelfth-century literature; but in fact one does not find in the works of the romantic school the same kind of humanity as in this scene. The melancholy of Begon at the thought of his isolation—"Bare is back without brother behind it" —is an adaptation of a common old heroic motive which is obscured by other more showy ideas in the romances. The conditions of life are here essentially those of the heroic age, an age which has no particular ideas of its own, which lives merely on such ideas as are struck out in the collision of lawless heavy bodies, in that heroic strife which is the parent of all things, and, among the rest, of the ideas of loyalty, fellowship, fair dealing, and so on. There is nothing romantic or idealist in Begon; he is merely an honest country gentleman, rather short of work.

He continues in the same strain, after the duchess has tried to dissuade him. She points out to him the risk he runs by going to hunt on his enemy's marches,—

> C'est en la marche Fromont le poësti,

—and tells him of her foreboding that he will never return alive. His answer is like that of Hector to Polydamas:—

> Diex! dist il, dame, merveilles avez dit:
> Ja mar croiroie sorciere ne devin;
> Par aventure vient li biens el païs,
> Je ne lairoie, por tot l'or que Diex fist,
> Que je n'i voise, que talens m'en est prins.

The hunting of the boar is as good as anything of its kind in history, and it is impossible to read it without wishing that it had been printed a few years earlier to be read by Sir Walter Scott. He would have applauded as no one else can this story of the chase and of the hunter separated from his companions in the forest. There is one line especially in the lament for Begon after his death which is enough by itself to prove the soundness of the French poet's judgment, and his right to a welcome at Abbotsford: "This was a true man; his dogs loved him":—

> Gentis hons fu, moult l'amoient si chien.

Begon came by his death in the greenwood. The forester found him there and reported him to Fromont's seneschal, who called out six of his men to go and take the poacher; and along with them went Thibaut, Fromont's nephew, an old rival of Begon. Begon set his back to an aspen tree and killed four of the churls and beat off the rest, but was killed himself at last with an arrow.

The four dead men were brought home and Begon's horse was led away:—

> En une estable menerent le destrier
> Fronce et hennit et si grate des pies
> Que nus de char ne li ouse aprochier.

Begon was left lying where he fell and his three dogs came back to him:—

> Seul ont Begon en la forest laissié:
> Et jouste lui revindrent si trois chien,
> Hulent et braient com fuissent enragié.

This most spirited passage of action and adventure shows the poet at his best; it is the sort of thing that he understands, and he carries it through without a mistake. It is followed by an attempt at another theme where something more is required of the author, and his success is not so perfect. He is drawn into the field of tragic emotion. Here, though his means are hardly sufficient for elaborate work, he sketches well. The character of Fromont when the news of his opponent's death is brought to him comes out as something of a different value from the sheer barbarism of *Raoul de Cambrai*. The narrative is light and wanting in depth, but there is no untruth and no dulness in the conception, and the author's meaning is perfectly clear. Fromont is different from the felons of his own household. Fromont is the adversary, but he is a gentleman. Even when he knows no more of the event than that a trespasser has been killed in the forest, he sends his men to bring in the body;—

Frans hons de l'autre doient avoir pitié

—and when he sees who it is (*vif l'ot véu, mort le reconnut bien*) he breaks out into strong language against the churls who have killed the most courteous knight that ever bore arms. Mingled with this sentiment is the thought of all the trouble to come from the revival of the feud, but his vexation does not spring from mere self-interest. Fromondin his son is also angry with Thibaut his cousin; Thibaut ought to be flayed alive for his foul stroke. But while Fromondin is thinking of the shame of the murder which will be laid to the account of his father's house, Fromont's thought is more generous, a thought of respect and regret for his enemy. The tragedy of the feud continues after this; as before, Fromont is involved by his irrepressible kinsmen, and nothing comes of his good thoughts and intentions.

Our wills and fates do so contrary run,
Our thoughts are ours, the ends none of our own.

This moral axiom is understood by the French author, and in an imaginative, not a didactic way, though his imagination is not strong enough to make much of it.

In this free, rapid, and unforced narrative, that nothing might be wanting of the humanities of the French heroic poetry, there is added the lament for Begon, by his brother and his wife. Garin's lament is what the French epic can show in comparison with the famous lament for Lancelot at the end of the *Mort d'Arthur* :—

> Ha ! sire Begues, li Loherains a dit
> Frans chevaliers, corajeus et hardis !
> Fel et angris contre vos anemis
> Et dols et simples a trestoz vos amis !
> Tant mar i fustes, biaus frères, biaus amis !

Here the advantage is with the English romantic author, who has command of a more subtle and various eloquence. On the other hand, the scene of the grief of the Duchess Beatrice, when Begon is brought to his own land, and his wife and his sons come out to meet him, shows a different point of view from romance altogether, and a different dramatic sense. The whole scene of the conversation between Beatrice and Garin is written with a steady hand ; it needs no commentary to bring out the pathos or the dramatic truth of the consolation offered by Garin.

She falls fainting, she cannot help herself ; and when she awakens her lamenting is redoubled. She mourns over her sons, Hernaudin and Gerin : "Children, you are orphans ; dead is he that begot you, dead is he that was your stay ! "—"Peace, madame," said Garin the Duke, "this is a foolish speech and a craven. You, for the sake of the land that is in your keeping, for your lineage and your lordly friends—some gentle knight will take you to wife and cherish you ; but it falls to me to have long sorrow. The more I have of silver and fine gold, the more will be my grief and vexation of spirit. Hernaudin and Gerin are my nephews ; it will be mine to suffer many a war for them, to watch late, and to rise up early."—"Thank you, uncle," said Hernaudin: "Lord! why have I not a little habergeon of my own? I would help you against your enemies!" The Duke hears him, and takes him in his arms and kisses the child. "By God, fair nephew, you are stout and brave, and like my brother in face and mouth, the rich Duke, on whom God have mercy!" When this was said, they go to bury the Duke in the chapel beyond Belin; the pilgrims see it to this day, as they come back from Galicia, from St. James.[1]

Roland, *Raoul de Cambrai*, and *Garin le Loherain* represent three kinds of French heroic poetry. *Roland* is the more purely heroic kind, in which the interest is concentrated on the passion of the hero, and the hero is glorified by every possible means of patriotism, religion, and the traditional ethics of battle, with the scenery and the accompaniments all chosen so as to bring him into relief and give him an ideal or symbolical value, like that of the statues of the gods. *Raoul* and *Garin*, contrasted with *Roland*, are two varieties of another species; namely, of the heroic poetry which (like the *Odyssey* and the Icelandic stories) represents the common life of an heroic age, without employing the ideal motives of great causes, religious or patriotic, and without giving to the personages

[1] One of the frequent morals of French epic (repeated also by French romance) is the vanity of overmuch sorrow for the dead.

> ἀλλὰ χρὴ τὸν μὲν καταθάπτειν ὅς κε θάνησιν
> νηλέα θυμὸν ἔχοντας, ἐπ' ἤματι δακρύσαντας.
> (Odysseus speaking) *Il.* xix. 228.

> "Laissiez ester," li quens Guillaumes dit;
> "Tout avenra ce que doit avenir;
> Li mort as mors, li vif voissent as vis;
> Duel sor dolor et joie sor joïr
> Ja nus frans hons nel devroit maintenir."
> Les cors enportent, les ont en terre mis.
> *Garin*, i. p. 262.

any great representative or symbolical import. The subjects of *Raoul* and *Garin* belong to the same order. The difference between them is that the author of the first is only half awake to the chances offered by his theme. The theme is well chosen, not disabled, like so many romantic plots, by an inherent fallacy of ethics or imagination; a story that shapes itself naturally, if the author has the wit to see it. The author of *Raoul de Cambrai*, unhappily, has "no more wit than a Christian or an ordinary man," and leaves his work encumbered with his dulness of perception; an evidence of the fertility of the heroic age in good subjects, and of the incompetence of some of the artists. *Garin*, on the other hand, shows how the common subject-matter might be worked up by a man of intelligence, rather discursive than imaginative, but alive to the meaning of his story, and before everything a continuous narrator, with the gift of natural sequence in his adventures. He relates as if he were following the course of events in his own memory, with simplicity and lucidity, qualities which were not beyond the compass of the old French verse and diction. He does not stop to elaborate his characters; he takes them perhaps too easily. But his lightness of spirit saves him from the untruth of *Raoul de Cambrai*; and while his ethics are the commonplaces of the heroic age, these commonplaces are not mere formulas or cant; they are vividly realised.

There is no need to multiply examples in order to prove the capacity of French epic for the same kind of subjects as those of the Sagas; that is, for the representation of strenuous and unruly life in a comprehensive and liberal narrative, noble in spirit and not much hampered by conventional nobility or dignity.

Roland is the great achievement of French epic, and there are other poems, also, not far removed from the severity of *Roland* and inspired by the same patriotic and religious ardour. But the poem of *Garin of Lorraine* (which begins with the defence of France against the infidels, but very soon passes to the business of the great feud—its proper theme), though it is lacking in the political motives, not to speak of the symbolical imagination of *Roland*, is significant in another way, because though much later in date, though written at a time when Romance was prevalent, it is both archaic in its subject and also comprehensive in its treatment. It has something like the freedom of movement and the ease which in the Icelandic Sagas go along with similar antique subjects. The French epic poetry is not all of it made sublime by the ideas of *Roland*; there is still scope for the free representation of life in different moods, with character as the dominant interest.

It should not be forgotten that the French epic has room for comedy, not merely in the shape of "comic relief," though that unhappily is sometimes favoured by the *chansons de geste*, and by the romances as well, but in the "humours" inseparable from all large and unpedantic fiction.

A good deal of credit on this account may be claimed for Galopin, the reckless humorist of the party of Garin of Lorraine, and something rather less for Rigaut the Villain Unwashed, another of Garin's friends. This latter appears to be one of the same family as Hreidar the Simple, in the Saga of Harald Hardrada; a figure of popular comedy, one of the lubbers who turn out something different from their promise. Clumsy strength and good-nature make one of the most elementary compounds, and may easily be misused (as in *Rainouart*) where the author has few scruples and no dramatic consistency. Galopin is a more singular humorist, a ribald and a prodigal, yet of gentle birth, and capable of good service when he can be got away from the tavern.

There are several passages in the *chansons de geste* where, as with *Rainouart*, the fun is of a grotesque and gigantic kind, like the fun to be got out of the giants in the Northern mythology, and the trolls in the Northern popular tales. The heathen champion Corsolt in the *Coronemenz Looïs* makes good comedy of this sort, when he accosts the Pope: "Little man! why is your head shaved?" and explains to him his objection to the Pope's religion: "You are not well advised to talk to me of God: he has done me more wrong than any other man in the world," and so on.[1]

Also, in a less exaggerated way, there is some appreciation of the humour to be found in the con-

[1] Respont li reis: "N'iés pas bien enseigniez,
Qui devant mei oses de Deu plaidier;
C'est l'om el mont qui plus m'a fait irier:
Mon pere ocist une foldre del ciel:
Tot i fu ars, ne li pot l'en aidier.
Quant Deus l'ot mort, si fist que enseigniez;
El ciel monta, ça ne volt repairier;
Ge nel poeie sivre ne enchalcier,
Mais de ses omes me sui ge puis vengiez;
De cels qui furent levé et baptisié
Ai fait destruire plus de trente miliers,
Ardeir en feu et en eve neier;
Quant ge la sus ne puis Deu guerreier,
Nul de ses omes ne vueil ça jus laissier,
Et mei et Deu n'avons mais que plaidier:
Meie est la terre et siens sera li ciels.
l.c., l. 522.

The last verse expresses the same sentiment as the answer of the Emperor Henry when he was told to beware of God's vengeance: "Celum celi Domino, terram autem dedit filiis hominum" (Otton. Frising. *Gesta Frid.* i. 11).

trast between the churl and the knight, and their different points of view; as in the passage of the *Charroi de Nismes* where William of Orange questions the countryman about the condition of the city under its Saracen masters, and is answered with information about the city tolls and the price of bread.[1] It must be admitted, however, that this slight passage of comedy is far outdone by the conversation in the romance of *Aucassin and Nicolette*, between Aucassin and the countryman, where the author of that story seems to get altogether beyond the conventions of his own time into the region of Chaucer, or even somewhere near the forest of Arden. The comedy of the *chansons de geste* is easily satisfied with plain and robust practical jokes. Yet it counts for something in the picture, and it might be possible, in a detailed criticism of the epics, to distinguish between the comic incidents that have an artistic value and intention, and those that are due merely to the rudeness of those common minstrels who are accused (by their rivals in epic poetry) of corrupting and debasing the texts.

There were many ways in which the French epic was degraded at the close of its course—by dilution

[1] Li cuens Guillaumes li comença à dire:
—Diva, vilain, par la loi dont tu vives
Fus-tu a Nymes, la fort cité garnie?
—Oïl, voir, sire, le paaige me quistrent;
Ge fui trop poures, si nel poi baillier mie.
Il me lessèrent por mes enfanz qu'il virent.
—Di moi, vilain, des estres de la vile.
Et cil respont:—Ce vos sai-ge bien dire
Por un denier .ii. granz pains i véismes;
La denerée vaut .iii. en autre vile:
Moult par est bone, se puis n'est empirie.
—Fox, dist Guillaume, ce ne demant-je mie,
Mès des paiens chevaliers de la vile,
Del rei Otrant et de sa compaignie.
l.c., ll. 903-916.

and expansion, by the growth of a kind of dull parasitic, sapless language over the old stocks, by the general failure of interest, and the transference of favour to other kinds of literature. Reading came into fashion, and the minstrels lost their welcome in the castles, and had to betake themselves to more vulgar society for their livelihood. At the same time, epic made a stand against the new modes and a partial compliance with them; and the *chansons de geste* were not wholly left to the vagrant reciters, but were sometimes copied out fair in handsome books, and held their own with the romances.

The compromise between epic and romance in old French literature is most interesting where romance has invaded a story of the simpler kind like *Raoul de Cambrai.* Stories of war against the infidel, stories like those of William of Orange, were easily made romantic. The poem of the *Prise d'Orange*, for example, an addition to this cycle, is a pure romance of adventure, and a good one, though it has nothing of the more solid epic in it. Where the action is carried on between the knights of France and the Moors, one is prepared for a certain amount of wonder; the palaces and dungeons of the Moors are the right places for strange things to happen, and the epic of the defence of France goes easily off into night excursions and disguises: the Moorish princess also is there, to be won by the hero. All this is natural; but it is rather more paradoxical to find the epic of family feuds, originally sober, grave, and business-like, turning more and more extravagant, as it does in the *Four Sons of Aymon*, which in its original form, no doubt, was something like the more serious parts of *Raoul de Cambrai* or of the *Lorrains*, but which in the extant version is expanded and made wonderful, a story of wild adventures, yet with traces still of its origin among the realities of the heroic age, the common matters of practical interest to heroes.

The case of *Huon of Bordeaux* is more curious, for there the original sober story has been preserved, and it is one of the best and most coherent of them all,[1] till it is suddenly changed by the sound of Oberon's horn and passes out of the real world altogether.

The lines of the earlier part of the story are worth following, for there is no better story among the French poems that represent the ruder heroic age—a simple story of feudal rivalries and jealousies, surviving in this strange way as an introduction to the romance of *Oberon.*

The Emperor Charlemagne, one hundred and twenty-five years old, but not particularly reverend, holds a court at Paris one Whitsuntide and asks to be relieved of his kingdom. His son Charlot is to succeed him. Charlot is worthless, the companion of traitors and disorderly persons; he has made enough trouble already in embroiling Ogier the Dane with the Emperor. Charlemagne is infatuated and will have his son made king:—

> Si m'aït Diex, tu auras si franc fiet
> Com Damediex qui tot puet justicier
> Tient Paradis de regne droiturier!

Then the traitor Amaury de la Tor de Rivier gets up and brings forward the case of Bordeaux, which has rendered no service for seven years, since the two brothers, Huon and Gerard, were left orphans. Amaury proposes that the orphans should be dispossessed. Charlemagne agrees at once, and with-

[1] Cf. Auguste Longnon, "L'élément historique de Huon de Bordeaux," *Romania*, viii.

draws his assent again (a painful spectacle!) when it is suggested to him that Huon and his brother have omitted their duties in pure innocence, and that their father Sewin was always loyal.

Messengers are sent to bring Huon and Gerard to Paris, and every chance is to be given them of proving their good faith to the Emperor.

This is not what Amaury the traitor wants; he goes to Charlot and proposes an ambuscade to lie in wait for the two boys and get rid of them; his real purpose being to get rid of the king's son as well as of Huon of Bordeaux.

The two boys set out, and on the way fall in with the Abbot of Clugni, their father's cousin, a strong-minded prelate, who accompanies them. Outside Paris they come to the ambush, and the king's son is despatched by Amaury to encounter them. What follows is an admirable piece of narrative. Gerard rides up to address Charlot; Charlot rides at him as he is turning back to report to Huon and the Abbot, and Gerard who is unarmed falls severely wounded. Then Huon, also unarmed, rides at Charlot, though his brother calls out to him: "I see helmets flashing there among the bushes." With his scarlet mantle rolled round his arm he meets the lance of Charlot safely, and with his sword, as he passes, cuts through the helmet and head of his adversary.

This is good enough for Amaury, and he lets Huon and his party ride on to the city, while he takes up the body of Charlot on a shield and follows after.

Huon comes before the Emperor and tells his story as far as he knows it; he does not know that the felon he has killed is the Emperor's son. Charlemagne gives solemn absolution to Huon. Then appears Amaury with a false story, making

Huon the aggressor. Charlemagne forgets all about the absolution and snatches up a knife, and is with difficulty calmed by his wise men.

The ordeal of battle has to decide between the two parties; there are elaborate preparations and preliminaries, obviously of the most vivid interest to the audience. The demeanour of the Abbot of Clugni ought not to be passed over: he vows that if Heaven permits any mischance to come upon Huon, he, the Abbot, will make it good on St. Peter himself, and batter his holy shrine till the gold flies.

In the combat Huon is victorious; but unhappily a last treacherous effort of his enemy, after he has yielded and confessed, makes Huon cut off his head in too great a hurry before the confession is heard by the Emperor or any witnesses:—

> Le teste fist voler ens el larris :
> Hues le voit, mais ce fu sans jehir.

The head went flying over the lea, but it had no more words to speak.

Huon is not forgiven by the Emperor; the Emperor spares his life, indeed, but sends him on a hopeless expedition.

And there the first part of the story ends. The present version is dated in the early part of the reign of St. Louis; it is contemporary with Snorri Sturluson and Sturla his nephew, and exhibits, though not quite in the Icelandic manner, the principal motives of early unruly society, without much fanciful addition, and with a very strong hold upon the tragic situation, and upon the types of character. As in *Raoul de Cambrai*, right and wrong are mixed; the Emperor has a real grievance against Huon, and Huon, with little fault of his own, is put apparently in the wrong. The interests involved are of the strongest possible. There was not a single lord among those to whom the minstrel repeated his story who did not know that he might have to look out for encroachments and injustice—interference at any rate—from the king, and treachery from his neighbours. No one hoped to leave his castles and lands in peace to his son, who did not also fear that his son might be left defenceless and his lands exposed to competition; a fear most touchingly expressed in the lament of William of Poitiers, when he set out on the first Crusade.[1]

Whatever general influences of law or politics or social economy are supposed to be at work in the story of *Huon of Bordeaux*,—and all this earlier part of it is a story of feudal politics and legal problems,—these influences were also present in the real world in which the maker and the hearers of the poem had their life. It is plain and serious dealing with matter of fact.

But after the ordeal of battle in which Huon kills the traitor, the tone changes with great abruptness and a new story begins.

The commission laid upon Huon by the implacable and doting Emperor is nothing less than that which afterwards was made a byword for all impossible enterprises—"to take the Great Turk by the beard." He is to go to Babylon and, literally, to beard the Admiral there, and carry off the Admiral's daughter. The audience is led away into the wide world of Romance. Huon goes to the East by way of Rome and Brindisi—naturally enough—but the real world ends at Brindisi; beyond that everything is magical.

[1] "Pos de chantar m'es pres talens:"—Raynouard, *Choix des poésies des Troubadours*, iv. p. 83; Bartsch, *Chrestomathie provençale*.

CHAPTER V

ROMANCE

AND THE OLD FRENCH ROMANTIC SCHOOLS

ROMANCE

AND THE OLD FRENCH ROMANTIC SCHOOLS

ROMANCE in many varieties is to be found inherent in Epic and in Tragedy; for some readers, possibly, the great and magnificent forms of poetry are most attractive when from time to time they forget their severity, and when the tragic strength is allowed to rest, as in the fairy interludes of the *Odyssey*, or the similes of the clouds, winds, and mountain-waters in the *Iliad*. If Romance be the name for the sort of imagination that possesses the mystery and the spell of everything remote and unattainable, then Romance is to be found in the old Northern heroic poetry in larger measure than any epic or tragic solemnity, and in no small measure also even in the steady course of the Icelandic histories. Possibly Romance is in its best place here, as an element in the epic harmony; perhaps the romantic mystery is most mysterious when it is found as something additional among the graver and more positive affairs of epic or tragic personages. The occasional visitations of the dreaming moods of romance, in the middle of a great epic or a great tragedy, are often more romantic than the literature which is nothing but romance from beginning to end. The strongest poets, Homer, Dante, and Shakespeare, have along with their strong reasoning enough of the lighter and fainter grace and charm to be the despair of all the "romantic schools" in the world. In the Icelandic prose stories, as has been seen already, there is a similar combination. These stories contain the strongest imaginative work of the Middle Ages before Dante. Along with this there is found in them occasionally the uncertain and incalculable play of the other, the more airy mode of imagination; and the romance of the strong Sagas is more romantic than that of the medieval works which have no other interest to rely upon, or of all but a very few.

One of the largest and plainest facts of medieval history is the change of literature in the twelfth century, and the sudden and exuberant growth and progress of a number of new poetical forms; particularly the courtly lyric that took shape in Provence, and passed into the tongues of Italy, France, and Germany, and the French romance which obeyed the same general inspiration as the Provençal poetry, and was equally powerful as an influence on foreign nations. The French Romantic Schools of the twelfth century are among the most definite and the most important appearances even in that most wonderful age; though it is irrational to contrast them with the other great historical movements of the time, because there is no real separation between them. French romance is part of the life of the time, and the life of the twelfth century is reproduced in French romance.

The rise of these new forms of story makes an unmistakable difference between the age that preceded them and everything that comes after. They are a new, fresh, and prosperous beginning in literature, and they imply the failure of the older manner of thought, the older fashion of imagination, represented in the epic literature of France, not to speak of the various Teutonic forms of heroic verse and prose that are related to the epic of France only by a remote common ancestry, and a certain general likeness in the conditions of "heroic" life.

The defeat of French epic, as has been noted already, was slow and long resisted; but the victory of romance was inevitable. Together with the influence of the Provençal lyric idealism, it determined the forms of modern literature, long after the close of the Middle Ages. The change of fashion in the twelfth century is as momentous and far-reaching in its consequences as that to which the name "Renaissance" is generally appropriated. The later Renaissance, indeed, in what concerns imaginative literature, makes no such abrupt and sudden change of fashion as was made in the twelfth century. The poetry and romance of the Renaissance follow naturally upon the literature of the Middle Ages; for the very good reason that it was the Middle Ages which began, even in their dark beginnings, the modern study of the humanities, and in the twelfth century made a remarkable and determined effort to secure the inheritance of ancient poetry for the advantage of the new tongues and their new forms of verse. There is no such line of division between Ariosto and Chrestien of Troyes as there is between Chrestien and the primitive epic.

The romantic schools of the twelfth century are the result and evidence of a great unanimous movement, the origins of which may be traced far back in the general conditions of education and learning, in the influence of Latin authors, in the interchange of popular tales. They are among the most characteristic productions of the most impressive, varied, and characteristic period in the Middle Ages; of that century which broke, decisively, with the old "heroic" traditions, and made the division between the heroic and the chivalric age. When the term "medieval" is used in modern talk, it almost always denotes something which first took definite shape in the twelfth century. The twelfth century is the source of most of the "medieval" influences in modern art and literature, and the French romances of that age are the original authorities for most of the "Gothic" ornaments adopted in modern romantic schools.

The twelfth-century French romances form a definite large group, with many ranks and divisions, some of which are easily distinguished, while all are of great historical interest.

One common quality, hardly to be mistaken, is that which marks them all as belonging to a romantic *school*, in almost all the modern senses of that term. That is to say, they are not the spontaneous product of an uncritical and ingenuous imagination; they are not the same sort of thing as the popular stories on which many of them are founded; they are the literary work of authors more or less sophisticated, on the look-out for new sensations and new literary devices. It is useless to go to those French books in order to catch the first fresh jet of romantic fancy, the "silly sooth" of the golden age. One might as well go to the *Légende des Siècles.* Most of the romance of the medieval schools is already hot and dusty and fatigued. It has come through the mills of a thousand active literary men, who know their business, and have an eye to their profits. Medieval romance, in its most characteristic and most influential form, is almost as factitious and professional as modern Gothic architecture. The twelfth-century dealers in romantic commonplaces are as fully conscious of the market value of their goods as any later poet who has borrowed from them their giants and enchanters, their forests and their magic castles;

and these and similar properties are used in the twelfth century with the same kind of literary sharpness, the same attention to the demands of the "reading public," as is shown by the various poets and novelists who have waited on the successes, and tried to copy the methods, of Goethe, Scott, or Victor Hugo. Pure Romance, such as is found in the old Northern poems, is very rare in the French stories of the twelfth century; the magical touch and the sense of mystery, and all the things that are associated with the name romance, when that name is applied to the *Ancient Mariner*, or *La Belle Dame sans Merci*, or the *Lady of Shalott*, are generally absent from the most successful romances of the great medieval romantic age, full though they may be of all the forms of chivalrous devotion and all the most wonderful romantic machines. Most of them are as different from the true irresistible magic of fancy as *Thalaba* from *Kubla Khan*. The name "romantic school" is rightly applicable to them and their work, for almost the last thing that is produced in a "romantic school" is the infallible and indescribable touch of romance. A "romantic school" is a company for the profitable working of Broceliande, an organised attempt to "open up" the Enchanted Ground; such, at least, is the appearance of a great deal of the romantic literature of the early part of the nineteenth century, and of its forerunner in the twelfth. There is this difference between the two ages, that the medieval romanticists are freer and more original than the moderns who made a business out of tales of terror and wonder, and tried to fatten their lean kine on the pastures of "Gothic" or of Oriental learning.

The romance-writers of the twelfth century, though they did much to make romance into a mechanic art, though they reduced the game to a system and left the different romantic combinations and conventions within the reach of almost any 'prentice hand, were yet in their way original explorers. Though few of them got out of their materials the kind of effect that appeals to us now most strongly, and though we think we can see what they missed in their opportunities, yet they were not the followers of any great man of their own time, and they chose their own way freely, not as bungling imitators of a greater artist. It is a disappointment to find that romance is rarely at its finest in the works that technically have the best right in the world to be called by that name. Nevertheless, the work that is actually found there is interesting in its own way, and historically of an importance which does not need to be emphasised.

The true romantic interest is very unequally distributed over the works of the Middle Ages, and there is least of it in the authors who are most representative of the "age of chivalry." There is a disappointment prepared for any one who looks in the greater romantic authors of the twelfth century for the music of the *Faery Queene* or *La Belle Dame sans Merci.* There is more of the pure romantic element in the poems of Brynhild, in the story of Njal, in the *Song of Roland*, than in the famous romances of Chrestien of Troyes or any of his imitators, though they have all the wonders of the Isle of Britain at their command, though they have the very story of Tristram and the very mystery of the Grail to quicken them and call them out. Elegance, fluency, sentiment, romantic adventures are common, but for words like those of Hervor at the grave of her father, or of the parting between Brynhild and Sigurd, or of Helgi and Sigrun, it would be vain to search in the romances of Benoit de Sainte More or of Chrestien. Yet these are the masters of the art of romance when it was fresh and strong, a victorious fashion.

If the search be continued further, the search for that kind of imaginative beauty which these authors do not give, it will not be unsuccessful. The greater authors of the twelfth century have more affinity to the "heroic romance" of the school of the *Grand Cyrus* than to the dreams of Spenser or Coleridge. But, while this is the case with the most distinguished members of the romantic school, it is not so with all the rest. The magic that is wanting to the clear and elegant narrative of Benoit and Chrestien will be found elsewhere; it will be found in one form in the mystical prose of the *Queste del St. Graal*—a very different thing from Chrestien's *Perceval*—it will be found, again and again, in the prose of Sir Thomas Malory; it will be found in many ballads and ballad burdens, in *William and Margaret*, in *Binnorie*, in the *Wife of Usher's Well*, in the *Rime of the Count Arnaldos*, in the *Königskinder*; it will be found in the most beautiful story of the Middle Ages, *Aucassin and Nicolette*; one of the few perfectly beautiful stories in the world, about which there is no need, in England at any rate, to say anything in addition to the well-known passages in which it has been praised. *Aucassin and Nicolette* cannot be made into a representative medieval romance: there is nothing else like it; and the qualities that make it what it is are the opposite of the rhetorical self-possession, the correct and deliberate narrative of Chrestien and his school. It contains the quintessence of romantic imagination, but it is quite unlike the most fashionable and successful romances.

There are several stages in the history of the great Romantic School, as well as several distinct sources of interest. The value of the best works of the school consists in their representation of the passion of love. They turn the psychology of the courtly amatory poets into narrative. Chaucer's address to the old poets,—"Ye lovers that can make of sentiment,"—when he complains that they have left little for him to glean in the field of poetry, does not touch the lyrical poets only. The narrative poetry of the courteous school is equally devoted to the philosophy of love. Narrative poets like Chrestien, when they turn to lyric, can change their instrument without changing the purport of their verse; lyric or narrative, it has the same object, the same duty. So also, two hundred years later, Chaucer himself or Froissart may use narrative or lyric forms indifferently, and observe the same "courteous" ideal in both.

In the twelfth-century narratives, besides the interest of the love-story and all its science, there was the interest of adventure, of strange things; and here there is a great diversity among the authors, and a perceptible difference between earlier and later usage. Courteous sentiment, running through a succession of wonderful adventures, is generally enough to make a romance; but there are some notable varieties, both in the sentiment and in the incidents. The sentiment comes later in the history of literature than the adventures; the conventional romantic form of plot may be said to have been fixed before the romantic sentiment was brought to its furthest refinement. The wonders of romantic story are more easily traced to their origin, or at least to some of their earlier forms, than the spirit of chivalrous idealism which came in due time to take possession of the fabulous stories, and gave new meanings to the lives of Tristram and Lancelot.

Variety of incident, remoteness of scene, and all

the incredible things in the world, had been at the disposal of medieval authors long before the French Romantic Schools began to define themselves. The wonders of the East, especially, had very early come into literature; and the Anglo-Saxon *Epistle of Alexander* seems to anticipate the popular taste for Eastern stories, just as the Anglo-Saxon version of *Apollonius of Tyre* anticipates the later importation of Greek romance, and the appropriation of classical rhetoric, in the twelfth and thirteenth centuries; as the grace and brightness of the old English poems of St. Andrew or St. Helen seem to anticipate the peculiar charm of some of the French poems of adventures. In French literature before the vogue of romance can be said to have begun, and before the epic form had lost its supremacy, the poem of the *Pilgrimage of Charlemagne*, one of the oldest extant poems of the heroic cycle, is already far gone in subjection to the charm of mere unqualified wonder and exaggeration—rioting in the wonders of the East, like the Varangians on their holiday, when they were allowed a free day to loot in the Emperor's palace.[1] The poem of Charlemagne's journey to Constantinople is unrefined enough, but the later and more elegant romances deal often in the same kind of matter. Mere furniture counts for a good deal in the best romances, and they are full of descriptions of riches and splendours. The story of

[1] See the account of the custom in the *Saga of Harald Hardrada*, c. 16. "Harald entrusted to Jarizleif all the gold that he had sent from Micklegarth, and all sorts of precious things: so much wealth all together, as no man of the North Lands had ever seen before in one man's hands. Harald had thrice come in for the palace-sweeping (*Polotasvarf*) while he was in Micklegarth. It is the law there that when the Greek king dies, the Varangians shall have a sweep of the palace; they go over all the king's palaces where his treasures are, and every man shall have for his own what falls to his hand" (*Fornmanna Sögur*, vi. p. 171).

Troy is full of details of various sorts of magnificence: the city of Troy itself and "Ylion," its master-tower, were built by Priam out of all kinds of marble, and covered with sculpture all over. Much further on in Benoit's poem (l. 14,553) Hector is brought home wounded to a room which is described in 300 lines, with particulars of its remarkable decorations, especially its four magical images. The tomb of Penthesilea (l. 25,690) is too much for the author:—

> Sepolture ot et monument
> Tant que se *Plenius* fust vis
> Ou *cil qui fist Apocalis*
> Nel vos sauroient il retraire:
> Por ço si m'en dei gie bien taire:
> N'en dirai plus, que n'oseroie;
> Trop halte chose envaïroie.

Pliny and the author of the Apocalypse are here acknowledged as masters and authorities in the art of description. In other places of the same work there is a very liberal use of natural history such as is common in many versions of the history of Alexander. There is, for example, a long description of the precious clothes of Briseide (Cressida) at her departure, especially of her mantle, which had been given to Calchas by an Indian poet in Upper India. It was made by nigromancy, of the skin of the beast *Dindialos*, which is hunted in the shadowless land by the savage people whose name is *Cenocefali*; and the fringes of the mantle were not of the sable, but of a "beast of price" that dwells in the water of Paradise:—

> Dedans le flum de Paradis
> Sont et conversent, ço set l'on
> Se c'est vrais que nos en lison.

Calchas had a tent which had belonged to Pharaoh:—

Diomedes tant la conduit
Qu'il descendi al paveillon
Qui fu al riche Pharaon,
Cil qui noa en la mer roge.

In such passages of ornamental description the names of strange people and of foreign kings have the same kind of value as the names of precious stones, and sometimes they are introduced on their own account, apart from the precious work of Arabian or Indian artists. Of this sort is the "dreadful sagittary," who is still retained in Shakespeare's *Troilus and Cressida* on the ultimate authority (when it comes to be looked into) of Benoit de Sainte More.[1]

A quotation by M. Gaston Paris (*Hist. litt. de la France*, xxx. p. 210), from the unpublished romance of *Ider* (Edeyrn, son of Nudd), shows how this fashion of rich description and allusion had been overdone, and how it was necessary, in time, to make a protest against it. Kings' pavilions were a favourite subject for rhetoric, and the poet of *Ider* explains that he does not approve of this fashion, though he has pavilions of his own, and can describe them if he likes, as well as any one :—

Tels diz n'a fors savor de songe,
Tant en acreissent les paroles :
Mes jo n'ai cure d'iperboles :
Yperbole est chose non voire,
Qui ne fu et qui n'est a croire,

---

[1] Il ot o lui un saietaire
Qui molt fu fels et deputaire :
Des le nombril tot contreval
Ot cors en forme de cheval :
Il n'est riens nule s'il volsist
Que d'isnelece n'ateinsist :
Cors, chiere, braz, a noz semblanz
Avoit, mes n'ert pas avenanz.
l. 12,207.

C'en est la difinicion :
Mes tant di de cest paveillon
Qu'il n'en a nul soz ciel qu'il vaille.

Many poets give themselves pains to describe gardens and pavilions and other things, and think they are beautifying their work, but this is all dreaming and waste of words ; I will have no such hyperbole. (*Hyperbole* means by definition that which is untrue and incredible.) I will only say of this pavilion that there was not its match under heaven.

The author, by his definition of *hyperbole*[1] in this place, secures an ornamental word with which he consoles himself for his abstinence in other respects. This piece of science is itself characteristic of the rhetorical enterprise of the Romantic School; of the way in which Pliny, Isidore, and other encyclopaedic authors were turned into decorations. The taste for such things is common in the early and the later Middle Ages ; all that the romances did was to give a certain amount of finish and neatness to the sort of work that was left comparatively rude by the earlier pedants. There many be discovered in some writers a preference for classical subjects in their ornamental digressions, or for the graceful forms of allegory, such as in the next century were collected for the Garden of the Rose, and still later for the *House of Fame*. Thus Chrestien seems to assert his superiority

[1] Chaucer, who often yields to the temptations of "Hyperbole" in this sense of the word, lays down the law against impertinent decorations, in the rhetorical instruction of Pandarus to Troilus, about Troilus's letter to Cressida (B. ii. l. 1037) :—

Ne jompre eek no discordaunt thing yfere
As thus, to usen termes of phisyk ;
In loves termes hold of thy matere
The forme alwey, and do that it be lyk;
For if a peyntour wolde peynte a pyk
With asses feet, and hede it as an ape,
It cordeth naught ; so nere it but a jape.

of taste and judgment when, instead of Oriental work, he gives Enid an ivory saddle carved with the story of Aeneas and Dido (*Erec*, l. 5337); or when, in the same book, Erec's coronation mantle, though it is fairy work, bears no embroidered designs of Broceliande or Avalon, but four allegorical figures of the quadrivial sciences, with a reference by Chrestien to Macrobius as his authority in describing them. One function of this Romantic School, though not the most important, is to make an immediate literary profit out of all accessible books of learning. It was a quick-witted school, and knew how to turn quotations and allusions. Much of its art, like the art of *Euphues*, is bestowed in making pedantry look attractive.

The narrative material imported and worked up in the Romantic School is, of course, enormously more important than the mere decorations taken out of Solinus or Macrobius. It is not, however, with the principal masters the most important part of their study. Chrestien, for example, often treats his adventures with great levity in comparison with the serious psychological passages; the wonder often is that he should have used so much of the common stuff of adventures in poems where he had a strong commanding interest in the sentiments of the personages. There are many irrelevant and unnecessary adventures in his *Erec*, *Lancelot*, and *Yvain*, not to speak of his unfinished *Perceval*; while in *Cliges* he shows that he did not rely on the commonplaces of adventure, on the regular machinery of romance, and that he might, when he chose, commit himself to a novel almost wholly made up of psychology and sentiment. Whatever the explanation be in this case, it is plain enough both that the adventures are of secondary value as compared with the psychology, in the best romances, and that their value, though inferior, is still considerable, even in some of the best work of the "courtly makers."

The greatest novelty in the twelfth-century narrative materials was due to the Welsh; not that the "matter of Britain" was quite overwhelming in extent, or out of proportion to the other stores of legend and fable. "The matter of Rome the Great" (not to speak again of the old epic "matter of France" and its various later romantic developments) included all known antiquity, and it was recruited continually by new importations from the East. The "matter of Rome," however, the tales of Thebes and Troy and the wars of Alexander, had been known more or less for centuries, and they did not produce the same effect as the discovery of the Celtic stories. Rather, it may be held that the Welsh stories gave a new value to the classical authorities, and suggested new imaginative readings. As Chaucer's *Troilus* in our own time has inspired a new rendering of the *Life and Death of Jason*, so (it would seem) the same story of Jason got a new meaning in the twelfth century when it was read by Benoit de Sainte More in the light of Celtic romance. Then it was discovered that Jason and Medea were no more, and no less, than the adventurer and the wizard's daughter, who might play their parts in a story of Wales or Brittany. The quest of the Golden Fleece and the labours of Jason are all reduced from the rhetoric of Ovid, from their classical dignity, to something like what their original shape may have been when the story that now is told in Argyll and Connaught of the *King's Son of Ireland* was told or chanted, ages before Homer, of a king's son of the Greeks and an enchantress beyond sea. Something indeed, and that of the highest consequence, as will be seen, was kept by Benoit from his reading of the *Metamorphoses*; the passion of Medea, namely. But the story itself is hardly distinguishable in kind from *Libeaux Desconus.* It is not easy to say how far this treatment of Jason may be due to the Welsh example of similar stories, and how far to the general medieval disrespect for everything in the classics except their matter. The Celtic precedents can scarcely have been without influence on this very remarkable detection of the "Celtic element" in the voyage of the Argonauts, while at the same time Ovid ought not to be refused his share in the credit of medieval romantic adventure. Virgil, Ovid, and Statius are not to be underrated as sources of chivalrous adventure, even in comparison with the unquestioned riches of Wales or Ireland.

There is more than one distinct stage in the progress of the Celtic influence in France. The culmination of the whole thing is attained when Chrestien makes the British story of the capture and rescue of Guinevere into the vehicle of his most finished and most courtly doctrine of love, as shown in the examples of Lancelot and the Queen. Before that there are several earlier kinds of Celtic romance in French, and after that comes what for modern readers is more attractive than the typical work of Chrestien and his school,—the eloquence of the old French prose, with its languor and its melancholy, both in the prose *Lancelot* and in the *Queste del St. Graal* and *Mort Artus.* In Chrestien everything is clear and positive; in these prose romances, and even more in Malory's English rendering of his "French book," is to be heard the indescribable plaintive melody, the sigh of the wind over the enchanted ground, the spell of pure Romance. Neither in Chrestien of Troyes, nor yet in the earlier authors who dealt more simply than he with their Celtic materials, is there anything to compare with this later prose.

In some of the earlier French romantic work, in some of the lays of Marie de France, and in the fragments of the poems about Tristram, there is a kind of simplicity, partly due to want of skill, but in its effect often impressive enough. The plots made use of by the medieval artists are some of them among the noblest in the world, but none of the poets were strong enough to bring out their value, either in translating *Dido* and *Medea*, or in trying to educate Tristram and other British heroes according to the manners of the Court of Champagne. There are, however, differences among the misinterpretations and the failures. No French romance appears to have felt the full power of the story of Tristram and Iseult; no French poet had his mind and imagination taken up by the character of Iseult as more than one Northern poet was possessed by the tragedy of Brynhild. But there were some who, without developing the story as Chaucer did with the story of Troilus, at least allowed it to tell itself clearly. The Celtic magic, as that is described in Mr. Arnold's *Lectures*, has scarcely any place in French romance, either of the earlier period or of the fully-developed and successful chivalrous order, until the time of the prose books. The French poets, both the simpler sort and the more elegant, appear to have had a gift for ignoring that power of vagueness and mystery which is appreciated by some of the prose authors of the thirteenth century. They seem for the most part to have been pleased with the incidents of the Celtic stories, without appreciating any charm of style that they may have possessed. They treated them, in fact, as they treated Virgil and Ovid; and there is about as much of the "Celtic spirit" in the

French versions of *Tristram*, as there is of the genius of Virgil in the *Roman d'Eneas.* In each case there is something recognisable of the original source, but it has been translated by minds imperfectly responsive. In dealing with Celtic, as with Greek, Latin, or Oriental stories, the French romancers were at first generally content if they could get the matter in the right order and present it in simple language, like tunes played with one finger. One great advantage of this procedure is that the stories are intelligible; the sequence of events is clear, and where the original conception has any strength or beauty it is not distorted, though the colours may be faint. This earlier and more temperate method was abandoned in the later stages of the Romantic School, when it often happened that a simple story was taken from the "matter of Britain" and overlaid with the chivalrous conventional ornament, losing its simplicity without being developed in respect of its characters or its sentiment. As an example of the one kind may be chosen the *Lay of Guingamor*, one of the lays of Marie de France;[1] as an example of the other, the Dutch romance of Gawain (*Walewein*), which is taken from the French and exhibits the results of a common process of adulteration. Or, again, the story of *Guinglain*, as told by Renaud de Beaujeu with an irrelevant "courtly" digression, may be compared with the simpler and more natural versions in English (*Libeaux Desconus*) and Italian (*Carduino*), as has been done by M. Gaston Paris; or the *Conte du Graal* of Chrestien with the English *Sir Perceval of Galles.*

Guingamor is one of the best of the simpler kind

[1] Not included in the editions of her works (Roquefort, Warnke); edited by M. Gaston Paris in the eighth volume of *Romania* along with the lays of *Doon*, *Tidorel*, and *Tiolet.*

of romances. The theme is that of an old story, a story which in one form and another is extant in native Celtic versions with centuries between them. In essentials it is the story of Ossian in the land of youth; in its chief motive, the fairy-bride, it is akin to the old Irish story of Connla. It is different from both in its definite historical manner of treating the subject. The story is allowed to count for the full value of all its incidents, with scarcely a touch to heighten the importance of any of them. It is the argument of a story, and little more. Even an argument, however, may present some of the vital qualities of a fairy story, as well as of a tragic plot, and the conclusion, especially, of *Guingamor* is very fine in its own way, through its perfect clearness.

There was a king in Britain, and Guingamor was his nephew. The queen fell in love with him, and was driven to take revenge for his rejection of her; but being less cruel than other queens of similar fortune, she planned nothing worse than to send him into the *lande aventureuse*, a mysterious forest on the other side of the river, to hunt the white boar. This white boar of the adventurous ground had already taken off ten knights, who had gone out to hunt it and had never returned. Guingamor followed the boar with the king's hound. In his wanderings he came on a great palace, with a wall of green marble and a silver shining tower, and open gates, and no one within, to which he was brought back later by a maiden whom he met in the forest. The story of their meeting was evidently, in the original, a story like that of Weland and the swan-maidens, and those of other swan or seal maidens, who are caught by their lovers as Weland caught his bride. But the simplicity of the French story here is in excess of what is required even by the illiterate popular versions of similar incidents.

Guingamor, after two days in the rich palace (where he met the ten knights of the king's court, who had disappeared before), on the third day wished to go back to bring the head of the white boar to the king. His bride told him that he had been there for three hundred years, and that his uncle was dead, with all his retinue, and his cities fallen and destroyed.

But she allowed him to go, and gave him the boar's head and the king's hound; and told him after he had crossed the river into his own country to eat and drink nothing.

He was ferried across the river, and there he met a charcoal-burner and asked for news of the king. The king had been dead for three hundred years, he was told; and the king's nephew had gone hunting in the forest and had never been seen again. Guingamor told him his story, and showed him the boar's head, and turned to go back.

Now it was after nones and turning late. He saw a wild apple-tree and took three apples from it; but as he tasted them he grew old and feeble and fell from his horse.

The charcoal-burner had followed him and was going to help him, when he saw two damsels richly dressed, who came to Guingamor and reproached him for his forgetfulness. They put him gently on a horse and brought him to the river, and ferried him over, along with his hound. The charcoal-burner went back to his own house at nightfall. The boar's head he took to the king of Britain that then was, and told the story of Guingamor, and the king bade turn it into a lay.

The simplicity of all this is no small excellence in

a story. If there is anything in this story that can affect the imagination, it is there unimpaired by anything foreign or cumbrous. It is unsupported and undeveloped by any strong poetic art, but it is sound and clear.

In the Dutch romance of *Walewein*, and doubtless in its French original (to show what is gained by the moderation and restriction of the earlier school), another story of fairy adventures has been dressed up to look like chivalry. The story of Walewein is one that appears in collections of popular tales; it is that of Mac Iain Direach in Campbell's *West Highland Tales* (No. xlvi.), as well as of Grimm's *Golden Bird.* The romance observes the general plot of the popular story; indeed, it is singular among the romances in its close adherence to the order of events as given in the traditional oral forms. Though it contains 11,200 lines, it begins at the beginning and goes on to the end without losing what may be considered the original design. But while the general economy is thus retained, there are large digressions, and there is an enormous change in the character of the hero. While Guingamor in the French poem has little, if anything, to distinguish him from the adventurer of popular fairy stories, the hero in this Dutch romance is Gawain,—Gawain the Courteous, in splendid armour, playing the part of Mac Iain Direach. The discrepancy is very great, and there can be little doubt that the story as told in Gaelic fifty years ago by Angus Campbell, quarryman, is, in respect of the hero's condition and manners, more original than the medieval romance. Both versions are simple enough in their plot, and their plot is one and the same: the story of a quest for something wonderful, leading to another quest and then another, till the several problems are solved and the adventurer returns successful. In each story (as in Grimm's version also) the Fox appears as a helper.

Mac Iain Direach is sent to look for the Blue Falcon; the giant who owns the Falcon sends him to the big Women of the Isle of Jura to ask for their white glaive of light. The Women of Jura ask for the bay filly of the king of Erin; the king of Erin sends him to woo for him the king's daughter of France. Mac Iain Direach wins all for himself, with the help of the Fox.

Gawain has to carry out similar tasks: to find and bring back to King Arthur a magical flying Chessboard that appeared one day through the window and went out again; to bring to King Wonder, the owner of the Chessboard, "the sword of the strange rings"; to win for the owner of the sword the Princess of the Garden of India.

Some things in the story, apart from the hero, are different from the popular versions. In *Walewein* there appears quite plainly what is lost in the Gaelic and the German stories, the character of the strange land in which the quests are carried out. Gawain has to pass through or into a hill to reach the land of King Wonder; it does not belong to the common earth. The three castles to which he comes have all of them water about them; the second of them, Ravensten, is an island in the sea; the third is beyond the water of Purgatory, and is reached by two perilous bridges, the bridge of the sword and the bridge under water, like those in Chrestien's *Lancelot*. There is a distinction here, plain enough, between the human world, to which Arthur and his Court belong, and the other world within the hill, and the castles beyond the waters. But if this may be supposed to belong to an older form of the story not evident in the popular versions, a story of adventures in the land of the Dead, on the other hand the romance has no conception of the meaning of these passages, and gets no poetical result from the chances here offered to it. It has nothing like the vision of Thomas of Erceldoune; the waters about the magic island are tame and shallow; the castle beyond the Bridge of Dread is loaded with the common, cheap, pedantic "hyperboles," like those of the *Pèlerinage* or of Benoit's *Troy*. Gawain is too heavily armoured, also, and even his horse Gringalet has a reputation of his own; all inconsistent with the lightness of the fairy tale. Gawain in the land of all these dreams is burdened still by the heavy chivalrous conventions. The world for him, even after he has gone through the mountain, is still very much the old world with the old stale business going on; especially tournaments and all their weariness. One natural result of all this is that the Fox's part is very much reduced. In the Gaelic story, Mac Iain Direach and his friend Gille Mairtean (the Lad of March, the Fox) are a pair of equals; they have no character, no position in the world, no station and its duties. They are quite careless, and they move freely. Gawain is slow, and he has to put in a certain amount of the common romantic business. The authors of that romantic school, if ever they talked shop, may have asked one another, "Where do you put your Felon Red Knight? Where do you put your doing away of the Ill Custom? or your tournaments?" and the author of *Walewein* would have had an answer ready. Everything is there all right: that is to say, all the things that every one else has, all the mechanical business of romance. The Fox is postponed to the third adventure, and there, though he has not quite grown out of his original likeness to the Gille Mairtean, he is evidently constrained. Sir Gawain of the romance, this courteous but rather dull and middle-aged gentleman in armour, is not his old light-hearted companion.

Still, though this story of *Gawain* is weighed down by the commonplaces of the Romantic School, it shows through all its encumbrances what sort of story it was that impressed the French imagination at the beginning of the School. It may be permitted to believe that the story of *Walewein* existed once in a simpler and clearer form, like that of *Guingamor*.

The curious sophistication of *Guinglain* by Renaud de Beaujeu has been fully described and criticised by M. Gaston Paris in one of his essays (*Hist. litt. de la France*, xxx. p. 171). His comparison with the English and Italian versions of the story brings out the indifference of the French poets to their plot, and their readiness to sacrifice the unities of action for the sake of irrelevant sentiment. The story is as simple as that of Walewein; an expedition, this time, to rescue a lady from enchantment. She is bewitched in the form of a serpent, and freed by a kiss (*le fier basier*). There are various adventures on the journey; it has some resemblance to that of Gareth in the *Morte d'Arthur*, and of the Red Cross Knight in Spenser, which is founded upon Malory's *Gareth*.[1] One of the adventures is in the house of a beautiful sorceress, who treats Guinglain with small consideration. Renaud de Beaujeu, in order to get literary credit from his handling of this romantic episode, brings Guinglain back to this enchantress after the real close of the story, in a kind of sentimental show-piece or appendix, by which the story is quite overweighted and thrown off its balance for the sake of a rhetorical demonstration. This of course belongs to the later period

[1] Britomart in the House of Busirane has some resemblance to the conclusion of *Libius Disconius*.

of romance, when the simpler methods had been discredited; but the simpler form, much nearer the fashion of popular stories, is still kept more or less by the English and the Italian rhymes of "Sir Lybeaux."

The most remarkable examples of the earlier French romantic methods are presented by the fragments remaining of the old Anglo-Norman poems on Tristram and Yseult, by Béroul and Thomas, especially the latter;[1] most remarkable, because in this case there is the greatest contradiction between the tragic capabilities of the story and the very simple methods of the Norman poets. It is a story that might test the tragic strength and eloquence of any poet in any age of the world; the poetical genius of Thomas is shown in his abstinence from effort. Hardly anything could be simpler. He does very little to fill out or to elaborate the story; he does nothing to vitiate his style; there is little ornament or emphasis. The story itself is there, as if the poet thought it an impertinence to add any harmonies of his own. If it were only extant as a whole, it would be one of the most notable of poems. Where else is there anything like it, for sincerity and for thinness?

This poet of *Tristram* does not represent the prevalent fashion of his time. The eloquence and the passion of the amorous romances are commonly more effusive, and seldom as true. The lost *Tristram* of Chrestien would probably have made a contrast with the Anglo-Norman poem in this respect. Chrestien of Troyes is at the head of the French Romantic School, and his interest is in the science of love; not in ancient rude and passionate stories, such as the

[1] Fr. Michel: *Tristan*. London, 1835. *Le Roman de Tristan* (Thomas) ed. Bédier; (Béroul) ed. Muret, *Anc. Textes*, 1902-1905. Cf. Gaston Paris, *Poëmes et Légendes*.

story of Tristram—for it is rude and ancient, even in the French of Thomas—not in the "Celtic magic," except for decorative and incidental purposes, but in psychology and analysis of the emotions, and in the appropriate forms of language for such things.

It is impossible (as M. Gaston Paris has shown) to separate the spirit of French romance from the spirit of the Provençal lyric poetry. The romances represent in a narrative form the ideas and the spirit which took shape as lyric poetry in the South; the romances are directly dependent upon the poetry of the South for their principal motives. The courtesy of the Provençal poetry, with its idealism and its pedantry, its psychological formalism, its rhetoric of antithesis and conceits, is to be found again in the narrative poetry of France in the twelfth century, just as, in the thirteenth, all the floods of lyrical idealism are collected in the didactic reservoir of the *Romaunt of the Rose*. The dominant interest in the French romances is the same as in the Provençal lyric poetry and in the *Romaunt of the Rose*; namely, the idealist or courteous science of love. The origins of this mode of thought are difficult to trace fully. The inquiry belongs more immediately to the history of Provence than of France, for the romancers are the pupils of the Provençal school; not independent practitioners of the same craft, but directly indebted to Provence for some of their main ideas and a good deal of their rhetoric. In Provence itself the origins are partly to be found in the natural (*i.e.* inexplicable) development of popular love-poetry, and in the corresponding progress of society and its sentiments; while among the definite influences that can be proved and explained, one of the strongest is that of Latin poetry, particularly of the *Art of Love*. About this there can be no doubt, however great may seem to be the interval between the ideas of Ovid and those of the Provençal lyrists, not to speak of their greater scholars in Italy, Dante and Petrarch. The pedantry of Ovid was taken seriously, for one thing, in an age when everything systematic was valuable just because it was a system; when every doctrine was profitable. For another thing, they found in Ovid the form, at least, of devotion, and again the *Art of Love* was not their only book. There were other writings of Ovid and works of other poets from whom the Middle Ages learned their lesson of chivalrous service; not for the most part, it must be confessed, from the example of "Paynim Knights," but far more from the classical "Legend of Good Women," from the passion of Dido and the other heroines. It is true that there were some names of ancient heroes that were held in honour; the name of Paris is almost inseparable from the name of Tristram, wherever a medieval poet has occasion to praise the true lovers of old time, and Dante followed the common form when he brought the names together in his fifth canto.

But what made by far the strongest impression on the Middle Ages was not the example of Paris or of Leander, nor yet the passion of Catullus and Propertius, who were then unknown, but the poetry of the loyalty of the heroines, the fourth book of the *Aeneid*, the *Heroides* of Ovid, and certain parts of the *Metamorphoses*. If anything literary can be said to have taken effect upon the temper of the Middle Ages, so as to produce the manners and sentiments of chivalry, this is the literature to which the largest share of influence must be ascribed. The ladies of Romance all owe allegiance, and some of them are ready to pay it, to the queens of the Latin poets.[1]

[1] A fine passage is quoted from the romance of *Ider* in the essay cited above, where Guenloïe the queen finds Ider near death and

Virgil's Dido and Ovid's Medea taught the eloquence of love to the French poets, and the first chivalrous lovers are those who have learned to think poorly of the recreant knights of antiquity.

The French romantic authors were scholars in the poetry of the Provençal School, but they also knew a good deal independently of their Provençal masters, and did not need to be told everything. They read the ancient authors for themselves, and drew their own conclusions from them. They were influenced by the special Provençal rendering of the common ideas of chivalry and courtesy; they were also affected immediately by the authors who influenced the Provençal School.

Few things are more instructive in this part of

thinks of killing herself, like Phyllis and other ladies of the old time, who will welcome her. It is the "Saints' Legend of Cupid," many generations before Chaucer, in the form of an invocation to Love, the tyrant :—

> Bel semblant ço quit me feront
> Les cheitives qui a toi sont
> Qui s'ocistrent par druerie
> D'amor ; mout voil lor compainie :
> D'amor me recomfortera
> La lasse Deïanira,
> Qui s'encroast, et Canacé,
> Eco, Scilla, Fillis, Pronné,
> Ero, Biblis, Dido, Mirra,
> Tisbe, la bele Hypermnestra,
> Et des autres mil et cinc cenz.
> Amor ! por quoi ne te repenz
> De ces simples lasses destruire ?
> Trop cruelment te voi deduire :
> Pechié feiz que n'en as pitié ;
> Nuls deus fors toi ne fait pechié !
> De ço est Tisbé al dessus,
> Que por lié s'ocist Piramus ;
> Amors, de ço te puet loer
> Car a ta cort siet o son per ;
> Ero i est o Leander :
> Si jo i fusse avec Ider,
> Aise fusse, ço m'est avis,
> Com alme qu'est en paraïs.

literature than the story of Medea in the *Roman de Troie* of Benoit de Sainte More. It might even claim to be the representative French romance, for it contains in an admirable form the two chief elements common to all the dominant school—adventure (here reduced from Ovid to the scale of a common fairy story, as has been seen already) and sentimental eloquence, which in this particular story is very near its original fountain-head.

It is to be noted that Benoit is not in the least troubled by the Latin rhetoric when he has to get at the story. Nothing Latin, except the names, and nothing rhetorical remains to show that the story came from Ovid, and not from Bletherieus or some other of his fellow-romancers in Wales,[1] so long, that is, as the story is merely concerned with the Golden Fleece, the Dragon, the Bulls, and all the tasks imposed on Jason. But one essential thing is retained by Benoit out of the Latin which is his authority, and that is the way in which the love of Medea for Jason is dwelt upon and described.

This is for medieval poetry one of the chief sources of the psychology in which it took delight,—an original and authoritative representation of the beginning and growth of the passion of love, not yet spoilt by the pedantry which later displayed itself unrestrained in the following generations of amatory poets, and which took its finest form in the poem of Guillaume de Lorris; but yet at the same time giving a starting-point and some encouragement to the later pedants, by its study of the different degrees of the passion, and by the success with which they are explained and made interesting. This is one of the masterpieces and one of the standards of composition

[1] Bletherieus, or Bréri, is the Welsh authority cited by Thomas in his *Tristan*. Cf. Gaston Paris, *Romania*, viii. p. 427.

in early French romance; and it gives one of the most singular proofs of the dependence of modern on ancient literature, in certain respects. It would not be easy to prove any real connexion between Homer and the Sagas, in order to explain the resemblances of temper, and even of incident, between them; but in the case of the medieval romances there is this direct and real dependence. The Medea of Apollonius Rhodius is at the beginning of medieval poetry, in one line of descent (through Virgil's Dido as well as Ovid's Medea); and it would be hard to overestimate the accumulated debt of all the modern poets whose rhetoric of passion, whether they knew it or not, is derived somehow from the earlier medieval masters of Dante or Chaucer, Boccaccio or Spenser.

The "medieval" character of the work of Chrestien and his contemporaries is plain enough. But "medieval" and other terms of the same sort are too apt to impose themselves on the mind as complete descriptive formulas, and in this case the term "medieval" ought not to obscure the fact that it is modern literature, in one of its chief branches, which has its beginning in the twelfth century. No later change in the forms of fiction is more important than the twelfth-century revolution, from which all the later forms and constitutions of romance and novel are in some degree or other derived. It was this revolution, of which Chrestien was one of the first to take full advantage, that finally put an end to the old local and provincial restrictions upon narrative. The older schools of epic are bound to their own nation or tribe, and to the family traditions. These restrictions are no hindrance to the poetry of Homer, nor to the plots and conversations of the Sagas. Within these local restrictions the highest form of narrative art is possible. Nevertheless the period of these restrictions must come to an end; the heroic age cannot last for ever. The merit of the twelfth-century authors, Benoit, Chrestien, and their followers, is that they faced the new problems and solved them. In their productions it may be seen how the Western world was moving away from the separate national traditions, and beginning the course of modern civilisation with a large stock of ideas, subjects, and forms of expression common to all the nations. The new forms of story might be defective in many ways, thin or formal or extravagant in comparison with some of the older modes; but there was no help for it, there was no progress to be made in any other way.

The first condition of modern progress in novel-writing, as in other more serious branches of learning, was that the author should be free to look about him, to reflect and choose, to pick up his ideas and his matter anyhow. He was turned out of the old limited region of epic tradition. The nations had several centuries to themselves, in the Dark Ages, in which they were at liberty to compose Homeric poems ("if they had a mind"), but by the twelfth century that time was over. The romancers of the twelfth century were in the same position as modern authors in regard to their choice of subjects. Their subjects were not prescribed to them by epic tradition. They were more or less reflective and self-conscious literary men, citizens of the universal world, ready to make the most of their education. They are the sophists of medieval literature; emancipated, enlightened and intelligent persons, with an apparatus of rhetoric, a set of abstract ideas, a repertory of abstract sentiments, which they could apply to any available subject. In this sophistical period, when the serious interest of national epic was lost, and when stories, collected from all the ends of the earth, were made the receptacles of a common, abstract, sentimental pathos, it was of some importance that the rhetoric should be well managed, and that the sentiment should be refined. The great achievement of the French poets, on account of which they are to be remembered as founders and benefactors, is that they went to good masters for instruction. Solid dramatic interpretation of character was beyond them, and they were not able to make much of the openings for dramatic contrast in the stories on which they worked. But they were caught and held by the language of passion, the language of Dido and Medea; language not dramatic so much as lyrical or musical, the expression of universal passion, such as might be repeated without much change in a thousand stories. In this they were happily guided. The greater drama, the stronger characters, appeared in due time; but the dramas and the novels of Europe would not have been what they are, without the medieval elaboration of the simple motives, and the practice of the early romantic schools in executing variations on Love and Jealousy. It may be remarked that there were sources more remote and even more august, above and beyond the Latin poets from whom the medieval authors copied their phrasing; in so far as the Latin poets were affected by Athenian tragedy, directly or indirectly, in their great declamatory passages, which in turn affected the Middle Ages.

The history of this school has no end, for it merges in the history of the romantic schools that are still flourishing, and will be continued by their successors. One of the principal lines of progress may be indicated, to conclude this discourse on Epic Poetry.

The twelfth-century romances are in most things the antithesis to Homer, in narrative. They are fanciful, conceited, thin in their drama, affected in their sentiments. They are like the "heroic romances" of the seventeenth century, their descendants, as compared with the strong imagination of Cervantes or Shakespeare, who are the representatives, if not of the Homeric line, at any rate of the Homeric principles, in their intolerance of the formally pathetic or heroic, and who have all the great modern novelists on their side.

But the early romantic schools, though they are generally formal and sentimental, and not dramatic, have here and there the possibilities of a stronger drama and a truer imagination, and seem at times almost to have worked themselves free from their pedantry.

There is sentiment and sentiment: and while the pathos of medieval romance, like some of the effusion of medieval lyric, is often merely formal repetition of phrases, it is sometimes more natural, and sometimes the mechanical fancy seems to quicken into true poetical vision, or at least to make room for a sane appreciation of real life and its incidents. Chrestien of Troyes shows his genius most unmistakably in his occasional surprising intervals of true description and natural feeling, in the middle of his rhetoric; while even his sustained rhetorical dissertations, like those of the *Roman de la Rose* in the next century, are not absolutely untrue, or uncontrolled by observation of actual manners. Often the rhetorical apparatus interferes in the most annoying way with the clear vision. In the *Chevalier au Lion*, for example, there is a pretty sketch of a family party—a girl reading a romance to her father in a garden, and her mother coming up and listening to the story—from which there is a sudden and annoying change to the common impertinences of the amatory professional novelist.

This is the passage, with the two kinds of literature in abrupt opposition :—

Messire Yvain goes into the garden, and his people follow; and he sees a goodly gentleman reclining on a cloth of silk and leaning on his elbow; and a maiden was sitting before him reading out of a romance, I know not whose the story. And to listen to the romance a lady had drawn near; that was her mother, and he was her father, and well might they be glad to look on her and listen to her, for they had no other child. She was not yet sixteen years old, and she was so fair and gentle that the God of Love if he had seen her would have given himself to be her slave, and never would have bestowed the love of her on any other than himself. For her sake, to serve her, he would have made himself man, would have put off his deity, and would have stricken himself with the dart whose wound is never healed, except a disloyal physician tend it. It is not right that any should recover from that wound, unless there be disloyalty in it; and whoever is otherwise healed, he never loved with loyalty. *Of this wound I could talk to you without end*, if it pleased you to listen; but I know that some would say that all my talk was idleness, for the world is fallen away from true love, and men know not any more how to love as they ought, for the very talk of love is a weariness to them! (ll. 5360-5396).

This short passage is representative of Chrestien's work, and indeed of the most successful and influential work of the twelfth-century schools. It is not, like some affected kinds of romance, entirely cut off from reality. But the glimpses of the real world are occasional and short; there is a flash of pure daylight, a breath of fresh air, and then the heavy-laden, enchanted mists of rhetoric and obligatory sentiment come rolling down and shut out the view.

It is possible to trace out in some detail a line of

progress in medieval romance, in which there is a victory in the end for the more ingenuous kind of sentiment; in which the rhetorical romantic forms are altered and strengthened to bear the weight of true imagination.

This line of progress is nothing less than the earlier life of all the great modern forms of novel; a part of European history which deserves some study from those who have leisure for it.

The case may be looked at in this way. The romantic schools, following on the earlier heroic literature, generally substituted a more shallow, formal, limited set of characters for the larger and freer portraits of the heroic age, making up for this defect in the personages by extravagance in other respects—in the incidents, the phrasing, the sentimental pathos, the rhetorical conceits. The great advantage of the new school over the old was that it was adapted to modern cosmopolitan civilisation; it left the artist free to choose his subject anywhere, and to deal with it according to the laws of good society, without local or national restrictions. But the earlier work of this modern enlightenment in the Middle Ages was generally very formal, very meagre in imagination. The progress of literature was to fill out the romantic forms, and to gain for the new cosmopolitan schemes of fiction the same sort of substantial contents, the same command of human nature and its variety, as belong (with local or national restrictions) to some at any rate of the earlier epic authors. This being so, one of the interests of the study of medieval romance must be the discovery of those places in which it departs from its own dominant conventions, and seems to aim at something different from its own nature: at the recovery of the fuller life of epic for the benefit of romance. Epic fulness of life within the limits of romantic form—that might be said to be the ideal which is *not* attained in the Middle Ages, but towards which many medieval writers seem to be making their way.

Chrestien's story of *Geraint and Enid* (Geraint has to take the name of *Erec* in the French) is one of his earlier works, but cannot be called immature in comparison with what he wrote afterwards. In Chrestien's *Enid* there is not a little superfluity of the common sort of adventure. The story of Enid in the *Idylls of the King* (founded upon the Welsh *Geraint*, as given in Lady Charlotte Guest's *Mabinogion*) has been brought within compass, and a number of quite unnecessary adventures have been cut out. Yet the story here is the same as Chrestien's, and the drama of the story is not the pure invention of the English poet. Chrestien has all the principal motives, and the working out of the problem is the same. In one place, indeed, where the Welsh romance, the immediate source of Tennyson's *Enid*, has shortened the scene of reconciliation between the lovers, the Idyll has restored something like the proportions of the original French. Chrestien makes Erec speak to Enid and renounce all his ill-will, after the scene in which "the brute Earl" is killed; the Welsh story, with no less effect, allows the reconciliation to be taken for granted when Geraint, at this point in the history, with no speech of his reported, lifts Enid on his own horse. The Idyll goes back (apparently without any direct knowledge of Chrestien's version) to the method of Chrestien.

The story of Enid in Chrestien is very unlike the other stories of distressed and submissive wives; it has none of the ineradicable falsity of the story of Griselda. How much is due to Chrestien for this can hardly be reckoned, in our ignorance of the materials he used. But taking into account the other passages, like that of the girl reading in the garden, where Chrestien shows a distinct original appreciation of certain aspects of life, it cannot be far wrong to consider Chrestien's picture of Enid as mainly his own; and, in any case, this picture is one of the finest in medieval romance. There is no comparison between Chrestien of Troyes and Homer, but it is not impious to speak of Enid along with Nausicaa, and there are few other ladies of romance who may claim as much as this. The adventure of the Sparrowhawk, one of the finest pieces of pure romance in the poetry of this century, is also one of the finest in the old French, and in many ways very unlike the commonplaces of chivalry, in the simplicity of the household where Enid waits on her father's guest and takes his horse to the stable, in the sincerity and clearness with which Chrestien indicates the gentle breeding and dignity of her father and mother, and the pervading spirit of grace and loyalty in the whole scene.[1]

In the story of Enid, Chrestien has a subject which recommends itself to modern readers. The misunderstanding between Enid and her husband, and the reconciliation, are not peculiarly medieval, though the adventures through which their history is worked out are of the ordinary romantic commonplace.

[1] The Welsh version has the advantage here in noting more fully than Chrestien the beauty of age in Enid's mother: "And he thought that there could be no woman fairer than she must have been in the prime of her youth." Chrestien says merely (at the end of his story, l. 6621):—

> Bele est Enide et bele doit
> Estre par reison et par droit,
> Que bele dame est mout sa mere
> Bel chevalier a an son pere.

Indeed the relation of husband and wife in this story is rather exceptionally divergent from the current romantic mode, and from the conventional law that true love between husband and wife was impossible. Afterwards, in his poem of *Lancelot* (*le Chevalier de la Charrette*), Chrestien took up and worked out this conventional and pedantic theory, and made the love of Lancelot and the Queen into the standard for all courtly lovers. In his *Enid*, however, there is nothing of this. At the same time, the courtly and chivalrous mode gets the better of the central drama in his *Enid*, in so far as he allows himself to be distracted unduly from the pair of lovers by various "hyperboles" of the Romantic School; there are a number of unnecessary jousts and encounters, and a mysterious exploit of Erec in a magic garden, which is quite out of connexion with the rest of the story. The final impression is that Chrestien wanted strength of mind or inclination to concentrate himself on the drama of the two lovers. The story is taken too lightly.

In *Cliges*, his next work, the dramatic situation is much less valuable than in *Enid*, but the workmanship is far more careful and exact, and the result is a story which may claim to be among the earliest of modern novels, if the Greek romances, to which it has a close relation, are not taken into account. The story has very little "machinery"; there are none of the marvels of the Faërie in it. There is a Thessalian witch (the heroine's nurse), who keeps well within the limits of possible witchcraft, and there is the incident of the sleeping-draught (familiar in the ballad of the *Gay Goshawk*), and that is all. The rest is a simple love-story (or rather a double love-story, for there is the history of the hero's father and mother, before his own begins), and the personages are merely true lovers, undistinguished by any such qualities as the sulkiness of Erec or the discretion of Enid. It is all pure sensibility, and as it happens the sensibility is in good keeping—not overdriven into the pedantry of the more quixotic troubadours and minnesingers, and not warped by the conventions against marriage. It is explained at the end that, though Cliges and Fenice are married, they are lovers still :—

> De s'amie a feite sa fame,
> Mais il l'apele amie et dame,
> Que por ce ne pert ele mie
> Que il ne l'aint come s'amie,
> Et ele lui autresi
> Con l'an doit feire son ami :
> Et chascun jor lor amors crut,
> N'onques cil celi ne mescrut,
> Ne querela de nule chose.
>
> *Cliges*, l. 6753.

This poem of Chrestien's is a collection of the finest specimens of medieval rhetoric on the eternal theme. There is little incident, and sensibility has it all its own way, in monologues by the actors and digressions by the author, on the nature of love. It is rather the sentiment than the passion that is here expressed in the "language of the heart"; but, however that may be, there are both delicacy and eloquence in the language. The pensive Fenice, who debates with herself for nearly two hundred lines in one place (4410-4574), is the ancestress of many later heroines.

> Meis Fenice est sor toz pansive ;
> Ele ne trueve fonz ne rive
> El panser dont ele est anplie,
> Tant li abonde et mouteplie.
>
> *Cliges*, l. 4339.

In the later works of Chrestien, in *Yvain*, *Lancelot*, and *Perceval*, there are new developments of romance, more particularly in the story of Lancelot and Guinevere. But these three later stories, unlike *Cliges*, are full of the British marvels, which no one would wish away, and yet they are encumbrances to what we must regard as the principal virtue of the poet—his skill of analysis in cases of sentiment, and his interest in such cases. *Cliges*, at any rate, however far it may come short of the *Chevalier de la Charrette* and the *Conte du Graal* in variety, is that one of Chrestien's poems, it might be said that one of the twelfth-century French romances, which best corresponds to the later type of novel. It is the most modern of them; and at the same time it does not represent its own age any the worse, because it also to some extent anticipates the fashions of later literature.

In this kind of romance, which reduces the cost of the "machinery," and does without enchanters, dragons, magic mists, and deadly castles, there are many other examples besides *Cliges*.

A hundred years after Chrestien, one of his cleverest pupils wrote the Provençal story of *Flamenca*,[1] a work in which the form of the novel is completely disengaged from the unnecessary accidents of romance, and reaches a kind of positive and modern clearness very much at variance in some respects with popular ideas of what is medieval. The Romance of the medieval Romantic School attains one of its highest and most distinctive points in *Flamenca*, and shows what it had been aiming at from the beginning—namely, the expression in an elegant manner of the ideas of the *Art of Love*, as understood in the polite society of those times. *Flamenca* is nearly contemporary with the *Roman de la Rose* of Guillaume de Lorris. Its inspiring ideas are the same, and though its influence on succeeding authors is indis-

[1] Ed. Paul Meyer, 1865, and, again, 1901.

cernible, where that of the *Roman de la Rose* is widespread and enduring, *Flamenca* would have as good a claim to be considered a representative masterpiece of medieval literature, if it were not that it appears to be breaking loose from medieval conventions where the *Roman de la Rose* makes all it can out of them. *Flamenca* is a simple narrative of society, with the indispensable three characters—the husband, the lady, and the lover. The scene of the story is principally at the baths of Bourbon, in the then present day; and of the miracles and adventures of the more marvellous and adventurous romances there is nothing left but the very pleasant enumeration of the names of favourite stories in the account of the minstrelsy at Flamenca's wedding. The author knew all that was to be known in romance, of Greek, Latin, or British invention—Thebes and Troy, Alexander and Julius Caesar, Samson and Judas Maccabeus, Ivain and Gawain and Perceval, Paris and Tristram, and all Ovid's *Legend of Good Women*—but out of all these studies he has retained only what suited his purpose. He does not compete with the Greek or the British champions in their adventures among the romantic forests. Chrestien of Troyes is his master, but he does not try to copy the magic of the Lady of the Fountain, or the Bridge of the Sword, or the Castle of the Grail. He follows the doctrine of love expounded in Chrestien's *Lancelot*, but his hero is not sent wandering at random, and is not made to display his courtly emotions among the ruins and shadows of the lost Celtic mythology, like Lancelot in Chrestien's poem. The life described in *Flamenca* is the life of the days in which it was composed; and the hero's task is to disguise himself as a clerk, so as to get a word with the jealously-guarded lady in church on Sundays, while giving her the Psalter to kiss after the

Mass. *Flamenca* is really the triumph of Ovid, with the *Art of Love*, over all his Gothic competitors out of the fairy tales. The Provençal poet has discarded everything but the essential dominant interests, and in so doing has gone ahead of his master Chrestien, who (except in *Cliges*) allowed himself to be distracted between opposite kinds of story, between the school of Ovid and the school of Blethericus; and who, even in *Cliges*, was less consistently modern than his Provençal follower.

Flamenca is the perfection and completion of medieval romance in one kind and in one direction. It is all sentiment; the ideal courtly sentiment of good society and its poets, made lively by the author's knowledge of his own time and its manners, and his decision not to talk about anything else. It is perhaps significant that he allows his heroine the romance of *Flores and Blanchefleur* for her reading, an older story of true lovers, after the simpler pattern of Greek romance, which the author of *Flamenca* apparently feels himself entitled to refer to with the condescension of a modern and critical author towards some old-fashioned prettiness. He is completely self-possessed and ironical with regard to his story. His theme is the idle love whose origin is explained by Ovid; his personages are nothing to him but the instruments of the symphony which he composes and directs: *sopra lor vanità che par persona*, over and through their graceful inanity, passes the stream of sentiment, the shifting, flickering light which the Provençal author has borrowed from Ovid and transferred for his own purposes to his own time. It is perhaps the first complete modern appropriation of classical examples in literary art; for the poem of *Flamenca* is classical in more than one sense of the term—classical, not only because of its comprehension of the spirit of the Latin poet and his code of manners and sentiment, but because of its clear proportions and its definite abstract lines of composition; because of the self-possession of the author and his subordination of details and rejection of irrelevances.

Many things are wanting to *Flamenca* which it did not suit the author to bring in. It was left to other greater writers to venture on other and larger schemes with room for more strength and individuality of character, and more stress of passion, still keeping the romantic framework which had been designed by the masters of the twelfth century, and also very much of the sentimental language which the same masters had invented and elaborated.

The story of the *Chastelaine de Vergi*[1] (dated by its editor between 1282 and 1288) is an example of a different kind from *Flamenca*; still abstract in its personages, still sentimental, but wholly unlike *Flamenca* in the tragic stress of its sentiment and in the pathos of its incidents. There is no plot in *Flamenca*, or only just enough to display the author's resources of eloquence; in the *Chastelaine de Vergi* there is no rhetorical expansion or effusion, but instead of that the coherent closely-reasoned argument of a romantic tragedy, with nothing in it out of keeping with the conditions of "real life." It is a moral example to show the disastrous result of breaking the first law of chivalrous love, which enjoins loyal secrecy on the lover; the tragedy in this case arises from the strong compulsion of honour under which the commandment is transgressed.

There was a knight who was the lover of the Chastelaine de Vergi, unknown to all the world.

[1] Ed. G. Raynaud, *Romania*, xxi. p. 145.

Their love was discovered by the jealous machinations of the Duchess of Burgundy, whom the knight had neglected. The Duchess made use of her knowledge to insult the Chastelaine; the Chastelaine died of a broken heart at the thought that her lover had betrayed her; the knight found her dead, and threw himself on his sword to make amends for his unwilling disloyalty. Even a summary like this may show that the plot has capabilities and opportunities in it; and though the scheme of the short story does not allow the author to make use of them in the full detailed manner of the great novelists, he understands what he is about, and his work is a very fine instance of sensitive and clearly-executed medieval narrative, which has nothing to learn (in its own kind, and granting the conditions assumed by the author) from any later fiction.

The story of the *Lady of Vergi* was known to Boccaccio, and was repeated both by Bandello and by Queen Margaret of Navarre.

It is time to consider how the work of the medieval romantic schools was taken up and continued by many of the most notable writers of the period which no longer can be called medieval, in which modern literature makes a new and definite beginning; especially in the works of the two modern poets who have done most to save and adapt the inheritance of medieval romance for modern forms of literature—Boccaccio and Chaucer.

The development of romance in these authors is not always and in all respects a gain. Even the pathetic stories of the *Decameron* (such as the *Pot of Basil*, *Tancred and Gismunda*, *William of Cabestaing*) seem to have lost something by the adoption of a different kind of grammar, a more learned rhetoric, in comparison with the best of the simple French stories, like the *Chastelaine de Vergi.* This is the case in a still greater degree where Boccaccio has allowed himself a larger scale, as in his version of the old romance of *Flores and Blanchefleur* (*Filocolo*), while his *Teseide* might be taken as the first example in modern history of the pernicious effect of classical studies. The *Teseide* is the story of Palamon and Arcita. The original is lost, but it evidently was a French romance, probably not a long one; one of the favourite well-defined cases or problems of love, easily understood as soon as stated, presenting the rivalry of the two noble kinsmen for the love of the lady Emily. It might have been made into one of the stories of the *Decameron*, but Boccaccio had other designs for it. He wished to write a classical epic in twelve books, and not very fortunately chose this simple theme as the groundwork of his operations. The *Teseide* is the first of the solemn row of modern epics; "reverend and divine, abiding without motion, shall we say that they have being?" Everything is to be found in the *Teseide* that the best classical traditions require in epic — Olympian machinery, catalogues of armies, descriptions of works of art to compete with the Homeric and Virgilian shields, elaborate battles, and epic similes, and funeral games. Chaucer may have been at one time tempted by all this magnificence; his final version of the story, in the *Knight's Tale*, is a proof among other things of his critical tact. He must have recognised that the *Teseide*, with all its ambition and its brilliancy of details, was a failure as a story; that this particular theme, at any rate, was not well fitted to carry the epic weight. These personages of romance were not in training for the heavy classical panoply. So he reduced the story of Palamon and Arcita to something not very different from what must have been its original scale as a romance. His modifications of Boccaccio here are a lesson in the art of narrative which can hardly be overvalued by students of that mystery.

Chaucer's procedure in regard to his romantic subjects is often very difficult to understand. How firm and unwavering his critical meditations and calculations were may be seen by a comparison of the *Knight's Tale* with its Italian source. At other times and in other stories he appears to have worked on different principles, or without much critical study at all. The *Knight's Tale* is a complete and perfect version of a medieval romance, worked out with all the resources of Chaucer's literary study and reflexion; tested and considered and corrected in every possible way. The story of *Constance* (the *Man of Law's Tale*) is an earlier work in which almost everything is lacking that is found in the mere workmanship of the *Knight's Tale*; though not, of course, the humanity, the pathos, of Chaucer. The story of *Constance* appears to have been taken by Chaucer from one of the least artificial specimens of medieval romance, the kind of romance that worked up in a random sort of way the careless sequence of incidents in a popular traditional tale. Just as the tellers of the stories in Campbell's *Highland Tales*, and other authentic collections, make no scruple about proportion where their memory happens to fail them or their irrelevant fancy to distract them, but go on easily, dropping out a symmetrical adventure here and there, and repeating a favourite "machine" if necessary or unnecessary; so the story of *Constance* forgets and repeats itself. The voice is the voice of Chaucer, and so are the thoughts, but the order or disorder of the story is that of the old wives' tales when the old wives are drowsy. All the principal situations occur twice over; twice the heroine is persecuted by a wicked mother-in-law, twice sent adrift in a rudderless boat, twice rescued from a churl, and so on. In this story the poetry of Chaucer appears as something almost independent of the structure of the plot; there has been no such process of design and reconstruction as in the *Knight's Tale.*

It is almost as strange to find Chaucer in other stories, as in the *Franklin's Tale* and the *Clerk's Tale*, putting up with the most abstract medieval conventions of morality; the Point of Honour in the *Franklin's Tale*, and the unmitigated virtue of Griselda, are hopelessly opposed to anything like dramatic truth, and very far inferior as motives to the ethical ideas of many stories of the twelfth century. The truth of *Enid* would have given no opportunity for the ironical verses in which Chaucer takes his leave of the Clerk of Oxford and his heroine.

In these romances Chaucer leaves some old medieval difficulties unresolved and unreconciled, without attempting to recast the situation as he found it in his authorities, or to clear away the element of unreason in it. He takes the framework as he finds it, and embroiders his poetry over it, leaving an obvious discrepancy between his poetry and its subject-matter.

In some other stories, as in the *Legend of Good Women*, and the tale of Virginia, he is content with pathos, stopping short of vivid drama. In the *Knight's Tale* he seems to have deliberately chosen a compromise between the pathetic mood of pure romance and a fuller dramatic method; he felt, apparently, that while the contrast between the two rivals admitted of drama, the position of the lady

Emily in the story was such as to prevent a full dramatic rendering of all the characters. The plot required that the lady Emily should be left without much share of her own in the action.

The short and uncompleted poem of *Anelida* gains in significance and comes into its right place in Chaucer's works, when it is compared with such examples of the older school as the *Chastelaine de Vergi.* It is Chaucer's essay in that delicate abstract fashion of story which formed one of the chief accomplishments of the French Romantic School. It is his acknowledgment of his debt to the artists of sensibility, the older French authors, "that can make of sentiment," and it proves, like all his writings, how quick he was to save all he could from the teaching of his forerunners, for the profit of "that fair style that has brought him honour." To treat a simple problem, or "case," of right and wrong in love, was a favourite task of medieval courtly poetry, narrative and lyric. Chaucer in his *Anelida* takes up this old theme again, treating it in a form between narrative and lyric, with the pure abstract melody that gives the mood of the actors apart from any dramatic individuality. He is one of the Extractors of Quintessence, and his *Anelida* is the formal spirit, impalpable yet definite, of the medieval courtly romance.

It is not here, but in a poem the opposite of this in fulness and richness of drama, that Chaucer attains a place for himself above all other authors as the poet who saw what was needed to transform medieval romance out of its limitations into a new kind of narrative. Chaucer's *Troilus and Criseyde* is the poem in which medieval romance passes out of itself into the form of the modern novel. What Cervantes and what Fielding did was done first by Chaucer;

and this was the invention of a kind of story in which life might be represented no longer in a conventional or abstract manner, or with sentiment and pathos instead of drama, but with characters adapting themselves to different circumstances, no longer obviously breathed upon by the master of the show to convey his own ideas, but moving freely and talking like men and women. The romance of the Middle Ages comes to an end, in one of the branches of the family tree, by the production of a romance that has all the freedom of epic, that comprehends all good and evil, and excludes nothing as common or unclean which can be made in any way to strengthen the impression of life and variety. Chaucer was not tempted by the phantasm of the Epic Poem like Boccaccio, and like so many of the great and wise in later generations. The substance of Epic, since his time, has been appropriated by certain writers of history, as Fielding has explained in his lectures on that science in *Tom Jones.* The first in the line of these modern historians is Chaucer with his *Troilus and Criseyde*, and the wonder still is as great as it was for Sir Philip Sidney :—

> Chaucer undoubtedly did excellently in his *Troylus* and *Cresseid*; of whom, truly I know not whether to mervaile more, either that he in that mistie time could see so clearely, or that wee in this cleare age walke so stumblingly after him.

His great work grew out of the French Romantic School. The episode of Troilus and Briseide in Benoit's *Roman de Troie* is one of the best passages in the earlier French romance; light and unsubstantial like all the work of that School, but graceful, and not untrue. It is all summed up in the monologue of Briseide at the end of her story (l. 20,308) :—

Dex donge bien a Troylus !
Quant nel puis amer ne il mei
A cestui[1] me done et otrei.
Molt voldreie aveir cel talent
Que n'eüsse remembrement
Des ovres faites d'en arriere :
Ço me fait mal à grant manière !

Boccaccio took up this story, from the Latin version of the Tale of Troy, the *Historia Trojana* of Guido. His *Filostrato* is written on a different plan from the *Teseide*; it is one of his best works. He did not make it into an epic poem; the *Filostrato*, Boccaccio's *Troilus and Cressida*, is a romance, differing from the older French romantic form not in the design of the story, but in the new poetical diction in which it is composed, and its new poetical ideas. There is no false classicism in it, as there is in his *Palamon and Arcita*; it is a novel of his own time, a story of the *Decameron*, only written at greater length, and in verse. Chaucer, the "great translator," took Boccaccio's poem and treated it in his own way, not as he had dealt with the *Teseide*. The *Teseide*, because there was some romantic improbability in the story, he made into a romance. The story of Troilus he saw was strong enough to bear a stronger handling, and instead of leaving it a romance, graceful and superficial as it is in Boccaccio, he deepened it and filled it with such dramatic imagination and such variety of life as had never been attained before his time by any romancer; and the result is a piece of work that leaves all romantic convention behind. The *Filostrato* of Boccaccio is a story of light love, not much more substantial, except in its new poetical language, than the story of *Flamenca*. In Chaucer the passion of Troilus is something different from the sentiment of romance; the changing mind of

[1] *i.e.* Diomede.

Cressida is represented with an understanding of the subtlety and the tragic meaning of that life which is "Time's fool." Pandarus is the other element. In Boccaccio he is a personage of the same order as Troilus and Cressida; they all might have come out of the Garden of the *Decameron*, and there is little to choose between them. Chaucer sets him up with a character and a philosophy of his own, to represent the world outside of romance. The Comic Genius claims a share in the tragedy, and the tragedy makes room for him, because the tragic personages, "Tragic Comedians" as they are, can bear the strain of the contrast. The selection of personages and motives is made in another way in the romantic schools, but this poem of Chaucer's is not romance. It is the fulfilment of the prophecy of Socrates, just before Aristophanes and the tragic poet had to be put to bed at the end of the *Symposium*, that the best author of tragedy is the best author of comedy also. It is the freedom of the imagination, beyond all the limits of partial and conventional forms.

NOTES AND ILLUSTRATIONS

APPENDIX

NOTE A (p. 133)

Rhetoric of the Western and Northern Alliterative Poems

ANY page of the Anglo-Saxon poets, and of the "Elder Edda," will show the difference between the "continuous" and the "discrete"—the Western and the Northern—modes of the alliterative verse. It may be convenient to select some passages here for reference.

(1) As an example of the Western style ("the sense variously drawn out from one verse to another"), the speech of the "old warrior" stirring up vengeance for King Froda (*Beowulf*, l. 2041 *sq.*; see above, p. 70):—

> þonne cwið æt beore se ðe beah gesyhð,
> eald æscwiga, se ðe eall geman
> garcwealm gumena (him bið grim sefa)
> onginneð geomormod geongum cempan
> þurh hreðra gehygd higes cunnian,
> wigbealu weccean, ond þæt word acwyð:
> "Meaht ðu, min wine, mece gecnawan,
> þone þin fæder to gefeohte bær
> under heregriman, hindeman siðe,
> dyre iren, þær hine Dene slogon,
> weoldon wælstowe, syððan Wiðergyld læg
> æfter hæleþa hryre, hwate Scyldingas?
> Nu her þara banena byre nathwylces,
> frætwum hremig, on flet gæð,
> mordres gylpeð ond þone maðþum byreð
> þone þe þu mid rihte rædan sceoldest!"

(The "old warrior"—no less a hero than Starkad himself, according to Saxo—bears a grudge on account of the slaying of Froda, and cannot endure the reconciliation that has been made. He sees the reconciled enemies still wearing the spoils of war, arm-rings, and even Froda's sword, and addresses Ingeld, Froda's son):—

Over the ale he speaks, seeing the ring,
the old warrior, that remembers all,
the spear-wrought slaying of men (his thought is grim),
with sorrow at heart begins with the young champion,
in study of mind to make trial of his valour,
to waken the havoc of war, and thus he speaks:
"Knowest thou, my lord? nay, well thou knowest the falchion
that thy father bore to the fray,
wearing his helmet of war, in that last hour,
the blade of price, where the Danes him slew,
and kept the field, when Withergyld was brought down
after the heroes' fall; yea, the Danish princes slew him!
See now, a son of one or other of the men of blood,
glorious in apparel, goes through the hall,
boasts of the stealthy slaying, and bears the goodly heirloom
that thou of right shouldst have and hold!"

(2) The Northern arrangement, with "the sense concluded in the couplet," is quite different from the Western style. There is no need to quote more than a few lines. The following passage is from the last scene of *Helgi and Sigrun* (*C.P.B.*, i. p. 143; see p. 72 above —"Yet precious are the draughts," etc.):—

Vel skolom drekka dýrar veigar
þótt misst hafim munar ok landa:
skal engi maðr angr-lióð kveða,
þótt mer á briósti benjar líti.
Nú ero brúðir byrgðar í haugi,
lofða dísir, hjá oss liðnom.

The figure of *Anadiplosis* (or the "Redouble," as it is called in the *Arte of English Poesie*) is characteristic of a certain group of Northern poems. See the note on this, with references, in *C.P.B.*, i. p. 557. The poems in which this device appears are the poems of the heroines (Brynhild, Gudrun, Oddrun), the heroic idylls of the North. In these poems the repetition of a phrase, as in the Greek pastoral poetry and its descendants, has the effect of giving solemnity to the speech, and slowness of movement to the line.

So in the *Long Lay of Brynhild* (*C.P.B.*, i. p. 296) :—

> svárar sifjar, svarna eiða,
> eiða svarna, unnar tryggðir ;

and (*ibid.*)—

> hann vas fyr utan eiða svarna,
> eiða svarna, unnar tryggðir ;

and in the *Old Lay of Gudrun* (*C.P.B.*, i. p. 319)—

> Hverr vildi mer hnossir velja
> hnossir velja, ok hugat mæla.

There are other figures which have the same effect :—

> Gott es at ráða Rínar malmi,
> ok unandi auði styra,
> ok sitjandi sælo nióta.
> *C.P.B.*, i. p. 296.

But apart from these emphatic forms of phrasing, all the sentences are so constructed as to coincide with the divisions of the lines, whereas in the Western poetry, Saxon and Anglo-Saxon, the phrases are made to cut across the lines, the sentences having their own limits, independent of the beginnings and endings of the verses.

NOTE B (p. 205)

The Meeting of Kjartan and King Olaf Tryggvason (*Laxdæla Saga*, c. 40)

Kjartan rode with his father east from Hjardarholt, and they parted in Northwaterdale ; Kjartan rode on to the ship, and Bolli, his kinsman, went along with him. There were ten men of Iceland all together that followed Kjartan out of goodwill; and with this company he rides to the harbour. Kalf Asgeirsson welcomes them all. Kjartan and Bolli took a rich freight with them. So they made themselves ready to sail, and when the wind was fair they sailed out and down the Borg firth with a gentle breeze and good, and so out to sea. They had a fair voyage, and made the north of Norway, and so into Throndheim. There they asked for news, and it was told them that the land had changed its masters; Earl Hacon was gone, and King Olaf Tryggvason come, and the whole of Norway had fallen under his sway. King Olaf was proclaiming a change of law; men did not take it all in the same way. Kjartan and his fellows brought their ship into Nidaros.

At that time there were in Norway many Icelanders who were men of reputation. There at the wharves were lying three ships all belonging to men of Iceland: one to Brand the Generous, son of Vermund Thorgrimsson; another to Hallfred the Troublesome Poet; the third ship was owned by two brothers, Bjarni and Thorhall, sons of Skeggi, east in Fleetlithe,—all these men had been bound for Iceland in the summer, but the king had arrested the ships because these men would not accept the faith that he was proclaiming. Kjartan was welcomed by them all, and most of all by Brand, because they had been well acquainted earlier. The Icelanders all took counsel together, and this was the upshot, that they bound themselves to refuse the king's new law. Kjartan and his mates brought in their ship to the quay, and fell to work to land their freight.

King Olaf was in the town; he hears of the ship's coming, and that there were men in it of no small account. It fell out on a bright day in harvest-time that Kjartan's company saw a number of men going to swim in the river Nith. Kjartan said they ought to go too, for the sport; and so they did. There was one man of the place who was far the best swimmer. Kjartan says to Bolli:

"Will you try your swimming against this townsman?"

Bolli answers: "I reckon that is more than my strength."

"I know not what is become of your hardihood," says Kjartan; "but I will venture it myself."

"That you may, if you please," says Bolli.

Kjartan dives into the river, and so out to the man that swam better than all the rest; him he takes hold of and dives under with him, and holds him under for a time, and then lets him go. After that they swam for a little, and then the stranger takes Kjartan and goes under with him, and holds him under, none too short a time, as it seemed to Kjartan. Then they came to the top, but there were no words between them. They dived together a third time, and were down longer than before. Kjartan thought it hard to tell how the play would end; it seemed to him that he had never been in so tight a place in his life. However, they come up at last, and strike out for the land.

Then says the stranger: "Who may this man be?"

Kjartan told his name.

The townsman said: "You are a good swimmer; are you as good at other sports as at this?"

Kjartan answers, but not very readily: "When I was in Iceland it was thought that my skill in other things was much of a piece; but now there is not much to be said about it."

The townsman said: "It may make some difference to know with whom you have been matched; why do you not ask?"

Kjartan said: "I care nothing for your name."

The townsman says: "For one thing you are a good man of your hands, and for another you bear yourself otherwise than humbly; none the less shall you know my name and with whom you have been swimming; I am Olaf Tryggvason, the king."

Kjartan makes no answer, and turns to go away. He had no cloak, but a coat of scarlet cloth. The king was then nearly dressed. He called to Kjartan to wait a little; Kjartan turned and came back, rather slowly. Then the king took from his shoulders a rich cloak and gave it to Kjartan, saying he should not go cloakless back to his men. Kjartan thanks the king for his gift, and goes to his men and shows them the cloak. They did not take it very well, but thought he had allowed the king too much of a hold on him.

Things were quiet for a space; the weather began to harden with frost and cold. The heathen men said it was no wonder they had ill weather that autumn; it was all the king's newfangledness and the new law that had made the gods angry.

The Icelanders were all together that winter in the town; and Kjartan took the lead among them. In time the weather softened, and men came in numbers to the town at the summons of King Olaf. Many men had taken the Christian faith in Throndheim, but those were more in number who were against it. One day the king held an assembly in the town, out on the point of Eyre, and declared the Faith with many eloquent words. The Thronds had a great multitude there, and offered battle to the king on the spot. The king said they should know that he had fought against greater powers than to think of scuffling with clowns in Throndheim. Then the yeomen were cowed, and gave in wholly to the king, and many men were christened; then the assembly broke up.

That same evening the king sends men to the Icelanders' inn to observe and find out how they talked. When the messengers came there, there was a loud sound of voices within.

Kjartan spoke, and said to Bolli: "Kinsman, are you willing to take this faith of the king's?"

"I am not," says Bolli, "for it seems to me a feeble, pithless thing."

Says Kjartan: "Seemed the king to you to have no threats for those that refused to accept his will?"

Says Bolli: "Truly the king seemed to us to come out clearly and leave no shadow on that head, that they should have hard measure dealt them."

"No man's underling will I be," says Kjartan, "while I can keep my feet and handle a sword; it seems to me a pitiful thing to be taken thus like a lamb out of the pen, or a fox out of the trap. I hold it a far better choice, if one must die, to do something first that shall be long talked of after."

"What will you do?" says Bolli.

"I will not make a secret of it," says Kjartan; "burn the king's house, and the king in it."

"I call that no mean thing to do," says Bolli; "but yet it will not be, for I reckon that the king has no small grace and good luck along with him; and he keeps a strong watch day and night."

Kjartan said that courage might fail the stoutest man; Bolli answered that it was still to be tried whose courage would hold out longest. Then many broke in and said that this talk was foolishness; and when the king's spies had heard so much, they went back to the king and told him how the talk had gone.

On the morrow the king summons an assembly; and all the Icelanders were bidden to come. When all were met, the king stood up and thanked all men for their presence, those who were willing to be his friends and had taken the Faith. Then he fell to speech with the Icelanders. The king asks if they will be christened. They make little sound of agreement to that. The king said that they might make a choice that would profit them less.

"Which of you was it that thought it convenient to burn me in my house?"

Then says Kjartan: "You think that he will not

have the honesty to confess it, he that said this. But here you may see him."

"See thee I may," says the king, "and a man of no mean imagination; yet it is not in thy destiny to see my head at thy feet. And good enough cause might I have to stay thee from offering to burn kings in their houses in return for their good advice; but because I know not how far thy thought went along with thy words, and because of thy manly declaration, thou shalt not lose thy life for this; it may be that thou wilt hold the Faith better, as thou speakest against it more than others. I can see, too, that it will bring the men of all the Iceland ships to accept the Faith the same day that thou art christened of thine own free will. It seems to me also like enough that thy kinsmen and friends in Iceland will listen to what thou sayest when thou art come out thither again. It is not far from my thought that thou, Kjartan, mayst have a better Faith when thou sailest from Norway than when thou camest hither. Go now all in peace and liberty whither you will from this meeting; you shall not be penned into Christendom; for it is the word of God that He will not have any come to Him save in free will."

There was much approval of this speech of the king's, yet chiefly from the Christians; the heathen men left it to Kjartan to answer as he would. Then said Kjartan: "We will thank you, Sir, for giving us your peace; this more than anything would draw us to accept your Faith, that you renounce all grounds of enmity and speak gently altogether, though you have our whole fortunes in your hand to-day And this is in my mind, only to accept the Faith in Norway if I may pay some small respect to Thor next winter when I come to Iceland."

Then answered the king, smiling: "It is well seen from the bearing of Kjartan that he thinks he has better surety in his strength and his weapons than there where Thor and Odin are."

After that the assembly broke up.

NOTE C (p. 257)

Eyjolf Karsson: an Episode in the History of Bishop Gudmund Arason, A.D. 1222 (from *Arons Saga Hjörleifssonar*, c. 8, printed in *Biskupa Sögur*, i., and in *Sturlunga*, ii. pp. 312-347).

Eyjolf Karsson and Aron stood by Bishop Gudmund in his troubles, and followed him out to his refuge in the island of Grimsey, lying off the north coast of Iceland, about 30 miles from the mouth of Eyjafirth. There the Bishop was attacked by the Sturlungs, Sighvat (brother of Snorri Sturluson) and his son Sturla. His men were out-numbered; Aron was severely wounded. This chapter describes how Eyjolf managed to get his friend out of danger and how he went back himself and was killed.]

Now the story turns to Eyjolf and Aron. When many of Eyjolf's men were down, and some had run to the church, he took his way to the place where Aron and Sturla had met, and there he found Aron sitting with his weapons, and all about were lying dead men and wounded. It is reckoned that nine men must have lost their lives there. Eyjolf asks his cousin whether he can move at all. Aron says that he can, and stands on his feet; and now they go both together for a while by the shore, till they come to a hidden bay; there they saw a boat ready floating, with five or six men at the oars, and the bow to sea. This was Eyjolf's arrangement, in case of sudden need. Now Eyjolf tells Aron that he means the boat for both of them; giving out that he sees no hope of doing more for the Bishop at that time.

"But I look for better days to come," says Eyjolf.

"It seems a strange plan to me," says Aron; "for I thought that we should never part from Bishop Gudmund in this distress; there is something behind this, and I vow that I will not go unless you go first on board."

"That I will not, cousin," says Eyjolf; "for it is shoal water here, and I will not have any of the oarsmen leave his oar to shove her off; and it is far too much for you to go afoot with wounds like yours. You will have to go on board."

"Well, put your weapons in the boat," says Aron, "and I will believe you."

Aron now goes on board; and Eyjolf did as Aron asked him. Eyjolf waded after, pushing the boat, for the shallows went far out. And when he saw the right time come, Eyjolf caught up a battle-axe out of the stern of the boat, and gave a shove to the boat with all his might.

"Good-bye, Aron," says Eyjolf; "we shall meet again when God pleases."

And since Aron was disabled with wounds, and weary with loss of blood, it had to be even so; and this parting was a grief to Aron, for they saw each other no more.

Now Eyjolf spoke to the oarsmen and told them to row hard, and not to let Aron come back to Grimsey that day, and not for many a day if they could help it.

They row away with Aron in their boat; but Eyjolf turns to the shore again and to a boat-house with a large ferry-boat in it, that belonged to the goodman Gnup. And at the same nick of time he sees the Sturlung company come tearing down from the garth, having finished their mischief there. Eyjolf takes to the boat-house, with his mind made up to defend it as long as his doom would let him. There were double doors to the boat-house, and he puts heavy stones against them.

Brand, one of Sighvat's followers, a man of good condition, caught a glimpse of a man moving, and said to his companions that he thought he had made out Eyjolf Karsson there, and they ought to go after him. Sturla was not on the spot; there were nine or ten together. So they come to the boat-house. Brand asks who is there, and Eyjolf says it is he.

"Then you will please to come out and come before Sturla," says Brand.

"Will you promise me quarter?" says Eyjolf.

"There will be little of that," says Brand.

"Then it is for you to come on," says Eyjolf, and for me to guard; and it seems to me the shares are ill divided."

Eyjolf had a coat of mail, and a great axe, and that was all.

Now they came at him, and he made a good and brave defence; he cut their pike-shafts through; there were stout strokes on both sides. And in that bout Eyjolf breaks his axe-heft, and catches up an oar, and then another, and both break with his blows. And in this bout Eyjolf gets a thrust under his arm, and it came home. Some say that he broke the shaft from the spear-head, and let it stay in the wound. He sees now that his defence is ended. Then he made a dash out, and got through them, before they knew. They were not expecting this; still they kept their heads, and a man named Mar cut at him and caught his ankle, so that his foot hung crippled. With that he rolls down the beach, and the sea was at the flood. In such plight as he was in, Eyjolf set to and swam; and swimming he came twelve fathoms from shore to a shelf of rock, and knelt there; and then he fell full length upon the earth, and spread his hands from him, turning to the East as if to pray.

Now they launch the boat, and go after him. And when they came to the rock, a man drove a spear into him, and then another, but no blood flowed from either wound. So they turn to go ashore, and find Sturla and tell him the story plainly how it had all fallen out. Sturla held, and other men too, that this had been a glorious defence. He showed that he was pleased at the news.

Note D (p. 360)

Two Catalogues of Romances

There are many references to books and cycles of romance in medieval literature—minstrels' enumerations of their stock-in-trade, and humorous allusions like those of Sir Thopas, and otherwise. There are two passages, among others, which seem to do their best to cover the whole ground, or at least to exemplify all the chief groups. One of these is that referred to in the text, from *Flamenca*; the other is to be found, much later, in the *Complaint of Scotland* (1549).

I. Flamenca (ll. 609-701)

Qui volc ausir diverses comtes
De reis, de marques e de comtes,
Auzir ne poc tan can si volc;
Anc null' aurella non lai colc,
Quar l'us comtet de Priamus,
E l'autre diz de Piramus;
L'us contet de la bell'Elena
Com Paris l'enquer, pois l'anmena;
L'autres comtava d'Ulixes,
L'autre d'Ector et d'Achilles;
L'autre comtava d'Eneas,
E de Dido consi remas
Per lui dolenta e mesquina;
L'autre comtava de Lavina
Con fes lo breu el cairel traire
A la gaita de l'auzor caire;
L'us contet d'Apollonices
De Tideu e d'Etidiocles;
L'autre comtava d'Apolloine
Comsi retenc Tyr de Sidoine;
L'us comtet del rei Alexandri
L'autre d'Ero et de Leandri;
L'us dis de Catmus quan fugi
Et de Tebas con las basti,
L'autre contava de Jason
E del dragon que non hac son;

L'us comte d'Alcide sa forsa,
L'autre con tornet en sa forsa
Phillis per amor Demophon ;
L'us dis com neguet en la fon
Lo bels Narcis quan s'i miret ;
L'us dis de Pluto con emblet
Sa bella moillier ad Orpheu ;
L'autre comtet del Philisteu
Golias, consi fon aucis
Ab treis peiras quel trais David ;
L'us diz de Samson con dormi,
Quan Dalidan liet la cri ;
L'autre comtet de Machabeu
Comen si combatet per Dieu ;
L'us comtet de Juli Cesar
Com passet tot solet la mar,
E no i preguet Nostre Senor
Que nous cujes agues paor ;
L'us diz de la Taula Redonda
Que no i venc homs que noil responda
Le reis segon sa conoissensa,
Anc nuil jorn ne i failli valensa ;
L'autre comtava de Galvain,
E del leo que fon compain
Del cavallier qu'estors Luneta ;
L'us diz de la piucella breta
Con tenc Lancelot en preiso
Cant de s'amor li dis de no ;
L'autre comtet de Persaval
Co venc a la cort a caval ;
L'us comtet d'Erec e d'Enida,
L'autre d'Ugonet de Perida ;
L'us comtava de Governail
Com per Tristan ac grieu trebail,
L'autre comtava de Feniza
Con transir la fes sa noirissa
L'us dis del Bel Desconogut
E l'autre del vermeil escut
Que l'yras trobet a l'uisset ;
L'autre comtava de Guiflet ;
L'us comtet de Calobrenan,
L'autre dis con retenc un an
Dins sa preison Quec senescal
Lo deliez car li dis mal ;

L'autre comtava de Mordret;
L'us retrais lo comte Duret
Com fo per los Ventres faiditz
E per Rei Pescador grazits;
L'us comtet l'astre d'Ermeli,
L'autre dis com fan l'Ancessi
Per gein lo Veil de la Montaina;
L'us retrais con tenc Alamaina
Karlesmaines tro la parti,
De Clodoveu e de Pipi
Comtava l'us tota l'istoria;
L'autre dis con cazec de gloria
Donz Lucifers per son ergoil;
L'us diz del vallet de Nantoil,
L'autre d'Oliveir de Verdu.
L'us dis lo vers de Marcabru,
L'autre comtet con Dedalus
Saup ben volar, et d'Icarus
Co neguet per sa leujaria.
Cascus dis lo mieil que sabia.
Per la rumor dels viuladors
E per brug d'aitans comtadors
Hac gran murmuri per la sala.

The allusions are explained by the editor, M. Paul Meyer. The stories are as follows: Priam, Pyramus, Helen, Ulysses, Hector, Achilles, Dido, Lavinia (how she sent her letter with an arrow over the sentinel's head, *Roman d'Eneas*, l. 8807, *sq.*), Polynices, Tydeus, and Eteocles; Apollonius of Tyre; Alexander; Hero and Leander; Cadmus of Thebes; Jason and the sleepless Dragon; Hercules; Demophoon and Phyllis (a hard passage); Narcissus; Pluto and the wife of Orpheus ("Sir Orfeo"); David and Goliath; Samson and Dalila; Judas Maccabeus; Julius Caesar; the Round Table, and how the king had an answer for all who sought him; Gawain and Yvain ("of the lion that was companion of the knight whom Lunete rescued"[1]);

[1] In a somewhat similar list of romances, in the Italian poem of *L'Intelligenza*, ascribed to Dino Compagni (st. 75), Luneta is named Analida; possibly the origin of Chaucer's Anelida, a name which has not been clearly traced.

of the British maiden who kept Lancelot imprisoned when he refused her love; of Perceval, how he rode into hall; Ugonet de Perida (?); Governail, the loyal comrade of Tristram; Fenice and the sleeping-draught (Chrestien's *Cliges*, see p. 357, above); Guinglain ("Sir Libeaus)"; Chrestien's *Chevalier de la Charrette* ("how the herald found the red shield at the entry," an allusion explained by M. Gaston Paris, in *Romania*, xvi. p. 101), Guiflet, Calobrenan, Kay punished for his railing accusations; Mordred; how the Count Duret was dispossessed by the Vandals and welcomed by the Fisher King (?); the luck of Hermelin (?); the Old Man of the Mountain and his Assassins; the Wars of Charlemagne; Clovis and Pepin of France; the Fall of Lucifer; Gui de Nanteuil; Oliver of Verdun; the Flight of Daedalus, and how Icarus was drowned through his vanity. The songs of Marcabrun, the troubadour, find a place in the list among the stories.

The author of *Flamenca* has arranged his library, though there are some incongruities; Daedalus belongs properly to the "matter of Rome" with which the catalogue begins, and Lucifer interrupts the series of *Chansons de geste*. The "matter of Britain," however, is all by itself, and is well represented.

II. The Complaynt of Scotland, c. vi.

(Ed. J. A. H. Murray, *E.E.T.S.*, pp. 62-64)

[This passage belongs to the close of the Middle Ages, when the old epic and romantic books were falling into neglect. There is no distinction here between literary romance and popular tales; the once-fashionable poetical works are reduced to their original elements. Arthur and Gawain are no more respected than the Red Etin, or the tale of the *Well at the World's End* (the reading *volfe* in the text has no defender); the Four Sons of Aymon have become what they were afterwards for Boileau (*Ep.* xi. 20), or rather for Boileau's gardener. But, on the whole, the list represents the common medieval taste in fiction. The *Chansons de geste* have provided the *Bridge of the Mantrible* (from *Oliver and Fierabras*, which may be intended in the *Flamenca* reference to Oliver), and the *Siege of Milan* (see *English Charlemagne Romances*, *E.E.T.S.*, part ii.), as well as the *Four Sons of Aymon* and *Sir Bevis.* The Arthurian cycle is popular; the romance of *Sir Ywain* (the Knight of the Lion) is here, however, the only one that can be definitely traced in the *Flamenca* list also, though of course there is a general correspondence in subject-matter. The classical fables from Ovid are still among the favourites, and many of them are common to both lists. See Dr. Furnivall's note, in the edition cited, pp. lxxiii.-lxxxii.]

Quhen the scheiphird hed endit his prolixt orison to the laif of the scheiphirdis, i meruellit nocht litil quhen i herd ane rustic pastour of bestialite, distitut of vrbanite, and of speculatioune of natural philosophe, indoctryne his nychtbours as he hed studeit ptholome, auerois, aristotel, galien, ypocrites, or Cicero, quhilk var expert practicians in methamatic art. Than the scheiphirdis vyf said: my veil belouit hisband, i pray the to desist fra that tideus melancolic orison, quhilk surpassis thy ingyne, be rason that it is nocht thy facultee to disput in ane profund mater, the quhilk thy capacite can nocht comprehend. ther for, i thynk it best that ve recreat our selfis vytht ioyus comonyng quhil on to the tyme that ve return to the scheip fald vytht our flokkis. And to begin sic recreatione i thynk it best that everie ane of vs tel ane gude tayl or fable, to pas the tyme quhil euyn. Al the scheiphirdis, ther vyuis and saruandis, var glaid of this propositione. than the eldest scheiphird began, and al the laif follouit, ane be ane in their auen place. it vil be ouer prolixt, and no les tideus to reherse them agane vord be vord. bot i sal reherse sum of ther namys that i herd. Sum vas in prose and sum vas in verse: sum vas stories and sum var flet taylis. Thir var the namis of them as eftir follouis: the taylis of cantirberrye, Robert le dyabil duc of Normandie, the tayl of the volfe of the varldis end, Ferrand erl of Flandris that mareit the deuyl, the taiyl of the reyde eyttyn vitht the thre heydis, the tail quhou perseus sauit andromada fra the cruel monstir, the prophysie of merlyne, the tayl of the giantis that eit quyk men, on fut by fortht as i culd found, vallace, the bruce, ypomedon, the tail of the three futtit dug of norrouay, the tayl quhou Hercules sleu the serpent hidra that hed vij heydis, the tail quhou the king of est mure land mareit the kyngis dochtir of vest mure land, Skail gillenderson the kyngis sone of skellye, the tail of the four sonnis of aymon, the tail of the brig of the mantribil, the tail of syr euan, arthour's knycht, rauf collȝear, the seige of millan, gauen and gollogras, lancelot du lac, Arthour knycht he raid on nycht viтht gyltin spur and candil lycht, the tail of floremond of albanye that sleu the dragon be the see, the tail of syr valtir the bald leslye, the tail of the pure tynt, claryades and maliades, Arthour of litil bertangȝe, robene hude and litil ihone, the meruellis of mandiueil, the tayl of the ȝong tamlene and of the bald braband, the ryng of the roy Robert, syr egeir and syr gryme, beuis of southamtoun, the goldin targe, the paleis of honour, the tayl quhou acteon vas transformit in ane hart and syne slane be his auen doggis, the tayl of Pirramus and tesbe, the tail of the amours of leander and hero, the tail how Iupiter transformit his deir love yo in ane cou, the tail quhou that iason van the goldin fleice, Opheus kyng of portingal, the tail of the goldin appil, the tail of the thre veird systirs, the tail quhou that dedalus maid the laborynth to keip the monstir minotaurus, the tail quhou kyng midas gat tua asse luggis on his hede because of his auereis.

INDEX

THE END

A CATALOGUE OF SELECTED DOVER BOOKS IN ALL FIELDS OF INTEREST

A CATALOGUE OF SELECTED DOVER BOOKS IN ALL FIELDS OF INTEREST

AMERICA'S OLD MASTERS, James T. Flexner. Four men emerged unexpectedly from provincial 18th century America to leadership in European art: Benjamin West, J. S. Copley, C. R. Peale, Gilbert Stuart. Brilliant coverage of lives and contributions. Revised, 1967 edition. 69 plates. 365pp. of text.

21806-6 Paperbound $3.00

FIRST FLOWERS OF OUR WILDERNESS: AMERICAN PAINTING, THE COLONIAL PERIOD, James T. Flexner. Painters, and regional painting traditions from earliest Colonial times up to the emergence of Copley, West and Peale Sr., Foster, Gustavus Hesselius, Feke, John Smibert and many anonymous painters in the primitive manner. Engaging presentation, with 162 illustrations. xxii + 368pp.

22180-6 Paperbound $3.50

THE LIGHT OF DISTANT SKIES: AMERICAN PAINTING, 1760-1835, James T. Flexner. The great generation of early American painters goes to Europe to learn and to teach: West, Copley, Gilbert Stuart and others. Allston, Trumbull, Morse; also contemporary American painters—primitives, derivatives, academics—who remained in America. 102 illustrations. xiii + 306pp. 22179-2 Paperbound $3.00

A HISTORY OF THE RISE AND PROGRESS OF THE ARTS OF DESIGN IN THE UNITED STATES, William Dunlap. Much the richest mine of information on early American painters, sculptors, architects, engravers, miniaturists, etc. The only source of information for scores of artists, the major primary source for many others. Unabridged reprint of rare original 1834 edition, with new introduction by James T. Flexner, and 394 new illustrations. Edited by Rita Weiss. $6\frac{5}{8}$ x $9\frac{5}{8}$.

21695-0, 21696-9, 21697-7 Three volumes, Paperbound $13.50

EPOCHS OF CHINESE AND JAPANESE ART, Ernest F. Fenollosa. From primitive Chinese art to the 20th century, thorough history, explanation of every important art period and form, including Japanese woodcuts; main stress on China and Japan, but Tibet, Korea also included. Still unexcelled for its detailed, rich coverage of cultural background, aesthetic elements, diffusion studies, particularly of the historical period. 2nd, 1913 edition. 242 illustrations. lii + 439pp. of text.

20364-6, 20365-4 Two volumes, Paperbound $6.00

THE GENTLE ART OF MAKING ENEMIES, James A. M. Whistler. Greatest wit of his day deflates Oscar Wilde, Ruskin, Swinburne; strikes back at inane critics, exhibitions, art journalism; aesthetics of impressionist revolution in most striking form. Highly readable classic by great painter. Reproduction of edition designed by Whistler. Introduction by Alfred Werner. xxxvi + 334pp.

21875-9 Paperbound $2.50

VISUAL ILLUSIONS: THEIR CAUSES, CHARACTERISTICS, AND APPLICATIONS, Matthew Luckiesh. Thorough description and discussion of optical illusion, geometric and perspective, particularly; size and shape distortions, illusions of color, of motion; natural illusions; use of illusion in art and magic, industry, etc. Most useful today with op art, also for classical art. Scores of effects illustrated. Introduction by William H. Ittleson. 100 illustrations. xxi + 252pp.
21530-X Paperbound $2.00

A HANDBOOK OF ANATOMY FOR ART STUDENTS, Arthur Thomson. Thorough, virtually exhaustive coverage of skeletal structure, musculature, etc. Full text, supplemented by anatomical diagrams and drawings and by photographs of undraped figures. Unique in its comparison of male and female forms, pointing out differences of contour, texture, form. 211 figures, 40 drawings, 86 photographs. xx + 459pp. 5⅜ x 8⅜.
21163-0 Paperbound $3.50

150 MASTERPIECES OF DRAWING, Selected by Anthony Toney. Full page reproductions of drawings from the early 16th to the end of the 18th century, all beautifully reproduced: Rembrandt, Michelangelo, Dürer, Fragonard, Urs, Graf, Wouwerman, many others. First-rate browsing book, model book for artists. xviii + 150pp. 8⅜ x 11¼.
21032-4 Paperbound $2.50

THE LATER WORK OF AUBREY BEARDSLEY, Aubrey Beardsley. Exotic, erotic, ironic masterpieces in full maturity: Comedy Ballet, Venus and Tannhauser, Pierrot, Lysistrata, Rape of the Lock, Savoy material, Ali Baba, Volpone, etc. This material revolutionized the art world, and is still powerful, fresh, brilliant. With *The Early Work,* all Beardsley's finest work. 174 plates, 2 in color. xiv + 176pp. 8⅛ x 11.
21817-1 Paperbound $3.00

DRAWINGS OF REMBRANDT, Rembrandt van Rijn. Complete reproduction of fabulously rare edition by Lippmann and Hofstede de Groot, completely reedited, updated, improved by Prof. Seymour Slive, Fogg Museum. Portraits, Biblical sketches, landscapes, Oriental types, nudes, episodes from classical mythology—All Rembrandt's fertile genius. Also selection of drawings by his pupils and followers. "Stunning volumes," *Saturday Review.* 550 illustrations. lxxviii + 552pp. 9⅛ x 12¼.
21485-0, 21486-9 Two volumes, Paperbound $10.00

THE DISASTERS OF WAR, Francisco Goya. One of the masterpieces of Western civilization—83 etchings that record Goya's shattering, bitter reaction to the Napoleonic war that swept through Spain after the insurrection of 1808 and to war in general. Reprint of the first edition, with three additional plates from Boston's Museum of Fine Arts. All plates facsimile size. Introduction by Philip Hofer, Fogg Museum. v + 97pp. 9⅜ x 8¼.
21872-4 Paperbound $2.00

GRAPHIC WORKS OF ODILON REDON. Largest collection of Redon's graphic works ever assembled: 172 lithographs, 28 etchings and engravings, 9 drawings. These include some of his most famous works. All the plates from *Odilon Redon: oeuvre graphique complet,* plus additional plates. New introduction and caption translations by Alfred Werner. 209 illustrations. xxvii + 209pp. 9⅛ x 12¼.
21966-8 Paperbound $4.00

ALPHABETS AND ORNAMENTS, Ernst Lehner. Well-known pictorial source for decorative alphabets, script examples, cartouches, frames, decorative title pages, calligraphic initials, borders, similar material. 14th to 19th century, mostly European. Useful in almost any graphic arts designing, varied styles. 750 illustrations. 256pp. 7 x 10. 21905-4 Paperbound $4.00

PAINTING: A CREATIVE APPROACH, Norman Colquhoun. For the beginner simple guide provides an instructive approach to painting: major stumbling blocks for beginner; overcoming them, technical points; paints and pigments; oil painting; watercolor and other media and color. New section on "plastic" paints. Glossary. Formerly *Paint Your Own Pictures.* 221pp. 22000-1 Paperbound $1.75

THE ENJOYMENT AND USE OF COLOR, Walter Sargent. Explanation of the relations between colors themselves and between colors in nature and art, including hundreds of little-known facts about color values, intensities, effects of high and low illumination, complementary colors. Many practical hints for painters, references to great masters. 7 color plates, 29 illustrations. x + 274pp.
20944-X Paperbound $2.75

THE NOTEBOOKS OF LEONARDO DA VINCI, compiled and edited by Jean Paul Richter. 1566 extracts from original manuscripts reveal the full range of Leonardo's versatile genius: all his writings on painting, sculpture, architecture, anatomy, astronomy, geography, topography, physiology, mining, music, etc., in both Italian and English, with 186 plates of manuscript pages and more than 500 additional drawings. Includes studies for the Last Supper, the lost Sforza monument, and other works. Total of xlvii + 866pp. 7⅞ x 10¾.
22572-0, 22573-9 Two volumes, Paperbound $10.00

MONTGOMERY WARD CATALOGUE OF 1895. Tea gowns, yards of flannel and pillow-case lace, stereoscopes, books of gospel hymns, the New Improved Singer Sewing Machine, side saddles, milk skimmers, straight-edged razors, high-button shoes, spittoons, and on and on . . . listing some 25,000 items, practically all illustrated. Essential to the shoppers of the 1890's, it is our truest record of the spirit of the period. Unaltered reprint of Issue No. 57, Spring and Summer 1895. Introduction by Boris Emmet. Innumerable illustrations. xiii + 624pp. 8½ x 11⅝.
22377-9 Paperbound $6.95

THE CRYSTAL PALACE EXHIBITION ILLUSTRATED CATALOGUE (LONDON, 1851). One of the wonders of the modern world—the Crystal Palace Exhibition in which all the nations of the civilized world exhibited their achievements in the arts and sciences—presented in an equally important illustrated catalogue. More than 1700 items pictured with accompanying text—ceramics, textiles, cast-iron work, carpets, pianos, sleds, razors, wall-papers, billiard tables, beehives, silverware and hundreds of other artifacts—represent the focal point of Victorian culture in the Western World. Probably the largest collection of Victorian decorative art ever assembled—indispensable for antiquarians and designers. Unabridged republication of the Art-Journal Catalogue of the Great Exhibition of 1851, with all terminal essays. New introduction by John Gloag, F.S.A. xxxiv + 426pp. 9 x 12.
22503-8 Paperbound $4.50

DESIGN BY ACCIDENT; A BOOK OF "ACCIDENTAL EFFECTS" FOR ARTISTS AND DESIGNERS, James F. O'Brien. Create your own unique, striking, imaginative effects by "controlled accident" interaction of materials: paints and lacquers, oil and water based paints, splatter, crackling materials, shatter, similar items. Everything you do will be different; first book on this limitless art, so useful to both fine artist and commercial artist. Full instructions. 192 plates showing "accidents," 8 in color. viii + 215pp. 8⅜ x 11¼. 21942-9 Paperbound $3.50

THE BOOK OF SIGNS, Rudolf Koch. Famed German type designer draws 493 beautiful symbols: religious, mystical, alchemical, imperial, property marks, runes, etc. Remarkable fusion of traditional and modern. Good for suggestions of timelessness, smartness, modernity. Text. vi + 104pp. 6⅛ x 9¼. 20162-7 Paperbound $1.25

HISTORY OF INDIAN AND INDONESIAN ART, Ananda K. Coomaraswamy. An unabridged republication of one of the finest books by a great scholar in Eastern art. Rich in descriptive material, history, social backgrounds; Sunga reliefs, Rajput paintings, Gupta temples, Burmese frescoes, textiles, jewelry, sculpture, etc. 400 photos. viii + 423pp. 6⅜ x 9¾. 21436-2 Paperbound $4.00

PRIMITIVE ART, Franz Boas. America's foremost anthropologist surveys textiles, ceramics, woodcarving, basketry, metalwork, etc.; patterns, technology, creation of symbols, style origins. All areas of world, but very full on Northwest Coast Indians. More than 350 illustrations of baskets, boxes, totem poles, weapons, etc. 378 pp. 20025-6 Paperbound $3.00

THE GENTLEMAN AND CABINET MAKER'S DIRECTOR, Thomas Chippendale. Full reprint (third edition, 1762) of most influential furniture book of all time, by master cabinetmaker. 200 plates, illustrating chairs, sofas, mirrors, tables, cabinets, plus 24 photographs of surviving pieces. Biographical introduction by N. Bienenstock. vi + 249pp. 9⅞ x 12¾. 21601-2 Paperbound $4.00

AMERICAN ANTIQUE FURNITURE, Edgar G. Miller, Jr. The basic coverage of all American furniture before 1840. Individual chapters cover type of furniture—clocks, tables, sideboards, etc.—chronologically, with inexhaustible wealth of data. More than 2100 photographs, all identified, commented on. Essential to all early American collectors. Introduction by H. E. Keyes. vi + 1106pp. 7⅞ x 10¾. 21599-7, 21600-4 Two volumes, Paperbound $11.00

PENNSYLVANIA DUTCH AMERICAN FOLK ART, Henry J. Kauffman. 279 photos, 28 drawings of tulipware, Fraktur script, painted tinware, toys, flowered furniture, quilts, samplers, hex signs, house interiors, etc. Full descriptive text. Excellent for tourist, rewarding for designer, collector. Map. 146pp. 7⅞ x 10¾. 21205-X Paperbound $2.50

EARLY NEW ENGLAND GRAVESTONE RUBBINGS, Edmund V. Gillon, Jr. 43 photographs, 226 carefully reproduced rubbings show heavily symbolic, sometimes macabre early gravestones, up to early 19th century. Remarkable early American primitive art, occasionally strikingly beautiful; always powerful. Text. xxvi + 207pp. 8⅜ x 11¼. 21380-3 Paperbound $3.50

THE ARCHITECTURE OF COUNTRY HOUSES, Andrew J. Downing. Together with Vaux's *Villas and Cottages* this is the basic book for Hudson River Gothic architecture of the middle Victorian period. Full, sound discussions of general aspects of housing, architecture, style, decoration, furnishing, together with scores of detailed house plans, illustrations of specific buildings, accompanied by full text. Perhaps the most influential single American architectural book. 1850 edition. Introduction by J. Stewart Johnson. 321 figures, 34 architectural designs. xvi + 560pp.
22003-6 Paperbound $4.00

LOST EXAMPLES OF COLONIAL ARCHITECTURE, John Mead Howells. Full-page photographs of buildings that have disappeared or been so altered as to be denatured, including many designed by major early American architects. 245 plates. xvii + 248pp. 7⅞ x 10¾.
21143-6 Paperbound $3.50

DOMESTIC ARCHITECTURE OF THE AMERICAN COLONIES AND OF THE EARLY REPUBLIC, Fiske Kimball. Foremost architect and restorer of Williamsburg and Monticello covers nearly 200 homes between 1620-1825. Architectural details, construction, style features, special fixtures, floor plans, etc. Generally considered finest work in its area. 219 illustrations of houses, doorways, windows, capital mantels. xx + 314pp. 7⅞ x 10¾.
21743-4 Paperbound $4.00

EARLY AMERICAN ROOMS: 1650-1858, edited by Russell Hawes Kettell. Tour of 12 rooms, each representative of a different era in American history and each furnished, decorated, designed and occupied in the style of the era. 72 plans and elevations, 8-page color section, etc., show fabrics, wall papers, arrangements, etc. Full descriptive text. xvii + 200pp. of text. 8⅜ x 11¼.
21633-0 Paperbound $5.00

THE FITZWILLIAM VIRGINAL BOOK, edited by J. Fuller Maitland and W. B. Squire. Full modern printing of famous early 17th-century ms. volume of 300 works by Morley, Byrd, Bull, Gibbons, etc. For piano or other modern keyboard instrument; easy to read format. xxxvi + 938pp. 8⅜ x 11.
21068-5, 21069-3 Two volumes, Paperbound $10.00

KEYBOARD MUSIC, Johann Sebastian Bach. Bach Gesellschaft edition. A rich selection of Bach's masterpieces for the harpsichord: the six English Suites, six French Suites, the six Partitas (Clavierübung part I), the Goldberg Variations (Clavierübung part IV), the fifteen Two-Part Inventions and the fifteen Three-Part Sinfonias. Clearly reproduced on large sheets with ample margins; eminently playable. vi + 312pp. 8⅛ x 11.
22360-4 Paperbound $5.00

THE MUSIC OF BACH: AN INTRODUCTION, Charles Sanford Terry. A fine, nontechnical introduction to Bach's music, both instrumental and vocal. Covers organ music, chamber music, passion music, other types. Analyzes themes, developments, innovations. x + 114pp.
21075-8 Paperbound $1.25

BEETHOVEN AND HIS NINE SYMPHONIES, Sir George Grove. Noted British musicologist provides best history, analysis, commentary on symphonies. Very thorough, rigorously accurate; necessary to both advanced student and amateur music lover. 436 musical passages. vii + 407 pp.
20334-4 Paperbound $2.75

A HISTORY OF COSTUME, Carl Köhler. Definitive history, based on surviving pieces of clothing primarily, and paintings, statues, etc. secondarily. Highly readable text, supplemented by 594 illustrations of costumes of the ancient Mediterranean peoples, Greece and Rome, the Teutonic prehistoric period; costumes of the Middle Ages, Renaissance, Baroque, 18th and 19th centuries. Clear, measured patterns are provided for many clothing articles. Approach is practical throughout. Enlarged by Emma von Sichart. 464pp. 21030-8 Paperbound $3.50

ORIENTAL RUGS, ANTIQUE AND MODERN, Walter A. Hawley. A complete and authoritative treatise on the Oriental rug—where they are made, by whom and how, designs and symbols, characteristics in detail of the six major groups, how to distinguish them and how to buy them. Detailed technical data is provided on periods, weaves, warps, wefts, textures, sides, ends and knots, although no technical background is required for an understanding. 11 color plates, 80 halftones, 4 maps. vi + 320pp. 6⅛ x 9⅛. 22366-3 Paperbound $5.00

TEN BOOKS ON ARCHITECTURE, Vitruvius. By any standards the most important book on architecture ever written. Early Roman discussion of aesthetics of building, construction methods, orders, sites, and every other aspect of architecture has inspired, instructed architecture for about 2,000 years. Stands behind Palladio, Michelangelo, Bramante, Wren, countless others. Definitive Morris H. Morgan translation. 68 illustrations. xii + 331pp. 20645-9 Paperbound $3.50

THE FOUR BOOKS OF ARCHITECTURE, Andrea Palladio. Translated into every major Western European language in the two centuries following its publication in 1570, this has been one of the most influential books in the history of architecture. Complete reprint of the 1738 Isaac Ware edition. New introduction by Adolf Placzek, Columbia Univ. 216 plates. xxii + 110pp. of text. 9½ x 12¾. 21308-0 Clothbound $10.00

STICKS AND STONES: A STUDY OF AMERICAN ARCHITECTURE AND CIVILIZATION, Lewis Mumford.One of the great classics of American cultural history. American architecture from the medieval-inspired earliest forms to the early 20th century; evolution of structure and style, and reciprocal influences on environment. 21 photographic illustrations. 238pp. 20202-X Paperbound $2.00

THE AMERICAN BUILDER'S COMPANION, Asher Benjamin. The most widely used early 19th century architectural style and source book, for colonial up into Greek Revival periods. Extensive development of geometry of carpentering, construction of sashes, frames, doors, stairs; plans and elevations of domestic and other buildings. Hundreds of thousands of houses were built according to this book, now invaluable to historians, architects, restorers, etc. 1827 edition. 59 plates. 114pp. 7⅞ x 10¾. 22236-5 Paperbound $3.50

DUTCH HOUSES IN THE HUDSON VALLEY BEFORE 1776, Helen Wilkinson Reynolds. The standard survey of the Dutch colonial house and outbuildings, with constructional features, decoration, and local history associated with individual homesteads. Introduction by Franklin D. Roosevelt. Map. 150 illustrations. 469pp. 6⅝ x 9¼. 21469-9 Paperbound $4.00

AGAINST THE GRAIN (A REBOURS), Joris K. Huysmans. Filled with weird images, evidences of a bizarre imagination, exotic experiments with hallucinatory drugs, rich tastes and smells and the diversions of its sybarite hero Duc Jean des Esseintes, this classic novel pushed 19th-century literary decadence to its limits. Full unabridged edition. Do not confuse this with abridged editions generally sold. Introduction by Havelock Ellis. xlix + 206pp. 22190-3 Paperbound $2.00

VARIORUM SHAKESPEARE: HAMLET. Edited by Horace H. Furness; a landmark of American scholarship. Exhaustive footnotes and appendices treat all doubtful words and phrases, as well as suggested critical emendations throughout the play's history. First volume contains editor's own text, collated with all Quartos and Folios. Second volume contains full first Quarto, translations of Shakespeare's sources (Belleforest, and Saxo Grammaticus), Der Bestrafte Brudermord, and many essays on critical and historical points of interest by major authorities of past and present. Includes details of staging and costuming over the years. By far the best edition available for serious students of Shakespeare. Total of xx + 905pp.
21004-9, 21005-7, 2 volumes, Paperbound $7.00

A LIFE OF WILLIAM SHAKESPEARE, Sir Sidney Lee. This is the standard life of Shakespeare, summarizing everything known about Shakespeare and his plays. Incredibly rich in material, broad in coverage, clear and judicious, it has served thousands as the best introduction to Shakespeare. 1931 edition. 9 plates. xxix + 792pp. (USO) 21967-4 Paperbound $3.75

MASTERS OF THE DRAMA, John Gassner. Most comprehensive history of the drama in print, covering every tradition from Greeks to modern Europe and America, including India, Far East, etc. Covers more than 800 dramatists, 2000 plays, with biographical material, plot summaries, theatre history, criticism, etc. "Best of its kind in English," *New Republic.* 77 illustrations. xxii + 890pp.
20100-7 Clothbound $8.50

THE EVOLUTION OF THE ENGLISH LANGUAGE, George McKnight. The growth of English, from the 14th century to the present. Unusual, non-technical account presents basic information in very interesting form: sound shifts, change in grammar and syntax, vocabulary growth, similar topics. Abundantly illustrated with quotations. Formerly *Modern English in the Making.* xii + 590pp.
21932-1 Paperbound $3.50

AN ETYMOLOGICAL DICTIONARY OF MODERN ENGLISH, Ernest Weekley. Fullest, richest work of its sort, by foremost British lexicographer. Detailed word histories, including many colloquial and archaic words; extensive quotations. Do not confuse this with the Concise Etymological Dictionary, which is much abridged. Total of xxvii + 830pp. 6½ x 9¼.
21873-2, 21874-0 Two volumes, Paperbound $6.00

FLATLAND: A ROMANCE OF MANY DIMENSIONS, E. A. Abbott. Classic of science-fiction explores ramifications of life in a two-dimensional world, and what happens when a three-dimensional being intrudes. Amusing reading, but also useful as introduction to thought about hyperspace. Introduction by Banesh Hoffmann. 16 illustrations. xx + 103pp. 20001-9 Paperbound $1.00

JOHANN SEBASTIAN BACH, Philipp Spitta. One of the great classics of musicology, this definitive analysis of Bach's music (and life) has never been surpassed. Lucid, nontechnical analyses of hundreds of pieces (30 pages devoted to St. Matthew Passion, 26 to B Minor Mass). Also includes major analysis of 18th-century music. 450 musical examples. 40-page musical supplement. Total of xx + 1799pp.
(EUK) 22278-0, 22279-9 Two volumes, Clothbound $15.00

MOZART AND HIS PIANO CONCERTOS, Cuthbert Girdlestone. The only full-length study of an important area of Mozart's creativity. Provides detailed analyses of all 23 concertos, traces inspirational sources. 417 musical examples. Second edition. 509pp. (USO) 21271-8 Paperbound $3.50

THE PERFECT WAGNERITE: A COMMENTARY ON THE NIBLUNG'S RING, George Bernard Shaw. Brilliant and still relevant criticism in remarkable essays on Wagner's Ring cycle, Shaw's ideas on political and social ideology behind the plots, role of Leitmotifs, vocal requisites, etc. Prefaces. xxi + 136pp.
21707-8 Paperbound $1.50

DON GIOVANNI, W. A. Mozart. Complete libretto, modern English translation; biographies of composer and librettist; accounts of early performances and critical reaction. Lavishly illustrated. All the material you need to understand and appreciate this great work. Dover Opera Guide and Libretto Series; translated and introduced by Ellen Bleiler. 92 illustrations. 209pp.
21134-7 Paperbound $1.50

HIGH FIDELITY SYSTEMS: A LAYMAN'S GUIDE, Roy F. Allison. All the basic information you need for setting up your own audio system: high fidelity and stereo record players, tape records, F.M. Connections, adjusting tone arm, cartridge, checking needle alignment, positioning speakers, phasing speakers, adjusting hums, trouble-shooting, maintenance, and similar topics. Enlarged 1965 edition. More than 50 charts, diagrams, photos. iv + 91pp. 21514-8 Paperbound $1.25

REPRODUCTION OF SOUND, Edgar Villchur. Thorough coverage for laymen of high fidelity systems, reproducing systems in general, needles, amplifiers, preamps, loudspeakers, feedback, explaining physical background. "A rare talent for making technicalities vividly comprehensible," R. Darrell, *High Fidelity*. 69 figures. iv + 92pp. 21515-6 Paperbound $1.00

HEAR ME TALKIN' TO YA: THE STORY OF JAZZ AS TOLD BY THE MEN WHO MADE IT, Nat Shapiro and Nat Hentoff. Louis Armstrong, Fats Waller, Jo Jones, Clarence Williams, Billy Holiday, Duke Ellington, Jelly Roll Morton and dozens of other jazz greats tell how it was in Chicago's South Side, New Orleans, depression Harlem and the modern West Coast as jazz was born and grew. xvi + 429pp.
21726-4 Paperbound $2.50

FABLES OF AESOP, translated by Sir Roger L'Estrange. A reproduction of the very rare 1931 Paris edition; a selection of the most interesting fables, together with 50 imaginative drawings by Alexander Calder. v + 128pp. 6½x9¼.
21780-9 Paperbound $1.25

LAST AND FIRST MEN AND STAR MAKER, TWO SCIENCE FICTION NOVELS, Olaf Stapledon. Greatest future histories in science fiction. In the first, human intelligence is the "hero," through strange paths of evolution, interplanetary invasions, incredible technologies, near extinctions and reemergences. Star Maker describes the quest of a band of star rovers for intelligence itself, through time and space: weird inhuman civilizations, crustacean minds, symbiotic worlds, etc. Complete, unabridged. v + 438pp. 21962-3 Paperbound $2.50

THREE PROPHETIC NOVELS, H. G. WELLS. Stages of a consistently planned future for mankind. *When the Sleeper Wakes,* and *A Story of the Days to Come,* anticipate *Brave New World* and *1984,* in the 21st Century; *The Time Machine,* only complete version in print, shows farther future and the end of mankind. All show Wells's greatest gifts as storyteller and novelist. Edited by E. F. Bleiler. x + 335pp. (USO) 20605-X Paperbound $2.50

THE DEVIL'S DICTIONARY, Ambrose Bierce. America's own Oscar Wilde—Ambrose Bierce—offers his barbed iconoclastic wisdom in over 1,000 definitions hailed by H. L. Mencken as "some of the most gorgeous witticisms in the English language." 145pp. 20487-1 Paperbound $1.25

MAX AND MORITZ, Wilhelm Busch. Great children's classic, father of comic strip, of two bad boys, Max and Moritz. Also Ker and Plunk (Plisch und Plumm), Cat and Mouse, Deceitful Henry, Ice-Peter, The Boy and the Pipe, and five other pieces. Original German, with English translation. Edited by H. Arthur Klein; translations by various hands and H. Arthur Klein. vi + 216pp.
20181-3 Paperbound $2.00

PIGS IS PIGS AND OTHER FAVORITES, Ellis Parker Butler. The title story is one of the best humor short stories, as Mike Flannery obfuscates biology and English. Also included, That Pup of Murchison's, The Great American Pie Company, and Perkins of Portland. 14 illustrations. v + 109pp. 21532-6 Paperbound $1.25

THE PETERKIN PAPERS, Lucretia P. Hale. It takes genius to be as stupidly mad as the Peterkins, as they decide to become wise, celebrate the "Fourth," keep a cow, and otherwise strain the resources of the Lady from Philadelphia. Basic book of American humor. 153 illustrations. 219pp. 20794-3 Paperbound $1.50

PERRAULT'S FAIRY TALES, translated by A. E. Johnson and S. R. Littlewood, with 34 full-page illustrations by Gustave Doré. All the original Perrault stories—Cinderella, Sleeping Beauty, Bluebeard, Little Red Riding Hood, Puss in Boots, Tom Thumb, etc.—with their witty verse morals and the magnificent illustrations of Doré. One of the five or six great books of European fairy tales. viii + 117pp. 8⅛ x 11. 22311-6 Paperbound $2.00

OLD HUNGARIAN FAIRY TALES, Baroness Orczy. Favorites translated and adapted by author of the *Scarlet Pimpernel.* Eight fairy tales include "The Suitors of Princess Fire-Fly," "The Twin Hunchbacks," "Mr. Cuttlefish's Love Story," and "The Enchanted Cat." This little volume of magic and adventure will captivate children as it has for generations. 90 drawings by Montagu Barstow. 96pp.
(USO) 22293-4 Paperbound $1.95

POEMS OF ANNE BRADSTREET, edited with an introduction by Robert Hutchinson. A new selection of poems by America's first poet and perhaps the first significant woman poet in the English language. 48 poems display her development in works of considerable variety—love poems, domestic poems, religious meditations, formal elegies, "quaternions," etc. Notes, bibliography. viii + 222pp.
22160-1 Paperbound $2.00

THREE GOTHIC NOVELS: THE CASTLE OF OTRANTO BY HORACE WALPOLE; VATHEK BY WILLIAM BECKFORD; THE VAMPYRE BY JOHN POLIDORI, WITH FRAGMENT OF A NOVEL BY LORD BYRON, edited by E. F. Bleiler. The first Gothic novel, by Walpole; the finest Oriental tale in English, by Beckford; powerful Romantic supernatural story in versions by Polidori and Byron. All extremely important in history of literature; all still exciting, packed with supernatural thrills, ghosts, haunted castles, magic, etc. xl + 291pp.
21232-7 Paperbound $2.50

THE BEST TALES OF HOFFMANN, E. T. A. Hoffmann. 10 of Hoffmann's most important stories, in modern re-editings of standard translations: Nutcracker and the King of Mice, Signor Formica, Automata, The Sandman, Rath Krespel, The Golden Flowerpot, Master Martin the Cooper, The Mines of Falun, The King's Betrothed, A New Year's Eve Adventure. 7 illustrations by Hoffmann. Edited by E. F. Bleiler. xxxix + 419pp. 21793-0 Paperbound $3.00

GHOST AND HORROR STORIES OF AMBROSE BIERCE, Ambrose Bierce. 23 strikingly modern stories of the horrors latent in the human mind: The Eyes of the Panther, The Damned Thing, An Occurrence at Owl Creek Bridge, An Inhabitant of Carcosa, etc., plus the dream-essay, Visions of the Night. Edited by E. F. Bleiler. xxii + 199pp. 20767-6 Paperbound $1.50

BEST GHOST STORIES OF J. S. LEFANU, J. Sheridan LeFanu. Finest stories by Victorian master often considered greatest supernatural writer of all. Carmilla, Green Tea, The Haunted Baronet, The Familiar, and 12 others. Most never before available in the U. S. A. Edited by E. F. Bleiler. 8 illustrations from Victorian publications. xvii + 467pp. 20415-4 Paperbound $3.00

MATHEMATICAL FOUNDATIONS OF INFORMATION THEORY, A. I. Khinchin. Comprehensive introduction to work of Shannon, McMillan, Feinstein and Khinchin, placing these investigations on a rigorous mathematical basis. Covers entropy concept in probability theory, uniqueness theorem, Shannon's inequality, ergodic sources, the E property, martingale concept, noise, Feinstein's fundamental lemma, Shanon's first and second theorems. Translated by R. A. Silverman and M. D. Friedman. iii + 120pp. 60434-9 Paperbound $1.75

SEVEN SCIENCE FICTION NOVELS, H. G. Wells. The standard collection of the great novels. Complete, unabridged. *First Men in the Moon, Island of Dr. Moreau, War of the Worlds, Food of the Gods, Invisible Man, Time Machine, In the Days of the Comet.* Not only science fiction fans, but every educated person owes it to himself to read these novels. 1015pp. 20264-X Clothbound $5.00

EAST O' THE SUN AND WEST O' THE MOON, George W. Dasent. Considered the best of all translations of these Norwegian folk tales, this collection has been enjoyed by generations of children (and folklorists too). Includes True and Untrue, Why the Sea is Salt, East O' the Sun and West O' the Moon, Why the Bear is Stumpy-Tailed, Boots and the Troll, The Cock and the Hen, Rich Peter the Pedlar, and 52 more. The only edition with all 59 tales. 77 illustrations by Erik Werenskiold and Theodor Kittelsen. xv + 418pp. 22521-6 Paperbound $3.50

GOOPS AND HOW TO BE THEM, Gelett Burgess. Classic of tongue-in-cheek humor, masquerading as etiquette book. 87 verses, twice as many cartoons, show mischievous Goops as they demonstrate to children virtues of table manners, neatness, courtesy, etc. Favorite for generations. viii + 88pp. 6½ x 9¼.
22233-0 Paperbound $1.25

ALICE'S ADVENTURES UNDER GROUND, Lewis Carroll. The first version, quite different from the final *Alice in Wonderland,* printed out by Carroll himself with his own illustrations. Complete facsimile of the "million dollar" manuscript Carroll gave to Alice Liddell in 1864. Introduction by Martin Gardner. viii + 96pp. Title and dedication pages in color. 21482-6 Paperbound $1.25

THE BROWNIES, THEIR BOOK, Palmer Cox. Small as mice, cunning as foxes, exuberant and full of mischief, the Brownies go to the zoo, toy shop, seashore, circus, etc., in 24 verse adventures and 266 illustrations. Long a favorite, since their first appearance in St. Nicholas Magazine. xi + 144pp. 6⅝ x 9¼.
21265-3 Paperbound $1.75

SONGS OF CHILDHOOD, Walter De La Mare. Published (under the pseudonym Walter Ramal) when De La Mare was only 29, this charming collection has long been a favorite children's book. A facsimile of the first edition in paper, the 47 poems capture the simplicity of the nursery rhyme and the ballad, including such lyrics as I Met Eve, Tartary, The Silver Penny. vii + 106pp. 21972-0 Paperbound $1.25

THE COMPLETE NONSENSE OF EDWARD LEAR, Edward Lear. The finest 19th-century humorist-cartoonist in full: all nonsense limericks, zany alphabets, Owl and Pussycat, songs, nonsense botany, and more than 500 illustrations by Lear himself. Edited by Holbrook Jackson. xxix + 287pp. (USO) 20167-8 Paperbound $2.00

BILLY WHISKERS: THE AUTOBIOGRAPHY OF A GOAT, Frances Trego Montgomery. A favorite of children since the early 20th century, here are the escapades of that rambunctious, irresistible and mischievous goat—Billy Whiskers. Much in the spirit of *Peck's Bad Boy,* this is a book that children never tire of reading or hearing. All the original familiar illustrations by W. H. Fry are included: 6 color plates, 18 black and white drawings. 159pp. 22345-0 Paperbound $2.00

MOTHER GOOSE MELODIES. Faithful republication of the fabulously rare Munroe and Francis "copyright 1833" Boston edition—the most important Mother Goose collection, usually referred to as the "original." Familiar rhymes plus many rare ones, with wonderful old woodcut illustrations. Edited by E. F. Bleiler. 128pp. 4½ x 6⅜. 22577-1 Paperbound $1.25

The Red Fairy Book, Andrew Lang. Lang's color fairy books have long been children's favorites. This volume includes Rapunzel, Jack and the Bean-stalk and 35 other stories, familiar and unfamiliar. 4 plates, 93 illustrations x + 367pp.
21673-X Paperbound $2.50

The Blue Fairy Book, Andrew Lang. Lang's tales come from all countries and all times. Here are 37 tales from Grimm, the Arabian Nights, Greek Mythology, and other fascinating sources. 8 plates, 130 illustrations. xi + 390pp.
21437-0 Paperbound $2.50

Household Stories by the Brothers Grimm. Classic English-language edition of the well-known tales — Rumpelstiltskin, Snow White, Hansel and Gretel, The Twelve Brothers, Faithful John, Rapunzel, Tom Thumb (52 stories in all). Translated into simple, straightforward English by Lucy Crane. Ornamented with headpieces, vignettes, elaborate decorative initials and a dozen full-page illustrations by Walter Crane. x + 269pp. 21080-4 Paperbound $2.50

The Merry Adventures of Robin Hood, Howard Pyle. The finest modern versions of the traditional ballads and tales about the great English outlaw. Howard Pyle's complete prose version, with every word, every illustration of the first edition. Do not confuse this facsimile of the original (1883) with modern editions that change text or illustrations. 23 plates plus many page decorations. xxii + 296pp.
22043-5 Paperbound $2.50

The Story of King Arthur and His Knights, Howard Pyle. The finest children's version of the life of King Arthur; brilliantly retold by Pyle, with 48 of his most imaginative illustrations. xviii + 313pp. 6⅛ x 9¼.
21445-1 Paperbound $2.50

The Wonderful Wizard of Oz, L. Frank Baum. America's finest children's book in facsimile of first edition with all Denslow illustrations in full color. The edition a child should have. Introduction by Martin Gardner. 23 color plates, scores of drawings. iv + 267pp. 20691-2 Paperbound $2.50

The Marvelous Land of Oz, L. Frank Baum. The second Oz book, every bit as imaginative as the Wizard. The hero is a boy named Tip, but the Scarecrow and the Tin Woodman are back, as is the Oz magic. 16 color plates, 120 drawings by John R. Neill. 287pp. 20692-0 Paperbound $2.50

The Magical Monarch of Mo, L. Frank Baum. Remarkable adventures in a land even stranger than Oz. The best of Baum's books not in the Oz series. 15 color plates and dozens of drawings by Frank Verbeck. xviii + 237pp.
21892-9 Paperbound $2.25

The Bad Child's Book of Beasts, More Beasts for Worse Children, A Moral Alphabet, Hilaire Belloc. Three complete humor classics in one volume. Be kind to the frog, and do not call him names . . . and 28 other whimsical animals. Familiar favorites and some not so well known. Illustrated by Basil Blackwell. 156pp. (USO) 20749-8 Paperbound $1.50

TWO LITTLE SAVAGES; BEING THE ADVENTURES OF TWO BOYS WHO LIVED AS INDIANS AND WHAT THEY LEARNED, Ernest Thompson Seton. Great classic of nature and boyhood provides a vast range of woodlore in most palatable form, a genuinely entertaining story. Two farm boys build a teepee in woods and live in it for a month, working out Indian solutions to living problems, star lore, birds and animals, plants, etc. 293 illustrations. vii + 286pp.
20985-7 Paperbound $2.50

PETER PIPER'S PRACTICAL PRINCIPLES OF PLAIN & PERFECT PRONUNCIATION. Alliterative jingles and tongue-twisters of surprising charm, that made their first appearance in America about 1830. Republished in full with the spirited woodcut illustrations from this earliest American edition. 32pp. 4½ x 6⅜.
22560-7 Paperbound $1.00

SCIENCE EXPERIMENTS AND AMUSEMENTS FOR CHILDREN, Charles Vivian. 73 easy experiments, requiring only materials found at home or easily available, such as candles, coins, steel wool, etc.; illustrate basic phenomena like vacuum, simple chemical reaction, etc. All safe. Modern, well-planned. Formerly *Science Games for Children*. 102 photos, numerous drawings. 96pp. 6⅛ x 9¼.
21856-2 Paperbound $1.25

AN INTRODUCTION TO CHESS MOVES AND TACTICS SIMPLY EXPLAINED, Leonard Barden. Informal intermediate introduction, quite strong in explaining reasons for moves. Covers basic material, tactics, important openings, traps, positional play in middle game, end game. Attempts to isolate patterns and recurrent configurations. Formerly *Chess*. 58 figures. 102pp. (USO) 21210-6 Paperbound $1.25

LASKER'S MANUAL OF CHESS, Dr. Emanuel Lasker. Lasker was not only one of the five great World Champions, he was also one of the ablest expositors, theorists, and analysts. In many ways, his Manual, permeated with his philosophy of battle, filled with keen insights, is one of the greatest works ever written on chess. Filled with analyzed games by the great players. A single-volume library that will profit almost any chess player, beginner or master. 308 diagrams. xli x 349pp.
20640-8 Paperbound $2.75

THE MASTER BOOK OF MATHEMATICAL RECREATIONS, Fred Schuh. In opinion of many the finest work ever prepared on mathematical puzzles, stunts, recreations; exhaustively thorough explanations of mathematics involved, analysis of effects, citation of puzzles and games. Mathematics involved is elementary. Translated by F. Göbel. 194 figures. xxiv + 430pp. 22134-2 Paperbound $3.00

MATHEMATICS, MAGIC AND MYSTERY, Martin Gardner. Puzzle editor for Scientific American explains mathematics behind various mystifying tricks: card tricks, stage "mind reading," coin and match tricks, counting out games, geometric dissections, etc. Probability sets, theory of numbers clearly explained. Also provides more than 400 tricks, guaranteed to work, that you can do. 135 illustrations. xii + 176pp.
20338-2 Paperbound $1.50

HOW TO KNOW THE WILD FLOWERS, Mrs. William Starr Dana. This is the classical book of American wildflowers (of the Eastern and Central United States), used by hundreds of thousands. Covers over 500 species, arranged in extremely easy to use color and season groups. Full descriptions, much plant lore. This Dover edition is the fullest ever compiled, with tables of nomenclature changes. 174 full-page plates by M. Satterlee. xii + 418pp. 20332-8 Paperbound $2.75

OUR PLANT FRIENDS AND FOES, William Atherton DuPuy. History, economic importance, essential botanical information and peculiarities of 25 common forms of plant life are provided in this book in an entertaining and charming style. Covers food plants (potatoes, apples, beans, wheat, almonds, bananas, etc.), flowers (lily, tulip, etc.), trees (pine, oak, elm, etc.), weeds, poisonous mushrooms and vines, gourds, citrus fruits, cotton, the cactus family, and much more. 108 illustrations. xiv + 290pp. 22272-1 Paperbound $2.50

HOW TO KNOW THE FERNS, Frances T. Parsons. Classic survey of Eastern and Central ferns, arranged according to clear, simple identification key. Excellent introduction to greatly neglected nature area. 57 illustrations and 42 plates. xvi + 215pp. 20740-4 Paperbound $2.00

MANUAL OF THE TREES OF NORTH AMERICA, Charles S. Sargent. America's foremost dendrologist provides the definitive coverage of North American trees and tree-like shrubs. 717 species fully described and illustrated: exact distribution, down to township; full botanical description; economic importance; description of subspecies and races; habitat, growth data; similar material. Necessary to every serious student of tree-life. Nomenclature revised to present. Over 100 locating keys. 783 illustrations. lii + 934pp. 20277-1, 20278-X Two volumes, Paperbound $6.00

OUR NORTHERN SHRUBS, Harriet L. Keeler. Fine non-technical reference work identifying more than 225 important shrubs of Eastern and Central United States and Canada. Full text covering botanical description, habitat, plant lore, is paralleled with 205 full-page photographs of flowering or fruiting plants. Nomenclature revised by Edward G. Voss. One of few works concerned with shrubs. 205 plates, 35 drawings. xxviii + 521pp. 21989-5 Paperbound $3.75

THE MUSHROOM HANDBOOK, Louis C. C. Krieger. Still the best popular handbook: full descriptions of 259 species, cross references to another 200. Extremely thorough text enables you to identify, know all about any mushroom you are likely to meet in eastern and central U. S. A.: habitat, luminescence, poisonous qualities, use, folklore, etc. 32 color plates show over 50 mushrooms, also 126 other illustrations. Finding keys. vii + 560pp. 21861-9 Paperbound $3.95

HANDBOOK OF BIRDS OF EASTERN NORTH AMERICA, Frank M. Chapman. Still much the best single-volume guide to the birds of Eastern and Central United States. Very full coverage of 675 species, with descriptions, life habits, distribution, similar data. All descriptions keyed to two-page color chart. With this single volume the average birdwatcher needs no other books. 1931 revised edition. 195 illustrations. xxxvi + 581pp. 21489-3 Paperbound $4.50

THE PRINCIPLES OF PSYCHOLOGY, William James. The famous long course, complete and unabridged. Stream of thought, time perception, memory, experimental methods—these are only some of the concerns of a work that was years ahead of its time and still valid, interesting, useful. 94 figures. Total of xviii + 1391pp.
20381-6, 20382-4 Two volumes, Paperbound $8.00

THE STRANGE STORY OF THE QUANTUM, Banesh Hoffmann. Non-mathematical but thorough explanation of work of Planck, Einstein, Bohr, Pauli, de Broglie, Schrödinger, Heisenberg, Dirac, Feynman, etc. No technical background needed. "Of books attempting such an account, this is the best," Henry Margenau, Yale. 40-page "Postscript 1959." xii + 285pp. 20518-5 Paperbound $2.00

THE RISE OF THE NEW PHYSICS, A. d'Abro. Most thorough explanation in print of central core of mathematical physics, both classical and modern; from Newton to Dirac and Heisenberg. Both history and exposition; philosophy of science, causality, explanations of higher mathematics, analytical mechanics, electromagnetism, thermodynamics, phase rule, special and general relativity, matrices. No higher mathematics needed to follow exposition, though treatment is elementary to intermediate in level. Recommended to serious student who wishes verbal understanding. 97 illustrations. xvii + 982pp. 20003-5, 20004-3 Two volumes, Paperbound $6.00

GREAT IDEAS OF OPERATIONS RESEARCH, Jagjit Singh. Easily followed non-technical explanation of mathematical tools, aims, results: statistics, linear programming, game theory, queueing theory, Monte Carlo simulation, etc. Uses only elementary mathematics. Many case studies, several analyzed in detail. Clarity, breadth make this excellent for specialist in another field who wishes background. 41 figures. x + 228pp. 21886-4 Paperbound $2.50

GREAT IDEAS OF MODERN MATHEMATICS: THEIR NATURE AND USE, Jagjit Singh. Internationally famous expositor, winner of Unesco's Kalinga Award for science popularization explains verbally such topics as differential equations, matrices, groups, sets, transformations, mathematical logic and other important modern mathematics, as well as use in physics, astrophysics, and similar fields. Superb exposition for layman, scientist in other areas. viii + 312pp.
20587-8 Paperbound $2.50

GREAT IDEAS IN INFORMATION THEORY, LANGUAGE AND CYBERNETICS, Jagjit Singh. The analog and digital computers, how they work, how they are like and unlike the human brain, the men who developed them, their future applications, computer terminology. An essential book for today, even for readers with little math. Some mathematical demonstrations included for more advanced readers. 118 figures. Tables. ix + 338pp. 21694-2 Paperbound $2.50

CHANCE, LUCK AND STATISTICS, Horace C. Levinson. Non-mathematical presentation of fundamentals of probability theory and science of statistics and their applications. Games of chance, betting odds, misuse of statistics, normal and skew distributions, birth rates, stock speculation, insurance. Enlarged edition. Formerly "The Science of Chance." xiii + 357pp. 21007-3 Paperbound $2.50

AMERICAN FOOD AND GAME FISHES, David S. Jordan and Barton W. Evermann. Definitive source of information, detailed and accurate enough to enable the sportsman and nature lover to identify conclusively some 1,000 species and sub-species of North American fish, sought for food or sport. Coverage of range, physiology, habits, life history, food value. Best methods of capture, interest to the angler, advice on bait, fly-fishing, etc. 338 drawings and photographs. l + 574pp. 6⅝ x 9⅜.
22383-1 Paperbound $4.50

THE FROG BOOK, Mary C. Dickerson. Complete with extensive finding keys, over 300 photographs, and an introduction to the general biology of frogs and toads, this is the classic non-technical study of Northeastern and Central species. 58 species; 290 photographs and 16 color plates. xvii + 253pp.
21973-9 Paperbound $4.00

THE MOTH BOOK: A GUIDE TO THE MOTHS OF NORTH AMERICA, William J. Holland. Classical study, eagerly sought after and used for the past 60 years. Clear identification manual to more than 2,000 different moths, largest manual in existence. General information about moths, capturing, mounting, classifying, etc., followed by species by species descriptions. 263 illustrations plus 48 color plates show almost every species, full size. 1968 edition, preface, nomenclature changes by A. E. Brower. xxiv + 479pp. of text. 6½ x 9¼.
21948-8 Paperbound $5.00

THE SEA-BEACH AT EBB-TIDE, Augusta Foote Arnold. Interested amateur can identify hundreds of marine plants and animals on coasts of North America; marine algae; seaweeds; squids; hermit crabs; horse shoe crabs; shrimps; corals; sea anemones; etc. Species descriptions cover: structure; food; reproductive cycle; size; shape; color; habitat; etc. Over 600 drawings. 85 plates. xii + 490pp.
21949-6 Paperbound $3.50

COMMON BIRD SONGS, Donald J. Borror. 33⅓ 12-inch record presents songs of 60 important birds of the eastern United States. A thorough, serious record which provides several examples for each bird, showing different types of song, individual variations, etc. Inestimable identification aid for birdwatcher. 32-page booklet gives text about birds and songs, with illustration for each bird.
21829-5 Record, book, album. Monaural. $2.75

FADS AND FALLACIES IN THE NAME OF SCIENCE, Martin Gardner. Fair, witty appraisal of cranks and quacks of science: Atlantis, Lemuria, hollow earth, flat earth, Velikovsky, orgone energy, Dianetics, flying saucers, Bridey Murphy, food fads, medical fads, perpetual motion, etc. Formerly "In the Name of Science." x + 363pp.
20394-8 Paperbound $2.00

HOAXES, Curtis D. MacDougall. Exhaustive, unbelievably rich account of great hoaxes: Locke's moon hoax, Shakespearean forgeries, sea serpents, Loch Ness monster, Cardiff giant, John Wilkes Booth's mummy, Disumbrationist school of art, dozens more; also journalism, psychology of hoaxing. 54 illustrations. xi + 338pp.
20465-0 Paperbound $2.75

THE PHILOSOPHY OF THE UPANISHADS, Paul Deussen. Clear, detailed statement of upanishadic system of thought, generally considered among best available. History of these works, full exposition of system emergent from them, parallel concepts in the West. Translated by A. S. Geden. xiv + 429pp.
21616-0 Paperbound $3.00

LANGUAGE, TRUTH AND LOGIC, Alfred J. Ayer. Famous, remarkably clear introduction to the Vienna and Cambridge schools of Logical Positivism; function of philosophy, elimination of metaphysical thought, nature of analysis, similar topics. "Wish I had written it myself," Bertrand Russell. 2nd, 1946 edition. 160pp.
20010-8 Paperbound $1.35

THE GUIDE FOR THE PERPLEXED, Moses Maimonides. Great classic of medieval Judaism, major attempt to reconcile revealed religion (Pentateuch, commentaries) and Aristotelian philosophy. Enormously important in all Western thought. Unabridged Friedländer translation. 50-page introduction. lix + 414pp.
(USO) 20351-4 Paperbound $2.50

OCCULT AND SUPERNATURAL PHENOMENA, D. H. Rawcliffe. Full, serious study of the most persistent delusions of mankind: crystal gazing, mediumistic trance, stigmata, lycanthropy, fire walking, dowsing, telepathy, ghosts, ESP, etc., and their relation to common forms of abnormal psychology. Formerly *Illusions and Delusions of the Supernatural and the Occult*. iii + 551pp. 20503-7 Paperbound $3.50

THE EGYPTIAN BOOK OF THE DEAD: THE PAPYRUS OF ANI, E. A. Wallis Budge. Full hieroglyphic text, interlinear transliteration of sounds, word for word translation, then smooth, connected translation; Theban recension. Basic work in Ancient Egyptian civilization; now even more significant than ever for historical importance, dilation of consciousness, etc. clvi + 377pp. 6½ x 9¼.
21866-X Paperbound $3.95

PSYCHOLOGY OF MUSIC, Carl E. Seashore. Basic, thorough survey of everything known about psychology of music up to 1940's; essential reading for psychologists, musicologists. Physical acoustics; auditory apparatus; relationship of physical sound to perceived sound; role of the mind in sorting, altering, suppressing, creating sound sensations; musical learning, testing for ability, absolute pitch, other topics. Records of Caruso, Menuhin analyzed. 88 figures. xix + 408pp.
21851-1 Paperbound $2.75

THE I CHING (THE BOOK OF CHANGES), translated by James Legge. Complete translated text plus appendices by Confucius, of perhaps the most penetrating divination book ever compiled. Indispensable to all study of early Oriental civilizations. 3 plates. xxiii + 448pp. 21062-6 Paperbound $3.00

THE UPANISHADS, translated by Max Müller. Twelve classical upanishads: Chandogya, Kena, Aitareya, Kaushitaki, Isa, Katha, Mundaka, Taittiriyaka, Brhadaranyaka, Svetasvatara, Prasna, Maitriyana. 160-page introduction, analysis by Prof. Müller. Total of 826pp. 20398-0, 20399-9 Two volumes, Paperbound $5.00

PLANETS, STARS AND GALAXIES: DESCRIPTIVE ASTRONOMY FOR BEGINNERS, A. E. Fanning. Comprehensive introductory survey of astronomy: the sun, solar system, stars, galaxies, universe, cosmology; up-to-date, including quasars, radio stars, etc. Preface by Prof. Donald Menzel. 24pp. of photographs. 189pp. 5¼ x 8¼.
21680-2 Paperbound $1.50

TEACH YOURSELF CALCULUS, P. Abbott. With a good background in algebra and trig, you can teach yourself calculus with this book. Simple, straightforward introduction to functions of all kinds, integration, differentiation, series, etc. "Students who are beginning to study calculus method will derive great help from this book." Faraday House Journal. 308pp. 20683-1 Clothbound $2.00

TEACH YOURSELF TRIGONOMETRY, P. Abbott. Geometrical foundations, indices and logarithms, ratios, angles, circular measure, etc. are presented in this sound, easy-to-use text. Excellent for the beginner or as a brush up, this text carries the student through the solution of triangles. 204pp. 20682-3 Clothbound $2.00

TEACH YOURSELF ANATOMY, David LeVay. Accurate, inclusive, profusely illustrated account of structure, skeleton, abdomen, muscles, nervous system, glands, brain, reproductive organs, evolution. "Quite the best and most readable account,' *Medical Officer*. 12 color plates. 164 figures. 311pp. 4¾ x 7.
21651-9 Clothbound $2.50

TEACH YOURSELF PHYSIOLOGY, David LeVay. Anatomical, biochemical bases; digestive, nervous, endocrine systems; metabolism; respiration; muscle; excretion; temperature control; reproduction. "Good elementary exposition," *The Lancet.* 6 color plates. 44 illustrations. 208pp. 4¼ x 7. 21658-6 Clothbound $2.50

THE FRIENDLY STARS, Martha Evans Martin. Classic has taught naked-eye observation of stars, planets to hundreds of thousands, still not surpassed for charm, lucidity, adequacy. Completely updated by Professor Donald H. Menzel, Harvard Observatory. 25 illustrations. 16 x 30 chart. x + 147pp. 21099-5 Paperbound $1.25

MUSIC OF THE SPHERES: THE MATERIAL UNIVERSE FROM ATOM TO QUASAR, SIMPLY EXPLAINED, Guy Murchie. Extremely broad, brilliantly written popular account begins with the solar system and reaches to dividing line between matter and nonmatter; latest understandings presented with exceptional clarity. Volume One: Planets, stars, galaxies, cosmology, geology, celestial mechanics, latest astronomical discoveries; Volume Two: Matter, atoms, waves, radiation, relativity, chemical action, heat, nuclear energy, quantum theory, music, light, color, probability, antimatter, antigravity, and similar topics. 319 figures. 1967 (second) edition. Total of xx + 644pp. 21809-0, 21810-4 Two volumes, Paperbound $5.00

OLD-TIME SCHOOLS AND SCHOOL BOOKS, Clifton Johnson. Illustrations and rhymes from early primers, abundant quotations from early textbooks, many anecdotes of school life enliven this study of elementary schools from Puritans to middle 19th century. Introduction by Carl Withers. 234 illustrations. xxxiii + 381pp.
21031-6 Paperbound $2.50

ADVENTURES OF AN AFRICAN SLAVER, Theodore Canot. Edited by Brantz Mayer. A detailed portrayal of slavery and the slave trade, 1820-1840. Canot, an established trader along the African coast, describes the slave economy of the African kingdoms, the treatment of captured negroes, the extensive journeys in the interior to gather slaves, slave revolts and their suppression, harems, bribes, and much more. Full and unabridged republication of 1854 edition. Introduction by Malcom Cowley. 16 illustrations. xvii + 448pp. 22456-2 Paperbound $3.50

MY BONDAGE AND MY FREEDOM, Frederick Douglass. Born and brought up in slavery, Douglass witnessed its horrors and experienced its cruelties, but went on to become one of the most outspoken forces in the American anti-slavery movement. Considered the best of his autobiographies, this book graphically describes the inhuman treatment of slaves, its effects on slave owners and slave families, and how Douglass's determination led him to a new life. Unaltered reprint of 1st (1855) edition. xxxii + 464pp. 22457-0 Paperbound $2.50

THE INDIANS' BOOK, recorded and edited by Natalie Curtis. Lore, music, narratives, dozens of drawings by Indians themselves from an authoritative and important survey of native culture among Plains, Southwestern, Lake and Pueblo Indians. Standard work in popular ethnomusicology. 149 songs in full notation. 23 drawings, 23 photos. xxxi + 584pp. 6⅝ x 9⅜. 21939-9 Paperbound $4.50

DICTIONARY OF AMERICAN PORTRAITS, edited by Hayward and Blanche Cirker. 4024 portraits of 4000 most important Americans, colonial days to 1905 (with a few important categories, like Presidents, to present). Pioneers, explorers, colonial figures, U. S. officials, politicians, writers, military and naval men, scientists, inventors, manufacturers, jurists, actors, historians, educators, notorious figures, Indian chiefs, etc. All authentic contemporary likenesses. The only work of its kind in existence; supplements all biographical sources for libraries. Indispensable to anyone working with American history. 8,000-item classified index, finding lists, other aids. xiv + 756pp. 9¼ x 12¾. 21823-6 Clothbound $30.00

TRITTON'S GUIDE TO BETTER WINE AND BEER MAKING FOR BEGINNERS, S. M. Tritton. All you need to know to make family-sized quantities of over 100 types of grape, fruit, herb and vegetable wines; as well as beers, mead, cider, etc. Complete recipes, advice as to equipment, procedures such as fermenting, bottling, and storing wines. Recipes given in British, U. S., and metric measures. Accompanying booklet lists sources in U. S. A. where ingredients may be bought, and additional information. 11 illustrations. 157pp. 5⅝ x 8⅛.
(USO) 22090-7 Clothbound $3.50

GARDENING WITH HERBS FOR FLAVOR AND FRAGRANCE, Helen M. Fox. How to grow herbs in your own garden, how to use them in your cooking (over 55 recipes included), legends and myths associated with each species, uses in medicine, perfumes, etc.—these are elements of one of the few books written especially for American herb fanciers. Guides you step-by-step from soil preparation to harvesting and storage for each type of herb. 12 drawings by Louise Mansfield. xiv + 334pp.
22540-2 Paperbound $2.50

CATALOGUE OF DOVER BOOKS

MATHEMATICAL PUZZLES FOR BEGINNERS AND ENTHUSIASTS, Geoffrey Mott-Smith. 189 puzzles from easy to difficult—involving arithmetic, logic, algebra, properties of digits, probability, etc.—for enjoyment and mental stimulus. Explanation of mathematical principles behind the puzzles. 135 illustrations. viii + 248pp.
20198-8 Paperbound $1.75

PAPER FOLDING FOR BEGINNERS, William D. Murray and Francis J. Rigney. Easiest book on the market, clearest instructions on making interesting, beautiful origami. Sail boats, cups, roosters, frogs that move legs, bonbon boxes, standing birds, etc. 40 projects; more than 275 diagrams and photographs. 94pp.
20713-7 Paperbound $1.00

TRICKS AND GAMES ON THE POOL TABLE, Fred Herrmann. 79 tricks and games—some solitaires, some for two or more players, some competitive games—to entertain you between formal games. Mystifying shots and throws, unusual caroms, tricks involving such props as cork, coins, a hat, etc. Formerly *Fun on the Pool Table.* 77 figures. 95pp. 21814-7 Paperbound $1.00

HAND SHADOWS TO BE THROWN UPON THE WALL: A SERIES OF NOVEL AND AMUSING FIGURES FORMED BY THE HAND, Henry Bursill. Delightful picturebook from great-grandfather's day shows how to make 18 different hand shadows: a bird that flies, duck that quacks, dog that wags his tail, camel, goose, deer, boy, turtle, etc. Only book of its sort. vi + 33pp. 6½ x 9¼. 21779-5 Paperbound $1.00

WHITTLING AND WOODCARVING, E. J. Tangerman. 18th printing of best book on market. "If you can cut a potato you can carve" toys and puzzles, chains, chessmen, caricatures, masks, frames, woodcut blocks, surface patterns, much more. Information on tools, woods, techniques. Also goes into serious wood sculpture from Middle Ages to present, East and West. 464 photos, figures. x + 293pp.
20965-2 Paperbound $2.00

HISTORY OF PHILOSOPHY, Julián Marias. Possibly the clearest, most easily followed, best planned, most useful one-volume history of philosophy on the market; neither skimpy nor overfull. Full details on system of every major philosopher and dozens of less important thinkers from pre-Socratics up to Existentialism and later. Strong on many European figures usually omitted. Has gone through dozens of editions in Europe. 1966 edition, translated by Stanley Appelbaum and Clarence Strowbridge. xviii + 505pp. 21739-6 Paperbound $3.00

YOGA: A SCIENTIFIC EVALUATION, Kovoor T. Behanan. Scientific but non-technical study of physiological results of yoga exercises; done under auspices of Yale U. Relations to Indian thought, to psychoanalysis, etc. 16 photos. xxiii + 270pp.
20505-3 Paperbound $2.50

Prices subject to change without notice.
Available at your book dealer or write for free catalogue to Dept. GI, Dover Publications, Inc., 180 Varick St., N. Y., N. Y. 10014. Dover publishes more than 150 books each year on science, elementary and advanced mathematics, biology, music, art, literary history, social sciences and other areas.

24401 46
155